T5-BAH-293

KILL AND CHILL

Restructuring Canada's Beef Commodity Chain

Both horrified and fascinated by a visit he made with his geography students to the Canada Packers Lethbridge plant, Ian MacLachlan searched for a book that would explain the main workings of the Canadian meat-packing industry. Finding very little available on the subject, he set about writing an account that is both an economic geography and a history of the meat-packing industry in Canada.

Comprehensive in its treatment of the whole system surrounding the industry, *Kill and Chill* traces the structural changes in Canada's cattle and beef commodity chain, beginning with calf production and cattle feeding on farms and feedlots. It describes the changes in cattle marketing, the development of meat packing – in particular the emergence of Canada's 'big three' meat-packing firms – and the rise of the industry's unions. Covering developments up to the end of the twentieth century, with the takeover of Maple Leaf Foods by the McCain family, MacLachlan concludes with an enlightening discussion of current trends in retail beef marketing.

IAN MACLACHLAN is an Associate Professor in the Department of Geography at the University of Lethbridge.

KILL and CHILL

Restructuring Canada's Beef Commodity Chain

Ian MacLachlan

UNIVERSITY OF TORONTO PRESS
Toronto Buffalo London

Toronto Buffalo London
Printed in Canada

ISBN 0-8020-0847-X (cloth)
ISBN 0-8020-7832-X (paper)

Printed on acid-free paper

National Library of Canada Cataloguing in Publication Data

MacLachlan, Ian
Kill and chill : restructuring Canada's beef commodity chain

Includes bibliographical references and index.
ISBN 0-8020-0847-X (bound) ISBN 0-8020-7832-X (pbk.)

1. Cattle trade – Canada. 2. Beef industry – Canada. I. Title.

HD9433.C22M32 2001 338.1'76213'0971 C2001-930525-7

This book has been published with the help of a grant from the Humanities and Social Sciences Federation of Canada, using funds provided by the Social Sciences and Humanities Research Council of Canada.

The University of Toronto Press acknowledges the financial assistance to its publishing program of the Canada Council for the Arts and the Ontario Arts Council.

University of Toronto Press acknowledges the financial support for its publishing activities of the Government of Canada through the Book Publishing Industry Development Program (BPIDP).

For Mary-jeanne and Moray,
Marianne and Howard

Contents

Acknowledgments ix

Tables xii

Figures xiii

Introduction 3

PART ONE: PRODUCING CATTLE

1 Calf Production: Breeding Beef Cows 13

2 Feedlot Alchemy: Turning Grain into Beef 52

3 Cattle Logistics: From Stockyards and Cattle Cars to Auction Marts and Cattle Liners 88

PART TWO: PROCESSING BEEF

4 Industrialization, Regulation, and Canada's Early Beef Packers 123

5 The Kill Floor at Mid-century: From the Knocking Box to the Hot Box 161

6 Canada's Beef Trust: The Rise and Fall of the Big Three 185

7 Organizing Kill-Floor Workers and Pattern Bargaining 245

8 An Industry Transformed: Meat-Packing Metamorphosis 245

PART THREE: MARKETING BEEF

9 Marketing Meat: From Branch House to Postmodern Retailing 291

10 Conclusion 326

References 331

Index 355

Acknowledgments

This book has been published with the help of a grant from the Humanities and Social Sciences Federation of Canada, using funds provided by the Social Sciences and Humanities Research Council of Canada. The research upon which it is based was also supported by a Social Sciences and Humanities Research Council of Canada Standard Research Grant. I am most grateful to the anonymous referees and the adjudication committee for their faith in this project. The grant enabled me to hire student research assistants to share in the process of discovery and to be trained in the methods of geography and social science research. Research assistants included Bonnie Brunner, Dawn Collins, Richard Crerar, Michelle Douville, Tammy Lopeter, Garnet Neufeld, and Ryo Sawada.

Two institutions provided a convivial and supportive atmosphere for analysis, writing, reflection, and discussion of ideas: the Department of Geography at the University of Lethbridge, and the Instituto de Geografía, Universidad Nacional Autónoma de México. Faculty colleagues at both institutions who gave technical assistance and shared their wisdom include Adrian Guillermo Aguilar, Quentin Chiotti, Geoffrey England, Bob Hironaka, Tom Johnston, Kurt Klein, María Salud Lozano, Francisco Galindo Maldonado, Omar Moncada Maya, Gilberto Aranda Osorio, Dennis Sheppard, and Ivan Townshend.

Many support staff, archivists, and librarians gave dedicated and sometimes inspired assistance far beyond the limits of their job descriptions: Marina Chiste, Diana Fancher, David Fraser, Rosemary Howard, Mary Ledwell, Marg McKeen, Susan Koop, Shelley Ross, Tina Tarini, and Linda Tkachenko. Archives that made their collections available included Canadian Pacific Railway Archives (Montreal), City of Edmonton Archives, Glenbow (Calgary), City of Lethbridge Archives, City of Toronto Archives, National Archives of Canada, and the Archives of Ontario.

At a greater distance, academics, research scientists, and others shared their expertise and offered sources and ideas in person and via the miracle of electronic mail: Jack Bamford, Roy Berg, Bob Blount, Merle Boyle, Michael Broadway, Ted Cochrane, Jacqueline Draper, Erana van Duren, Simon Evans, Kevin Grier, Merle Faminow, Brian Freeze, Tom Golden, Temple Grandin, Fraser Hart, Bill Heffernan, Lester Jeremiah, Jim Lemon, Chris Mayda, Tim McAllister, Gordon McGregor, Joel Novek, Brian Page, Jimmy Skaggs, and Ike Tagg. Other sources of assistance from government regulators and industry groups are also gratefully acknowledged: Cindy Delaloye, Anne Dunford, Margaret Fisher, Joanne Lemke, Julie McAuley, Cindy McCreath, Heather Reti, Ray Thibert, and Joel Yan.

The book relies heavily on semi-structured interviews with producers and processors. They gave unstintingly of their time. Producer respondents included Darlene Bowen, Jim and Denise Calderwood, Edgar Cornish, Dick and Simon DeBoer, Bob and Trudy Desjardins, Bob Dobson, Gerald Doris, Paul Hamilton, Glenn Logan, Rod MacLaren, George Montgomery, Marvin and Barbara Prusky, Paul Runnions, Mike Sullivan, Wayne Telford, and Cor Van Raay. Meat packing corporate executives, plant managers, and packinghouse workers included Brent Altwasser, Vic Azzopardi, Al Baerg, Guy Bonneau, Arthur Child, Marcel Garreau, Leo Giroux, Jim Gough, George Hall, Norm Haugen, Ross Held, Charles Horlings, John Howard, Arthur Humphries, Daryl Hutchings, Dean Iler, Mark Ishoy, Mike de Jonge, Denzil Logan, Lloyd MacLeod, Jeffrey McMullen, Danny Phillip, Barry Reimer, Saul Tabachnik, Andre Viau, Ron Weiland, and Heinz Woehr. Kip Connolly and Norm Leclaire provided a valuable union perspective.

Six respondents read part or all of the working manuscript. Their critical insights, incisive comments, and corrections were indispensable: Bill Goetz, Michael Landry, Ted Haney, Karen Schwartzkopf-Genswein, and two others who preferred to be anonymous. One anonymous reader, who was once a highly placed executive, took vigorous exception to my interpretation of Canada Packers' role as the industry leader in pattern bargaining. His criticisms were invaluable as they prompted me to gather additional data to reinforce my argument. I fear that some of these people will not agree with everything in this book. Nevertheless, they were generous with their time, cooperative, and remarkably accommodating.

From our first meeting at the Learneds, Virgil Duff at the University of Toronto Press was an enthusiastic supporter of the project and he provided much helpful advice on getting it started. Kate Baltais did an outstanding job of copyediting the manuscript and provided much helpful advice on getting it finished. In between these two, Chris Bucci and Anne Laughlin at UTP were responsible for getting it right. Any remaining gaffes are mine alone.

Last on the list but first in my thoughts, is my wife, Diane Clark. Diane took Christmas holidays in cheerless archives, included packing plant visits in our summer vacation plans, and detoured down countless dusty concession roads in search of 'just one more interview.' She read the entire manuscript and, as always, was my most observant and perceptive critic. She was incredibly tolerant of a ramshackle fence and delays in many other household chores.

Lethbridge, Alberta
16 July 2000

Tables

1.1 Regional structure of the Canadian cattle herd, 1 January 2000 20
1.2 Regional structure of the Canadian cattle herd, 1 January 1976 22
3.1 Interprovincial flows of slaughter cattle, 1959 118
3.2 Interprovincial flows of slaughter cattle, 1997 119
4.1 Net earnings per carcass: Harris Abattoir, 1909 143
4.2 Profit and loss statement of William Davies Company Limited, 1913–1917 157
6.1 Slaughter capacity and profitability: Canada Packers' Plants, 1946–1955 191
7.1 Selected hourly wage rates in Edmonton packing plants of Canada Packers, Burns & Co., and Swift Canadian, 1943 226
8.1 Rationalization of cattle slaughter and processing in Alberta, 1987–1998 287
9.1 Beef carcass grades by region, 1999 304

Figures

I.1 The cattle–beef commodity chain 4
1.1 Canadian cattle cycles, 1 January, 1950–2000 18
1.2 Spatial distribution of beef cows in Canada, 1996 23
1.3 Beef cow and steer herd size distribution, 1996 26
2.1 Spatial distribution of steers in Canada, 1996 57
2.2 Steer herd size distribution, 1976 and 1996 62
2.3 Feedlot bunk capacity in Alberta, 1999 80
3.1 Direct-to-packer sales as a percentage of total cattle slaughter, 1929–1985 95
3.2 West to east shipments of slaughter cattle by railway and highway, 1952–1998 98
3.3 Cattle shipments from Canada's public stockyards at their peak, 1965 104
3.4 Slaughter cattle shipments from public stockyards in Canada, 1945–1992 109
3.5 The Ontario Stock Yards industrial complex, 1983 113
3.6 Lethbridge Stock Yard cattle sales, 1950–1977 117
4.1 Cattle kill floor c. 1880 139
4.2 'The way it is played' 156
7.1 'Divide they conquer – United we stand' 236
7.2 Wage differentials in Canadian packinghouses, 1947 239
7.3 Wage differentials in Canadian packinghouses, 1969 240
7.4 Labour grades at Burns and Company, 1955 241
7.5 National wage convergence at Canada Packers, 1947–1980 243

8.1 Twin rail restraining and stunning system 251
8.2 Wages in meat packing as a percentage of wages in manufacturing industries, 1961–1997 273
8.3 Base wages in selected large packing plants, 1993 277
8.4 Base and starting wages in Canada's largest beef plants, 1998 278
8.5 Big three slaughter capacity in Canada, 1960 282
8.6 Federally inspected cattle slaughter by region, 1950–1999 284
8.7 Selected large federally inspected slaughter plants in Canada, 1990 286
9.1 Per capita beef consumption in Canada, 1960–1999 312

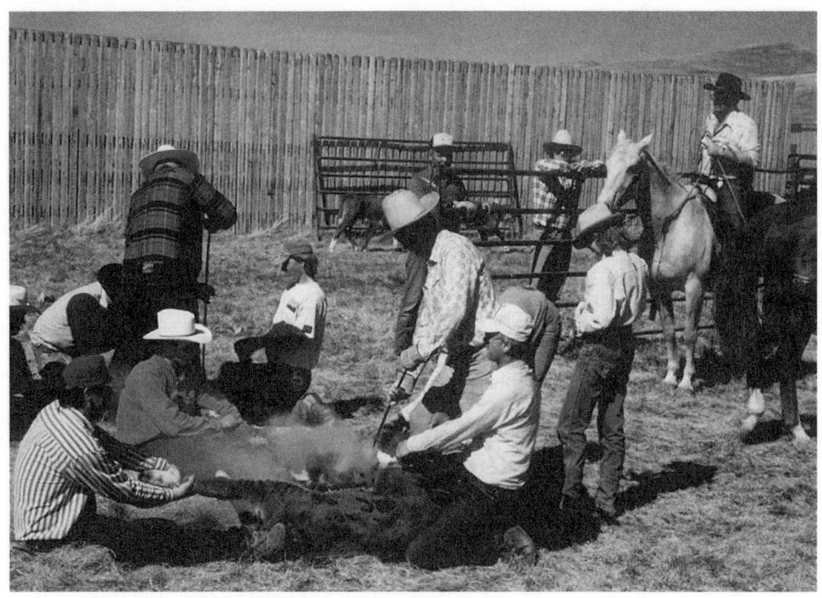

Branding flat-ass on a foothills ranch in Southern Alberta. Horses are used to drag the calves into the centre of the corral, where they are restrained for vaccination, branding, and castration of the bull calves. The palisade on the west side of the corral is a windbreak. Ball caps and the steel gates are the only indication that this photograph was taken in the 1990s and not the 1890s. (Ian MacLachlan)

A large feedlot with a capacity of 25,000 head of cattle covers a quarter section (160 acres) of land northwest of Picture Butte, Alberta, in the heart of feedlot alley. The towering feed mill at the main entry to the feedlot is its most conspicuous feature. A large catch basin to store runoff is on the opposite side. Centre pivots for irrigation leave their distinctive pattern on the two fields on the right, and an irrigation canal is visible in the far distance. The two large buildings accommodate office space and a lunch room, and are used to care for cattle and to store machinery. The other rectangular features are stacks of straw bales to be used as bedding for the cattle when conditions are wet. Mounds of manure are visible at the centre of each of the empty pens. (Ian MacLachlan)

Loading dehorned Hereford steers from a small Alberta trackside receiving yard near Picture Butte in 1944. The cattle driver keeps a cudgel at the ready in case cattle baulk as they are driven up the loading chute. (Harry Rowed/ National Archives of Canada/PA-155467)

Lethbridge Stock Yards looking north on a busy sale day in 1973. The orthogonal layout of pens and alleys was typical of the many small stockyards on the Prairies; most of the open pens are not in use. The stockyard was located directly adjacent to the CPR's Crowsnest Pass line so that cattle originating in the Kootenay ranch country of British Columbia could be unloaded for the

mandatory rest stop en route to Winnipeg or points east. The two-storey stockyard office building accommodated packer buyers, own-account cattle dealers, and commission firms, as well as Agriculture Canada officials. By the 1970s the yard relied more on truck deliveries of local livestock than on the railway, and it was finally closed in 1974. (Sir Alexander Galt Museum and Archives)

Loading three- to four-year-old steers from a small trackside receiving yard at Dunmore, North-West Territories (just east of present-day Medicine Hat, Alberta), on the Canadian Pacific mainline around the turn of the century. Typical of the semi-feral scrub cattle raised on the open range, they were not routinely dehorned. This caused considerable bruising in crowded livestock cars, labelled at that time as 'stable cars.' (William James Topley/National Archives of Canada/PA-026189)

A Judas goat leads sheep to slaughter in 1920. For many years animals from Toronto's Union Stockyard were routinely led across St Clair Avenue, past a typical grocery store, and along a residential side yard to reach the livestock ramp of Gunn's packing plant (to the left). This plant became an integral part of Canada Packers head-office operations in 1927. (John Boyd/National Archives of Canada/PA-084576)

Reflected in the placid waters of the Otonabee River, Canada Packers' five-storey Peterborough plant dates back to 1884. The plant predated the arrival of the railway and originally received farm-dressed hogs by river scow. Beef killing operations ended in 1959, and the plant was closed in 1962 and demolished in 1964. A livestock ramp and cattle pens are visible to the left. Additions made of different building materials exemplify the gradual expansion of plants of this age. (Archives of Ontario, C262-7-13, CPM 29, A0 4615)

Originally built as the Harris Abattoir (Western), this plant in St-Boniface was the second largest of Canada Packers' meat-packing plants when this photograph was taken, looking north about 1960. The adjacent St-Boniface Union Stockyards are clearly visible to the northeast. The plant depended on railway access: the tracks on the east side of the plant bring livestock to the plant using five white loading chutes. The tracks on the west side are adjacent to a large loading dock for transferring hanging beef from the cold storage building to reefer cars for shipment to eastern markets. A truck-loading facility was added in the foreground to handle the growing shipment of fresh and processed meats by semitrailer truck. A livestock ramp conveys cattle from the large livestock holding area behind the office building over the railway tracks to the fifth-storey kill floor. The large tanks to the left of the chimney contain fats and oils produced by the rendering operations, while the small white building to the northwest is the ice plant required to chill the reefer cars. (Archives of Ontario, C262-7-13, CPM 2.14 A04617)

Built in 1913, Toronto Municipal Abattoir was one of the few examples of direct municipal ownership and control of livestock processing in Canada. It is a distinguished piece of architecture with large arched windows on the second storey to provide light for the kill floor. The plant had access to the harbourfront railway tracks of the Grand Trunk (later Canadian National Railways) for shipment of cattle. (City of Toronto Archives, SC 231-513)

The Union Jack flutters against an azure sky at Canada Packers' award-winning Edmonton plant in 1936 when it was completed. With a capacity of 3,000 hogs per week and a battery of eight massive curing vats, each the size of a single-car garage, it was built primarily to produce bacon for export to Britain in response to the Ottawa Agreements of 1932. Typical of 1930s-vintage plants, it processed cattle, sheep, and calves as well. I-beams over the railway track just outside the cold storage area of the plant were used to transfer ice to the rooftop bunkers of reefer cars for shipping chilled meats to eastern markets and to tidewater for export. Much of the ice for this plant was cut from the North Saskatchewan River. (Archives of Ontario, C262-7-13, CPM 2.3, A04618)

The Harris Abattoir (Western) soon after it was built in St-Boniface, Manitoba, in 1925, immediately adjacent to St-Boniface Union Stockyards, just east of the City of Winnipeg. The windowless structure bearing the sign is the cold storage area immediately beside railway tracks for shipping fresh chilled meats to eastern and export markets. To its left, the five-storey windowed building is the main processing area of the plant. A livestock ramp conveys cattle to the fifth-storey kill floor. The single track running past the large tanks is for inedible by-products and the oils produced by the rendering plant. The small white building in the centre foreground is a mechanical ice plant, an innovation at a time when many plants were still using ice cut from nearby rivers and lakes. The stone building in the far distance on the right side is King George V School. (Archives of Ontario, C262-6-8, HA H1, AO 4613)

Swift Premium, 'the two most trusted words in meat.' Swift Canadian's Edmonton plant dates back to 1908. By the 1960s the five-storey plant complex had diversified and expanded in all directions, concealing all evidence of the original structure. The windowed building on the left contains offices and laboratories, while the cooler is at the centre. Railway tracks, livestock pens, and loading docks are hidden from street view at the rear of the plant. This plant was purchased by Gainers, Burns, and then Maple Leaf Foods. It was finally closed in 1997. (City of Edmonton Archives, EA-267-41)

Opened in 1970, Canada Packers' Red Deer plant was the last of a generation of dedicated beef kill and chill plants in Western Canada. Its slaughter capacity of 800 head per day was quite a respectable volume in the early 1970s, but was uneconomically small by the late 1980s. Built of concrete block painted white in a one-storey configuration, the western beef plants were bleak-looking structures built close to the edge of smaller cities. Note that there is no stockyard and no rail access for cattle. All cattle are delivered to the covered stock pens to the right by semitrailer with a large area for washing the livestock trailers to the rear of the plant. Only two doors provide access to railway reefer cars for shipping chilled beef to the eastern market, while semitrailers serving both eastern and local markets were loaded through the four truck docks. (Archives of Ontario, C262-7-13, CPM 2.10, A0 4616)

A Cargill Foods plant just north of High River, Alberta, looking west in 2000. Finished cattle are unloaded into covered pens on the north side of the plant. The plant is served by a rail line between the east side of the plant and the settling ponds in the foreground. However, cattle are shipped in and boxed beef is shipped out in highway semitrailers, which are parked on the west side of the plant. (Ian MacLachlan)

Cattle kill floor of the Toronto Municipal Abattoir in 1917. The carcasses at the left are at half hoist while the centre carcass is being split using a hand saw. Only one interior light is visible, underscoring the importance of large windows to admit natural daylight to processing and manufacturing operations. (City of Toronto Archives, RG8, Series 55, Item 157)

Cattle kill floor using siding bed technology, which was not displaced by on-the-rail processing until after 1950. The two carcasses in the foreground rest on pritch plates, while siders remove the hide from the abdomen in what is clearly a cooperative process. In the middle ground two carcasses are at 'half hoist' to remove the hide from the rump. Hide removal is completed at full hoist in the far distance and the carcass is shifted to a moving rail. In the 1940s workers were still equipped with soft hats (in lieu of helmets) and hand saws were used to remove the feet. The scabbard hanging by a chain from the waist of the worker is similar to those worn up to the present day as the meat cutter's 'badge of office.' (Archives of Ontario C262-7-13, CPM 2.3a, A0 4619)

The hide-off area of a Canada Packers cattle line in the 1940s. At the far left the carcass is eviscerated and the viscera are placed on the conveyor table, a relatively new innovation at that time. Just left of centre, a carcass is split with a reciprocating saw, one of the earliest power tools in use for dressing beef. Note the heavy wooden ceiling beams required to support the overhead rail. (Archives of Ontairo, C262-7-13, CPM 2.3a, A0 4620)

KILL AND CHILL

Restructuring Canada's Beef Commodity Chain

Introduction

The meat-packing industry is the central link in a long value added chain that begins on the farm or ranch with calf production and ends when the consumer picks out a Styrofoam tray in the supermarket meat department. Adjacent links in the chain may be articulated by arm's length market transactions or simply as an accounting entry at factory cost between two divisions of an agribusiness conglomerate. Each of the links in the value added chain has a location. This location may be a thousand kilometres from its adjacent link or it could be just across the fence or through the cooler doors. The commodity chain knits together diverse activities in different locations. The links between places change with the passage of time. It is difficult to look at the distribution of economic activity in space and not ask, 'But what was here before?' We need a historical backdrop to provide a temporal context for understanding the development of the value added chain.

These three dimensions could be conceived as the outline of a cube with the vertical progression from calf to hamburger patty on the y-axis. Space, from western livestock surplus regions to eastern livestock deficit regions, would be the x-axis. The history of corporate organization, technological development, and the regulatory environment of the chain through time would be represented by the z-axis pointing into the page, starting in the 1870s and finishing in 2000. In this industrial geography, the description of the imaginary cube is organized according to the first of these contextual dimensions, giving pride of place to the sequence in which value is added in the chain. Part 1 deals with producing cattle, an agricultural activity that begins with the pro-

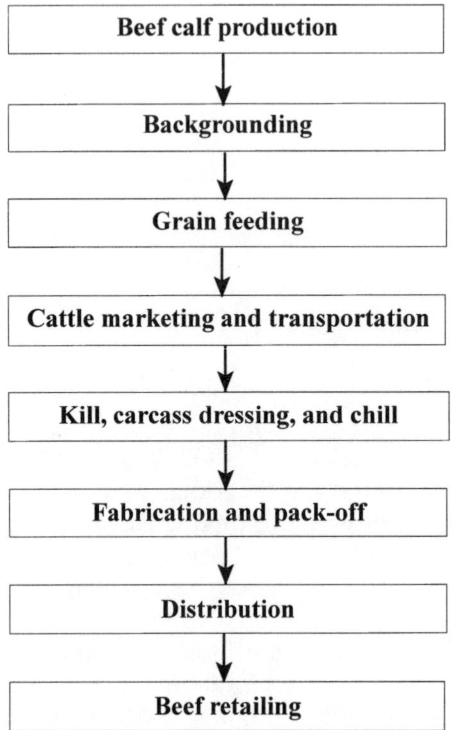

Figure I.1. The cattle–beef commodity chain.

duction of calves and culminates with the marketing of finished slaughter cattle. Part 2 is concerned with processing beef as an industrial activity situated mainly in the meat-packing industry. Part 3 deals with marketing beef and the retail meat trade (Figure I.1).

The Agroindustrial Commodity Chain

An agroindustrial commodity chain is a sequence of discrete economic activities linked by transactions that articulate farms to firms and ultimately to final demand in the form of consumers. Value added is simply the value of outputs minus the value of inputs. The added value is the product of the factors of production (land, labour, capital, and entrepreneurship) that are combined with inputs from other industries to produce a socially useful good or service. The output of one activity becomes the input of the next activity and value is added within each link of the chain that represents a different industry. The value added chain articulates industries into a production system.

Different industries have different firm-size distributions. Thus, the transactions between adjacent links in the chain are almost invariably asymmetric. Buyer and seller do not have equal influence in the negotiation of the price. Commercial farmers have long felt a sense of powerlessness as they sell most of their agricultural products (crops, livestock, and milk) to much larger industrial scale processors 'in the city.' Few agroindustrial commodity chains in Canada have had a greater or more persistent imbalance than the meat-packing oligopsony in which (focusing only on the larger players) 15,000 calf producers sell feeder cattle to 400 feeders, who in turn sell finished slaughter cattle to a dozen or so meat-packing plants.

The asymmetry, however, does not end there. There are marked differences in turnover and margin between agricultural production and food processing. Agriculture is generally a low-turnover, high-margin business, and few types of agriculture have as low a turnover as the production of cattle. Combining gestation, maturation, and finishing, it takes more than two years from conception to slaughter of a steer, compared with less than a year for a pig, and scarcely three months for a broiler chicken. The value added to beef cattle is large, but this must be offset by the slow turnover.

Meat packing, however, is a high-turnover, low-margin business. Meat-packing firms have massive revenues and massive costs. Their profit is an extraordinarily small percentage of their revenues. That is not to say that the meat packers are not profitable, for they usually are. But the essence of value added in meat packing is in the huge volume of livestock inputs, enormous tonnage of beef output, and rapid turnover in between. After all, you either sell it or smell it.

The links in the value added chain are often so widely separated in space that the common carriers providing specialized transportation services for living animals or perishable products are rightly considered as value added links in their own right. In other cases the links of the value added chain thrive because of their very proximity. Chicago's Union Stock Yards has always been the prototype of the U.S. meat-packing industrial complex, while Toronto, Winnipeg, and Calgary used to be the best-known Canadian exemplars. Perhaps the most notable thing about these classic examples of meat-packing industrial complexes is that every one of them has been abandoned and dismantled in the past two decades, with scarcely a trace remaining.

The cattle–beef value added chain is truly a commodity chain. The prices of both cattle and beef are cyclical over the long term and volatile over the short run. Cattle are a crude resource product, and the price and supply depend on natural cyclical factors such as the gestation period, random climatic shocks such as drought, and the breeding and culling decisions of thousands of cattle producers. The meat-packing industry is constantly responding to price changes that it cannot control or predict, despite widespread allegations of collusion and price manipulation from both agricultural producers and domestic consumers.

Whether the adjacent links in the chain are spatially remote, next door, or integrated under one roof, the value added chain articulates places just as it articulates industries. The value added chain is the mechanism by which changes in demand or supply make themselves felt, channelling global events to localities, sometimes changing places forever, most notably when investments in meat-packing plants are made or unmade. Changes in consumer preferences, one might say food fashions, have been manifest in declining per capita beef consumption. The full impact of consumer taste preferences is transmitted along the value added chain from the supermarket all the way to the calf producer hundreds or thousands of kilometres away.

The structure of this book parallels the cattle–beef commodity chain. The first chapter describes the regional structure of the beef cow herd in Canada and outlines the fundamental components of beef calf production. Most beef calves are produced on specialized farms known as cow-calf operations or ranches, but they are also very commonly found on mixed farms to provide an alternative source of income, especially for part-time farmers. A historical outline of the development of cattle breeding in Canada is provided to explain one of the key strategic decisions of calf production and to put the development of exotic crossbreeds into a temporal context.

While cattle have always been specially fattened in preparation for slaughter, large-scale grain-based cattle feedlots created a new mode of factory farm production during the post–Second World War era. Cattle finishing takes place in every province, but Chapter 2 focuses on the large-scale feedlots of Alberta, where about 70 per cent of Canada's beef cattle spend their last months being grain-finished in preparation for slaughter. Cattle finishing adds value to calves close to the site of their production, and it is an important step in the diversification of the western economy. Until the mid-1980s cattle feeding in western Canada was discouraged by statutory grain rates (the 'Crow rate'). Rapid growth of large-scale feedlots since that time may be traced to changes in federal transportation and agricultural policy. Cattle feeding is a localized activity, and it has a localized impact. Some of the immediate odour and environmental problems stemming from intensive livestock operations are serious enough to prompt calls for new regulatory instruments that may have an impact on the profitability and scale of future cattle feeding in southern Alberta.

At the beginning of the twentieth century, cattle marketing required an extensive infrastructure to manage the care and transportation of a living product that might be slaughtered thousands of miles from where it was produced. Chapter 3 reviews the issues unique to the marketing of a product weighing half a tonne or more, which has enormous natural variation, is vulnerable to many hazards when removed from its home range, and must be carefully confined lest it simply walk away. Stockyards were the publicly regulated facilities for the loading, containment, and marketing of cattle and other livestock. They were located in most metropolitan areas between Montreal and Vancouver and were the principal attraction for the large-scale integrated packing houses that were built in the first half of the century. Cattle logistics and marketing have changed profoundly as livestock railcars have been phased out and replaced by semitrailer cattle liners, and the sale of cattle has shifted from head-to-head competitive bidding by 'commission men' in a metropolitan stockyard to sales direct to the packer. Two short case studies are presented, one of the Ontario Stock Yards in Toronto, Canada's largest public stockyard, and the other of the Lethbridge Stock Yard, typical of the smaller Prairie receiving yards from whence cattle began their long journeys eastward.

In Canada, the slaughter and dressing out of cattle became an industrial-scale activity in the closing years of the nineteenth century. Chapter 4 discusses how industrial meat packing evolved in Canada. Slaughter was driven out of built-up commercial areas, and urban butcher shops relinquished their traditional roles in the purchase and dispatch of live animals to concentrate on retailing. But the industrialization of meat-packing was not even or complete. Rural slaughter remained significant until the 1950s, and some still goes on. Unlike the United States, Canada debated the merits of a system of public abattoirs following the European model. This movement in favour of publicly owned and operated slaughter facilities, however, was pre-empted by the construction of integrated packing plants by the private sector between 1890 and 1914. As cattle slaughter became an industrial activity, the division of labour deepened, and parts of the carcass-dressing process began to be done on the rail. The disassembly of livestock suspended by their hind legs on a packinghouse rail was the inspiration for Henry Ford's first automobile assembly line. The natural animate variability in cattle and the nature of organic tissue required more labour-intensive technology than automobile manufacturing but in other respects the turn-of-the century meat-packing industry in North America was the prototype for the Fordist revolution.

The earliest industrial packing plants were developed from urban butcher shops, rural cattle dealers, and cattle producers. In most cases killing and dressing cattle was a sideline, and industrial meat packers made their big money from exporting bacon, ranching and cattle dealing, and retailing. Scant years after creating truly industrial concerns, the early meat-packing scions such as William Davies, Senator Patrick Burns, and Sir Joseph Flavelle became the controversial and roundly detested subjects of a variety of scandals related to sanitation, adulteration of the product, and manipulation of prices to the detriment of both livestock producers and meat consumers. None of these allegations was ever proven in Canada. But it was clear to all that meat packing became almost unbelievably profitable when times were good. Thus, the meat packing industrialists were publicly excoriated, not for their failings, but for their very conspicuous accomplishments in a capitalist society.

Chapter 5 addresses the modern kill floor, classifying meat-packing in three categories: farm slaughter (uninspected), small-scale meat packers (provincially inspected), and integrated large-scale meat-packers (federally inspected but largely obsolete). Canada Packers, once Canada's largest meat-packing enterprise, revolutionized cattle dressing when it developed the first continuous on-the-rail beef-dressing technology in the late 1940s, one of the few innovations in meat packing that diffused from Canada to the United States. Humane animal handling and slaughter issues came to the fore in the 1950s, as social pressure was brought to bear on meat-packing technology. Regulatory change forced meat packers to revise their practices on the kill floor. In the 1960s, many small-scale packers were forced to renovate their facilities to meet the provisions of provincial inspection legislation or, indeed, to close their facilities and focus on another line of business. Responding to all of these factors, the meat packers began to shift their beef operations to Alberta, closer to the source of fed cattle.

Chapter 6 picks up the story of Canada's 'big three' meat packers (Canada Packers, Swift Canadian, and Burns and Company) in 1928. By then, all of the original founders had given way to a new generation of corporate meat packers, who were expanding to operate as national firms in what was becoming a national industry. The big three were regularly pilloried as a ruthless oligopoly that was the subject of several inquiries into alleged manipulation of the market and unfair market control. None of the inquiries ever succeeded, but they fixed the packers in the public mind as a combine to be hobbled. Paradoxically, all three firms disintegrated as a result of the very competition that they had always insisted was in everyone's best interest. At the same time and in the same way as happened in the United States, all three meat packers were acquired in leveraged buyouts as their asset values exceeded their ability to generate profit. In a few short years from 1987 to 1995 the last of the old oligopoly exited the beef-processing sector to be replaced by an entirely new oligopoly that controls as much of the beef-packing industry as the big three had up to the previous decade.

Chapter 7 addresses the labour process in meat-packing, highlighting the division of labour and the unique packing-house workforce. It describes the emergence of the United Packinghouse Workers of America in the 1930s and shows how, with favourable wartime labour controls, it was able to countervail the bargaining power of the big three. Labour relations in the Canadian meat-packing industry were modelled after those in the United States. A tradition of pattern bargaining developed, and wages gradually converged on a national standard. When the labour relations system of the United Packinghouse Workers reached its pinnacle in 1980, each of the big three had a master agreement that was national in scope, that was negotiated nationally, that paid the same wage premiums for equivalent packing-house occupations, and was only pennies away from a national wage that applied from the Atlantic to the Pacific. No sooner had the system of labour relations reached this remarkable degree of convergence than it began to disintegrate, a process that became complete when the last Canada Packers' beef-processing plants were closed down in 1991.

The denouement in the transformation of Canada's meat-packing industry is described in Chapter 8. Restructuring was rapid and comprehensive and no part of the industry was left untouched. It included technology change and increasing returns to scale, the boxed beef revolution, and the advent of carcass fabrication (first in central distribution centres and later as an integral part of cattle processing), the rise of a new generation of meat packers in new locations, and the collapse of the system of pattern bargaining that had developed in the immediate post-war era. The result was a new geography of cattle and beef processing.

Chapter 9 deals with a variety of components in the meat-marketing process, past and present. The industrialization of meat-packing depended on the refrigerated shipment and refrigerated warehousing of large quantities of perishable fresh meats. A system of branch houses to distribute their perishable products in widely dispersed markets became an important competitive advantage of the big three. The gradual demise of the branch-house system parallelled the inexorable rise of the large supermarket chains. Refrigerated beef shipments shifted from the packer-owned branch house to the chain-owned distribution centre, and eventually direct to the individual supermarket retailer. The specialized handling and equipment that swinging sides of beef required became obsolete with the advent of boxed beef, the last nail in the coffin of the packer-owned distribution apparatus.

One of the most significant factors in the restructuring of the meat-packing industry in Canada and the United States has been the long decline of per capita consumption of red meat in general and beef in particular. While the year-to-year changes have not been smooth, the industry endured a twenty-two-year slide in per capita beef consumption (with a few blips) that was exacerbated by a downward phase in the beef cycle. The combined result was that the number of cattle slaughtered in federally inspected facilities in Canada declined for nine of the fourteen years between 1977 and 1991. This demonstrates the close relationship between consumers, processors, and producers in a long commodity chain that persists despite sweeping structural changes in every link from farm to firm to final demand by consumers.

The concluding discussion in Chapter 10 summarizes the key factors that have influenced the cattle–beef commodity chain, emphasizing the rationalization of meat-packing plants and the industry's shift to the west.

Part One

PRODUCING CATTLE

ONE

Calf Production: Breeding Beef Cows

The pastoral landscape of southern Alberta's foothills on a sunny day in spring is unforgettable. Spring rains have transformed the mixed grass prairie from the dun of winter to shamrock. The azure sky is uninterrupted by clouds, so the eye is drawn immediately to the horizon, scalloped by receding sets of verdant hills rising west to the snow-capped Rockies in the far distance. It is May 1994, and I am driving my old station wagon along a rutted track about thirty kilometres west of Granum. Cresting yet another rise, the branding corrals of the Calderwood Ranch come into view in the draw below.

The corrals are surrounded by about a dozen pick-up trucks and my station wagon immediately identifies me as a stranger 'from town.' Surrounding the trucks, five hundred Hereford cows mill nervously, while inside the corrals, five hundred calves are bawling at the top of their lungs. They were rounded up early this morning on horseback, driven down from the hills to the corrals, and then separated from their mothers for the first time in their lives, accounting for all the ruckus.

This is a traditional community branding, and labour is supplied by a dozen or so nearby ranchers. Next week there will be another branding, and the Calderwoods will go off to another ranch to provide their labour in exchange for the many services provided today. It is a hard day's work that culminates with a barbecue, consisting of thinly sliced beef braised in a tangy orange sauce, lots of cold beer, and socializing after the enforced isolation of a long winter.

There is a distinct division of labour in a community branding. 'Heelers,' the men and women who bring their own horses to the branding, ride into the calf pen and 'heel' the nearest calf by dropping a loop of the lariat immediately in front of its hind hooves. They pull the loop tight to ensnare the hind legs once the animal has stepped inside, wind a 'dally' round the saddle horn and ride into the branding area, dragging the unwilling calf on braced fore legs behind them. A pair of the strongest young men wrestle the calf to the ground and remove the lariat. The wrestler in front kneels on the calf's neck and bends and twists the fore leg. The hind-end wrestler holds one calf leg extended while sitting 'flat-ass,' his foot braced against the other hock. This technique (known as 'flat-assing') completely immobilizes the calf and exposes both the side for branding and, for male calves, the scrotum for cutting. Middle-aged women use a large stainless steel hypodermic needle to vaccinate against a variety of cattle diseases, then they apply an ear punch to pierce the cartilage and attach a plastic tag to repel flies. The most skilled work is the castration of the bull calves using a stockman's jack-knife. The bottom of the scrotum is slit from side to side, and the testes are squeezed out and drawn about a foot from the body. The blunt bottom end of the blade is used to carefully pare away the blood vessels from each stretched spermatic cord before it is cut and snaps elastically back into the scrotum. The operation takes about fifteen seconds after which the castrator drops the two thumb-sized testes into a plastic ice cream bucket. Branding is done by two older men; the task requires experience but less stamina. The brand is complex and requires three separate branding irons which are heated in a small propane furnace. It takes less than a minute to apply the three irons and the calves bawl a little. Occasionally a calf that missed dehorning immediately after birth is discovered. Dehorning is accomplished by applying a dehorning iron to the horn buttons and seems extremely painful, far worse than branding. The calf bellows in protest until the last of the living horn tissue is burned away. The calf is then released and makes its way out of the corral, somehow finding its mother in a sea of white-faced cows. The couple slowly make their way back into the hills.

As producers of animals, cattle people are drawn together by a common annual reproductive cycle: the fundamentals of cattle production are shared among diverse culture regions and cattle breeds. From the shaggy Highland cattle of Argyll, Scotland, to the humped Africander of South Africa, all cattle producers superimpose a 285-day-gestation imperative on the vicissitudes of world beef prices, weather, and the grassland resource. Nevertheless, there are sharp regional differences in animal husbandry practices that in some ways are deeply rooted in tradition, while being in constant flux to cope with the dynamics of the changing environment and marketplace.

It is not surprising that cattle producers are jealous of their independence; flexibility is essential if they are to respond to conditions that are always changing. Calf production is a traditional pursuit, and strategies such as breed selection, calving times, or feeding regimes are passed down the generations even though they may not always be functional or well adapted to current conditions. According to Mike Sullivan in Peterborough County: 'We have always backgrounded and the calf prices ... like last year was a year that we shouldn't have backgrounded. We should have sold the calves last fall and sold the corn. But you do the same thing year after year so you kind of stick with it.' Consistent with this adherence to traditional methods is political conservatism, 'innate suspicion,' and an 'independent frontier mentality' manifest most clearly as a distrust of collectives and any form of regulation (Creative Research Group 1983: 8). Unlike dairy or hog production, for example, beef producers need not answer to any marketing board.

The irony is that while the sector is bound by tradition, there is probably a wider strategic repertoire among cow-calf operators than is found in any other type of livestock production. In the absence of a central market or producer cooperative, there is more scope and incentive to use different production strategies, breeding philosophies, and land management systems. The dairy farmer milks cows twice a day, 365 days a year, and gets a monthly check. The dedicated cow-calf producer, who sells yearlings in spring, gets most of the year's income in a single annual check. Despite their freedom to exercise different options, cow-calf operators function in much the same way from one year to the next. It seems paradoxical that cattle producers as a group demand the freedom to react flexibly and rapidly to market conditions, yet most develop one strategy and mode of operation and stick with it. However, there are always a few proud mavericks, who are not afraid to try something radically different and somehow succeed at it.

The strategy used by cow-calf producers depends in large measure on the working roles of the partners operating the farm. In some cases, the farm operator works full-time on the farm while a spouse works full- or part-time off the farm, taking little active role in the farm business. In other cases, family farms are true partnerships with all activities shared equally. Notwithstanding the abiding importance of tradition and conservatism among cattle producers, farm families, no less than their urban counterparts, are challenging traditional gender roles in the division of labour. Darlene and Claude Bowen in Ontario's clay belt are a case in point:

In the group of producers that we know here in Timiskaming, there are many wives who are as capable of managing the operation as their husbands. They can calve cows, run equipment, make management decisions, and keep the records. They take a very active role. They are partners and without them, many farm operations would not operate effectively.

My husband has worked away a lot, on pipeline and road construction. One year he left the day after Christmas and did not return until the middle of April. My sons, who were young teenagers at the time, helped me calve all the cows and kept everything fed and operating smoothly until he returned. Another year he left in May and came back in November. The joke around here is that he usually leaves at the beginning of haying or calving season. It was beneficial from a financial point of view because we could keep everything paid off, increase livestock inventories, and make capital investments in the farm. In the beef industry you can't afford to carry debt. Your income comes in a large burst in one season and this must be spread over the full year.

We have always viewed the time that Claude worked away as an opportunity to invest in the farm. It wouldn't have been possible for this to happen if our sons and myself were not committed to staying here and assuming responsibility. It also required a great deal of trust and confidence on Claude's part to leave the operation in our hands. This is the way it works with a lot of couples. My husband is as capable in the house as he is outside. It isn't just the outside work we share, we share everything.

Doug and Trudy Desjardins of Renfrew County are siblings with a more rigid division of labour in the shared management of their cow-calf enterprise.

DOUG: We each of us have our specialty here, right? I look after the crops and the growing of the crops and the machinery end of it. And Trudy is just the dictionary of genetics. Like, we have 170 some cows in our herd and she knows every cow generations and generations back.

TRUDY: And our marketing books. So I'm the marketing person. You have to understand that Doug and I each own our own land, our own machinery, our own cattle, but we do everything, we co-mingle it to make two ... So that makes more book work for me but in the end we split everything.

Clearly, the opportunities to finance farm expansion, and the approach to feeding, breeding, and marketing depend on the division of labour within the farm household and opportunities for off-farm employment. Some cow-calf operators are high-income urban professionals who raise cattle as an avocation and part-time activity. In other cases, calf producers are proud to declare that they have never taken an off-farm job, which is adduced as a measure of their proficiency as farmers.

In many ways the fundamental aspects of calf production have remained unchanged over the past hundred years. Calf production relies on a natural process driven by the rhythm of the seasons, the land base, and the gestation cycle. Although the technical responses may have changed, the key decision points in the annual reproduction process are no different than they were a century ago. Thus, calf production is the most traditional of all stages in the cattle–beef commodity chain.

Overview of Calf Production in Canada

The long commodity chain that leads to the roast on the Canadian dinner table, the fast-food hamburger patty, and worldwide exports of Canadian beef and beef by-products begins with bovine reproduction and the birth, nurture, and growth of calves. While a significant number of calves are created as a by-product of the dairy farm sector, our focus here is mainly on beef cattle and the farms that produce them. 'Cow-calf operations' maintain herds of beef cows, ideally, each cow produces one calf per year. Ranches are cow-calf operations based on large areas of uncultivated grazing land that is usually leased from the provincial government.

Beef cattle are a commodity, differentiated by breed, age, sex, and conformation characteristics. As such, their price is determined exogenously on world markets, and calf producers consider themselves to be price takers. Like any other commodity, the price of cattle is cyclical with a typical wavelength of ten to twelve years. Since cows can only produce one calf a year (unlike hogs, for example, which farrow 2.4 times a year, producing an annual average of twenty-five live offspring), the supply of cattle responds quite slowly to an increase in prices. The commodity cycle is quite long. In Canada, cattle numbers grew rapidly from 1951 to 1964 and again from 1969, reaching an all-time high in 1975. Numbers bottomed in 1987 and peaked again in 1996 (Figure 1.1).

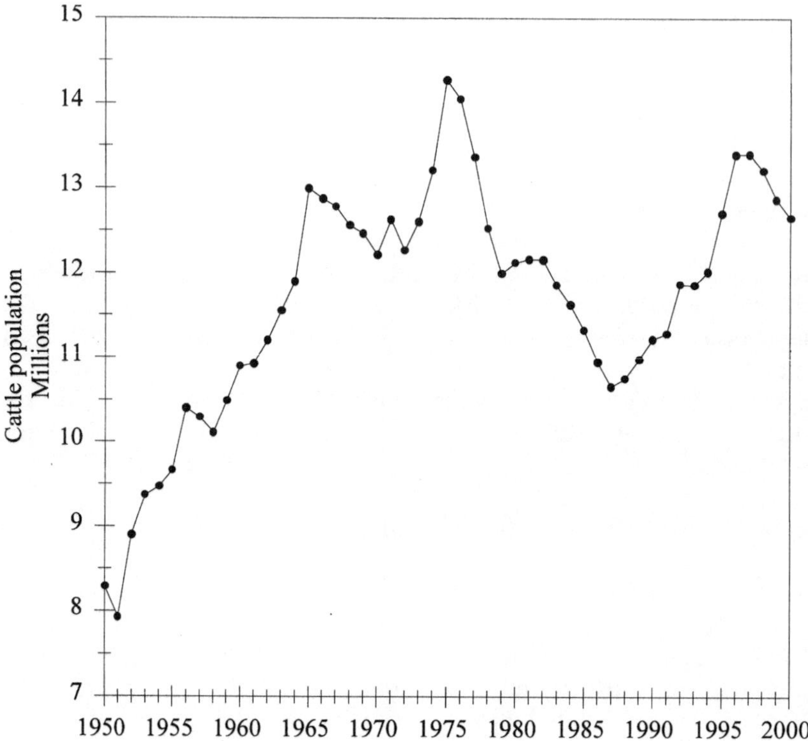

Figure 1.1. Canadian cattle cycles, 1 January, 1950–2000. Source: Agriculture Canada *Livestock Market Review*, various years.

Canada's cattle population increased by an average 5.5 per cent per year between 1972 and 1975. This period of growth in the national cattle herd was well in excess of the fastest rates of human population growth anywhere in the world. Cattle numbers then dropped by 25 per cent between 1975 and 1987, as a result of Prairie drought in the early 1980s superimposed on a trend towards lower beef consumption, lower cattle slaughter, and heavier carcass weights.

Although no region in Canada is untouched by the cyclical behaviour of the cattle population, the amplitude of the cattle cycle tends to be lower in eastern Canada and more volatile in the west. Western Canada has a much stronger supply response to price changes and most of the cyclical correction over the past forty years has taken place in the Prairies (Schissel et al. 1995: 178), one of the many components that contributes to western Canada's boom-and-bust type of economy.

Crude and semiprocessed commodities such as cattle and beef remain vitally important to Canada's balance of international trade, so much so, in fact, that Canadian economic history is often interpreted by the 'staples theory,' proposed by Harold Adams Innis (Watkins 1963). As a staple industry, calf production shares many of the characteristics of other Canadian resource exports: They are the foundation of Canada's economic history and of Canada's comparatively high standard of living. As a commodity industry, calf production is inherently cyclical and vulnerable to exogenous changes on world markets and climatic anomalies.

The Regional Structure of Calf Production in Canada

The provincial distribution of Canada's cattle herd is sharply regionalized. Table 1.1 breaks out the cattle population by province and by function. Dairy cows and dairy replacement heifers (which will be classed as dairy cows after their first calf is born) are primarily intended to produce milk. However, when dairy cows become too old to produce milk they are culled for slaughter and, in the aggregate, in the 1980s, accounted for about 12 per cent of Canada's beef production (Fairbairn 1989: 9). Because milk may only be sold within the province where it is produced, and since fluid milk is comparatively expensive to transport over large distances, every metropolitan area in Canada is surrounded by a belt of dairy farms. Thus dairy cows are distributed in much the same way as the human population. (Table 1.1). The one exception is Quebec, with a large dairy herd concentrated in the St Lawrence Lowlands and south to the international boundary with a small outlier in the Lac St-Jean region. In the 1931 Census of Agriculture, dairy cows made up 44.3 per cent of the total national cattle herd, but by 2000 they constituted only 9.0 per cent. A structural shift away from dairy cattle in favour of the beef breeds underlies regional changes in the distribution of the national cattle herd taken as a whole.

Beef cows and beef replacement heifers are intended mainly to produce calves for slaughter. Steers (castrated male cattle) and slaughter heifers are intended to be fattened for slaughter without ever reproducing. Relatively poor quality farmland in most of Atlantic Canada accounts for its remarkably small beef cattle population, although Prince Edward Island, using potato by-products as feed, has a greater

Table 1.1 Regional structure of the Canadian cattle herd, 1 January 2000

	Dairy cows & replacement heifers	Beef cows & replacement heifers	Steers & slaughter heifers	Human population[a]	Beef cows per farm[b]
Number in thousands					
Newfoundland	5.2	1.0	0.2	568.5	8
PEI	22.8	18.2	26.9	129.8	21
Nova Scotia	35.8	32.7	8.7	899.9	18
New Brunswick	28.6	24.6	11.4	723.9	19
Quebec	605.0	239.0	58.0	6,896.0	27
Ontario	551.0	460.0	327.0	10,084.9	23
Manitoba	64.5	582.0	79.0	1,091.9	47
Saskatchewan	46.5	1,199.0	70.0	988.9	50
Alberta	139.0	1,885.0	1,165.0	2,545.6	63
British Columbia	109.5	289.0	27.5	3,282.0	44
Canada	1,607.9	4,730.5	1,773.7	27,296.9	45
Percentage of total[c]					
Newfoundland	0.3	0.0	0.0	2.1	
PEI	1.4	0.4	1.5	0.5	
Nova Scotia	2.2	0.7	0.5	3.3	
New Brunswick	1.8	0.5	0.6	2.7	
Quebec	37.6	5.1	3.3	25.3	
Ontario	34.3	9.7	18.4	37.0	
Manitoba	4.0	12.3	4.5	4.0	
Saskatchewan	2.9	25.4	4.0	3.6	
Alberta	8.6	39.9	65.7	9.3	
British Columbia	6.8	6.1	1.6	12.0	
Canada	99.9	100.1	100.1	99.8	

[a]1996 Census; Yukon and NWT included in total for Canada
[b]Average number of beef cows per farm reporting beef cows in 1996 Census
[c]Percentages do not total 100 because of rounding.
Source: Computed from Statistics Canada 1998 Catalogue 93-358-XPB; 23-603-UPE

percentage of the national steer herd than its tiny population would warrant. Quebec has historically been a large producer of dairy cattle and hogs rather than beef cattle. With one-quarter of the Canadian population, Quebec's beef cow herd is a paltry 5.1 per cent of the national total. Ontario has Canada's fourth-largest beef cattle herd, but beef cows and slaughter cattle are under-represented when compared with Ontario's dairy cow herd and human population. The Prairie provinces account for 77.4 per cent of Canada's beef cows and 74.1 per cent of Canada's slaughter cattle. Beef cattle outnumber humans in both Saskatchewan and Alberta. Saskatchewan has one-quarter of the national beef cow herd, in part a response to many years of policies to diversify the province's agricultural base away from 'king wheat.' Surprisingly, Saskatchewan has only 5.9 per cent of the steers and slaughter heifers, which is evidence of the large numbers of weaned calves and yearlings it exports on the hoof to Alberta, Ontario, and the United States for finishing. With 6.1 per cent of Canada's beef cows, British Columbia has only 1.6 per cent of the national herd of slaughter cattle, showing that it, too, ships most of its feeder cattle out of province, mainly to Alberta and the state of Washington. Alberta, of course, has the largest beef cow and slaughter cattle population of any Canadian province. It has nearly 40 per cent of Canada's beef cows and replacement heifers and more than 65 per cent of the steers and slaughter heifers.

Table 1.2 provides a structural profile in 1976, just after the historical peak of the cattle population illustrated in Figure 1.1. The regional structure of Canada's dairy herd has not changed significantly, but its size has contracted dramatically from 2.54 million dairy cows and dairy replacement heifers in 1976 to only 1.61 million in 2000. Only the dairy herds of Newfoundland and British Columbia were spared from this national decline. With respect to beef cows and replacement heifers, Alberta has increased its share quite modestly, mainly at the expense of Ontario and Saskatchewan. But the really dramatic change between 1976 and 2000 is in the distribution of steers and slaughter heifers. Alberta increased its share of slaughter cattle from 30 per cent to 65 per cent, while Ontario dropped from 40.5 per cent to 18.4 per cent. Until the late 1970s, large numbers of feeder calves were shipped east by rail for feeding on Ontario corn and eventual slaughter in the Toronto region. Thus, a good proportion of the 40.5 per cent of steers and slaughter heifers on Ontario farms on 1 January 1976 were actually born on the Prairies in the spring of 1975. By 2000, the transcontinental traffic in live cattle on the hoof has greatly diminished, and most Canadian beef cattle are grain-finished in Alberta, which accounts for the change in the locational structure of the national beef herd.

Statistics Canada does not collect data for beef calves in its Census of Agriculture, and beef cows therefore provide the best measure of the spatial distribution of calf production (Figure 1.2). Almost every census subdivision in Canada produces some calves for eventual consumption as beef. Many mixed farms keep ten to twenty beef cows to

Table 1.2 Regional structure of the Canadian cattle herd, 1 January 1976

	Dairy cows & replacement heifers	Beef cows & replacement heifers	Steers & slaughter heifers	Human population[a]	Beef cows per farm[b]
Number in thousands					
Newfoundland[c]	2.7	1.6	0.1	557.7	6
PEI	32.6	18.0	26.3	118.2	9
Nova Scotia	49.0	35.3	16.4	828.6	11
New Brunswick	37.8	32.5	12.9	677.3	12
Quebec	1,034.0	281.0	71.0	6,234.4	11
Ontario	895.0	600.4	904.6	8,264.5	15
Manitoba	112.0	569.8	196.2	1,021.5	29
Saskatchewan	91.0	1,388.4	306.6	921.3	32
Alberta	186.0	1,862.9	652.1	1,838.0	41
British Columbia	104.0	261.0	50.0	2,466.6	30
Canada	2,544.1	5,050.9	2,236.2	22,992.6	27
Percentage of total[d]					
Newfoundland	0.1	0.0	0.0	2.4	
PEI	1.3	0.4	1.2	0.5	
Nova Scotia	1.9	0.7	0.7	3.6	
New Brunswick	1.5	0.6	0.6	2.9	
Quebec	40.6	5.6	3.2	27.1	
Ontario	35.2	11.9	40.5	35.9	
Manitoba	4.4	11.3	8.8	4.4	
Saskatchewan	3.6	27.5	13.7	4.0	
Alberta	7.3	36.9	29.2	8.0	
British Columbia	4.1	5.2	2.2	10.7	
Canada	100.0	100.1	100.1	99.5	

[a]1976 Census; Yukon and NWT included in total for Canada
[b]Average number of beef cows per *farm reporting* beef cows in 1976 Census
[c]Cattle population for Newfoundland was interpolated from other years
[d]Percentages do not add to 100 because of rounding.
Source: Statistics Canada 1998 Catalogue 93-358-XPB; 23-603-XPE

graze fallow and stubble on land whose primary purpose is to produce crops and to help diversify farm revenues. Small beef cow herds are ubiquitous throughout the Great Lakes, St Lawrence, and Ottawa Valley Lowlands, especially on marginal crop land along the edge of uplands such as the Canadian Shield, where pastures are lush, but topography and soil conditions do not favour crops with higher returns per acre. More specialized cow-calf operations are found in

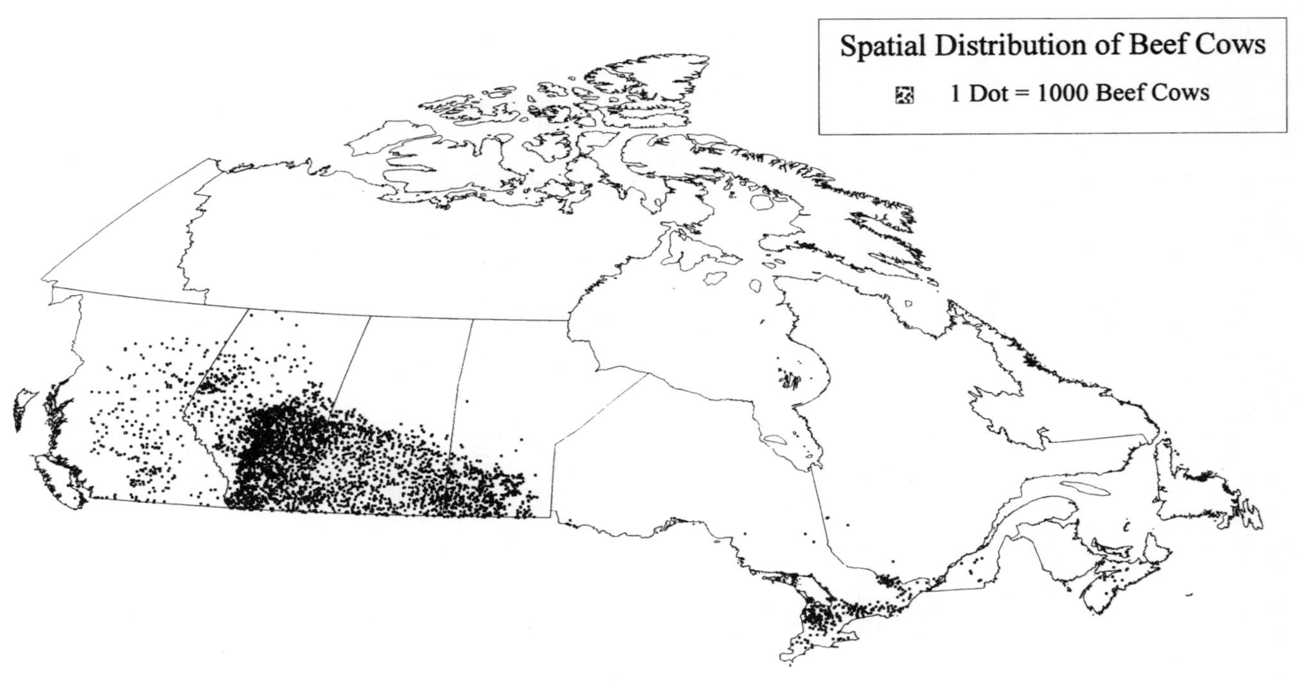

Figure 1.2. Spatial distribution of beef cows in Canada, 1996. Source: Raw data from Statistics Canada, Census of Agriculture 1996.

southern Ontario at the south end of the Bruce Peninsula in Grey and Bruce Counties, in a narrow belt between the shore of Lake Ontario and the Canadian Shield, and up the Ottawa Valley as far as Pembroke. Smaller, but locally important, concentrations of beef cows are also found on the south side of the St Lawrence River in the Eastern Townships and Beauce regions of Quebec, along the upper Saint John and Kennebecasis River valleys of New Brunswick, Queen's County in central Prince Edward Island, and in Nova Scotia from the Annapolis Valley along the Fundy Lowlands to Antigonish.

But over three-quarters of Canada's beef cows are in the Prairie west, 40 per cent in Alberta alone. The greatest concentration is found in a rectangle with its southern base covering nearly the entire east–west extent of Alberta along the U.S. border. Its eastern boundary extends straight north along the Saskatchewan boundary line. Highway 2 joining Cardston near the U.S. border through Calgary and Edmonton to Athabasca, approximates the western boundary.

On southern Alberta's 'dry land' (so called because it is not served by irrigation infrastructure) conditions are generally too arid for any but the most drought-resistant grain and oilseed crops. As many erstwhile homesteaders discovered in the 1930s, the only sustainable use for the most arid lands of Alberta and Saskatchewan is grazing. Sustainable stocking densities are determined by the local rainfall regime, in some places no more than one animal for every fifty acres of range. Palliser's Triangle, with its base running along the 49th parallel from the border of British Columbia and Alberta and 100 degrees west longitude (south of Brandon, Manitoba) and its apex at 52 degrees north (just southeast of Saskatoon), is Canada's most arid region outside of the frigid 'desert' of the far north (Spry 1968: 9, 255). The influence of Palliser's Triangle can be seen on Figure 1.2 by the lower beef cattle densities in southeastern Alberta and southwestern Saskatchewan, even though there are few competing uses for dry land that averages 30 to 40 centimetres of rain per year.

The park belt region is a transitional vegetation zone between Palliser's Triangle and woodlands: subalpine forest to the west and boreal forest to the north. It is clearly visible because of its higher stocking densities, although it is also ideal for the cultivation of grain. Along the narrow western margin of the park belt, higher elevations bring about an earlier killing frost that reduces the amount of wheat grown, leaving more land available for grazing. Hence, there is a pronounced concentration of beef cows along a north–south axis jammed in between a line joining Edmonton and Calgary and the Rocky Mountain front. During his expedition of exploration (1857–60), John Palliser observed that this axis of land intervening between the arid zone and the Rockies was so narrow that its eastern boundary was always within sight of the Rocky Mountains. Like similarly situated Switzerland and Tyrol, it had superb nutritious grasses and was better watered than the arid zone, making it ideal for cattle grazing (Spry 1968: 19–20). A second advantage of this narrow axis are the warm Chinook winds of winter that regularly blow across the Rockies from the Pacific, melting whatever snow may lie in their path. In the Chinook belt of southern Alberta it is not at all unusual to have no snow cover in midwinter, which has made the region favourable for winter grazing of livestock (Hobbs 1970: 6). This can be discerned on Figure 1.2 as the dense, nearly vertical line of dots running from the 49th parallel due north to the centre of Alberta.

Scale of Production

Cow-calf operations are concerned with reproduction of beef cattle and their size is typically measured in reproductive units, that is the number of beef cows that are kept by the farm. The minimum efficient scale for a full-time dedicated cow-calf operation is typically considered to be 100 cows. The scale of cow-calf operations in Alberta is larger than in any other province, with an average of sixty-three beef cows per cow-calf farm that reports at least one beef cow. Eastern Canadian farms average less than half this size of herd. While average beef-cow herd size has grown markedly since 1976 (Tables 1.1 and 1.2), not a single province has an average even close to the minimum efficient size. Turning to the Canada-wide herd size distribution for beef cows in 1996 (Figure 1.3), only 6.8 per cent of the cow-calf operations had in excess of 122 cows, and they accounted for 32 per cent of the total number of beef cows. The famous Douglas Lake Ranch, southwest of Kamloops, British Columbia, is the largest cow-calf operation in Canada. It controls over 500,000 acres of grazing land: 163,00 acres are deeded and 350,000 acres are leased from the provincial government. On this land, the ranch winters some 15,000 head of cattle and produces over 6,500 calves per year (Wooliams 1979; Douglas Lake Ranch 2000).

The Douglas Lake Ranch, however, is a conspicuous anomaly. In 1996, the modal cow herd size category was eighteen to forty-seven cows, well below the arbitrary 100 cow minimum size threshold. The 84 per cent of all cow-calf operations with fewer than seventy-eight head

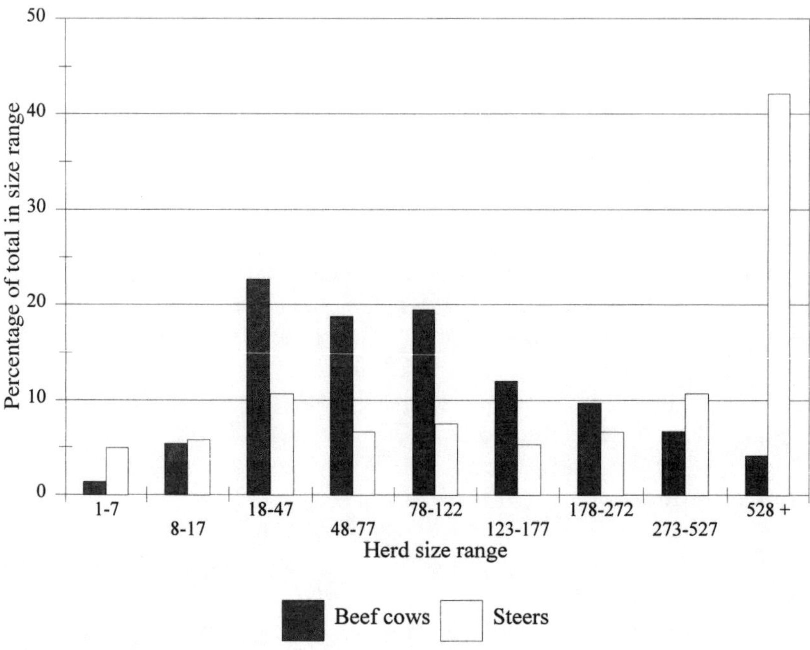

Figure 1.3. Beef cow and steer herd size distribution, 1996. Source: Statistics Canada, Census of Agriculture 1996, special tabulation.

account for nearly one half (48.1 per cent) of Canada's beef cows. Small-scale producers comprise a heterogeneous mixture of hobby farmers, part-time operators, and truly mixed farms that choose to produce below minimum scale to leave resources for other agricultural activities.

The size distribution of steer herds (mainly being fed and finished for slaughter) stands in marked contrast to the herd size distribution for beef cows (mainly breeding stock). Some 42 per cent of Canada's steers are found on only 404 cattle-feeding operations, which constitute less than one per cent of all farms reporting steers. Unlike cattle feeding, which is concentrated on a small number of very large feedlots, most cow-calf production takes place on a very large number of smaller operations.

In fact, full-time operation is atypical of most calf producers. One-half of beef-cattle farm operators (50.3 per cent) reported some non-farm employment for the operator in 1995 (Statistics Canada 1997:

Table 7). If the data included non-farm work by the operator's spouse, who in many cases effectively subsidizes farm operations, the number would be much higher. Hobby farmers may keep a small beef-cow herd for recreational purposes; indeed, beef cattle are the livestock of choice among hobby farmers. 'Many small herds of beef cattle are a source of prestige rather than profit for their owners, because they primp up the place where the hobby farmer plays cowboy on the weekends' (Hart and Mayda 1998: 60). The farm's flow of income (or losses) and depreciation expenses may be attractive for tax purposes, so the producer may be indifferent to the price obtained for calves and the overall profitability of the enterprise.

Full-time cow-calf operators regard part-time farmers with a mixture of envy and admiration. Hobby farmers may have the resources to own and operate a large ostentatious tractor, late model pickup truck, and colour-matched stock trailer, as well as a wide range of expensive agricultural machinery, luxuries that a full-time farmer may not be able to afford. On the other hand, part-timers may rent out their land at favourable rates and pay cash for services such as plowing the lane in winter, cutting and baling hay, or feeding livestock while they are on vacation. By purchasing supplies and expensive new equipment and machinery, hobby farmers support agricultural equipment dealers, which are then also available for the full-timers.

For many part-time farmers, off-farm work is a form of diversification to guard against market downturns. In addition to caring for ninety beef cows, Mike Sullivan of Peterborough County, who repairs farm machinery said:

> I think that if I was doing nothing else but looking after the cows, I could actually keep more. I could probably keep up to 150 with some part-time help. But trying to do another job like machinery repair or whatever, I just can't keep any more cattle. I'm sort of at my limit, I think. And I just wouldn't want to get into that, get locked into that, where I have nothing else to fall back on. Getting locked into the beef operation where I had nothing else to fall back on because it runs in cycles. And I've seen the cycles come and go. And in the low end of the cycle, unless there's something else to fall back on it's pretty hard to survive.

One of the advantages of large-scale cow-calf farms is that the larger operations can keep more than one bull and maintain separate groups of cows bred for different qualities and for sale in different markets. The larger cow-calf operators typically divide their animals among different pastures. In part, this is necessary because each pasture has a finite grazing capacity. It is also advantageous to apportion different qualities of forage and feed to animals at different stages of the growth and life cycle and to separate cows and bulls that produce replacement heifers from those that produce calves destined for sale and slaughter. Typically, first-calf heifers are separated from the mature cows so that they may be bred to a bull specially selected to yield low birth weight calves and to ensure that the first-calf heifers do not have to compete with larger cows to get a good diet while they are pregnant (Rode et al. 1992: 26). But separating pasturage in this way is not feasible for a herd of less than fifty cows.

Large-scale calf producers also benefit from their ability to assemble and market large homogeneous lots of feeder cattle. Ontario feedlot operators prefer to purchase a 'pot load' (semitrailer cattle liner filled with up to sixty calves) of homogeneous cattle from Alberta: 'They can phone out West and say, "I need 500 calves, I'd like a Charolais cross mix, I'd like all steers, I'd like them all preconditioned," and they can get that from one producer! ... They brought in 200 head of heifers and they looked like clones, they were all the same! They'd all come from one farm. We can't do that in Ontario with herds of 20 because of the differences in management systems.'

Fundamentals of Calf Production

Although the scale of production varies enormously between regions, the goal of calf production is common to all: to produce the greatest number of weaned calves, with the heaviest weaning weights, at the lowest cost. There are seven strategic variables in calf production: breeding, beef cows, beef bulls, calving, weaning of calves, culling of unproductive breeding stock, and pasture management.

Beef Cows

A female calf is known as a heifer. Some heifers are destined for slaughter (slaughter heifers), while others are chosen to become part of the breeding cow herd (replacement heifers). Heifers are typically bred shortly after turning one year of age, and first–calf heifers are the most likely to have calving difficulties. In the year after she has borne her first calf, she may still be marketed as a 'heiferette,' but after giving birth, she joins the breeding-cow herd. Replacement heifers are usually selected from among the best heifer calves produced within a 'closed herd.' A closed herd relies entirely on replacement heifers produced in-house as its breeding stock. Commercial beef cows have a productive lifespan of eight to fifteen years, and they are expected to produce one calf every year. Open cows (cows that have not conceived), cows that have difficulty giving birth, and cows that fail to wean a healthy calf are liable to be culled from the breeding herd and shipped off to the auction mart and then to the slaughterhouse.

Management of the cow herd involves decisions about what breed or cross-breed is best suited to the local environment and regional market conditions. Few commercial operators keep registered purebred cows, however. Registered cows are almost exclusively found in the hands of a very small number of full-time registered purebreeders, and occasionally they are owned and bred as a matter of great pride by hobby farmers. Some commercial cows are of a single identifiable breed (straight bred), while others are cross-bred to combine the best qualities of two or more separate breeds.

Most cow-calf operators have a 'survival of the fittest philosophy' and believe that any cow that is unable to thrive under rigorous conditions should be marketed for slaughter to make room for those that are more self-reliant: 'I like my cows, but I take a real hard attitude about them having to pay their own way, carrying their weight. So I don't get up in the middle of the night when the cows are calving. I check them before dark, I check them at first light, and I often get a 100 per cent [calf] crop with the help of some twins maybe. Because any cow that ever gave me any trouble, away she went. And after a few generations of that, your troublemakers are gone.'

Most beef cows are not quartered inside in the winter months, although they may have access to a lean-to or windbreak. In Ontario they are often wintered on broken scrubby pastures or 'in the bush,' where they are expected to scavenge for themselves to supplement the hay provided daily as winter feed. Calving begins in March, and in the normal course of events it takes place outdoors with minimal intervention. In bad weather or when a cow has serious calving problems such as a prolapsed uterus, a small calving shed may be available for temporary shelter. But in the main, beef cows are left in the open where they get more exercise and have fewer health problems than animals confined in a shelter.

Most heifers are first impregnated in June at an age of fourteen to fifteen months and they 'calve out' the next March after a gestation period of nine and a half months. Some ranchers avoid breeding yearling heifers because of high maternal mortality and the poor quality of calves from young mothers. In eastern Canada, calving is more closely monitored, and first-calf heifers give birth at or even before the age of two years. In Ontario, one of the newest concepts is the heifer development centre. With encouragement from the Ontario government, a number of these centres were established in various regions of the province beginning in 1991. A heifer development centre brings in other farmers' heifers at weaning time, feeds them through the winter, breeds them, and sends them back home in September as bred heifers. They are fed to gain at a modest rate in order to grow them out properly so they can calve as two-year-olds. Monthly measurements chart weight, frame scores, and even pelvic dimensions to develop high-quality maternal breeding stock. First-calf heifers are artificially inseminated using semen from a bull that is specially selected for ease of calving by young mothers. Thus, the pregnant heifer is well prepared for a lifetime of successful reproduction before she goes back to her home farm to give birth and join the breeding-cow herd (Paul Hamilton, Interview).

Beef Bulls

Artificial insemination is rarely used by beef producers, so commercial beef herds require bulls to breed the cows. Unlike cows, bulls are typically responsible for twenty to fifty calves per year depending on the area and ruggedness of grazing land. Bulls sire 100 to 300 calves in a lifetime, assuming a six-year breeding life. Because of the long generational interval and the low reproductive rate of cattle, breeding has traditionally relied upon a carefully selected purebred bull to provide important traits from outside the gene pool, while cows are typically sourced from replacement heifers born and raised within the herd. The bull is thus 'half the herd' and is considered to be a critical element in the hereditary traits of the herd such as its health and manageability and the productivity of its calves. Bulls are typically purchased for $1,500 to $4,000 at winter bull sales.

Cow-calf producers of any size keep at least two bulls. 'Maternal bulls' are selected to produce replacement heifers with good maternal qualities such as high fertility, ability to give birth without assistance, adequate milk production, and the instincts to wash, suckle, and succour their newborns. The heifer calves of maternal bulls are destined to join the breeding-cow herd. 'Terminal bulls' are bred with the progeny of the maternal bulls to produce healthy calves with high weights at weaning and good carcass traits. All of the calves sired by a terminal bull are intended for slaughter. Progeny testing is used to reveal which terminal bulls tend to produce calves with good marbling, yield, and efficient weight gain ratios.

The purchase of a maternal bull is a critical decision, because the traits will stay with the herd for future generations. The best way of verifying the ability of a maternal bull to produce good mothering cows is to examine the bull's mother, something that Trudy Desjardins of Renfrew County feels very strongly about:

> I always go and scout my maternal bulls. Terminal bulls, I don't. The reason being anything I buy for terminal purposes won't stay here long. So, I'm not as concerned about the udder and things like that so I don't go see the mother or siblings, or anything else. When it's a maternal bull that's going to have a long-lasting effect on our cow herd, that's when I go.
>
> [Interviewer: Do you just sort of lean on the fence?]
>
> Oh no! I check them all over. I ask to see the mother. And it's a real opportunity to chat just the same as we're doing and you can ask a lot of questions and see if there's consistency in the answers. And I have found that a lot of bulls are put on the market and if you actually go and see the mother, she has a poor udder, she's got poor feet and for a cow, to be retaining females from that – that's not what I want.

On average, bulls have a shorter reproductive life than cows and are only active and fertile for three to six years. By the end of the early summer breeding season, it is usually clear which bulls are no longer fertile. Infertile breeding stock are typically culled in late summer to avoid the expense of feeding an unproductive animal over the winter. However, the market price for older cows and bulls reaches a seasonal low in fall when most other producers are facing the same culling decisions. Thus, the timing of the culling decision often depends on how much winter feed is on hand.

Calving

In a beef herd, the measure of calving success is the number of live births as a percentage of the number of cows in the herd. In Alberta, with a large proportion of cattle grazing on open and unsupervised range land, an 89 per cent calf crop is typical. Ontario has a calving success rate of 95 per cent, the highest in Canada (Schissel et al. 1995:

186). On some eastern Canadian cow-calf operations the calving percentage approaches and even exceeds 100 per cent thanks to twin births and careful monitoring and intervention during calving.

Most calf producers believe that late winter or early spring calving is desirable, so that the calf is weaned by September or October and is growing well before the next winter. The earlier the calf is born, the heavier it will be when sold as a weaned calf the next fall. This may be especially important for pure-breeders to get the jump on the next year's market for purebred bulls and replacement heifers. Weaning in the early fall gives pregnant cows an opportunity to get their strength back and increase calcium levels before winter and calving again the next spring.

There are, however, also arguments in favour of fall calving and differences in calving practices among producers help to spread the supply of finished cattle ready for slaughter throughout the year. Advocates of fall calving cite moderate weather conditions in late summer and early fall when cows are giving birth. Calving takes place in clean dry pastures without the accumulation of manure and melt water that is inevitable in barns or pens during the spring. Weaned calves sell at a premium in the spring because of their scarcity, and late calving cows or cows that are still 'open' (not pregnant) after the normal breeding season are available at a substantial discount. When the breeding season starts in late October, there is an ample supply of idle bulls nearby, which may be available for a modest rent.

Some large-scale producers have two calving seasons, one in spring and one in fall. Split calving makes better use of the bulls as there are two separate breeding periods, and one bull could service fifty to sixty cows and heifers a year instead of only twenty-five to thirty in a single breeding season. If a spring-calving cow is found to be open in the fall, she can be bred again and join the fall-calvers. There are two separate marketing periods and two annual flows of income instead of one.

Calves must be 'preconditioned' for sale at some point after birth. On a traditional western Canadian ranch using spring calving, branding, castration, vaccination, and hormone administration typically take place at a round-up in late May or June. In Ontario, castration and dehorning is often done within twenty-four hours of birth. On a traditional ranch these operations are still done 'flat-ass' using nothing but muscle power to restrain the calf flat on the ground. Conventional cow-calf producers are equipped with a 'calf-table,' a miniature cattle squeeze that secures the calf and then pivots ninety degrees to lay the immobilized calf in its side. On older calves dehorning may be accomplished with electrodes or a red-hot steel cylinder that fits around the horn button and cauterizes its root. Caustic paste is also used, but this may cause problems if rain water causes the caustic solution to run into the calves' eyes.

Castration methods vary widely. Most western calf producers cut the testes out with a jackknife. It leaves an open wound, but is sure to have the desired effect. Some producers use a Burdizzo emasculator, a clamping tool that is applied to the scrotum and squeezed shut, crushing the sperm ducts and breaking the connection with the testes. According to Edgar Cornish of Peterborough County: 'We pinch down here, we don't cut 'em. I guess it's whatever a person gets used to. In this part of the country a lot of people just pinch 'em. That way you don't have an open wound where they get an infection ... it's like any technique – if you do it quite a bit you can be good at it' (Edgar Cornish, Interview). In the District of Timiskaming, Darlene and Claude Bowen prefer to apply sheep elastics to bull calves within hours of birth. The testes are numb within a few hours and eventually just drop off. This, they feel, is less stressful than castrating at an age of four or five months, and there is no precocious mounting behaviour in the interim. In Renfrew County, Trudy and Doug Desjardins believe in leaving their calves intact for their first four months of life to take advantage of the hybrid vigour and testosterone naturally present in a bull calf. If left intact much after four months, however, the bull calves develop secondary male characteristics and begin to look 'staggy' or masculine.

Branding is common practice in Saskatchewan, Alberta, and British Columbia, but it is avoided in eastern Canada where ear tags are considered to be sufficient identification. Advocates of branding complain that tags may fall off and are impossible to read at a distance. Theft of cattle also remains a significant problem in the west's open-range environments (Mitchell 1996; *Lethbridge Herald* 1999), which the highly visible brand helps to discourage. Electronic identification systems have been developed which use subcutaneous implants that give off a programmed signal which may be read with a sensing device. Once again, it is necessary to get very close to the animal to read the implant. Opponents of branding are concerned about causing unnecessary pain to young calves. They also point out that a branded hide is discounted by about $10, reducing the value of the finished animal to both the packing house and the producer.

Weaning

As mass production operations, feedlots prefer to receive a standardized feeder calf that can be put directly into a pen with fifty to 150 others of the same size for a set period of high-energy grain feeding. Feeder calves that come from diverse cow-calf operators, however, are often a mixed bag that have not always been preconditioned in the same way, if at all. The calves coming from hobby farmers may not have been properly dehorned, for example. They are likely to be stressed and traumatized after being separated from their mothers, crowded into a cattle liner for twelve or fifteen hours, and prodded through one or two auction barns. For these reasons, newly weaned calves may be slow to begin feeding properly, are more vulnerable to disease, and have a high rate of mortality.

Specialized calf-weaning centres provide a seven-week custom conditioning and weaning program to prepare calves for marketing and feeding. Some 300 to 600 newly weaned calves enter the centre at one time and stay for two months. The centre is a sort of nursery school for calves who must learn to feed themselves. Its goal is to reduce the mortality of calves that would otherwise be thrust directly onto a high-energy feeding regime in a feedlot. The cattle arrive at the weaning centre as little as thirty minutes after leaving their place of birth. Bob Dobson of Renfrew County gives a vivid sense of the time, care, and empathy that an Ottawa Valley farmer lavishes on calves:

> The [newly weaned] calves spend more time walking and bawling instead of eating. So, we walk down to the pen – and I'll go down there ten or a dozen, if I have time maybe even fifteen times a day – the pen is down at the barn, it's 300 feet away I guess, and the noise floats up here quite nicely. But as soon as I walk down there, climb over the edge of the pen and into the pen everything's very quiet again for a little while. 'Oh, there's something new in here, it's not another calf, it's not another calf feeling miserable for itself, it's somebody walking across the pen.' So then you just walk back and forth across the pen a couple of times and they look at you and then they start kind of following you a little bit you know, and they calm down again. And if you have any lying down in the back of the pen you quietly get them up and bring them out, bring them past the water trough, bring them past the other water trough, bring them past the bale of hay, you know, bring them past the little box with whole oats in it ... If they're lying down they're not eating, they're not probably getting enough to drink, they're really feeling pretty sorry

> for themselves. It's a sad day ... I want them to eat because a full calf is a healthy calf ...
>
> We'll have feed on both sides of the pen. We'll give them whole oats because whole oats is better for their stomach, for their rumen, than ground feed or even rolled feed. And we'll give them first cut real nice fine grassy hay. We'll put big troughs of water, on both sides of the pen. And the pen is half inside, half outside with a good high roof in the pole barn, knee deep in straw and very dry in there. And we've gone now six to seven years with a mortality rate of 1/4 of 1 per cent ... So, it seems to be working.

Calf-weaning centres are clearly labour intensive, representing a real innovation in the traditionally land-intensive cow-calf industry. Proponents argue that healthier calves and lower mortality rates justify the additional expense, especially in eastern Canada.

Pasture Management and Community Pastures

Range and pasture management is critical to maintain the optimal size of herd on the available land without negatively affecting the regenerative powers of the grass. Thus, the condition of grass must be monitored and animals moved before any damage is done to the long-term health of the forage. In most regions of Canada, winter conditions are so severe that it is necessary to provide winter feed, delivering hay to wherever the cattle are wintering. In the B.C. interior, for example, winter pastures are typically located at lower elevations to facilitate supplementary feeding for up to five months of the year. A daily supplementary ration of ten pounds of hay and lots of water to wash it down produce roughly one pound of gain per day (Acton and Woodward 1961: 21).

In eastern Canada there is virtually no grazing land available for lease through the government. Instead, about half of all cow-calf operators in Ontario rent nearby parcels from farm owners who do not require all the land they own (Creative Research Group 1983: 13). In eastern Canadian cow-calf operations with at least twenty beef cows, an average of 25 per cent of the land is rented compared with 41 per cent of the land area of western Canadian operations (Schissel et al. 1995: 187).

In many cases, the fencing on rented land is in poor condition which makes it better suited for crops that cannot walk away. Thus, some cow-calf operators choose to keep their animals on the home farm, where they can keep an eye on them and where it pays to make a substantial investment in fencing to prevent the escape of valuable stock. In other cases, a very substantial investment in tile drains or commercial fertilizer has been made on the home farm that can only earn a reasonable return if it is used for higher value crops such as grain or forage. In that event, the cattle are pastured on rented land, and dilapidated fences are augmented with electric fencing, which is cheap to install and easily retrieved when the rental agreement is dissolved.

The rent charged for private land in Ontario might be a cash payment in the order of $10 to $20 per acre or it could be an informal agreement to supply a dressed and wrapped beef carcass each year in lieu of rent. A crop-sharing agreement may be arranged in which the cow-calf operator receives half the hay crop in exchange for supplying the labour and equipment to cut and bale it.

Unlike the mixed farms of the eastern provinces, much of western Canada's calf production takes place on specialized ranches and cow-calf operations that depend on public grazing land leased from provincial governments. Along with the homestead quarter section, the large-scale calf producer in southern Alberta needs to control, via a long-term grazing lease, hundreds and sometimes thousands of acres of grass to sustain an economic scale of calf production. A survey of Alberta cow-calf operators with ten or more cows showed that cow-calf farms controlled an average of 3,632 acres per farm, at an average stocking density of 13.2 acres per animal unit. And of that pastureland, 70 per cent was rented – most from the provincial government (Ross et al. 1988: 12). The terms of a grazing lease typically permit the erection of improvements (such as fencing, watering facilities, and temporary shelters to protect cattle from the weather) and they prohibit overgrazing. But leased grazing land is not closely regulated and it is seldom inspected.

At the height of the Great Depression in 1935, when Prairie agriculture was on the ropes, the federal government passed the Prairie Farm Rehabilitation Act, which led to the creation of the Prairie Farm Rehabilitation Administration (PFRA) in 1939. The PFRA was responsible for a wide range of regional development programs to curb soil erosion through the distribution of tree seedlings to plant shelter belts and the promotion of new cultivation techniques for soil conservation. The PFRA also provided water through the construction of large-scale dams and reservoirs such as Saskatchewan's Gardner Dam and Lake Diefenbaker and by encouraging the excavation of thousands of small-scale farm reservoirs known on the Prairies as 'dugouts.'

From the point of view of cattle grazing, however, the PFRA's community pasture program has undoubtedly had the greatest influence. Beginning in 1937, the PFRA began to receive badly eroded lands from the provinces of Manitoba, Saskatchewan, and Alberta. Most of this land had been abandoned by unsuccessful farmers during the drought years of the 1930s and was acquired by the provinces in an attempt to recover delinquent taxes. The tax recovery lands were generally arid and beyond the range of irrigation infrastructure. Much of this land was still covered in native vegetation. But some portions had been cultivated and then abandoned under dust bowl conditions and had become severely eroded. Under the PFRA, these marginal lands were acquired and consolidated into large parcels. On land that was eroded and barren after misguided efforts to crop it, the first step in rehabilitation was to plant drought-resistant grasses. Out-of-work farmers were paid to dig the post holes and string the wire necessary to fence these large expanses for livestock grazing. As the community pastures were reseeded, they began to receive cattle in the summer months to help local farmers maintain livestock year round and diversify their operations. By the 1980s, eighty-seven community pastures, mainly in Saskatchewan, covered 2.2 million acres, providing grazing for 230,000 head of cattle (Prairie Farm Rehabilitation Administration 1987).

The community pastures benefit Prairie farmers in three ways. First, they provide summer grazing land to supplement limited pasturage on deeded land. Land costs and the limited carrying capacity of dry land pasture limit a farmer's ability to run a large enough herd to benefit from economies of scale.

Second, most community pastures maintain a high-quality bull herd to breed cows. Good quality bulls are expensive to buy and feed, especially for small cow herds that require servicing for only a few weeks of the year. Third, community pastures provide preconditioning services for calves such as branding, dehorning, and castration in the spring when farmers are busy putting in the crop. Like the privately operated calf weaning and heifer development centres of Ontario, the PFRA functions as a subcontractor to farmers who pay a daily fee per head of cattle for their specialized services.

Unlike the United States, where most of the western grazing land is owned and leased by the federal government's Bureau of Land Management, most of the grazing land in western Canada is operated and leased by provincial governments. The community pastures of the PFRA represent the only federal government involvement in Canada's rangelands and they occupy a small fraction of the total western grazing land.

Feeding and Marketing Options

The traditional nineteenth-century ranch feeding regimen saw steers fed on grass until the age of four, when they were considered 'grass-finished' and driven over a trail to the railhead and thence by railcar to slaughter. The life of the average slaughter animal is now little more than a year. Assuming the traditional spring-calving regimen, the contemporary calf producer may choose from among three basic strategies (Haney 1997; Ross et al. 1988: 9–10).

1 Feeder calves may be shipped to a feedlot as soon as they are weaned in the fall, at six to seven months of age. They will be in the feedlot for six to seven months, a 'long keep,' and be ready for slaughter in the spring, a year to fourteen months after birth. This is especially appropriate for the calves of the large exotic breeds with a weaning weight of 270 to 320 kilograms. They would produce too large a carcass if they were pastured any length of time after weaning.
2 Mid-sized calves, with a weaning weight of 230 to 270 kilograms, may be backgrounded (kept on grass, hay, or silage with a little grain as a supplement) for their first winter, becoming 'yearlings' the spring after they are born. Yearlings weighing 360 to 410 kilograms may then be transferred to a feedlot in spring for four to five months of grain finishing and be ready for slaughter in the fall.
3 Smaller calves with a weaning weight of 160 to 230 kilograms and those born late in the calving season may be backgrounded for an entire year on pasture to gain weight. They would then be sold to a feedlot as 'long yearlings' in the fall. As long yearlings, they may require as little as three months of grain finishing (a 'short keep') before going to slaughter in the winter, at about eighteen months of age. These older slaughter cattle have the shortest time on a grain-finishing diet, yet they may have the most marbling.

These options become even more complex when potential changes in ownership and location are considered. A producer may retain ownership of a calf from its birth to unloading at the slaughterhouse gate; this is especially common among the larger cow-calf operators of southern Ontario. Or there may be as many as three arm's-length market transactions and changes of ownership between calving and slaughter. Cattle may remain on the same farm all their lives, or they may be trucked through a series of different auction rings to a number of different locations for each specialized phase of maturation, growth, and feeding. In other words, the production of a slaughter steer may be operationally and spatially integrated or dispersed. While there are many options, most calf producers sell weaned calves at fall stocker sales and do not attempt to grain-finish cattle to slaughter weight themselves. Unlike hog production, where fully integrated (farrow to finish) operations under one roof are the rule, cattle production is less integrated, and the two principal sectors (calf production and feedlots) are usually articulated through the cattle marketing system.

Of course, heifer calves offer more flexibility than steer calves. If prices are high in the spring, a farmer might sell every yearling on the operation to leave room for the next calf crop. If prices are low and farmers are not short of money, they might sell only the yearling steers and breed every one-year-old heifer they have, hoping for higher prices in the next year. Thus, the cow herd expands and contracts based on market expectations and management strategy.

Marketing is another activity in which there are wide differences in attitude. According to Mike Sullivan: 'I like selling through the auction barn. Everybody gets a chance to bid on those cattle and I've got prices through the auction barn that I wouldn't dream of asking here at home.' Trudy Desjardins, who sells mainly Aberdeen Angus crossbred yearlings, avoids the local auction markets: 'If we were to market our calves here in Renfrew county we would be literally slaughtered because it's only order buyers that buy at our local sales barns and blacks here have always been associated with being a Holstein cross. So they really hit you hard here. But what they do is buy our calves dirt cheap and then they sell them, you know, put them on the market again in Ontario. But that's once again knowing your market, so we always take the cattle to where the feedlot people are – in Cookstown [successor to the Ontario Stock Yards].'

Canadian Cattle Breeding Revolution

Cattle of the Western world had two functions up to the eighteenth century: motive power as draft animals and the production of milk for dairy products. When they were too old or too diseased to fulfil either of these primary functions, cattle were slaughtered as a source of meat.

The main requirement for draft oxen was strength and mass. Thus, tall big-boned cattle were bred for hauling loads over muddy roads and fields (McFall 1927: 80). Distinctive races of cattle emerged in different regions but there were no cattle breeds per se.

By the middle of the eighteenth century, as the enclosure movement and the loss of common grazing lands was sweeping European agriculture, the desirability of breeding animals to improve their traits began to gain sway. The gradual replacement of oxen by draft horses during Britain's agricultural revolution and the increasing demand for tender beef were also critical factors in the newfound emphasis on meat-producing qualities. Robert Bakewell (1726–95) of Leicestershire is credited with the first scientific approach to breeding cattle for the production of meat despite the fact that his work preceded the acceptance of Mendel's pioneering genetics research by over a century. Maxims such as 'breed the best to the best' survive to the present as methods of selection based on inbreeding. Bakewell's goal was efficiency, to maximize weight gain per unit of feed and to increase the weight of the most valuable cuts of meat per unit of total live weight (Winters 1948: 27–31): 'All is useless that is not beef ... You can get beasts to weigh where you want them to weigh, i.e., in roasting places and not boiling places' (Bakewell quoted in Pawson 1957: 50). Bakewell selected for improved meat-production efficiency by developing a system for evaluating the offspring of particular bulls and cows that is known today as progeny testing. As the first scientific cattle breeder, Bakewell was not concerned with esthetic traits such as colour, shape, or symmetry of the horns, but paradoxically these were the very features that came to dominate nineteenth-century cattle breeding.

To protect the integrity of cattle that were bred to suit the agroclimatic conditions of specific regions, systems for identifying and registering pure breeds developed. Herd books were established in Britain for Shorthorns (then known as Durhams) in 1822, Herefords in 1846, and Aberdeen Angus in 1862. Thus, pedigreed cattle breeds first emerged in the mid-nineteenth century in Great Britain.

By the late nineteenth century, the legacy of Bakewell's applied breeding experiments had been corrupted into cattle-breeding practices based not on science but on a dysfunctional folklore. The ostensible goal of intensive and repetitive inbreeding was to establish specific desirable characteristics within closed purebred herds and flocks. Fathers were bred to daughters, sons were bred to mothers, and brothers were bred to sisters. It is little wonder, then, that a counterproductive breeding philosophy developed that was based on the merits of long bloodlines and the importance of particular bodily phenotypes.

The Pure Breed Esthetic

Purebred cattle from Britain began to enter North America almost from their inception and a purebreed esthetic emerged by the late nineteenth century. It became commonly accepted that purebred cattle (like other domesticated species) were intrinsically superior to scrub or mongrel cattle. The most popular method of breeding was phenotypic selection. And the phenotypes that were selected tended to be those which conformed best to the breed type: an arbitrary scheme of 'fancy points' (Winters 1948: 275). While they may also have had superior traits such as weight gain and feed conversion efficiency, purebreds developed a value as show ring performers creating an incentive for pure breeders to continue to select for breed characteristics.

Until 1850, farmers in Upper Canada took greater interest in improving horse breeds than cattle, but after that time the growth of cattle exports and local livestock markets prompted an interest in the improvement of cattle. Shorthorns became the dominant breed of beef cattle in the nineteenth century as draft oxen all but disappeared by 1900 (Jones 1946: 269–70). Registered beef cattle from Britain began to enter Canada in significant numbers in the 1880s. The first Canadian associations to promote the British cattle breeds were the Canadian Shorthorn Association in 1886, Canadian Hereford Association in 1890, and the Canadian Aberdeen Angus Association in 1906. In 1900, federal legislation conferred legitimacy on incorporated breed associations by granting them the exclusive right to register purebred stock and by establishing a nationwide system for keeping pedigree records. By 1913, Shorthorns were 'unquestionably the most popular breed in the world' and in Canada they outnumbered Herefords, the next most popular breed, by six to one (Arkell 1914: 252; Fairbairn 1989: 16–17; Spencer 1913: 19).

With the development of herd books and detailed records of ancestry, pedigree became the dominant criterion for selection. Each breed had certain diagnostic traits, and when these were all present, an animal 'conformed to type': the generally accepted conformation, colour, and all of the fancy points that characterize a breed. It was assumed, usually without recourse to scientific experimentation, that the type conferred functional advantages in the form of efficiency of feed conversion, carcass value for sale as meat, and ability to thrive under specific environmental conditions and to reproduce successfully and reliably.

This had two implications. First, cattle came to be judged and selected based on appearance by those who subscribed to that breed's particular esthetic. This was so, even though it was known that there were sometimes substantial differences between assessments of cattle on the hoof and carcasses on the rail and between the assessed rail grade and the actual cut-out value (Winters 1948: 162). This was not overly serious from the producer's point of view, because the cattle buyers of the day also subscribed to the breed esthetic, and type was at least of some use in meeting market demands for particular cuts of meat. Second, but more serious because it was physiologically and economically dysfunctional, was the failure to assess how well type conformed with production efficiency.

Nevertheless, highly bred cattle began to command enormous prices in the late nineteenth century, culminating in 1873 when 8th Duchess of Geneva, a Shorthorn, was sold for $40,600 at auction in New York: 'Fads in breeding had been carried too far, pedigree alone was of value, animals of the desired bloodlines were retained on breeding herds irrespective of individual merit and disaster was not long in overtaking the mad speculative craze that took possession of Shorthorn breeders in America as well as in England' (Spencer 1913: 18).

The widespread belief in the pedigree as the standard of excellence was not uprooted among even the well informed until after the 1920s (Winters 1948: 39), and it seems likely that the farmers and livestock breeders of the day were even slower to grasp the implications of advances in the science of animal breeding. Cross-breeding was considered to be wrong; animals that were not the offspring of purebred parents were not eligible for registration, impairing their value as commodities. In 1917, Saskatchewan's Livestock Commissioners bemoaned the poor quality and lack of uniformity among cattle marketed by Saskatchewan cattle producers. In part this was a result of the lack of grain-finishing to a consistent weight standard and in part it was due to the use of inferior herd sires: 'One stockman from Swift Current shipped his cattle to Omaha. There were 22,000 head in the yards along with his own and to use his own words: "I was ashamed of my own stock when I got there. Their cattle were more uniform and better bred"' (Saskatchewan 1917: 33).

Scientific Breeding

Canadian cross-breeding experiments began in the 1930s, and the genetic principles of hybridization began to spread from one species to another. One of the most influential Canadian experiments in cattle breeding was conducted by a research team that included Grant MacEwan, later lieutenant governor of Alberta (Shaw and MacEwan 1938). Shaw and MacEwan placed a herd of 160 purebred beef cows composed of equal numbers of Angus, Herefords, Galloways, and Shorthorns on a community pasture north of Swift Current, Saskatchewan. For each of four years they bred the cows to a different breed of bull: Angus, Hereford, Galloway, and Shorthorn. They monitored the hardiness and rustling capabilities of the cows under open-range conditions with no shelter and nothing but natural sources of water. Winter feed was only provided when grazing conditions became perilous. They also carefully tested the growth performance and carcass traits of the progeny, paying special attention to the merits of the purebreds in comparison with the cross-breds. The advantage long imputed to purebreds was not scientifically measurable: 'Without stretching the imagination it would be impossible to conclude from this project that any single breed or crossbreed is greatly superior or greatly inferior to all others. Perhaps one of the most significant things has been the similarity between the groups in point of utility and suitability. Certain differences already shown, however, may have significance. From the data presented, the crossbreds appear to have had a slight advantage over the purebreds in rate of gain, finish and suitability of carcasses' (Shaw and MacEwan 1938: 192).

Decades passed before breeding practices took full cognizance of these seminal findings. The conclusions on the merits of cross-breeds required such careful qualification that they do not seem very impressive. But the very fact that 'mongrel' cross-breeds were even *slightly* superior to registered breeds dealt a heavy blow to the purebred cattle esthetic. Registered pure breeders had guarded and inflated the value of their pedigreed bulls based on the mythic superiority of 'pure' bloodlines extending back to prizewinning British cattle of the nineteenth century. Shaw and MacEwan showed that the emperor had no clothes; there was no measurable basis in fact, especially under strenuous Canadian range conditions, for the alleged superiority of purebred cattle.

A revolution in Canadian breeders' attitudes towards cross-breeding began in the late 1950s. In part, it was driven by the dissemination of Canadian breeding research. In part, the change in attitude may be traced to innovative experiments in Texas that had crossed Hereford, Shorthorn, and Aberdeen Angus with Brahman cattle originating in tropical India. Synthetic breeds such as the Beefmaster, Santa Gertrudis, and Brangus combined the superb carcass characteristics of the British breeds with the Brahmans' hardy adaptation to the torrid climatic conditions of Texas.

The first and best known of the Canadian synthetic breeds was developed in Alberta by Harry Hays (later Senator Harry Hays) with a cross of Holstein, Hereford, and Brown Swiss. Hays's philosophy was to develop an animal that gained weight quickly, converting milk and later grass to beef as efficiently as possible. Hays also required rugged cattle that could survive under Alberta range conditions with a minimum of winter feeding and hoof trimming, reproducing annually without assistance. In 1975 the 'Hays Converter' became the first synthetic crossbred to become recognized and registered as a pure breed in Canada.

Cattalo and Cross-breeding for the Canadian Range

With the disastrous winters of 1884–5 and 1906–7 in mind, western Canadian breeding experiments have emphasized the ability to thrive in the cold and to rustle for grass under snow. As early as 1915, Canada's Department of Agriculture attempted to develop a range animal that would combine the North American bison's hardiness with the meat qualities of domestic beef cattle: 'Bison have huge flat heads that they swing from side to side like a snow shovel, plowing a swath to the grass. Cattle stand and starve, their noses a few inches above cured carbohydrates' (Manning 1995: 127). Protected by their heavy hides, bison tend to face into storms, while cattle tend to drift in the direction that the storm is blowing until they are stopped by some obstacle. After a severe winter storm on the Prairies, a herd of cattle may be found dead in a great putrefying pile, bogged down in snow, entrapped on the windward side of a fence.

The 'Cattalo' experiments were conducted in southern Alberta in the early 1950s. The mating of bison bulls with domestic cattle females failed because of the very high mortality of both calves and cows at birth. All of the successful matings were between domestic bulls and bison females. The female hybrids of the cattle–bison cross were able to conceive normally, however, the 'first cross' male hybrids all proved to be sterile. Thus, it was necessary to cross the female hybrids back with domestic bulls. Eventually some fertile one-eighth-bison and one-quarter-bison males were produced through these 'back-crosses.' The first true Cattalo were reproduced when these hybrid males were fertile enough to be bred with female hybrids (Logan and Sylvestre 1950).

The Cattalo had heavier hair coats and were more willing and able to graze under harsh winter conditions than were cattle. Unlike horses, they did not paw through the snow, but instead burrowed down into the snow with their muzzles to reach the grass below (Smoliak and Peters 1955). However, Cattalo did not perform favourably in calving percentage, efficiency of feedlot gains, or carcass grade relative to domestic Herefords (Peters 1957; Peters and Slen 1966). The search for hardier beef cattle shifted to crosses of domestic cattle breeds.

Beginning in the 1950s, experiments at the Manyberries Range Research Station in southeastern Alberta explored the advantages of crossing Hereford, Shorthorn, and Angus cows with Brahman bulls under rigorous winter range conditions. The 'hybrid vigour' of virtually all crosses produced more hardy animals (especially important on the Canadian Prairies), cows that calved with fewer losses, produced more milk, and raised bigger calves that gained weight faster after weaning. Indeed, the Manyberries experiment was terminated when six of the remaining eleven purebred Hereford cows perished in the cold winter of 1964–5 (Peters and Slen 1967), a rate of mortality far above the Brahman–Hereford crosses even though the Brahman was considered to be a tropical breed!

The mythic superiority of purebred cattle died hard, however, especially given the clout of the breed associations who were able to maintain the elitism surrounding the pedigree, despite research that had demonstrated the merits of cross-breeding:

> It is almost impossible to make a comparative analysis between breeds. The advocates of each breed have almost a religious fanaticism on the subject of their favorite. When someone has spent 25 years developing a fine herd of a particular breed, he develops a blind spot about any favorable qualities of another breed.
>
> The universities and government agencies are afraid to touch the subject because of the partisan outcries that would come from their friends and supporters on the publication of any unfavorable comparisons. (Oppenheimer 1971: 64)

Herefords gained their dominance in Alberta and Saskatchewan after they were the only breed to survive the rigours of the 1906–7 winter (Jacobs 1993). As late as the 1960s, commercial Herefords accounted for 80 per cent of the total beef herd in western Canada. Most of the remainder were Shorthorns and Aberdeen Angus. Despite the fact that the purebred British cattle did not perform particularly well as calf producers or beef converters (a fact which was seldom measured in any case), the purebred esthetic was extolled by both the beef-cattle producers and beef cattle buyers: 'If you go to a fall calf sale, there is nothing more inspiring than a sale ring filled with 50 popping good calves, all marked the same. That uniform color earns dollars. It really shouldn't count but eye-appeal can't be ignored if you want the top price. You can't get uniform color in your calves by rotational crossing' (Jacobs 1993: 166).

By the 1960s, the most common rationale for cross-breeding came to be 'heterosis' or 'hybrid vigour.' Heterosis referred to almost any favourable domestic animal property: rate and efficiency of gain, fertility, or general robustness. Cross-breeding brings a new infusion of genes into any close-bred herd, but it was also motivated to exploit particular complementarities between breeds. Complex systems of cross-breeding emerged to produce superior breeding stock with maternal bulls and slaughter animals with terminal bulls.

Exotic Cross-breds

Because of the allure of the breed esthetic and the traditional fear of 'mongrelization' among breeders of pedigreed beef cattle, cross-breeding did not come into its own until the sudden onslaught of the European 'exotics' in the late 1960s. Preston and Willis (1970: 425) observed that cattle producers in the plains states tended to get better prices and earn higher profits from 'inferior' cross-breeds than was the case for the purebred Hereford and Angus steers that predominated in the Midwest. By the 1980s, two-thirds of the cattle marketed were cross-breeds (Fairbairn 1989: 19), and 90 per cent of Alberta's commercial cow-calf herds were cross-bred (Basarab: 1994). Most commercial beef producers now depend on cross-breeds, and straight-bred herds have become anomalies. Thus, 'cross-breed' has come to be an accolade rather than an epithet.

'Exotic cattle' or simply 'exotics' are continental European breeds of beef cattle that are characterized by their large size and generally lighter colouring. While some exotic blood had filtered into Canada via the United States and Mexico in the 1950s, it was not until 1966 that exotic cattle were able to surmount opposition from breeders of British cattle concerning hoof and mouth disease (aftosa). In 1965, Canada's Department of Agriculture resurrected the quarantine station on Grosse Isle, upstream from Quebec City, and converted it from the detection of cholera among human immigrants to guarding Canada's beef and dairy herd from European sources of aftosa. When demand for exotics exceeded the capacity of the Grosse Isle station, a new facility was built on the French island colony of St Pierre (Fairbairn 1989: 15). In the next ten years the heretofore conservative cattle industry was overwhelmed by over a dozen new exotic breeds, the most common of which were Charolais, Simmental, and Limousin. Along with the exotic breeds came an entirely new philosophy of the merits of cross-breeding, which was assisted by the advent of artificial insemination for beef cattle. At first cross-bred steers (cross-bred bulls had no value) were so suspect and undervalued that they had to be sold 'rail grade,' that is, at a price based on the weight of the dressed and graded carcass hanging on the packing-house rail. By the 1980s, exotic cross-breds were so highly valued that livestock markets consistently awarded them a premium price *on the hoof*.

During the early 1970s the west enjoyed a resource boom propelled largely by rising fossil fuel prices. The beef industry rode the coat-tails of the western boom and sales of exotic cattle in grand ballrooms of luxury hotels seemed consistent with all the other excesses of the cowboy nouveau riche. In 1974, a one quarter interest in Cadet Roussel, a Charolais bull, sold at auction for $81,000 (MacEwan 1982: 198). The steady rise in prices for exotic bulls, their semen, and cross-bred heifers slowed by the mid-1970s, but not before there had been a revolution in the prevailing ideas about cattle breeds on the part of both cattle producers and packing-house cattle buyers. Cattle have grown much larger during the thirty years since exotics first entered Canada. They grow faster on less feed and are slaughtered younger. While most calf producers use unregistered commercial cattle, none have been left untouched by the impact of exotic breeds on the North American cattle gene pool.

Beef-Cattle Breeding Technology

While dairy cattle had long been bred to achieve measurable efficiency results in pounds of milk and butterfat per unit of input, the beef-cattle industry seemed preoccupied with arbitrary and traditional standards of show-ring conformation and ancestral lineage expressed in the pedigree. The assessment of beef cattle was visual and subjective with terms such as 'reputation cattle' used as an assurance of quality (Rosaasen and Lokken 1986: 847). The dairy producer was selling a commodity with qualities that were easily measured without impairing the reproductive capacity of the animal that produced it. The beef-cattle producer was selling a live animal on the hoof, the final value of which could only be determined after its death. Given the variety of conformations and breeds, the value of live beef cattle was more difficult to determine; beef is a more subjectively differentiated commodity than is whole milk.

Quality control has become one of the watchwords of modern manufacturing production, and the consistency of livestock quality has become a growing issue. The problem in measuring quality and the creation of value in beef production has always been that the meat (and ultimately the value of the animal) could only be evaluated in the cooler when it is graded, that is, the day after slaughter.

Until recently, it was not possible to scientifically assess the grade potential of live cattle. Experienced buyers rely on cues such as breed, sex, overall fatness, and time on feed to judge marbling potential, but marbling (intramuscular fat) is difficult to predict on a live animal (Jeremiah et al. 1970). In the absence of any hard data, cattle are often overfed to ensure that the carcass will attain sufficient marbling to gain an A grade. This causes the accumulation of excess back fat (subcutaneous fat), one of the most serious quality problems in the beef industry (Brethour 1994: 1425).

Ultrasound technology now provides a means for measuring the body composition of live animals. It is a non-invasive and non-destructive method of measuring marbling on live cattle. The equipment for ultrasound testing is exactly the same as is used for pregnant women, except that a larger sensor is used along the animal's flanks, and the operator has to be trained to detect different densities and depths of fat. While ultrasound testing is still at the experimental stage, it has the potential to provide livestock producers with vital information on thickness of subcutaneous fat, intramuscular fat, and total yield of red meat (measured using the area of the longissimus dorsi (rib-eye) muscle between the eleventh and twelfth rib).

Ultrasound testing provides breeders with the data they need to select more reliably for superior carcass characteristics and so improve seed-stock cattle. Ultrasound may also assist in sorting slaughter cattle into uniform groups as they go into the feedlot, making it easier to meet consumer demand for consistency, to gear production for demanding niche markets, and to target carcasses to exact packer specifications. Sorted cattle should reach the same level of finish at the same time, shortening the time cattle spend in the feedlot and increasing efficiency.

Artificial insemination (AI) is accomplished by confining a cow or heifer in a cattle squeeze and manually injecting semen deep into her vagina. Despite the widespread availability of AI, natural insemination by bulls is still preferred by 90 per cent of Alberta calf producers (Ross et al. 1988: 10). Consistent with other aspects of western calf production, insemination by bulls makes more intensive use of land and less intensive use of capital and labour.

Semen is collected by inducing a bull to mount another bovine or a dummy, directing the 30 to 45-centimetre penis into a warm lubricated artificial vagina and collecting the ejaculate in a pipette. The semen is typically frozen for transportation and storage. To select semen, the producer can thumb through illustrated catalogues of different breeds of bulls and compare statistics on birth weight, weaning weight and calving ease, among many other performance measures. A single dose of frozen semen is sold in a vial for as little as $5, but conception is never guaranteed.

Artificial insemination requires that the cow or heifer has come into estrus (ovulated), which occurs on a twenty-one-day cycle. The detection of estrus is the principal technical problem in using the procedure, especially when cows are dispersed over open range land. The onset of estrus may be detected by observation as cows in heat tend to mount other cows and to be mounted themselves. Another method is to use a 'gomer' (an intact bull with a surgically altered penis) equipped with a dye-filled marker under his chin. After mounting and futile attempts to copulate, the gomer leaves a tell-tale stain on the back of the cow in estrus. Cows must be observed every twelve hours to detect these marks.

Thus, AI is both capital and labour intensive in relation to the land required to maintain a small group of bulls. AI has long been favoured for dairy cattle because dairy bulls are notoriously dangerous to manage; because dairy cows are closely confined and easy to observe; and because estrus may be managed and coordinated ('heat-synchronized') by administering a hormone to the whole herd simultaneously. These procedures are more difficult and costly with free-ranging beef cattle. Inevitably some cows are missed and remain open. For this reason, even those calf producers who do use AI, only run their AI programs for about three weeks before turning out the 'clean-up bull' to impregnate naturally any cows that may have been missed or failed to conceive from AI. Although impractical under range conditions, AI and other bioengineering techniques have contributed to enormous improvements in the performance and efficiency of beef cattle in the conversion of low-value grass and grain to high-value beef. Cloning and genetic modification will undoubtedly become the next issue facing the cow-calf fraternity.

Conclusion

The production of calves is the most traditional phase in the cattle–beef commodity chain. Breeding cows and rearing calves for sale has probably changed less than any other type of livestock specialty. The majority of beef cows are still bred naturally, beef calves are suckled naturally by a cow, and the main source of food for both is natural, standing grass augmented with hay in winter. Yet superimposed on its traditionalism are two unique features. First, the structure of the industry has changed enormously over time. Most beef calves are born and raised on large specialized farms with large beef cow herds. Yet a sizeable minority of Canada's beef calves are raised in small numbers as an avocation of part-time farmers. The spatial distribution of beef cows has also changed. Calf production has shifted westward to the cheapest source of large areas of grazing land, closer to the feedlots, the next link in the value added chain.

Second, while the cow-calf industry is traditional in many respects, calf production is inherently creative and even entrepreneurial. Unlike the feedlot or packinghouse, where mass production demands an invariant and repetitive cycle of work, the cow-calf producer is constantly improvising in response to the weather and market conditions for both feed and cattle. This applies to everything from timing the calving, culling cows, to acquiring the right combination of bulls to serve the herd. Often the course that is ultimately chosen is selected because it leaves the most latitude to manoeuvre in future decisions. But all that said, the calf producer will often justify a choice with, 'That's just the way we've always done it.'

There is terrific variety among cow-calf operations. Some producers are proud that they have never worked off the farm, while others could not function without off-farm income. On some stock farms the gender roles seem unchanged from the nineteenth century, while in others the new-age farm household has made most traditional gender roles obsolete. Some will justify watering their cattle along a river bank (causing erosion and pollution downstream) because that is what their fathers did. Others have spent thousands of dollars to prevent cattle from trampling stream banks and polluting groundwater with manure in a deep and sincere ethical commitment to make their farms environmentally sustainable. Some crop the home fields and keep their cattle on rented grass. Others keep the cattle at home where they can keep an eye on them and crop the rented land. There is such a huge variety in farm behaviour that generalizations are perilous, and the results of attitudinal farm surveys are frustratingly ambiguous because there is simply no consensus.

Technological change in calf production is most strongly manifest in the methods of cross-breeding. Beef cattle are larger than they once were; indeed, the contemporary challenge is to keep carcass size down to avoid the overweight discounts applied by packers. The breeds and hide colours have changed, and some of the breeding philosophies have been revised, yet the fundamentals of breeding have remained the same. Cow-calf farms remain relatively unaffected by technological change and continue to be deeply traditional in their ways.

TWO

Feedlot Alchemy: Turning Grain into Beef

As you begin your final approach to Calgary International Airport from the east, the fine-grained monotony of the mile-square sections of the Dominion Land Survey system begins to resolve into variegated 160-acre quarter sections. Some are dominated by the inscribed green circle created by a gigantic centre pivot irrigation apparatus, others are the yellow-to-green gradations of dry pasture, and here and there one sees the rich dark chocolate colour of manure that indicates a feedlot, an intensive livestock operation that grain-feeds cattle to slaughter weight.

In a land approach, the Prairie feedlot signals itself from miles away by the fifteen-metre-high 'leg' of its feed mill with augers radiating out in all directions. The feed mill is a complex of cylindrical grain storage bins interconnected by sloping augers for transferring grain. With the demise and demolition of many country grain elevators, the feed mill has become the new sentinel and symbol of agroindustry on the Prairie landscape.

The feedlot is a grid of pens each holding up to 250 animals; larger feedlots have a one-time capacity of 25,000 feeder cattle or more. Concrete feed bunks run along the front of each pen, positioned to receive a carefully measured stream of feed from the feed truck's auger.

The animals in each pen are typically homogeneous with respect to ownership, sex, breed, and size. Despite the popularity of exotic crossbreeds, white-faced ruddy brown Herefords are still a mainstay of western Canadian feedlots. The white faces look up as one and stare as I approach the feed bunk; it feels like the first day of class. One begins to back away in distrust of the camera-toting stranger, and suddenly they all take flight towards the back of the pen. By spring the pens seldom have much straw bedding and tons of wet manure have accumulated in each one. The cattle stand hock-deep in their own excrement, but they don't seem to mind.

Overview of Cattle Feeding in Canada

Cattle feeding is a higher volume and more capital intensive phase in the value added chain than cow-calf operations. Cattle feeders take weaned calves or yearlings as their raw material and produce finished slaughter cattle at the precise weight, fat content, and body conformation required for processing. North American consumers prefer the marbled texture and pure white fat covering that only grain feeding gives. Grass-finished beef has less marbling, and its fat has a distinctive yellow tint because of the beta-carotene in grass.

On many mixed farms, cattle feeding is a seasonal sideline to produce a source of income in spring, add value to grain and hay produced on the farm (especially when grain prices are low), and provide a use for farm machinery and labour that would otherwise be idle in the winter months. Small-scale cattle feeding helps to diversify farm activities and add value to bull calves that have no place in milk production. Many small-scale cow-calf operators still feed their own calves to market weight, especially in Atlantic Canada (Agriculture Canada 1983). Cattle feeding is also a way to be more self-reliant, and farmers may finish one or two animals to stock the freezer and supply their domestic needs.

At the other extreme, feedlots holding tens of thousands of cattle are highly specialized operations found principally in Alberta. To make the most of invested capital, large scale feedlots, those with a one-time capacity in excess of 10,000 head of cattle, run all year long and buy most of their grain, although most grow their own silage. The average feeding period is 120 days; a feedlot operating at full capacity could do three 'turns' a year, but two and a half turns is more typical.

Feeder cattle arrive by cattle liner and are unloaded into special receiving pens for new arrivals. Within twenty-four hours of delivery the new entrants to the feedlot are put through centralized processing facilities. Each animal is cycled through the cattle squeeze where, depending on how they were preconditioned, the new animals may need to be branded or dehorned, vaccinated against common feedlot diseases, and injected with vitamin and mineral supplements. A numbered tag is punched into the ear and a growth hormone pellet is usually implanted; ears are not used for human consumption. Feedlot heifers may also receive melengestrol acetate, a synthetic progesterone administered as a feed additive to suppress the onset of estrus and maintain normal behaviour and feed intake (Cheeke 1993: 109).

After processing, the cattle are moved to a pen and kept together as a familiar herd group. For some of the young feeder calves this is a traumatic time as they have just been weaned and may have left their mothers and open grassland only hours earlier. New entrants to the feedlot are typically given a three- to four-week adjustment period during which the percentage of grain in the ration is gradually increased. New feeder calves begin with hay for the first two weeks and then the proportion of grain in the feed is gradually increased from 10 per cent up to 85 per cent or more.

In large feedlots, cattle alleys run behind the pens while feed alleys run in front of the pens and along the feed bunks to separate cattle and truck traffic. Feed trucks equipped with augers drive down the feed alleys delivering the twice daily ration of grain and silage to scores of cattle pens. At one end of the feedlot will be one or more silage pits (bunker silos); these are immense barn-sized excavations, shored up with concrete, filled with chopped barley (grain, leaves, and stems), and packed down the previous fall by a massive four-wheel drive tractor. Covered with heavy gauge polyethylene and weighted down with truck tires, the pit undergoes anaerobic decomposition to produce a pungent forage rich in energy from the concentration of alcohols and sugars produced by fermentation. Feedlot operators do not typically use the tall tower silos associated with dairy farms of eastern Canada. Tower silos are costly and bunker silos seem to work just as well for barley chop. Minor spoilage around the edges of the bunker where the silage may be exposed to oxygen is a small price to pay considering the lower capital cost. A front-end loader seems to be in constant action to transfer silage from the silo to the feed truck for distribution to pens.

The feed mill is the most visible piece of feedlot equipment, and it is usually situated near the main road access for deliveries of grain and feed supplements. The feed mill needs to be separated from cattle receiving and shipping facilities yet close to feed alleys to simplify the distribution of feed grain to the pens. Milling is a critical activity in Alberta feedlots, as the seed coat of each grain of barley must be cracked to be digestible yet not pulverized into dust that may cause bloat. To achieve precisely the right texture, barley is 'tempered' with hot water so that the hull may be broken without crushing the kernel (Hironaka and Freeze 1992).

The Geography of Cattle Feeding

As an intermediate stage in the beef-production process, large-scale cattle feeding is drawn to calf producers, packing plants, or some point intervening between the two, subject always to the availability of grain and water. Calf producers are drawn to range and pasture in large parcels which are not suitable for cash crops.

Until the 1960s, cattle slaughter was located close to local markets and major transportation nodes in the railway net. In the United States, this left room for two intervening regions that were blessed with the capacity to produce vast quantities of cheap grain. The Midwestern corn belt centred on Iowa was ideally situated to feed cattle which had been funnelled in from all over the United States and Canada. The corn belt had the deep soils, prolonged high summer temperatures, and rainfall required to produce corn. In 2000 just two corn belt states, Kansas and Nebraska, fed 40.1 per cent of the heifers and steers marketed annually in the United States. A second major cattle feeding region developed later in the sorghum growing region of Texas and the southern Great Plains, drawn by large quantities of young feeder calves produced locally and imported from Mexico. Texas alone accounts for 25.3 per cent of all fed cattle marketed in the United States (United States Department of Agriculture 2000a).

In Canada, the most prominent intervening region between Alberta and the markets of the Windsor–Quebec Axis is the Canadian Shield which is unsuitable for commercial grain production. To the east, Quebec and Atlantic Canada are deficient in grain, while to the west, Manitoba and Saskatchewan suffer from such severe winter conditions that they are at a disadvantage in finishing cattle despite their proximity to both feed grain and feeder cattle (Canada 1969: 161). Thus, large-scale feeding has become polarized between Alberta, with 69.3 per cent of Canada's fed cattle production, and 2,000 miles away in southern Ontario, with 18.3 per cent. In the tug-of-war between grass and grain in the west and metropolitan markets of the east, the resource base has proven to be the anchor.

Most of the 'feedlots' in Eastern Canada are concentrated in southern Ontario. But a feedlot in southern Ontario is quite different from a feedlot in Alberta. Ontario farmers sometimes finish fifty or so cattle using their own corn grain and silage. A feedlot with a capacity of 300 head is considered large, and only a handful of Ontario feedlots have a one-time capacity of over 1,000 head. In Alberta, on the other hand, feedlots of less than 3,000 head are considered to be uneconomic, while the largest operations feed in excess of 25,000 head of cattle on a quarter section (160 acres) parcel, although much additional land is required to provide feed and dispose of manure.

Seventy per cent of all Canadian cattle on feed were regionally concentrated in Alberta in 1999, and in that province feeding has become concentrated in the hands of a few hundred large-scale operations. With 40 per cent of the Canadian beef-cow herd, Alberta is also Canada's leading calf producer. Roughly one-half of Alberta's agricultural land base is unsuitable for cultivated crops and is devoted to cattle grazing. Much of the remaining acreage is devoted to grain and oilseed production. Given present world prices for grain and the cost of transportation, a sizeable grain surplus is available for use as animal feed. Thus, Alberta has the resource base to support both calf production and cattle feeding.

The number of steers in each census subdivision is used as a proxy measure for the spatial distribution of cattle feeding (Figure 2.1). Within southern Alberta, feedlots are concentrated in a broad swathe along Highway 2 running from Edmonton south to Calgary and Cardston, with Lethbridge County as the undisputed giant followed by Newell County, centred on the town of Brooks.

Setting the feedlot titans aside, Figure 2.1 also shows that small numbers of steers are fed for slaughter in almost every one of Canada's agricultural census subdivisions. The most significant concentrations outside of Alberta are found in Bruce and Huron counties to the east of the Lake Huron shore and in the Regional Municipality of Kitchener-Waterloo. But every one of the 49,361 steers in Bruce County, Ontario's cattle-feeding capital, could be accommodated in Alberta's largest feedlot. Smaller concentrations of steers are found south of Montreal between Cowansville and St-Jean-sur-Richelieu, south of Quebec City along the Rivière Chaudière, and in Queen's County in the centre of Prince Edward Island.

Cattle Feeding and Irrigation in Western Canada

In his report on the findings of the Palliser Expedition (1857–60), John Palliser concluded that the vast arid region covering southern Alberta and Saskatchewan, now known as Palliser's Triangle, would 'forever be comparatively useless' (Spry 1968: cx) and certainly unsuitable for agriculture. Palliser's pessimistic forecast has been discredited in the many irrigation districts that are provided with melt water from the Rocky Mountain snowpack. Channelled east by the St Mary, Belly, Oldman, Bow, and Red Deer rivers that drain into the South

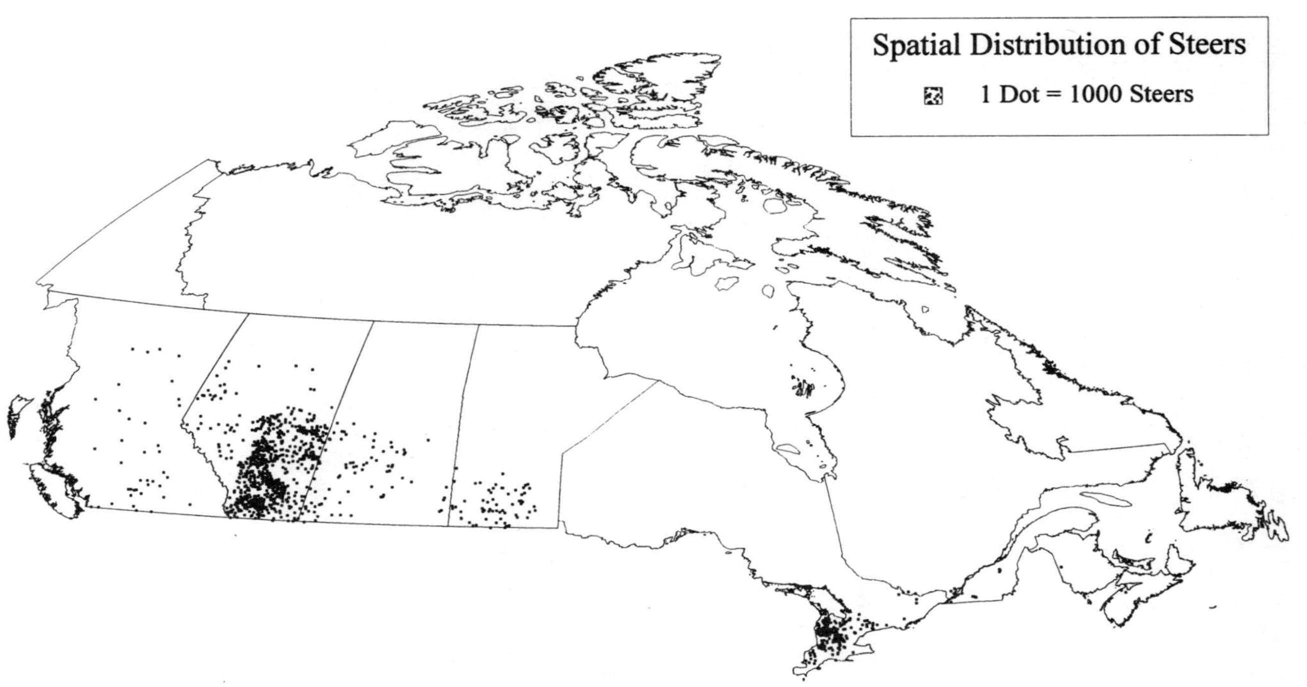

Figure 2.1. Spatial distribution of steers in Canada, 1996. Source: Raw data from Statistics Canada, Census of Agriculture 1996.

Saskatchewan River, impounded behind the Oldman and St Mary dams and in scores of smaller reservoirs, precipitation from the Pacific provides the water resource upon which irrigation districts depend.

Irrigation has been vital to agriculture in the arid regions of southern Alberta since the migration of a small band of Mormons from Utah to Cardston in 1887, bringing with them a pragmatic knowledge of the engineering of small-scale ditches, and flood irrigation of fields in the arid lands of the west (Dawson 1936). In the Lethbridge area, the Alberta Railway and Irrigation Company began the first large-scale irrigation project in 1899. The project passed into the hands of the Canadian Pacific Railway (CPR), and with the influx of agricultural settlers between 1900 and 1910, further irrigation infrastructure was developed on the north side of the Bow River between Medicine Hat and Calgary (Mackintosh 1934: 107–8). By 1925, there were 5,200 miles of irrigation ditches in southern Alberta, yet less than one-quarter of the irrigable land area had actually been supplied with water (Morton 1938: 146). Water supplies were expanded again in the postwar period with the completion of the St Mary River Dam in 1951 and the Oldman River Dam forty years later. Until the 1970s, most irrigation was based on excavated reservoirs and channels, gravity flow, and distribution to plants by simply flooding fields on a periodic basis.

Technological change and massive investments by both the public and private sectors in hydraulic infrastructure expanded the land under irrigation in the 1970s (Johnston and Sundstrom 1995; Raby 1965). Between 1973 and 1988 many of the irrigation districts installed pressurized distribution systems using buried pipes in lieu of ditches, increasing the land area that had access to irrigation water. Individual farmers took advantage of the new water supply and invested in both side-roll and centre-pivot irrigation equipment to improve the quantity and regularity of water delivery (McKnight 1979). Between 1965 and 1985, the land area under irrigation doubled, reaching 1.1 million acres in 1995. In 1998, forage crops (led by alfalfa) accounted for 43 per cent of Alberta's irrigated land, while cereal grains (led by barley) accounted for a further 34 per cent. While enhanced irrigation increased southern Alberta's capacity to produce forage and feed grain, it also made good quality water available to build feedlots in areas otherwise too dry to sustain the needs of growing cattle. Of course, it is still necessary to excavate a reservoir or 'dugout' adjacent to the feedlot to provide a source of water from October to April, when irrigation water transmission systems are inactive and feedlot activity reaches its annual peak (Alberta Agriculture 1999b: Table 1; Ross et al. 1990: 28–9).

In the unirrigated portions of the arid region of southern Alberta, stock watering is dependent on the vicissitudes of rain, snow melt, and natural water courses. A dryland feedlot of any size is not viable; 20,000 head of feeder cattle require up to 250,000 gallons of water per day in warm weather. Thus, very large dugouts are required; the rule of thumb is that the rain-fed dugout capacity should be equal to two years' supply of water, which further increases dugout costs for dryland feedlots (Ross et al. 1990: 31). Water and the large-scale irrigation infrastructure to gather, contain, and channel it have been essential to southern Alberta's cattle-feeding industry: 'Where would Alberta's cattle feeding industry be without irrigation? Most likely it would have remained, on average, farm-based, small scale, feeding hay and surplus or damaged feed grains. Although feed supplies would be adequate to support the current number of cattle being fed, water supplies would likely be insufficient in the South, or at least, insufficient to support a large number of large-scale feedlots. Eventually competition from large-scale U.S. feedlots would have taken the business away, and left Alberta as a supplier of calves and backgrounded yearlings' (Freeze 1993: 32).

With 31.7 per cent of its farm area supplied with irrigation water in 1996, Lethbridge County housed 139,000 steers over one year of age. Vulcan County, immediately to the north, has a larger land base and is situated closer to the largest cattle processors, yet it had only 17,000 steers in 1996. Most of Vulcan is dry land, only 4.6 per cent of its farm land has access to irrigation water (Statistics Canada 1997). Access to irrigation water is an essential prerequisite to cattle feeding in the arid zone of southern Alberta.

Northern Alberta receives more rainfall than the south does, and irrigation is not usually required. With its low cost, rain-fed crop land, northern Alberta produces most of the province's feed grain. Between 1984 and 1988, northern Alberta produced an average of 51 per cent of the barley, 68 per cent of the oats, and 63 per cent of the tame hay grown in the province. But the northern region of Canada's largest beef-producing province accounted for only 12 per cent of the cattle slaughter capacity and marketed only 16 per cent of the province's slaughter steers in 1988, a fair proxy of cattle feeding activity. The cost savings of ready access to feed grain and sufficient rainfall to make capital investment in irrigation infrastructure unnecessary are offset by lower temperatures in winter (which increases feed requirements per unit of gain) and the problem of feedlot 'gumbo,' the blend of mud and manure that builds up after snow melt and spring rain. Manure is more difficult to spread and takes longer to decompose on the wetter fields of the Prairie park belt. On balance, southern Alberta has a cost advantage over the north because of its location with respect to existing slaughter plants and the U.S. export market (Ross et al. 1990: 31–2). Thus, northern Alberta specializes in the production of feed grains and calves, while the south is the premiere cattle-feeding region in the province and in Canada as a whole.

Economies of Scale in Feedlots

Following trends established in the United States (Hart and Mayda 1998; United States International Trade Commission 1993; Winsberg 1996), Canada's cattle feeding industry is becoming highly concentrated. In Alberta, in 1990, 69 per cent of the slaughter cattle producers sold fewer than 100 cattle annually, but collectively they sold only 4.3 per cent of the cattle. On the other hand, the 2.6 per cent of producers who sold more than 1,000 slaughter cattle in 1990 under the National Tripartite Stabilization Program were responsible for 71.3 per cent of cattle sales in Alberta (Alberta Agriculture 1991: 5). By 2000, just eleven Alberta feedlots, each with a capacity of over 20,000 head, could accommodate 34.9 per cent of the cattle on feed in the province (CanFax 2000).

Economies of scale are vital to cattle feeding, which accounts for the dominance of large operations in the overall production of slaughter cattle. Larger feedlots can spread their fixed costs over a larger number of cattle, and over a full year's operation in contrast to the seasonal operations of smaller farm-based feedlots. Economies of scale on variable costs are also important for feedlots. These include the cube-square law, the principle of multiples, and the principle of bulk transactions (Berry et al. 1997: 245–6).

The cube-square law relates costs to the linear dimensions of space, while the revenue-earning capacity increases with its area or volume. The surface area (and revenue capacity) of a cattle pen increases as the product of its dimensions, while the cost of the fencing merely increases in proportion to its perimeter. Thus, the cube-square law rewards large animal pens and pastures. The volumetric storage capacity of a bunker silo increases as the product of its dimensions, while its construction costs increase only as its surface area. The volume of a cylindrical granary or tower silo increases as $\pi r^2 h$, while its surface area increases only as $2\pi rh$. Because of their need for animal confinement and bulk storage of feed and supplements, feedlots are especially sensitive to the cube-square law.

The second source of economies of scale is the principle of multiples. Cattle feeding requires many specialized types of capital equipment in different proportions (e.g., one and a half grain trucks for each combine). Larger operators require more separate pieces of equipment and they are better able to achieve the lowest common multiple and have the optimal mixture of equipment and back-ups when machinery fails.

The third important component of variable cost economies of scale is the principle of bulk transactions. Large-scale farm operations are able to negotiate better prices when they are buying large volumes of inputs on the open market such as pharmaceuticals, feed supplements, and grain. Large feedlots can obtain feeder cattle at lower cost because they purchase them in larger quantities. Large feedlots are able to market larger numbers of cattle at a premium because they are able to ship uniform truck loads of cattle more regularly with the specific weight and conformation characteristics demanded by the largest packing houses. Large packing plants pay top prices for standardized inputs and discount livestock that do not meet weight, grade, or sex specifications. Finally, large feedlots can devote more management resources to market research and price hedging strategies, enhancing their ability to make more informed decisions on prices, timing of sale, and marketing.

In most agricultural activities, the long-run average cost curve is 'L-shaped': average costs diminish rapidly at first as scale increases (increasing returns to scale) and then flatten out so that there is little or no incentive to grow larger (constant returns to scale). Cow-calf operations reach the point of constant returns to scale at a much smaller number of animals than feedlots do. As a consequence, the cow-calf sector tends to have many very small-scale producers, while the feeding of slaughter cattle tends to be concentrated in the hands of a relatively small number of larger operators. To illustrate the growing importance of scale in cattle feeding, Figure 2.2 portrays the size distribution of herds on farms reporting steers, a proxy for feedlots, using Census of Agriculture data for 1976 and 1996.

Focusing on the 1996 data, steer herds of one to seventeen represent the large number of micro-feeding operations that constitute 90 per cent of all the farms reporting steers, yet account for only 21.3 per cent of the total number of steers on farms. These include small census farms operated by part-time farmers practising recreational back-

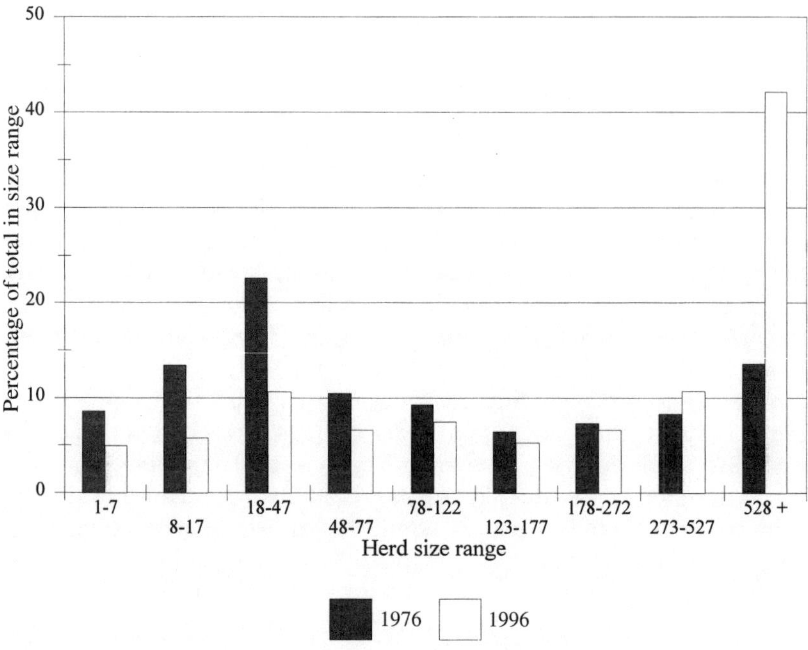

Figure 2.2. Steer herd size distribution, 1976 and 1996. Source: Statistics Canada, Census of Agriculture 1996, special tabulation.

grounding, but they also include mixed farms that specialize in some other agricultural activity but choose to be self-sufficient in beef. Back in 1976, 92.6 per cent of all the farms reporting steers kept fewer than forty-eight animals and in aggregate were responsible for 44.6 per cent of the total national steer herd.

Turning to the large herd size classes in Figure 2.2, it is clear that the size distribution of feedlots has changed dramatically to take advantage of the economies of scale in this sector. In 1976, the 254 'farms' (feedlots) feeding over 528 steers had 13.6 per cent of the national total. By 1996, 404 farms with over 528 steers (less than 1 per cent of all farms reporting steers) were responsible for 42 per cent of the herd. Because cattle feeding is more sensitive to economies of scale than calf production, it is becoming more concentrated in the hands of large producers (Ehrensaft 1987).

In normative economic theory, rational economic cattle feeders should increase the size of their operations until they reach the production scale that minimizes average total costs. This mythic point occurs at different scales on different farms depending on a host of different factors that are specific to each farm and farmer, and it varies from place to place and over time depending on markets and technology. For instance, a study in Saskatchewan found that cow–calf-feeder operators (farms with beef cows selling at least some feeder cattle) reached minimum cost size at 619 head of feeder cattle, while commercial feedlots reached their minimum cost at 7,240 head of slaughter cattle (Leung et al. 1991: 78–9). It is little wonder that there is great dispersion in the steer herd size distribution and all feedlots are not the same size; there is no universal optimum.

The cost to produce one pound of gain per head of cattle drops very quickly as the number of cattle increases, up to about 25,000 head of cattle. At this point, diseconomies of scale begin to set in and create a disincentive to further growth. Rising costs of manure disposal 'loom as the virtually undisputed diseconomy for the larger feedlots,' according to the Colorado Cattle Feeders' Association (Canadian International Trade Tribunal 1993: 88–9). Preston and Willis (1970: 426) found that 30,000 head was the practical maximum that one manager and one feed mill could handle. To grow larger, they suggested, it would be better to build a completely separate feedlot in a different location. Some large cattle feeding enterprises in Alberta have done just that and operate multiple feedlots in the 25,000 to 30,000 head range. However, the economics of cattle feeding seem to be rewarding ever larger scales of operation, and Alberta feedlots are reaching 50,000 head while in the United States quite a number now exceed 100,000 head (Krause 1991).

Cattle-Feeding Strategy

Large-scale feedlots are intensely competitive enterprises. Based on their location, cattle-handling facilities and the state of cattle markets, feedlot operators may elect from among different strategies: the type and age of cattle to be fed, choice of feed ration, and the level of integration between adjacent links in the commodity chain.

Types of Cattle in Feedlots

Castrated steer cattle are preferred by consumers as the source of premium cuts of beef, and steers are regarded as the sex class of choice among cattle feeders. Steers are available and attractive for feeding since they are not required for herd replacement, they do not fight like bulls, they grow faster than heifers and do not come into heat, and most importantly, steers command a premium price per pound over all other types of slaughter cattle.

The number of slaughter heifers available to go on feed depends on the cattle cycle. If herds are being expanded, more heifers will be withheld for breeding and fewer will be sold for feeding. Heifers are typically lighter than steers at weaning, when they enter the feedlot, and when they are finished for slaughter. They are usually priced lower and convert feed to meat less efficiently than steers. Heifers are also more difficult to manage at estrus, although most feedlots prevent estrus with hormones. Most feedlot operators specialize in either steers or heifers. To avoid fighting or mounting behaviour which would interfere with feeding and weight gain, steers and heifers are never held in the same pen.

Among beef-cattle producers, black and white Holsteins are contemptuously labelled 'magpies.' Holstein bull calves are produced in large volumes by the dairy industry, and some dairy producers feed and finish their own bull calves as a sideline. A 100-cow dairy farm will produce nearly fifty bull calves per year, thus, a small-scale finishing operation is an attractive proposition for some dairy farmers. But most eastern dairy farmers auction their bull calves as soon as possible so they can be slaughtered before weaning as milk-fed veal for specialty markets in Montreal and Toronto. In western Canada, the veal market is small, so dairy bull calves are more typically steered and grain-fed to finish weight. A pen full of Holsteins has become a common, if incongruous sight in Alberta feedlots, where the white-and-black hide stands out against the primarily brown and tan beef cattle (Thomas 1989).

Backgrounding on Grass

If cattle enter the feedlot as newly weaned calves, they will be there for a longer period and consume far more expensive grain and concentrate than older cattle. They tie up capital for a longer period of time than older cattle and have a higher death rate especially if they are newly weaned. Young calves gain weight slowly, as they must also produce bone and muscle using expensive grain.

For these reasons many feedlots prefer to purchase stocker cattle which have been backgrounded on grass for anywhere from three to six months after weaning. The goal of backgrounding is to feed weaned calves on grass and build skeletal size as the physiological 'background' for the later addition of meat and fat. While cattle feeding traditionally uses grain and silage-based feeds, backgrounding uses mainly grass and hay to build frame size before a short period of grain-finishing in preparation for marketing.

Backgrounding may be an integral part of cow-calf operations, a specialized and separate phase in the cattle commodity chain, or an adjunct to feedlot operations. Some hobby farmers buy yearlings in the spring, allow them to graze on pasture land during the summer, and sell them in the fall for grain-finishing. This form of recreational backgrounding only requires that pastures have adequate grass for the number of cattle being fed, a source of water, a block of salt, and adequate fences. Less labour, expertise, or capital is required than for breeding beef cows, and once the cattle are sold in the fall, the empty pasture has time to recover before grazing resumes the next spring. Feedlot backgrounding, on the other hand, typically confines cattle in grass paddocks of one-to-three acres with a manger at one end. The diet is predominantly grass and roughage, supplemented with grain or silage.

Backgrounding is becoming more popular because backgrounded cattle take less time to grain-finish. Capital-intensive feedlots prefer heavy, backgrounded feeder cattle which gain weight very rapidly under feedlot conditions. Heavier animals will cost considerably more but the capital investment may be turned over very rapidly, as heavy yearlings may be on feed for only three months before reaching slaughter weight (O'Mary 1983: 108). Many feedlot operators are becoming unwilling to accept newly weaned calves because they require more care and are more susceptible to stress and disease.

Backgrounding is an especially attractive option for cattle with relatively low weaning weights (notably the British breeds) which need to add frame size on grass before finishing on grain. If newly weaned calves of the smaller British beef breeds were to go directly to grain feeding they might finish under 500 kilograms, too light a weight to get the best price as slaughter cattle. If they remain on grain after they have reached the optimal degree of fat covering, by the time they have reached the required weight they will be carrying too much subcutaneous fat to attain the top grade designation. Thus, backgrounding adds the necessary frame size and weight on which the final high-energy grain finish may be applied (Marlowe 1983: 85).

The larger European exotic cattle breeds such as Charolais or Limousin are more likely to go directly to the feedlot after they are weaned. The fast growing large-framed breeds have weaning weights in excess of 250 kilograms, and if these large weaned calves were backgrounded before feeding they would be too heavy for marketing by the time they were finished. If they are grass-fed for too long, the carcass will be too big to lay on enough fat to grade and still be within the margin of tolerance preferred by the slaughter plants (520 to 610 kilograms). Cattle are typically subject to a discount if they exceed 700 kilograms since some packing houses are not well equipped to handle oversized carcasses, and oversized steaks or roasts are difficult to sell in the domestic market.

Cattle-Feeding Rations

A second dimension of strategic choice by cattle feeders is the source of feed. Some of the smaller feeders are quite proud of the fact that they are also farmers and that they produce all of the feed grains, silage, and forage in the summer months that they feed to their cattle in the winter. This vertically integrated strategy internalizes the production of inputs and avoids unpredictable feed-grain markets. Other feeders believe that they should focus on their core competency as commercial stock raisers and purchase all of their inputs at arm's length so that they may concentrate on developing their competitive edge in the large-scale confinement, feeding, and marketing of cattle for slaughter.

The ingredients used in cattle feed vary by region. The principal elements of the ration are quite flexible: grain corn and corn silage in the Midwest, rolled barley and barley silage on the northern plains, and sorghum (milo) on the southern plains of the United States. Some cattle feeding was originally established to consume agricultural wastes. For example, by-products from cottonseed oil and sugar mills were used in Texas, citrus rinds were used in California's earliest feedlots, while sugar beet tops and beet pulp from sugar mills were a factor in the growth of southern Alberta's feeding industry. In the late 1940s, sugar beet farmers in southern Alberta fed beet pulp from local area sugar refineries to as many as 50,000 cattle each winter (*Lethbridge Herald* 1950: 12). In the Maritime provinces, cull potatoes, waste from fruit and vegetable processing plants (e.g., apple pomace), and spent grains from breweries and distilleries are still used to supplement cattle rations. However, the demand for cattle feed has far outgrown the availability of food-processing by-products, and most cattle are fed grain products produced specifically for that use.

In Alberta, barley is the principal component of the livestock diet. New cattle entering the feedlot are accustomed to a diet of grass and hay. They need to be started on a high-carbohydrate diet of hay and silage, and over a period of two to three weeks they undergo a 'step-up program' in which grain is gradually introduced and increased while the hay and silage is gradually reduced. After the first two weeks, a typical finishing-ration diet would be 85 per cent (by weight) rolled barley grain. Barley grain is typically purchased from grain farms in central Alberta and Saskatchewan where there is sufficient moisture that it can be grown on dry land. When the price of wheat is low, especially if it is frost damaged or low quality, it may be combined with barley grain. About 15 per cent of the diet is barley silage. Barley silage has a higher moisture content and lower value per unit of weight than grain, so it is usually grown by the feedlot operator on irrigated land within a few kilometres of the feedlot. Every feedlot seems to have its own feeding idiosyncrasy. The basic barley grain and silage diet is often supplemented with pelletized commercial feeds to add specific minerals or vitamins to the diet, and it may be augmented with molasses or food-processing by-products. Feed additives in minute concentrations are used to make up for local mineral deficiencies and to increase the daily rate of gain or feed efficiency (weight gain per weight of feed consumed).

The goal of cattle feeding is to add weight at the fastest possible rate and the lowest possible cost. Performance is measured in terms of weight gain per day and conversion efficiency, that is, weight gain per unit of feed input. On a high-energy ration, feeder cattle consume up to 10 kilograms of feed and 40 litres of water to gain up to 1.7 kilograms of body weight per day. Average daily gain and feed efficiency decrease in severe weather conditions, while feed consumption increases. In general, feed costs per kilogram of gain decrease as the rate of gain increases (Alberta Agriculture 1986). Thus, there is a powerful incentive to manage feeding programs to maximize the rate of gain. The variable cost of feed per unit of increase is lower, and cattle that attain maturity sooner can be sold faster to release the capital investment locked up in livestock. When cattle have achieved their optimal weight (approximately 540 kilograms for heifers and 590 kilograms for steers) and have sufficient fat covering, they are considered to be 'finished.'

While grain-finishing is essential to satisfy consumer preferences for beef marbled with pure white fat, grain is not the ideal food for cattle. The ruminant's four stomachs are well adapted to digestion of the complex long-chain carbohydrates (cellulose) of grasses, but not to the high-energy starches and proteins in a grain ration. A significant percentage of the livers from grain-fed animals may be condemned in the packing house because they are abscessed – a result of the excessive bile production required to digest a diet rich in grain.

If feeding is poorly managed and cattle are given wet or finely ground grain or excessive quantities of green alfalfa, they may suffer, and even die, from bloat as the rumen fills rapidly with the frothy gaseous product of digestion run amok. During the digestion process, microflora in the rumen produce gas (mainly methane) which is gradually released when cattle belch. High-energy rations may prompt such a rapid digestion process that there is a build-up of methane trapped in the rumen. The rumen swells rapidly, giving the entire animal a bloated appearance, putting pressure on the diaphragm, and making breathing difficult. In extreme cases, it is necessary to cannulate the rumen (pierce the rumen with a sharp steel tube) to release the pressurized methane. This, and several other feed-related disorders, point to the careful dietary management and emergency intervention that is required in the cattle-feeding and -finishing process. For bloat and a host of other cattle diseases, feedlots are equipped with hospital areas and facilities to care for sick cattle.

Integration

The third strategic dimension is the degree of integration between cattle feeding and adjacent activities in the value added chain. Some feedlots are owned by calf producers or their immediate families. In such cases, calf production and cattle feeding are managed as an integrated process. Other feeders buy and sell their own feeder cattle in an arm's length transaction. This can be risky, as the buying prices of feeder cattle and feed grains and the selling price of slaughter cattle are volatile. Custom feedlots insulate themselves from much of the risk of unfavourable fluctuations in cattle and grain markets. They typically own a few pens of cattle on their own account, but most of their cattle are owned by others who pay a daily fee per head for the accommodation and feeding of their animals. Custom feeding of cattle owned by third parties reduces risk for the feedlot operator, as the daily fee per animal for feed and yardage is guaranteed while the owner absorbs the risk of low selling prices when the animals are finished. A growing number of the cattle housed in custom feedlots are owned by beef-packing firms. This is a form of backward integration which ensures that the packer has a captive supply of finished cattle.

In some cases, the feeder sells cattle to a packing plant months before they are finished, for delivery on a set date in the future. This is known as a forward contract. The feedlot agrees to deliver a specified quantity (typically in truck load lots) of cattle of specified weight and sex on a future date. Whether forward contracting is, in fact, a form of vertical integration is open to debate (Uvacek 1983: 17). But there is no question that forward contracts and custom-feeding agreements are growing as an important form of strategic alliance between packing plants and feedlots.

Origins of Cattle Feeding

The spatial separation of cattle feeding from calf production is millennia old. It can be traced to the earliest days of transhumance in which animals were moved from calving areas in the sheltered valleys, where they had wintered, to fatten on the succulent summer grasses of subalpine pastures. In ancient Britain there was a spatial division of labour between Celtic cattle breeding and Saxon cattle feeding. By the end of the eighteenth century, 100,000 cattle per year were being driven south from calving grounds in the Scottish Lowlands to East Anglia and the Home Counties where they were purchased and fattened on turnips and hay to recover from the long drive in preparation for slaughter (Trow-Smith 1959: 172). Commercial cattle feedlots appeared before the end of the seventeenth century near Boston and were observed in the Midwestern corn belt by the 1840s. Like the Scottish droving industry of eighteenth-century Britain, the gruelling trail drives of the 1860s and 1870s that were required to get Longhorn cattle to the railhead at places such as Abilene, Kansas, generally left them in emaciated condition. Thus, the Texas ranchers soon became dependent on corn belt feeders to finish cattle before the final rail journey to the packing houses of Chicago. By the 1870s, commercial feedlots, operated as adjuncts to mixed farms in Kansas and Nebraska, were preparing fat cattle for the national slaughter market (Skaggs 1986). By the 1920s, the preference for fed beef was becoming apparent as U.S. consumers were prepared to pay a substantial price premium for grain-finished beef (Clemen 1923: 266).

Canada was comparatively slow in developing a cattle-feeding industry, and most of the cattle exported from Canada in the nineteenth-century were finished for slaughter either in the United States or on English pastures. In nineteenth century Ontario, an intensive feeding industry developed based primarily on by-products. Cattle were purchased in the fall and fed through the winter to gain weight prior to slaughter in the spring (Reaman 1970: 129). Breweries, distilleries, and flour mills were the largest domestic processors of grain, and many of these operated their own cattle- or hog-feeding operations to consume waste and spent grain. In 1877, up to 3,000 cattle at one time were being stall-fed on distillery swill in preparation for export from Toronto (*Canadian Illustrated News* 1877). Ontario distilleries such as Gooderham and Worts (Toronto), J.P. Wisers (Prescott), and Seagrams (Waterloo) provided by-products to nearby cattle feeders until 1916 when wartime regulations discouraged the production of alcoholic beverages. Some of Canada's earliest meat packers operated these distillery-based feeding operations as a living hedge on rising cattle prices. When markets fluctuated upwards, the packers could simply withdraw from the market and kill their buffer stocks for a few days (Canada 1934: 619; Child 1960: 127, 144, 149; Ontario Sessional Papers 1887: 83).

Until the Second World War, and notwithstanding Alberta's romantic ranching heritage, cattle feeding in Ontario was far more important than it was in any of the Prairie provinces. Ontario was a significant calf producer in its own right, and a large proportion of the feeder calves born in western Canada were shipped to Ontario for grain-finishing on both corn and small grains augmented with roots (McFall 1927: 506–8).

Two factors encouraged active cattle feeding in Western Canada. First, the arrival of the CPR in 1885 created new markets to repay a greater expenditure on cattle feed. Second, the disastrous winter of 1886 in which a large proportion of the western herd perished of cold and starvation had clearly demonstrated the fickle nature of Alberta winters and the risk of relying exclusively on natural range-land grazing. By the 1890s, the winter feeding of cattle with natural and cultivated sources of hay to augment grazing became prudent and accepted practice. With winter feeding and more nutritious diets, cattle could be sold as two-year-olds, which was half the average lifespan of grass-finished cattle in the nineteenth century (Vrooman 1941), speeding the turnover of capital wrapped up in livestock. In the late nineteenth century, the introduction of horse-powered machines for mowing and baling hay reduced the labour costs of providing winter feed to livestock (Lutz 1980: 9).

By 1909, J.G. Rutherford, Canada's livestock commissioner, was advocating a revolution in the way cattle were finished for the British export market. Because the cattle had spent most of their lives on unconfined range land, they were wild and excitable when they were penned to await the arrival of railway cars. Western cattle spent many days cramped in stock cars as they made their way to Montreal, and when navigation was closed by ice, tidewater ports at Saint John, New Brunswick, Portland, Maine, or Boston, Massachusetts. After a brief period of feed, water, and rest they were then loaded on ships for a two-week voyage tied to a stanchion deep in the dark hold of a rolling ship. It was little wonder that they arrived in England much shrunken from their departure weight and sold at a substantial discount relative to cattle from the United States. Rutherford argued for changes in the way cattle were finished prior to shipping and improvements in cattle husbandry (Rutherford 1909: 9–10).

Two methods for finishing cattle were in use at that time. The earliest and most widely practised method was 'stall-feeding' in which cattle were tied up in a stable in early September, where they remained, not going outside until they were sold in mid-April. In essence, stall-feeding was a confinement system identical to the way dairy cows were managed at that time. The grain ration of two pounds of feed per day (augmented with silage, straw, hay, and roots) was gradually increased over the winter to ten pounds per day. The second method was to feed cattle outside for the whole winter, sheltered only from the wind. There were concerns that the expensive feed ration would be wasted as cattle would use up more energy keeping warm than they would gain as weight. Rutherford (1909: 12) observed, 'It must be borne in mind, however, that cattle that are not stabled grow a coat of hair more resembling in its density that of a beaver than that of a steer, and that this provision aids greatly in conserving the animal heat.' When Rutherford compared the profitability of the two systems, he found that the outside system generated a net profit per steer of $7.05 while the stall-fed animals earned only $5.52, and this was before capitalizing the high cost of a stable compared with the negligible capital costs of feeding outside in an existing field (Rutherford 1909: 13). By 1909, grain farmers from Manitoba to Alberta were grain-finishing anywhere up to 150 big three-year-old steers as a winter sideline.

The development of a grain-finishing sector in Alberta was interrupted in 1913 when the Underwood Tariff gave Canadian cattle free entry to U.S. markets. The best quality Canadian stocker calves and feeder cattle began to be exported to the United States for grain-finishing. Only the lower quality stock tended to remain in Canada for domestic consumption (Foran 1998: 13). After the U.S. export market was blocked by postwar tariffs, and Canadian cattle prices had plummeted along with most other agricultural commodities, there was a new incentive to add more value in Canada. In 1920, Alberta's Department of Agriculture began to experiment with cattle feeding on indigenous grains and was soon touting cattle feeding as the profitable end of the cattle industry (Foran 1998: 18).

Despite these advances, Canada was believed to be poorly suited to finishing cattle on grain. There was ample grassland in Alberta available at low cost, but the province did not possess the climatic advantages of the more southerly states to make it competitive in grain production. Feed corn has not been grown in most parts of western Canada because thermal conditions, measured as 'corn heat units,' are insufficient for it to ripen it within the frost-free period (Putnam and Putnam 1970: 27). Thus, it would be more profitable to export stocker cattle to the United States for finishing. Second, corn-finishing as practised in the Midwestern United States was considered to be superior to the barley which was more widely available in Alberta and western Canada (Foran 1998: 17).

To some degree, the failure of the Prairies to develop an indigenous feeding industry may also be assigned to the innate conservatism of western Canadian livestock producers: 'It is perhaps safe to say that the greatest problem in connection with beef cattle production in Western Canada arises out of the fact that there is no beef cattle finishing tradition in the country. The average beef producer thinks in terms of an intermediate product rather than in terms of an ultimate product and his conscience is not hurt when his cattle are marketed as stockers and feeders' (Sinclair 1931: 434).

A paradigm shift to grain-finishing of cattle was a long time in coming. One factor that encouraged grain-finishing was Canada's first beef grading system (Sinclair 1931). Beginning in 1929, government graders were employed to assess and stamp beef carcasses according to a consistent national standard for 'choice' (red brand) and 'good' (blue brand). For the first time, the consumer had an unambiguous and authoritative basis to justify a premium price. Once the red brand was established as a target, feeders had a greater incentive to produce a higher quality product.

As a solution to the problem of low grain prices in the 1930s, Canada's Department of Agriculture began to encourage the sale of younger stock for finishing in Ontario and in the grain-growing regions of the Prairies (Booth 1936: 58–60). Exporting anything less than Canada's very best quality grain to the glutted European markets in the 1930s was folly. But since the production of substandard wheat was inevitable, western Canadian farmers were encouraged to feed lower grades of wheat to livestock and, in so doing, to become more diversified: 'Our low-grade wheat used at home will be ultimately exported in the form of bacon or fatted cattle and bring satisfactory returns' (Morton 1938: 154). Experimental work suggested that low-grade grain would yield a higher return if marketed through a steer than if it were sold through an elevator (Spencer 1913: 72).

While the foundation for grain-finishing cattle can be traced to the turn of the century, the large-scale grain-feeding and -finishing of cattle in the complex of open-air pens comprising a specialized feedlot is a development of the post–Second World War era. The growth of the feedlot sector was driven by two basic market forces: supply and demand.

Demand Pull and Supply Push

In both the United States and in Canada, grain finishing of cattle was driven by demand from the emerging retail chain store giants and the manipulation of consumer food preferences using the emergent science of marketing and mass advertising (Skaggs 1986: 178–81; Uvacek 1983: 11–14). One of the dominant symbols of the post–Second World War period of economic growth and prosperity is the planned suburban shopping plaza, anchored by a supermarket chain store. Chain stores revolutionized the way North Americans shopped for food. In the urban commercial landscape, corner grocers, dry goods merchants, butchers, fishmongers, and fruit stores soon went the way of vaudeville theatres and the livery stable.

National competitors such as A&P and a host of regional chains (e.g., Overwaitea in British Columbia and Loblaws in Ontario) were locked in a battle for market share. There was little scope for competitive advantage in lower prices. Prices were already cut to the bone and margins on groceries were lower than for any other retail category. Branded grocery products could not be differentiated from those sold in other stores. The advertising of loss leaders had its limits, and premium stamps were soon offered by every chain.

The meat counter, however, was one area that constituted a large proportion of the grocery basket, in which the store added some value, and in which the chains could claim a quality advantage. In 1963, Canada's Dominion Store chain began to trumpet a new slogan: 'It's mainly because of the meat,' advertising that it sold only red-brand beef, then Canada's top grade. Consumer preferences shifted in favour of red meat, a barbecue was added to every suburban patio, and steak became a staple. Like the hula hoop and drive-in curb service, the consumer innovation that began in California soon diffused all over North America and into Canada.

A taste for the most juicy and tender beef had been created by the chain stores, and pressure was on the beef industry to fulfil the demand for this high-quality, high-margin product. This was the 'demand pull' that prompted the feedlot revolution. Red-brand carcasses could only be consistently produced from animals fed on a high-energy feed ration.

Over much of the early post–Second World War period world markets were glutted with grain and prices were generally low. Canada's Prairies had bumper crops and not even enormous grain sales to the Soviet Union and China were sufficient to clear the market or raise prices. Cattle feeding became a means of adding value to an oversupply of low-priced grain. The 1956–7 crop year generated unprecedented wheat surpluses that could only be disposed of as animal feed. In 1957–8 British Columbia's ranchers sold all of their yearlings as well as their two-year-olds (Weir 1964: 117). From that time on, no rancher could afford to return to selling two-year-olds because it would require the loss of a year's income. Instead, they added more cows to produce more calves on the limited grazing land available and held the calves for a shorter period. The lush pastures formerly used for grass-finishing market steers became breeding pastures (Weir 1964: 154), as every cattle feeder became a competitor on world grain markets.

Based on cheap feed grain and whatever frost- or moisture-damaged grain might be unsuitable for human consumption, commercial and custom cattle feedlots in western Canada, in general, and southern Alberta in particular, grew rapidly in the late 1960s and early 1970s (Horner 1980: 105). The price of feed grain began to increase in 1973–4, and this increase was instrumental in the collapse of Canada's cattle population which reached its all-time high in 1975 (Figure 1.1). The cow-calf operator and cattle-finisher had become as vulnerable to world grain prices as grain farmers.

When cattle supplies and cattle prices began to climb rapidly in 1982 (the only cause for optimism in Alberta at that time), cattle-feeding resumed the growth that had begun in the late 1960s. Alberta was feeding 1.27 million cattle in 1987, 1.86 million in 1992, and 2.41 million in 2000 – representing 69.3 per cent of Canada's total fed cattle production

(Johnson 1993; CanFax 2000). But the second growth spurt had as much to do with government policies that favoured domestic grain consumption and livestock production as it did with grain prices.

Public Policy and Cattle Feeding in Western Canada

Cattle people are known for their conservatism, especially in Alberta. As rural populists, cattle folk have been as distrustful of government intervention as they have of the railway and freight rates, collusion by the big eastern beef packers, and absentee ranching interests from overseas. It is therefore a paradox that the industry owes much to government initiatives. The impetus for ranching in western Canada was a direct outcome of Sir John A. Macdonald's National Policy and his ambitious plans for western Canada. In the beginning, the cattle industry depended on government procurement, government railway subsidies, and the innovation of the long-term grazing lease (Breen 1983; Evans 1983). The government brought one of the earliest cattle herds into Alberta, the government provided subsidies to improve breeding stock, and the government provided training in animal husbandry to improve the competitiveness of Canadian cattle production. The government subsidized grain transportation and created a cattle-feeding industry in eastern Canada, while federally regulated stockyards made long distance west to east rail movement of finished cattle feasible. Thus, an important theme in understanding the history and geography of Canada's cattle economy is the importance of state intervention and agricultural policy.

The Crow Rate and the Crow Offsets

Given its huge size and small population, it is little wonder that incentives to build and invest in transportation infrastructure, the regulation of transportation industries, and the manipulation of freight rates have all been key components in nation-building in Canada. And given the importance of grain exports in Canada's trade structure, it is no surprise that the grain industry has traditionally been a higher priority than livestock in general or cattle in particular. The Crow rate had its origins as an incentive for the CPR to build a second transmountain railway line in 1897 to consolidate Canadian control over the rich resources of British Columbia's Kootenay district. In return for the incentives, the CPR agreed in 1897 to reduce its freight rate on grain to half a cent per ton-mile. The low rate was eventually applied to all railways carrying grain to all export shipping points on the Pacific, Hudson Bay, and at the Lakehead. Almost from its inception, it was recognized that the Crow rate created a disincentive for raising livestock as a component in mixed farming: 'The reduction of freight rates on wheat, consequent upon the development of the railroads, together with inadequate local markets for surplus live stock, tended to encourage the growing of wheat and to discourage the breeding and feeding of live stock. Pastures were broken up, barns left unused or converted into horse stables, straw piles were burned [instead of feeding the straw to cattle], "money came easy" and wheat was crowned King' (Spencer 1913: 75).

As time passed, the Crow rate fell further and further behind the actual cost of moving grain. By 1976, the Crow rate covered only about 30 per cent of the actual cost of moving grain by rail (Snavely et al. 1982). By 1981, it cost only 22 cents per hundredweight to move a car load of grain from Saskatoon to Thunder Bay, but $7.67 per hundredweight to move a car load of fresh meat by rail from Saskatoon to Ottawa (Wilson 1981: 169). The prescient observations made by J.S. Spencer were as apt in the 1970s as they had been in 1913. The impact of the Crow rate on Prairie agriculture was to encourage grain farmers to grow more wheat for export at artificially low freight rates, and to discourage adding any value to the grain in situ – most notably to discourage the western Canadian livestock industry from feeding grain to animals. Instead, there was an incentive to grow wheat for export, to produce calves on extensive range land not suitable for grain production, and ship the weaned calves east for finishing on Ontario corn. By the 1920s, beef production was much more important in Ontario than in any of the Prairie provinces, and Ontario was regarded as Canada's real cattle-fattening centre (McFall 1927: 507).

Western grain would be wasted on Alberta livestock, as it cost so much more to ship animals or meat than it did to ship crude grain. Prices of feed grain were levered up by the Crow rate, making it less attractive to feed animals locally. Marginal crop land that would otherwise be used as grazing land for animals was cultivated for grain (Gilson and Wilson 1993: 37–41). It was estimated that cattle production in Alberta was reduced by at least 21 per cent below the levels that could have been expected without the Crow rate (MacEachern 1978: 28). This was especially important because cattle production and meat products have a much greater growth-inducing impact on the economy than does grain. The multiplier for wheat was 1.59. That is, for every dollar of wheat output (strictly speaking, final demand), $1.59 in total economic activity was created to supply the direct and indirect inputs required to grow and market the grain. The multipliers for beef cattle and for meat products, were 2.16 and 2.83 respectively. Clearly, the livestock and meat sectors had high multiplier effects in comparison with other agricultural sectors (Josling and Trant 1966: 61–2; MacEachern 1978: 29). By encouraging cattle feeding and cattle slaughter in central Canada, statutory grain rates directed the growth-inducing effects of the livestock and meat sectors towards the heartland and away from the Prairie west.

While in theory the Crow rate should have discouraged the production and export of livestock, it may have had the opposite effect. The impact of the crow Rate on the railways was to discourage them from reinvesting in their grain-handling infrastructure. The western grain transportation system was in disarray by the late 1970s because of the obsolescence of infrastructure which created the problem of 'shut-in grain' with no place but cattle feedlots to put it all (Kerr and Ulmer 1984: 18). Paradoxically, then, the Crow rate may have actually have helped western cattle interests.

In late 1983, the Western Grain Transportation Act (WGTA) was passed which allowed the price of moving grain to gradually increase, transferring the real costs of the Crow rate from the railways (which had simply passed the costs on to their other customers) to the government. The Crow rate was finally abolished on 1 August 1995, some ninety-eight years after its inception, providing a real incentive to feed western grain to western livestock and, indirectly, to increase cattle slaughter and beef fabrication as well.

From the viewpoint of livestock producers, the WGTA did not change anything: they were still paying higher prices for feed grains than they otherwise would. Indeed, to the extent that government payments of over $700 million per year to the railways improved grain-handling equipment, the WGTA could even make matters worse as there would be less 'shut-in grain' and even higher prices. To assist livestock producers in offsetting the negative impacts of the WGTA, each of the Prairie provinces brought in programs to subsidize the cost of feed grain: Manitoba's Livestock Development Program, Saskatchewan's Feed Grain Adjustment Program, and Alberta's Feed Grain Market Adjustment Program (Canadian International Trade Tribunal 1993: 117).

Alberta's Feed Grain Market Adjustment Program began operating in 1985. Livestock producers could apply for an amount equal to the 'market distortion' created by the WGTA which was calculated as $21 per tonne of grain (mainly wheat, oats, and barley, but virtually every feed grain was eligible), provided that it was fed to livestock. On 1 April 1987, the program was renamed the Alberta Crow Benefit Offset Program, and the subsidy was reduced to $13 per tonne. On 1 September 1989, the value of the offset was reduced still further to $10 per tonne. The subsidy was paid directly to livestock producers who grew their own grain and issued as a voucher to producers who purchased grain at arm's length. By subsidizing feed grain expenditures, the Alberta program made intensive grain-feeding of cattle more remunerative and encouraged the establishment of many new feedlots in the 1980s.

Tripartite Stabilization Program

The other important livestock policy in recent years was the National Tripartite Stabilization Program (NTSP), an insurance scheme that came into effect on 1 April 1986. As a *tripartite* program it was funded by premiums shared equally between the federal government, the provincial governments (except Quebec and Newfoundland), and those beef-cattle producers who chose to participate. In essence, the program was intended to stabilize cattle producers' revenues. If the monthly average selling price of cattle fell below a support price calculated to guarantee a margin, the plan would make up the difference and pay the producer. Separate plans were designed for feeder calves, feeder cattle, and slaughter cattle. The program was designed to be 'actuarially sound,' that is, for payouts to be fully covered by the premiums received from the three participants (Agriculture Canada 1989).

At almost the same time as the NTSP was launched, the U.S. government had applied countervailing duties on Canadian hog imports in 1985, followed by duties on pork in 1989. This experience and a sabre-rattling investigation of the Canadian industry by the U.S. International Trade Commission (U.S. ITC 1987), caused great concern due to the potential for similar countervailing duties on cattle or beef.

The dip in slaughter-cattle prices in 1991 was sufficient to trigger large NTSP payments to producers of slaughter cattle, mainly feedlot operators. According to Gary Sargent, general manager of the Alberta Cattle Commission, 'The Americans felt the pain of low prices too, but they saw Canadians getting $190-an-animal payouts and didn't feel that was fair' (quoted in Carter 1993a: 22). The Canadian Cattlemen's

Association was soon lobbying for an end to the NTSP for cattle, as the risk of countervailing duties by the United States outweighed the benefits of stabilization (Gilson and Wilson 1993).

Of course, cattle producers could have employed different methods to reduce risk. In comparison with private strategies for risk reduction such as hedging of cattle on feed or the purchase of live cattle options, participation in the NTSP yielded higher net incomes because of the subsidy aspect of the NTSP: two-thirds of the premium costs were borne by government (Freeze et al. 1990: 248). The U.S. ITC investigated the operation and payout record for cattle plans under the NTSP. Because the Canadian cattle supply was so much smaller than that of the United States, the trade commission found that the NTSP would have a small impact on the U.S. market at a national scale, however, it was potentially large in some regions (U.S. ITC 1993: 5–6). For instance, the Washington Cattlemen's Association argued that the NTSP was a trade-distorting program as the reduction of risk and the guarantee of a margin would encourage Canadian cow-calf producers to expand production, reducing prices in the Pacific northwest (Canadian International Trade Tribunal 1993: 138). The NTSP was terminated on 31 December 1993; however, it may have helped to 'prime the pump' by encouraging the establishment of many new feedlots during the eight-year window of opportunity it created, while the stabilization program was in existence.

Feedlot Alley: Intensive Cattle-Feeding Issues in Alberta

The greatest concentration of cattle feeding activity in all of Canada is in the County of Lethbridge which is centred roughly on the City of Lethbridge, 200 kilometres south of Calgary and 100 kilometres north of the Montana border (Figure 2.3). Counting only feedlots with a capacity of 1,000 cattle or more, Lethbridge County accounts for 35 per cent of Alberta's total feedlot capacity. Much of the remaining 65 per cent is distributed as a great T-shaped zone of cattle feeding that extends north from the Milk River to Edmonton with a cross-bar corresponding roughly to Highway 16: the east–west Yellowhead Route.

Within Lethbridge County cattle feeding capacity is even further concentrated on the north side of the Oldman River in the Lethbridge Northern Irrigation District (LNID). A line running northeast from the Village of Monarch to Picture Butte and on to Turin has become known as 'Feedlot Alley.' In 1995, the feedlots then in place in this area had a

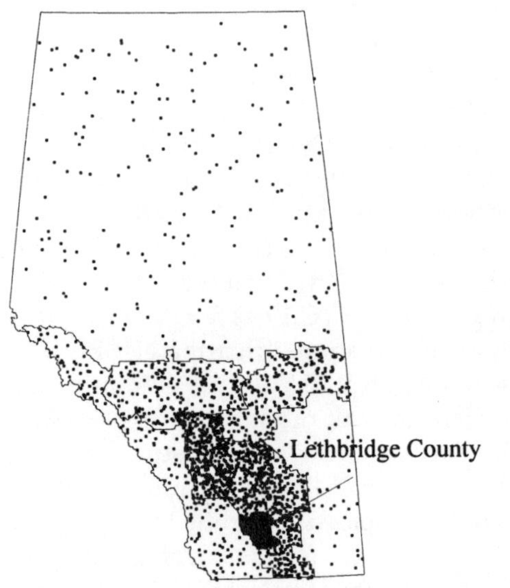

Figure 2.3. Feedlot bunk capacity in Alberta, 1999. Source: Canadian Cattlemen's Association, CanFax Cattle on Feed.

one-time capacity for some 325,000 head of cattle, approximately double the volume in 1990 (Bennett and McCarley 1995: 5). By 2000, Lethbridge County had a bunk capacity of 524,200 head of cattle (CanFax 2000). Such a concentration of feedlots, together with a considerable number of other intensive livestock operations (ILOs) such as hog, dairy, and chicken barns, poses a number of health and environmental concerns for local residents – but the most controversial concerns are manure management, odour, and water pollution.

Manure Management

Manure is composed of urine and fecal material. Mature feeder cattle produce twenty to twenty-five kilograms (wet weight) of manure per day which amounts to approximately two tonnes for each animal over the duration of a ninety-day stay in the feedlot (Fairbank 1983: 197).

Most western Canadian grain farmers do not depend on manure as a fertilizer. From the 1890s onward, Prairie agriculture was distinctive because of its reliance on specialized grain farms and the lack of livestock other than draft animals. Unlike Ontario and Quebec farms, with their large dairy herds, the spreading of cattle manure was never a part of the grain-growing tradition (MacEwan 1980: 112). Soil fertility for the production of wheat was maintained by fallowing, and after the lessons of the 'Dirty Thirties' had been learned, with crop rotation and commercial fertilizer. Commercial fertilizers often give comparable or higher crop yields at less expense than animal excrement, and synthetic fertilizer may be blended in the precise ratio required for specific soil or crop needs.

Spreading manure requires large quantities of energy to broadcast a bulky and low-value nutrient. The break-even point, where the cost of manure transport exceeds its nitrogen and phosphate nutrient value, is only 18 kilometres from the feedlot gate (Freeze and Sommerfeldt 1985). Thus, for large feedlots, manure has become less valued as a fertilizer resource and is perceived more as a noxious waste product that is costly to discard. Far from crop farmers paying for manure as a productive input, feedlot operators with insufficient land to absorb the manure they produce must now pay farmers to remove the excrement and apply it to crop land (Canadian International Trade Tribunal 1993: 89). The nutrient content of manure decreases significantly during storage, handling, and spreading. Because of the volatilization of ammonia, for example, only 25 per cent of the available nitrogen excreted by the animal is available in the soil for uptake by plants (Bennett and McCarley 1995). The management of large volumes of manure and its associated odour and fly problems has become a critical problem for feedlot operators.

Stream pollution and fish kills resulting from poor feedlot design in the late 1950s led to the first feedlot licensing and regulatory requirements in Kansas (Fairbank 1983: 201). Since that time feedlot operators have begun to feel threatened by the public and by provincial and municipal authorities. They feel that outsiders do not understand their business and they are concerned that costly regulations will be imposed which are impractical and even counterproductive because regulators and the public do not appreciate the day-to-day realities of feeding livestock.

Nevertheless, there have also been some appalling examples of negligence and irresponsibility on the part of some feedlot operators. One of the most spectacular examples in Canada was in 1997 when Western Feeders in Mossleigh, Alberta (southeast of Calgary), was charged under both the federal Fisheries Act and Alberta's Environmental Protection and Enhancement Act with dumping over 30 million litres of cattle pen run-off which flowed into West Arrowwood Creek and eventually the Bow River, 'killing everything in its path.' According to a local area farmer: 'It was a deliberate release that killed everything in the stream ... It was like putting fish into a sceptic tank' (*Globe and Mail* 1998a). Western Feedlots pled guilty to the charges and was sentenced to a total penalty of $120,000 in October 1998 (Alberta Environmental Protection 1998). Public concerns about the negative impacts of intensive livestock production have grown in both rural and urban areas. The conflict is often painted by feedlot operators as one between heroic farmers and naive urbanites who move to country residential properties only to discover the negative externalities of commercial agriculture. But many of the critics of contemporary feedlot practices are themselves farmers who view the feedlots and large-scale hog barns as the interlopers in the pastoral landscape.

Manure collects in animal pens, especially in the areas immediately adjacent to feed bunks and water troughs, and an accumulation of half a metre of manure in early spring is not unusual. Manure clean-out is seldom attempted until after the pen has been emptied, and its occupants shipped off to slaughter. Front-end loaders are used to either empty the pen and stockpile the manure elsewhere in the feedlot or simply to push the manure into a mound in the centre of the pen where it dries and becomes a favoured place for the next generation of feeder cattle to lie down at night. In daylight the manure pile is often chosen by the largest and most dominant cattle to stand on so that they can survey their domain. Once all of the pens have central mounds of manure, the excess must be removed from pens and stockpiled until the soil has thawed sufficiently to spread it.

Manure is not spread on snow or frozen soil to avoid contaminating spring run-off and prevent a sudden surge of fecal matter into surface waters. For that reason, manure must be stored until late spring when the ground has thawed and fields are dry enough to support heavy machinery to incorporate it into the soil. While some can be given away to nearby farmers, feedlots in western Canada typically own a section or more of land to absorb the manure produced the preceding winter. Alberta's Code of Practice for the Safe and Economic Handling of Animal Manures specifies that a 10,000-head feedlot requires 1,400 acres of irrigated land or 2,800 acres of the dark-brown soils of southern and central Alberta to dispose of manure (Alberta Agriculture, Food and Rural Development 1995: 33). At recommended rates of application, the land area required for manure disposal is roughly equivalent to the acreage required to grow the amount of barley silage required by a feedlot of that size (MacAlpine et al. 1997: 14). However, the Code of Practice, is coming under fire: it is not legislated, it is not enforced, and there are no penalties for failing to adhere to it. Second, there is some question about the long-term sustainability of the rates of manure application that the code prescribes. The Code of Practice is used as a guideline by municipalities approving development permits, and a new or expanded feedlot is normally required to demonstrate that it has the requisite land base to spread its waste.

The Irrigation Branch of Alberta Agriculture, Food and Rural Development investigated the manure produced from some 258 intensive livestock operations in relation to the land available in the Lethbridge Northern Irrigation District. The nutrient content of just over 1 million tonnes of manure produced annually (two-thirds was solid manure from beef-cattle and poultry operations) was evaluated in relation to the nutrient requirements of the crops commonly grown under irrigation (principally grain and forages but with some potatoes and sugar beets). Assuming that all feedlots were operating at full capacity all year long, the study found that 24 per cent of the feedlots did not own sufficient land to spread the manure they would generate, at a rate of 60 tonnes of manure per hectare, the maximum recommended rate on irrigated land. However, many of these feedlots make arrangements to spread the manure on neighbouring parcels, especially on land they rent to grow barley for silage. After some years of heavy manure application it may be necessary to reduce the quantity applied to avoid an excessive build-up of nitrates in the root zone. The study concluded: 'About one third of the ILO's in the LNID portion of the County of Lethbridge have sufficient land for repeated, annual application of manure at agronomic and environmentally responsible rates of 20–30 Mg ha^{-1}. The total amount of cultivated land in the entire study area is insufficient for agronomic utilization of all the manure potentially produced by existing ILO's. Further expansion of the livestock feeding industry in the study area is severely limited by the scarcity of cultivated land available for manure disposal' (Bennett and McCarley 1995: 16).

While further research on the capacity of soils to support the application of manure is required, it appears that further expansion of feedlots and other intensive livestock operations in the County of Lethbridge would be unwise. Yet, the local county council debated and turned down a proposal to limit further growth of its intensive livestock industry. The council learned that 75 per cent of the local intensive livestock operators were planning to expand their operations and decided against limiting growth as it would be 'unfair' and 'undemocratic' (Helmer 1998a: A1).

The Smell of Money

The smell is the first thing most people notice; it is called 'the smell of money.' The removal and spreading of manure releases the very worst of feedlot odours. Alberta's Code of Practice requires that manure be incorporated into the soil within forty-eight hours of spreading by ploughing, tillage, or direct injection into the soil (Alberta Agriculture 1995: 16). There are inevitably exceptions, however. Manure may simply be broadcast (scattered with a manure-spreading machine coupled to a tractor) on forage crops such as alfalfa, provided that the land is not subject to run-off and the spreading does not pose a nuisance in conflict with other land uses. Manure in combination with collected water run-off may be sprayed on fields as a thin slurry through the nozzles of large-scale irrigation apparatus. Finally, incorporation of manure into soil is not necessary if it can be demonstrated that it does not cause an odour or run-off problem.

Feedlot operators protest that they have little flexibility in when they can spread and incorporate manure since soil moisture and weather conditions are outside their control. An unexpected machinery breakdown may prevent incorporation within the forty-eight-hour period. The apocryphal June wedding that was marred when the neighbouring feedlot operator chose that particular Saturday to clean out his pens is common folklore in southern Alberta. In an attempt to avoid this type of problem, Alberta has drafted minimum distance separation guidelines depending on the size of feedlot and intensity of neighbouring uses. For example, the minimum distance separation between an 18,000-head feedlot and a single country residence is 3,230 feet, just under one kilometre (Alberta Agriculture 1999: 13). When the wind is blowing, as it often does, and the manure is freshly applied, as it sometimes is, one kilometre – even ten kilometres – is not far enough. While fresh manure, especially liquid hog manure, has an appalling and inescapable stench that seriously interferes with people's ability to enjoy being out of doors, odours are not considered to be a public health problem. Feedlot odours are treated as a land use issue and are regulated through the land development approval process by local and regional planning authorities.

Water Pollution

Two separate water pollution problems may be caused by manure in the large volumes found in a feedlot. First, surface run-off from feedlot pens and temporary stockpiles can make its way into irrigation canals and natural watercourses, elevating nitrate and phosphate concentration above safe levels, and introducing fecal coliform bacteria into water at levels that threaten the purity of drinking water. Second, limitations in the land base create an incentive for feedlot operators to apply excessive quantities of manure to crop land, reaching and sometimes exceeding the capacity of the soil to absorb it, eventually resulting in the pollution of groundwater which ultimately makes its way to surface water or into wells for drinking water.

Water is vital to raising livestock, and in southern Alberta most intensive livestock facilities are located within irrigation districts that supply and administer the flow of irrigation water within their confines. Irrigation canals run throughout these districts to supply field irrigation apparatus, to recharge feedlot dugouts for livestock, and to provide drinking water for many rural residents and urban municipalities. Although they are often protected by berms or engineered to be higher than the surrounding fields, these canals are vulnerable to pollution by overland run-off and groundwater contamination if the animal wastes generated by intensive livestock facilities are not properly contained.

Feedlots are normally designed to channel and divert uncontaminated overland run-off away from and around the site. Slope and elevation are critical variables in the feedlot location decision. Not only does good drainage reduce the total amount of contaminated water that must be managed, but it also helps to keep livestock pens and cattle drier. Contaminated run-off from within the feedlot must be contained within the property, and it is typically impounded in a lined catch basin that includes manure-contaminated wash water. The catch basin may simply dry out through evaporation over the summer but feedlots with irrigation infrastructure usually also pump the slurry of manure, rain, and wash water through a centre-pivot irrigation system onto adjacent fields. To maintain a margin for unexpected events, catch basins must maintain eighteen inches of 'free-board,' that is, they should never be intentionally filled higher than a line eighteen inches from the top of the basin. The bottom of the basin must be at least three feet above the water table and lined with a layer of virtually impermeable material which is typically made of naturally occurring local clay. Some are lined with concrete or a flexible synthetic membrane (Alberta Agriculture 1995: 9). Feedlot visitors are always toured by the catch basin, and feedlot operators are fond of declaring that there is no seepage and that liquid waste is fully contained at all times under all weather conditions. It is difficult not to feel a little sceptical about these claims. In any case, it is very difficult to detect a catch-basin leak or to measure its severity.

It has been concluded that agricultural practices are contributing to a degradation in water quality. The concentration of fecal coliform bacteria in both surface and irrigation water often exceeds human and livestock drinking water guidelines (Canada-Alberta Environmentally Sustainable Agriculture Committee 1998: 29). Agricultural sources are the most obvious culprit, although wildlife and humans are also contributors. This environmental problem becomes a public health issue when the concentration of fecal coliforms in tap water exceeds Canadian standards. The imposition of 'boil water orders' by local health authorities is an occasional – but alarming – occurrence in the towns and villages of Feedlot Alley. Some suggest that living with episodic boil-water orders is a price that must be paid for the benefits of intensive livestock operations. But as water quality problems come to be felt right in the home, there is growing public concern and debate over the costs and benefits of a local economy that depends on intensive livestock confinement.

In May 2000, an *E. Coli* outbreak in the municipal water supply of Walkerton, Ontario, infected several thousand people and caused at least six deaths, although it was implicated in 15 more. The source of contamination was traced to a municipal well adjacent to a cow-calf operation, although the severity of the outbreak was largely a result of faulty chlorination, failure to test the municipal water supply conscientiously, and a long delay before the water contamination problem was made public (*Lethbridge Herald* 2000b; *Toronto Star* 2001). Many people in Feedlot Alley know that they face a similar risk and that the events of Walkerton could be replayed in the Oldman River basin. But boil water orders have become an accustomed part of domestic life in southern Alberta communities, and the region is protected by greater awareness and greater vigilance over the quality of the water supply.

Conclusion

Feedlots are a comparatively new feature on the economic landscape of Alberta and, to a much lesser extent, elsewhere in Canada. Together with intensive hog and poultry operations, they are the prototype of industrial agriculture. A modern feedlot has little of the feeling of a family farm or generations'-old commitment to the land that one senses on a ranch that raises calves. Instead, feedlots are much more like a small factory. The owner typically commutes to the feedlot each day and works on a computer in an office. Feedlots employ about one worker for every 3,000 head of cattle. They have the ambience of a small business; the social centre of the feedlot is the lunchroom where employees gather for coffee, it is no farm kitchen. Feeding cattle is becoming routinized, much of the work is repetitive and varies little from one season to another. You do not walk around the feedlot, you drive. It is hard to get lost as the gridiron made up of pens separated by alleys is quite like the street pattern of a small Prairie city and the feed-mill leg and bunker silo loom above all else as landmarks on Alberta's new economic landscape.

Economies of scale are vital to these agricultural enterprises. They are becoming increasingly entrepreneurial and businesslike, as the procurement of grain and the marketing of cattle becomes more like commodity trading than farming. In common with cow-calf operations, no two feedlots are quite alike. They have different philosophies on where to procure cattle, the precise constituents of the feeding ration, and most of all in marketing. Unlike cow-calf operations, feedlots are mass production operations with less scope to manoeuvre or to innovate over the short term. Once cattle are purchased they must be fed and sold as quickly as possible to keep up with payments to the bank. Whether cattle prices are high or low, the task is the same: to keep a steady stream of grain and silage in front of tens of thousands of steer noses. Keep them eating, keep them gaining, keep them healthy, and somehow, get rid of all that manure.

THREE

Cattle Logistics: From Stockyards and Cattle Cars to Auction Marts and Cattle Liners

In 1969, I can remember riding my bicycle to the Côte des Neiges underpass which took traffic under Montreal's major east-west Canadian Pacific Railway line. I went to watch the cattle trains with forty carloads or more of livestock, clanking their way into a maze of trackage and freight yards that led eventually to the city's east-end stockyard. You could see the steers peering through the slats. You could hear them mooing. You could smell that barnyard smell. These animals had come from the great ranches and feedlots of far away Alberta, with rest stops in St-Boniface, Manitoba, and even the wilds of White River in Northern Ontario. This seemed very exotic to a city kid who had never travelled west of Toronto and had never been on a farm. I had no idea that I was witnessing the end of an era, when cattle on the hoof were shipped over two thousand miles by rail from the western grazing periphery to slaughter in the industrial east.

There are no railway cattle cars left in Canada. The last west-to-east cattle train made its way east in 1987. Cattle now move much shorter distances to slaughter, and they are shipped in great aluminum semitrailers known as cattle liners or possum bellies. With two decks for cattle and three for hogs, these highway leviathans provide a direct connection from the feedlot to the unloading chute of the slaughterhouse.

The best place to see cattle in long-distance transit now is in the dozens of cattle liners queued in the receiving lot of a major packing plant at about 5:00 in the morning. These steers were loaded yesterday at feedlots all over the Prairie west, and they will be chilling carcasses by lunch time. The cattle are packed in tightly to reduce risk of injury in the event of sudden braking. In the crush, stress, heat of the trailer and without food or water, cattle may lose up to 12 per cent of their body weight; this is known as 'shrink.' By the end of a long trip, the broad backs of animals on the lower deck are covered in manure splattered through the slatted floor of the top deck. But the many hours in a highway cattle liner are more humane than the four days that cattle spent shivering in frigid stock cars in Prairie winters in the early nineteen hundreds, or the constant harassment and punishment meted out in cattle drives of up to six weeks in the late nineteenth century.

The cattle commodity chain becomes progressively more concentrated in ownership and space as value is added. Calf production is distributed among thousands of calf producers in every province, while cattle feeding is concentrated among a few hundred large feedlots, mainly in Alberta. Cattle slaughter is still more concentrated in about a dozen large plants. Cattle producers and processors are articulated through a market and transportation system to transfer cattle between producers and processors. This is cattle logistics.

The geography of cattle movement changed dramatically between the 1960s and 1980s. In 1960, large numbers of western cattle were still shipped to the east where the main markets were to be found. Stockers moved from calf producers on the Prairies and foothills to rural cattle-finishers in Ontario, usually with an intervening stop at the Ontario Stock Yards in Toronto. Finished cattle also moved from west to east by rail (mainly between July and November) to provide a significant proportion of the slaughter cattle processed through public stockyards in Montreal and Toronto for onward shipment to packing plants. By the 1980s, the west–east shipment of slaughter cattle had slowed to a trickle, and now it is only occasionally warranted when supplies of Ontario and Quebec cattle are insufficient to supply the eastern beef plants.

Overview of Cattle Marketing

The commodity chain for cattle and beef is complex and involves a number of highly specialized activities, each with its own geography. Between the newborn calf and the 1,300-pound steer in the knocking box, the bovine moves through a series of spatially distinct establishments and may change ownership up to half a dozen times. The cattle-marketing system functions in a price discovery and property transfer process facilitated by different types of marketing functionaries.

Meat-packing firms employ professional 'cattle buyers,' paying them a salary to acquire cattle of the required sex, age, and conformation at the lowest possible price to keep the packing plant in continuous operation. They drive the dusty rural roads from feedlot to feedlot to assess the cattle offered for sale, offer a price for cattle that fulfils their plant's current requirements, and arrange for delivery 'just-in-time' for the cattle to enter the kill floor. They also attend the regular sales at auction marts in their territory. Purchasing cattle is a critical activity that requires fine judgment and expertise. Cattle buyers must be able to look over a pen of cattle and assess their carcass grade and yield percentage (carcass weight as a percentage of live weight) within a 1 per cent margin of error.

The cattle buyer is concerned with acquiring cattle in truckload cattle lots that are uniform in sex, weight, and grade characteristics. Packinghouses are not able to hold more than a one-day supply of cattle; they are not equipped to feed cattle, and their pens have limited capacity. Thus, the buyer must acquire and deliver the requisite quantities of cattle on a just-in-time basis. To keep the packing plant in continuous operation, buyers must coordinate shipments with the plant's beef manager so that cattle arrive hours before slaughter. The cattle buyer's job is crucial to the profitability of the packinghouse.

Commission firms typically act as selling agents for cattle sellers, usually cow-calf operators, but sometimes for backgrounders or feedlot operators. Commission firms do not ever take ownership of the cattle. They are paid a commission on a per head or percentage basis for sorting diverse lots of cattle, combining small lots into larger homogeneous and saleable groups, and presenting them to packer buyers for the slaughterhouse or to order buyers for backgrounders or feedlot operators.

Commission firms may also act as order buyers or cattle brokers, operating on a commission paid by the parties who place the order, usually on a per head basis. Order buying is a service to buy specific types and ages of cattle on behalf of backgrounders or feedlot operators. They may also purchase cattle on behalf of packers in regions where the livestock population is too widely dispersed to support direct sales through packer buyers.

Livestock dealers buy and sell cattle on their own account, unlike commission firms. They are essentially *arbitrageurs* who buy small and irregular lots of cattle, sort and assemble them into large uniform lots, and resell them to feedlots, packinghouses, or to distant markets where prices are higher. Dealers often operate at the fringes of the industry where cattle production is limited or purchases are not routine (Lesser 1993: 217).

The Price Discovery Process

To the typical consumer the idea of 'price discovery' seems ridiculous: 'Just read the tag!' Cattle, however, are a commodity whose price is changing hour by hour and from place to place. There is no tag. Prices are determined by negotiation between buyers and sellers. Prices may be determined by a private negotiation ('private treaty'), by public auction in which low bids gradually rise until the selling price is reached, or by 'Dutch auction' in which the bids start high and gradually fall until someone finally punches a button, turning a bid into a price.

Private Treaty

Until 1960 the majority of Canadian cattle were sold at public stockyards for a price negotiated between a 'commission man' and a cattle buyer in a 'private treaty.' Cattle producers would deliver their livestock to the stockyard in the afternoon and consign the animals to one of the bonded and licensed commission firms. The livestock would be driven into the alley that was assigned to that commission firm, confined in a pen, and given feed and water.

The next morning when the market officially opened for trading, each commission firm would take a group of registered cattle buyers down its alley to show and describe the livestock in various pens. The buyers would establish their bidding sequence by coin toss and the commission firm would offer the cattle to the buyers in the order established by toss. All of the buyers would have a chance to bid on the cattle, and in the event that two firms settled on the same price, the coin toss would prevail. If the final bid was too low, the commission firm had the right to 'pass' the lot and wait for stronger market conditions. Once the cattle were sold, the 'alley boys' would drive the animals out of the commission firm's pen, onto the weigh scale, and then to the new owner's pen or sometimes directly across the street to the packinghouse (Friesen 1995: 48).

Community Auction Sales

Community auctions, auction marts, or country yards are interchangeable terms for small-scale stockyards that sell cattle by public auction. Unlike public stockyards, they provide no livestock services, keep few animals overnight, have no direct link with slaughter plants, and rely entirely on highway transportation of livestock. Community auctions began to develop in Canada in the 1940s as trucking of livestock became less costly and the dominant position of the public stockyard began to weaken (Reaman 1970: 132). Community auction sales were innovative in two ways. Located uniformly over the rural landscape in small towns, community auctions decentralized cattle marketing. In 1955, over 60 per cent of the livestock consigned to auction marts in the United States originated within a twenty-five-mile radius of the market (Ives 1966: 53).

Second, the cattle prices which resulted from competitive bidding by public outcry became a matter of public record, providing a rich daily database for sellers and buyers to use in charting market trends. Open and competitive bidding benefited producers, as the transaction became transparent. Buyers appreciated having the opportunity to bid on every lot of livestock coming up for sale. In an effort to compete with the auction marts, and following the lead of the big federally regulated stockyards in the United States, most of the public stockyards in western Canada introduced auction selling in 1950 (Canada, Department of Agriculture 1950).

Auction marts operate only one or two days a week or seasonally. They are a ready source of cash for farmers selling small lots or individual animals. The type of animals sold at an auction vary with the seasons. In spring, the auctions tend to attract buyers for small-scale slaughter plants specializing in the slaughter of older cows which are often culled from the breeding herd in the spring if the cow fails to produce a healthy calf. Spring auctions also see dairy bull calves for sale to specialized feeders of milk-fed veal and yearlings destined for grain-finishing. In the fall, the emphasis changes as livestock auctions sell large numbers of recently weaned stockers, ready to be wintered on hay and grass, but there are also aged open slaughter cows which have been culled after weaning their last calves. In winter months, auction marts advertise bull sales which attract cow-calf producers needing a new bull for their cow herd.

Some feeders prefer not to deal in cattle that have been through a sales ring because of the risk of disease from being exposed to a large number of cattle in an unaccustomed environment. Auction sales are a stressful experience for cattle. They are confronted by sometimes aggressive handlers, exposed to hundreds of animals of different species, and it may be the first time that they have ever been off pasture. Unloading, loading, sorting, and moving cattle from one pen to another, and coercing cattle to move around and appear fit and healthy in the sales ring is a part of the constant activity in any auction market. The most common tool for guiding cattle is the 'stockman's cane,' a sturdy wooden cane with a crook at one end. The stockman's cane is like a badge of office for cattle handlers and a symbol of the auction ring. It seems that every animal that comes within range gets lightly whacked across the back to encourage movement. The stockman's cane is also a defensive weapon to club an animal in the rare instance when cattle become aggressive. Electric prods with a trigger to deliver a painful shock are occasionally necessary as the only way to load animals on a truck.

Electronic and Satellite Auctions

Electronic auctions were first developed in Canada as an integral component of the Ontario hog marketing board system in 1961 (*Canadian Food Industries* 1961), and they had spread to most other provinces by end of the 1960s. Microcomputer and network technology replaced the rustic teletypes of the early auctions and the electronic auction began to spread to cattle when the Ontario Cattlemen's Association established an electronic auction in 1982. Known as OLEX (Ontario Livestock Exchange), the system is based in Kitchener-Waterloo but available province-wide. The electronic cattle auction is held twice a week and OLEX now accounts for approximately 40 per cent of Ontario cattle sales. The electronic auction of the *Fedération des Producteurs de Bovins du Québec* accounts for 50 per cent of slaughter-cattle sales in the province of Quebec (McAuley 1995: 150; Ontario 1988: 30).

In an electronic auction the selling process begins when a cattle producer with cattle to sell telephones or e-mails the market with a list of the cattle for sale, well in advance of the auction. A representative of the market (a 'field man') drives to the farm, inspects the livestock, describes the animals by breed, sex, grade, and estimated weight. This information, along with the name of the field man who made the assessment and the location of the cattle for sale, is placed on the auction's computer for viewing by potential buyers. The auction begins at an appointed time, and a relatively low bid is offered to get the bidding process started. The bids in cents per pound live weight go up in increments of a quarter of a cent, as, one after another, potential buyers key in their bids. When there is no response for fifteen seconds, the bidding is finished, and the highest bidder owns the cattle subject to pre-established conditions of sale such as the location of the weigh scale to be used and the delivery date (Friesen 1995: 97).

Similar to live auctions, electronic auctions are popular for older cull cows, and bulls which are expected to be thin, will not achieve a quality grade, and are mainly differentiated by weight. Young feeder cattle may also be sold by electronic auction, but prime backgrounded cattle that are ready for finishing are more likely to be sold directly by the backgrounder to the feedlot. Most slaughter cattle are sold directly to packer buyers.

Satellite auctions use video cameras and satellite links to convey a detailed image of livestock characteristics to a much wider audience than can be seated in the sales ring of a country yard. They have been used to auction stocker cattle originating in northern Ontario to cattle feeders in southern Ontario, and they are also becoming popular for premium quality bull sales directed to buyers all over North America.

Direct-to-Packer Sales

Direct-to-packer sales have become the dominant marketing channel for fed cattle from large-scale feedlots. Feedlots are more geographically concentrated and their product, finished cattle for slaughter, are typically sold in large truck-load lots, forty cattle at a time. Packer buyers are, therefore, willing and able to visit individual feedlots and negotiate to buy the cattle directly from the feeder. Direct-to-packer sales save on the transportation costs, yardage fees, stress, and carcass shrink involved in shipping cattle to an auction ring. Terms of sale include a delivery date which could be the following day or a 'forward contract' for delivery several months in the future. Unlike the auction mart, where price discovery is based on a public bidding process among a group of competing buyers, direct-to-packer sales are based on a private treaty between a professional buyer of slaughter cattle and a cattle feeder. Thus, the seller has less information to assess the offered price (Canada 1982: 9). For this reason, the Canadian Cattlemen's Association operates CanFax, a widely used non-profit information service that provides buyers and sellers with a weekly report of cattle prices and market trends in Canada.

In Canada, direct-to-packer sales have grown fairly steadily since the 1920s, exceeding 90 per cent of cattle sales by 1985 when Agriculture Canada stopped collecting the data necessary to compute the percentage (Figure 3.1). The remaining 8 to 10 per cent of slaughter cattle sold through auction markets are mainly older animals culled from the breeding herd. Three factors account for the growing popularity of direct-to-packer sales. First, as livestock trucking became commonplace in the 1920s, independent livestock truckers preferred to deliver

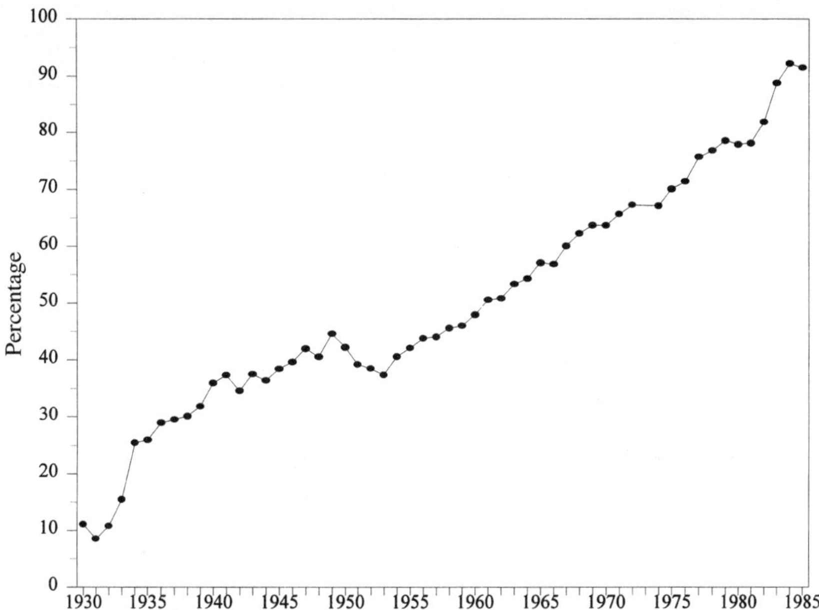

Figure 3.1. Direct-to-packer sales as a percentage of total cattle slaughter, 1929–1985. Source: Agriculture Canada, *Livestock Market Review*, various years.

livestock directly to packing plants instead of stockyards, obviating the need to wait to see if the cattle would sell and to take any returns back to the farmer. Second, increasing concentration of the industry in the hands of large packing firms in the 1930s meant that there were fewer small and medium-sized packers to bid on livestock at the public stockyards. Once a direct offer had been made on the ranch or farm, it was believed that collusion among packer buyers would ensure that no packing firm would make a higher offer if those same cattle later appeared at a stockyard (Canada 1935: 161–2). Packer direct sales were further encouraged by the advent of large-scale feedlots in the 1960s which tend to be regionally concentrated, making it easy for packer buyers to call at each feedlot to evaluate cattle and bid on them. Direct-to-packer sales are especially dominant in western Canada, while auction markets account for a larger proportion of slaughter-cattle sales in Quebec and Ontario (McAuley 1995: 149–50; Smith 1980: 18).

There are two main pricing systems for direct-to-packer sales. If the feedlot has a truck scale (and most of the large ones do), a truck load of animals may be sold on a 'live weight' basis less a reduction for 'shrink' in transit. A shrink factor ranging from 2 to 5 per cent is typical, depending on the distance from feedlot to packing plant and the prevailing temperatures. In Alberta, where the bulk of slaughter cattle are youthful and of high quality, the vast majority of packer direct sales are on a live weight basis.

Cattle may also be priced on a carcass weight basis which means that the decapitated and eviscerated carcass will be weighed as it hangs from the rail, just before it goes in the cooler (hot carcass weight). This weight multiplied by the price per pound determines the feedlot's revenue for the animal. Carcass weight pricing formulas may include a complex array of discounts for different carcass grades and yields. Selling cattle 'on the rail' tends to spread the grading risk between the seller and buyer, while selling on a live weight basis means that the packer will lose out if the carcasses do not grade as highly as the buyer anticipated. Carcass basis pricing is the norm for direct-to-packer sales in all provinces except Alberta.

Transportation

Live cattle were among the earliest western commodities to be carried on Canadian railways. Indeed, the CPR made such a large investment in specialized rolling stock for cattle that they balked at the refrigerated shipment of carcasses in reefer cars for many years (Silver 1994). Ice-cooled and later mechanically chilled reefers were more expensive than cattle cars, and their tare weight was also greater, thus the movement of chilled meat required greater capital costs for rolling stock and greater line-haul costs because of the burden of non-revenue freight on the back haul (Canadian Transport Commission 1975: 37). Livestock cars were also used for general freight in the nineteenth century, while reefers made the return trip empty. Discrimination against beef carcass shipments in reefers and more favourable freight rates on live cattle became another of the west's many grievances about its industrial underdevelopment relative to Ontario and the east.

The railway cattle shipment system consisted of a network of railway-owned facilities for yarding and loading cattle, hogs, and sheep in western Canada. Some of these were full-fledged receiving yards under government regulation but there were also hundreds of concentration points consisting of a track-side pen and a loading chute.

There were three primary way stations for the rest and feeding of cattle in transit. The west-to-east cattle shipments began as far west as Kamloops in British Columbia's Interior Plateau and Nelson in the Selkirk Mountain Trench. These cattle were shipped east over the Rogers Pass through the Selkirk Mountains to Calgary and over the Crowsnest Pass to Lethbridge where cattle were unloaded for the compulsory four-hour stop for rest, water, and feed at the stockyard. While some of these cattle could be sold in Alberta for local slaughter, most were 'through billed' to the east.

After the rest stop, B.C. cattle continued east to be joined by Prairie cattle entrained at stockyards such as Prince Albert in the north and Moose Jaw in the south, as the rails funnelled east to Winnipeg where the next major rest station was located. Winnipeg witnessed rapid growth in the eastward shipment of cattle for export through its yard, beginning in 1887, when shipments of live cattle were inaugurated. The CPR doubled the capacity of the Winnipeg yard in 1890 to handle the growth as increasing trainloads of cattle moved eastward (Silver 1994: 20). As forty hours was the maximum allowable time that livestock could be held in railway cars without food or water, stockyards were required north of Lake Superior on the Canadian Shield, midway between Winnipeg and Toronto. On the CPR line, the yard was in White River and on the CNR it was at Hornepayne. The White River and Hornepayne stockyards watered and fed the cattle from up to 100 cattle cars a day. As cattle trains began to make the Winnipeg-to-Toronto run in less than forty hours, the stockyards of northern Ontario became obsolete. All but ten pens (for emergencies) were demolished in White River's stockyard in 1976 (Houston 1985: 61).

A standard thirty-six-foot railway livestock car carried twenty to thirty-two head of live cattle, the carcass equivalent of about 10,000 pounds, while a railway reefer car equipped with overhead rails could transport some 25,000 pounds of swinging or carcass beef. In other words, railway cars carrying cattle or swinging beef bulked out long before they weighed out. With boxed beef sitting on the floor, the maximum for the same size of reefer was 40,000 pounds (Canada 1961: 328). Live cattle shipments by rail began to tail off in the 1970s for two reasons. First, semi-trailer cattle liners were making inroads as the preferred mode for shipping livestock. Second, it was far more efficient to ship chilled beef which had been killed and dressed on the Prairies than it was to move live animals on the hoof filled with valueless paunch manure, bone, and viscera to stockyards in inner-city Montreal and

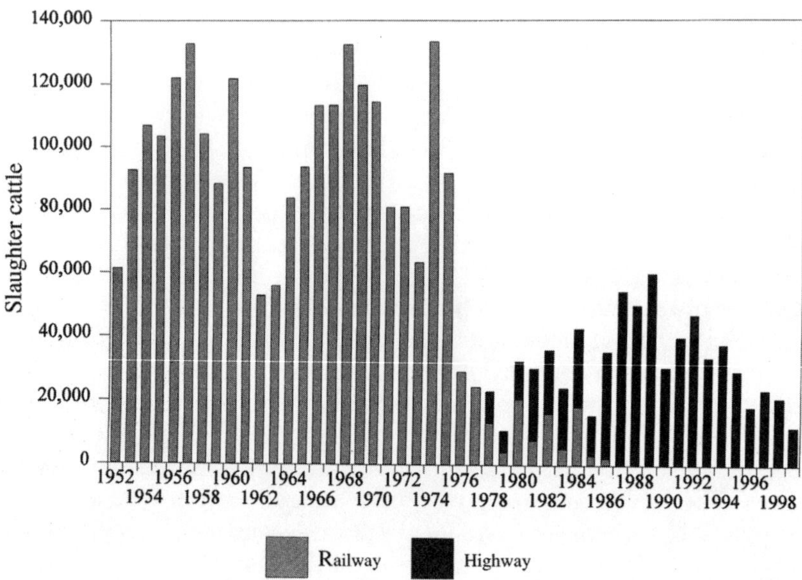

Figure 3.2. West to east shipments of slaughter cattle by railway and highway, 1952–1998. Source: Agriculture Canada, *Livestock Market Review,* various years.

Toronto. By 1961, a steadily increasing quantity of the beef sold in Ontario and Quebec had been killed in western Canada and shipped east in carcass form (Canada Packers 1961, Annual Report: 6). The peak of west–east flows of cattle by rail came in 1975, coinciding with the peak in the cattle cycle, and it diminished rapidly thereafter (Figure 3.2).

Truck shipment of livestock began in the 1920s, and by 1933 it already accounted for 24 per cent of cattle delivered to stockyards while rail captured the remaining 76 per cent (Canada 1934: 574). Livestock arriving by truck typically came directly from farms located relatively close to the stockyards. Tractor-semitrailer rigs had come into general use by the late 1940s, although at twenty-six feet in length and with wooden slatted sides, they looked very different from the present-day sixty-foot all-aluminum cattle liners. In 1945, 42 per cent of all cattle delivered to slaughter plants or stockyards moved by truck and 58 per cent by rail. By 1957, 72.5 per cent moved by truck and only 27.5 per cent moved by rail (Canada, Department of Agriculture 1957). Trucking became especially dominant for short-haul livestock movements. By 1961, for example, railway shipment of livestock within Ontario, where most shipments travelled less than 200 miles, had become of negligible importance (Weijs and Contini 1963: 40).

Rail remained king for long-distance cattle shipment because rail freight rates were so much lower. For example, the rail rate for a 100-mile shipment terminating in the Union Stock Yards of Toronto in 1933 was 17.5 cents per hundredweight, while the same trip by truck would have cost 35 to 40 cents per hundredweight (Canada 1934: 558). The tractor-drawn cattle liner semitrailer rig began to make serious inroads into the transcontinental shipment of cattle in the 1970s and had completely displaced railway stock cars within ten years (Figure 3.2). The railway cattle car inventory (both single-deck and double-deck rail cars) was becoming heavily depreciated by the 1980s. As continuous west–east shipments of slaughter cattle gave way to the shipment of feeder calves (mainly in the fall) the frequency of usage did not justify their repair or replacement (Kerr and Ulmer 1984: 37).

Most of the railway facilities for unloading cattle for the mandatory rest, feed, and water stops have been dismantled. The end of the great cattle trains may be attributed to two fundamental structural changes. First, semitrailer cattle liners displaced the train because of their ability to provide timely and reliable door-to-door service at low cost, dispensing with the need for stressful stockyard terminals. Second, as the locus of the industry shifted from east to west, fewer surplus feeder or slaughter cattle were available for shipment from the Prairies and those which were, found ready markets closer at hand in the northwestern United States.

Shrinkage and Bruising in Transport

Cattle sold on a live weight basis are normally docked for a percentage of the live body weight at the origin to cover the inevitable weight reduction or 'shrink' in transit. Four per cent is a typical shrink allowance, but the exact amount varies depending on the length of the trip and prevailing temperatures. Much of shrink is simply caused by defecation, urination, dehydration, and normal metabolic weight losses, as the animal has no opportunity to eat or drink during the hours it spends in a cattle liner or in the time it spends in the lairage waiting for slaughter. Up to 25 per cent of the live weight of cattle is the contents of the alimentary tract. A transit time of twenty-four hours from feedlot to packing plant is not unusual, and after a fast of that length the gut is likely to shed a considerable portion of its contents. Of greater concern is the shrink caused by dehydration and the stress resulting from the crowding, movement, and heat in cattle trailers which causes a weight loss in the carcass itself, drying the meat and reducing its market value (Tarrant and Grandin 1993: 120).

Carcass bruising is the cause of substantial losses, as bruised tissues must be trimmed away. While bruising may be caused by all kinds of cattle-handling equipment, truck transportation is the most common culprit, especially during violent cornering and braking. Some of this may be controlled when there are incentives. For example, one study showed that cattle sold by live weight had twice as many bruises as those sold on a carcass basis (Tarrant and Grandin 1993: 116). At even medium densities, horned cattle are responsible for significant carcass bruising, warranting the painful dehorning procedure.

Regulations under Canada's Health of Animals Act require that cattle not be confined in a truck trailer for longer than forty-eight hours without being unloaded for rest, water, and feed unless they will reach their final destination without being confined longer than fifty-two hours (Agriculture Canada 1991: 23) This seems like a long time; however, the trauma of loading and unloading needs to be balanced against the benefits of rest and feed (Grandin 1994a: 375).

Cattle Markets and Stockyards

Until the establishment of cattle markets and before the arrival of the railway, cattle producers relied on local butchers and itinerant drovers to convert cattle to cash. The local butcher might have no competing buyers and, from the butcher's point of view, disposing of large quantities of fresh beef in an age before refrigeration meant that beef prices might have to be reduced to ensure that the supply was exhausted before putrefaction set in. The itinerant drover would scour the countryside in search of relatively small lots of cattle. Once purchased, the cattle had to be driven to a wharf along the Great Lakes for export, to an urban market or, in the late nineteenth century, to the nearest railway loading facility.

Periodic Cattle Markets

Agricultural fairs and exhibitions emerged in the eighteenth century to provide periodic markets for livestock (Trow-Smith 1959: 224). Agricultural fairs permitted producers and buyers to share information which made for a more equitable price discovery process than an isolated transaction between a drover and farmer. Annual fairs with cattle markets became a feature of farm life in the Maritimes and in Upper Canada in the 1820s.

As cattle prices increased in the 1860s, in response to demand during the Civil War south of the border, monthly fairs were established in the heart of Ontario's cattle country, for example, in Goderich (1864); Fergus, Harriston, and Georgetown (1865); and Waterloo (1866). In the Ottawa Valley, fall fairs became institutions in Almonte, Carp, Douglas, Eganville, and Renfrew in the 1860s for the purpose of selling long yearlings for export to the United States. By the 1870s, there were some twenty-five monthly cattle fairs in southern Ontario, many of them tributary to the big monthly fair at Guelph, where the cattle were driven by local drovers for resale into larger herds for export to the United States (Jones 1946: 282–4).

The Durham Cattle Fair on the Saugeen River in the heart of Ontario's Grey County is a good example of these early fairs. Beginning in the early 1860s, it operated on the third Tuesday of every month, and as many as twenty buyers would arrive in town by stage coach the day before the sale. Equipped with the traditional stockman's cane, the buyers would walk a mile or more out of town and intercept farmers driving their cattle to the market. Flourishing U.S. silver dollars, the buyers would attempt to strike a pre-emptive deal before the farmer could reach the market. The cattle purchased on the market day would be driven sixteen miles to Mount Forest where there would be another monthly sale the following day. This left the field free for socializing, shopping, and not a small amount of drinking and boisterous behaviour. As draft oxen went out of use, the fair gradually shifted to horse trading and declined as a cattle market in the 1880s (Marsh 1931: 293–5). By the 1880s, the Great Western and Grand Trunk had woven a skein of track through much of southern Ontario and the monthly fairs changed function, eventually fading from the scene.

Municipal Cattle Markets

The most famous of the world's great urban cattle markets was Smithfield which was established in 950 A.D. Originally located beyond London's city walls, the six-acre market was encroached upon and gradually hemmed in as the city grew around it. The market was surrounded by the businesses it attracted: slaughterhouses, triperies, bone-boiling houses, and gut-scraperies (Perren 1978: 33). By 1808, Smithfield was hopelessly overcrowded with no room to expand, and in 1855 it moved to a new location with direct rail access (Perren 1978: 41). Thus, Smithfield became the prototype for a cycle of suburban location, overgrowth by the city, and relocation to even more distant suburban locations. Throughout the late nineteenth and early twentieth centuries the cattle markets and stockyards of North America would repeat the Smithfield experience.

In Canada, the first urban cattle markets were integral components of permanent public markets established by provinces and municipalities as the commercial infrastructure of the largest settlements. The province of Nova Scotia passed legislation in 1779 establishing a public market for the sale of livestock in the town of Halifax (Rasmussen 1995: 47). The St Lawrence Market, Toronto's first public market, was established in 1803 in the heart of the city. The original structure was rebuilt in 1850, when the present-day St Lawrence Hall was built. Butchers' stalls had doors that faced out to the street to admit the animals which had been purchased for slaughter and doors on the inside to admit customers from the arcade (Mulvany 1884). As livestock marketing and congestion grew, there was pressure to shift the livestock section of the market to a new location that would not interfere with downtown traffic. In 1877, livestock sales were moved to a new municipally owned facility at the corner of Bathurst and Wellington Streets which became known as the Western Cattle Market.

Public Stockyards

Public stockyards are extensive facilities for the unloading, enclosure, care, sale, and transhipment of large volumes of livestock (MacLachlan 1998b). Facilities include pens arranged in a network of numbered alleys, unloading chutes for trucks and railway cars, cattle scales, and one or more auction rings. Public stockyards in Canada were federally regulated under the terms of the Live Stock and Live Stock Products Act (1917) and were typically located in large-scale metropolitan centres at strategic points in the railway network.

The impetus for stockyards arose with the long-distance shipment of livestock that became possible with the expansion of railway networks deep into the continental interior in the late nineteenth century. Many stockyards functioned as transhipment points for feeding and watering cattle that were destined for shipment further east. Others were situated at strategic nodes in the rail grid and evolved into terminals and livestock markets as meat-packing facilities were attracted to adjacent sites. Established in 1865, Chicago's Union Stock Yards was the first large rail-based livestock terminal in North America. It became the model for nearly 100 stockyards in the Midwest and Plains of the United States and Canada. The facility was formed to unify and replace seven competing stockyards operated by nine of the largest railroads (Cronon 1991: 210). The 'union' moniker, indicating some form of joint venture among competing railroads, was soon applied to many other stockyards from the Union Stock Yards, San Antonio (1894), to the Union Stock Yards of Toronto (1903). The establishment of these and many other stockyards was the catalyst for investment in large-scale slaughterhouses and the development of a basic livestock and meat industry serving national markets.

Responding to suspicions of wartime profiteering and collusion among the large-scale meat packers, the Canadian government enacted the Live Stock and Live Stock Products Act in 1917. Henceforth, the federal government would regulate activities in each stockyard and the market transactions in its associated Livestock Exchange. In 1939, the act was amended to prohibit the purchase or sale of livestock by a stockyard 'proprietor,' a safeguard already in place in the United States to keep the meat packers at arm's length from the operation of livestock markets.

Often termed 'public stockyards,' they were public only in the sense that they were closely regulated and supervised by the federal government's Department of Agriculture. Some were owned by the railways as a joint venture between two or more companies (e.g., Union Stock Yards in St-Boniface, just east of Winnipeg and Montreal Stock Yard), others by a holding company ultimately owned by a single railway (e.g., Calgary Stock Yards and Lethbridge Stock Yards owned by Western Stock Yards, a subsidiary of the CPR). Some were owned by independent private limited liability firms (e.g., Saskatoon, Moose Jaw, and Edmonton), while others were owned or operated by livestock cooperatives (e.g., Regina, Prince Albert, and Vancouver). Only one public stockyard, the Ontario Stock Yards, was actually owned by the government after it was purchased from U.S. interests in 1944. Each stockyard had a livestock exchange and all buyers, dealers, or commission agents had to be members of the exchange if they were to do business there (Canada 1961: 46–7). The smaller Prairie yards in centres such as Lethbridge or Prince Albert were known as 'receiving yards,' since they were mainly in the business of consolidating livestock from farms and ranches for onward shipment to 'terminal yards' such as those in Montreal and Toronto (Figure 3.3). Montreal's stockyard handled

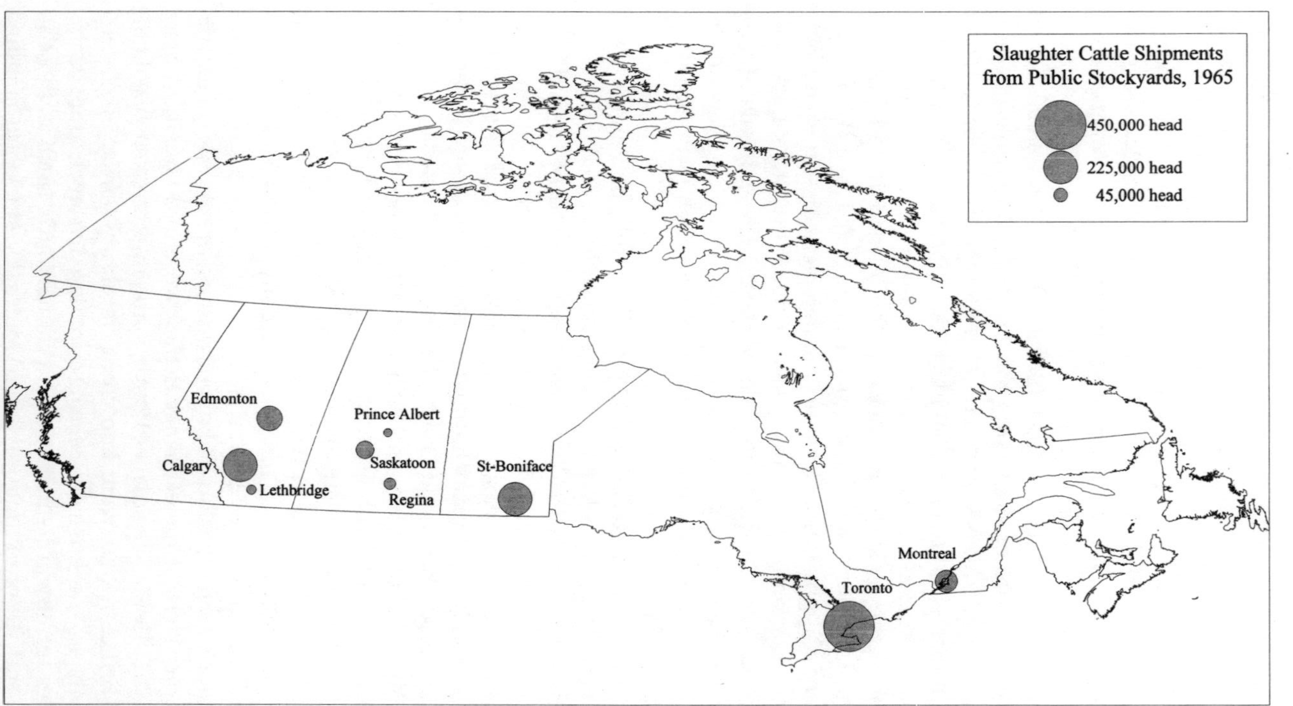

Figure 3.3. Cattle shipments from Canada's public stockyards at their peak, 1965. Source: Raw data from Agriculture Canada, *Livestock Market Review*, 1965.

smaller volumes than Toronto, reflecting the small numbers of beef cattle on Quebec farms and the smaller number of slaughter cattle that were railed east of Toronto.

To facilitate the daily price quotation and sale of cattle, an unofficial Canada-wide livestock grading system was developed in the 1930s. Steers and heifers were designated in four categories, namely, choice, good, medium, and common; cows were classified as good, medium, common, and 'canners and cutters,' while bulls were either good or common. Cattle grades are reliable indicators of the animal's quality but there is no direct relationship between the unofficial cattle grade used for quoting price ranges and the official carcass grade (described in Chapter 8).

The stockyard was significant to many western Canadian cities as the nucleus of an agroindustrial complex that propelled rapid urban growth in the first two decades of the twentieth century. There was a close relationship among railways, stockyards, livestock exchanges, commission firms, and livestock dealers, slaughter and packing concerns, animal by-products processors, and a host of specialist suppliers. The shared savings accruing from the proximity of vertically linked operations that processed every component of the carcass, the availability of a large semiskilled butcher workforce, and tacit acceptance of noxious environmental externalities were the sources of localization economies that made stockyards a dynamic engine of growth.

Most of the marketing in stockyards occurred from September to November; at other times the yards stood half-empty. The actual sale of cattle took place under the auspices of the stockyard's livestock exchange which was also federally regulated. Other than size, rail access, federal regulation, and breadth of facilities, the traditional difference between a public stockyard and an auction market was that the former used commission agents to make most sales by private treaty while auction marts used live auctions exclusively. However, most federally regulated public stockyards in the United States and Canada began to add auction rings in the 1950s, blurring the distinction between community auctions and public stockyards. Late in 1960, the Ontario Stock Yards introduced auction selling – it was the last public stockyard in Canada to do so (Canada 1961: 49). However, the public stockyards were closely regulated by the federal government which meant that they lacked the flexibility of the less-regulated country yards. (Lesser 1993: 286).

The heyday of terminal public stockyards came in the 1920s prior to the advent of paved highways and intercity trucking, when they handled 90 per cent of the cattle destined for federally inspected slaughter in the United States. By the 1930s terminal public stockyards were in decline both in the number of yards and in the number of cattle handled (Lesser 1993: 286). Direct farm-to-packer sales were undermining the role of public markets. And the trend towards trucking cattle from the farm gate to the slaughterhouse door was cutting into the volume of slaughter cattle that stockyards handled.

However, almost as many agricultural interests seemed in favour of retaining the stockyards as were bypassing the federally regulated markets and shipping directly. In 1934, the Honourable D.G. Mackenzie, minister of agriculture for the province of Manitoba, commented: 'At the end of another five years our public stockyards will be put out of business' with 'disastrous' effects on producers because 'it would eliminate the only competitive markets' available at that time (Canada 1935: 163). The federally regulated public stockyards were thought to protect beef producers in other respects as well. The stockyards had 'type registering beam scales' (which printed the weight directly on a ticket) that were authoritative, accurate, and tamper-proof. The scales were operated by trained and bonded 'scalemen' who ensured that fair weights were recorded. Cattle sold directly, on the other hand, were subject to weighing and grading decisions by the packer. As the stockyards lost business to packer direct sales, the fixed costs of public stockyards had to be spread over smaller numbers of cattle and yardage fees increased.

Producers have always been concerned that they are in an inferior bargaining position relative to cattle buyers who may conspire to hold prices down. In Saskatchewan, collusion was alleged to constitute a 'serious menace' to western Canada's livestock industry:

> A Saskatchewan feeder was made an offer in Saskatchewan for a bunch of choice steers by a Winnipeg packinghouse who are represented at Montreal. He declined the offer as being too low and shipped to Montreal. At Montreal he could not get a single bid on his cattle, high or low. He was being punished by the system. His loss was so great that it put him out of the cattle feeding business for good.
>
> If a feeder ships to St Boniface market he is approached by one buyer only. A dozen others may be sitting on the fence looking on, but he can get no other offer except from the one man. (Saskatchewan 1917: 41)

The obvious rebuttal to this allegation is that the original offer was a fair price to begin with, and no higher offers were received simply because no canny buyer would pay more. By the late 1930s, the accounts of collusion had changed very little, but in addition to the dominance of public livestock exchange markets by the largest meat packers, growing packer direct sales were also thought to be eroding the role of public markets in the process of price discovery (*Canadian Cattlemen* 1938; Canada 1934: 1293; 1935: 162).

The decline in stockyard activity which had begun in the 1930s accelerated into the 1950s. There were eleven public stockyards in Canada in 1950 but the last was closed in 1994. At the very time that terminal public stockyards reached their peak, small-scale country auction marts began to grow in numbers. In the United States there were fewer than 200 auction marts in 1930 but by 1952 they numbered 2,500 (Ives 1966: 53). In Canada there were fewer than twenty country auctions in 1948, but this had increased to 112 in 1959: sixty-eight in eastern Canada and forty-four in western Canada (Canada 1960: 189). In 1974, country auctions handled twice as many cattle as the remaining public stockyards which had become increasingly inefficient and imposed higher costs on producers and consumers. Thus, the federal government's Commission of Inquiry into the Marketing of Beef and Veal recommended the closure of the public stockyards (Canada 1976: 114).

In summary, there were four main reasons for the gradual disappearance of stockyards from the commodity chain:

1 Packers began procuring their slaughter cattle directly from producers in the 1920s, and by the 1950s, community auctions began to appropriate a growing share of the market for stocker cattle, as it made little sense to truck animals into central Toronto or Calgary to sell them to a feedlot operator who would then have to truck them back out to the country.
2 Metropolitan packing plants began closing in significant numbers in the 1950s, as the industry shifted to smaller centres in cattle-feeding regions in the United States. The first harbinger of this shift was the exodus of meat-packing plants in Chicago's Packingtown which began in 1954. All of the major plants had closed by 1970, prompting the closure of Chicago's Union Stock Yards in August 1971. Despite the fact that packer direct sales had removed the price discovery process from the stockyards' confines, the stockyards still received a

steady stream of income for handling, feeding, and yarding cattle that were sold directly. In many cases the packers simply walked their daily kill across the street from stockyard to packing plant. The stockyards offered considerable buffer capacity to minimize the chance of disruptions in the flow of livestock to the kill floor. As the big metropolitan packing plants closed down in the 1980s, the stockyards lost the yardage and loading fees they had earned from handling slaughter cattle.

3 Short-haul railway transportation of livestock was in decline by the 1950s. In 1961, 200 kilometres was considered a 'reasonable' distance for trucking livestock and 80 per cent of the livestock in Canada was produced within 200 kilometres of a public stockyard (Canada 1961: 51). By the 1980s, railway cattle transportation had all but disappeared, even for Alberta-to-Ontario shipments, in favour of highway 'cattle liners' which are less efficient on congested inner-city streets. Thus, a strategic location in the rail network no longer conferred any advantage on public stockyards (Williams and Stout 1964). Massive public investment in highway construction and improvements in semitrailer truck technology permitted trucking to supplant railways in livestock transportation, as it has for many other commodities.

4 Finally, at the beginning of the twentieth century, the stockyards were typically sited on the edge of their metropolitan regions. Land was cheaper and the large parcel size required by a stockyard could only be found on the edge of the city. A discreet suburban location removed many of the unseemly sights and smells of the stockyard from the noses and eyes of the public. In the case of Calgary's stockyard, cattle were still being trailed in from the country as late as the Second World War, with only the occasional urban stampede caused by barking dogs or flapping laundry (Friesen 1995: 24). By the 1980s, Canada's stockyards, like London's Smithfield market, had become surrounded by residential tracts and other intensive land uses that drove up land costs and caused traffic congestion, slowing the inflow of cattle trucks which was especially inefficient for feeder cattle which would then have to be turned around and shipped out of the city after they were sold. The noxious sights, smells, and sounds of the stockyard became an increasing source of friction with downwind residents in metropolitan centres.

The volumes of slaughter cattle handled by the public stockyards were always volatile, tracking the cattle cycle and total number of

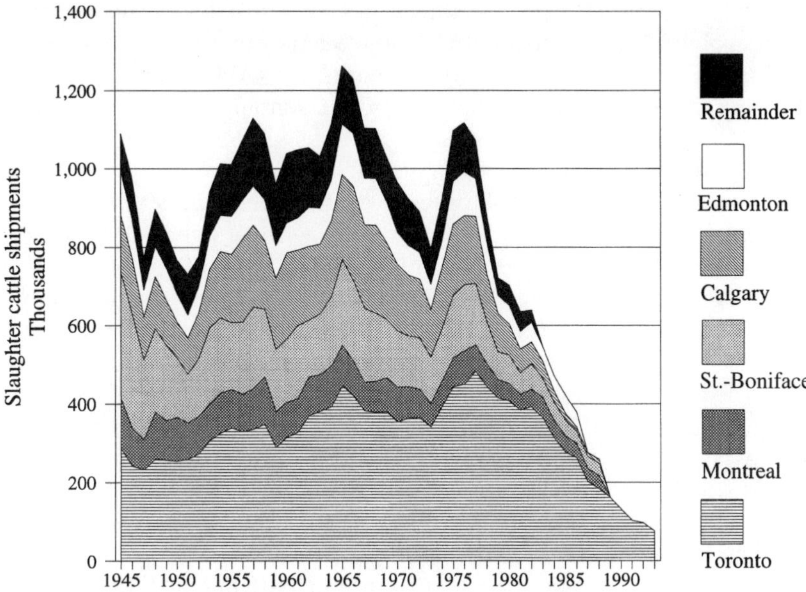

Figure 3.4. Slaughter cattle shipments from public stockyards in Canada, 1945–1992. Source: Agriculture Canada, *Livestock Market Review*, various years.

cattle slaughtered (Figure 3.4). The smaller western yards were shut down in the late 1970s and most of the larger western yards disappeared en masse in 1988. In most cases the marketing operations, mainly for stockers, were shifted to auction marts immediately outside the metropolitan area. For example, the sales operations formerly in Montreal were shifted east to St-Hyacinthe. Toronto's Ontario Stock Yards struggled along until February 1994, when the final auction was held and cattle sales shifted fifty kilometres north to Cookstown.

The passing of the public stockyard leaves two issues in its wake. First, the closure of stockyards and associated packing plants released large quantities of industrial land with rail access in the centre of cities. This presents a prime opportunity for inner-city redevelopment. On the former site of its stockyard, Chicago has a huge industrial park awaiting investment and development. Following the closure of the Ontario Stock Yards in 1994, Toronto's stockyard district is being redeveloped for large-scale industrial and retail space such as Canada's largest Home Depot store. Second, a network of small-scale country yards replaced public stockyards. These auction marts have helped to reinforce the economic base of agricultural service centres across southern Ontario and throughout western Canada.

Ontario Stock Yards: Canada's Biggest Cattle Market

Cattle sales in Toronto's St Lawrence Market were transferred to the Western Cattle Market in 1877, and the growth in livestock volumes was so rapid that it soon outpaced the physical limitations of the site. In 1887, the Provincial Board of Health began considering sanitary conditions at the Western Market in light of a proposal to expand it to hold an additional 1,100 cattle, 1,100 sheep, and 300 pigs. The board was concerned about the environmental impact of an additional fifty-six tons of manure and 2,500 gallons of urine. The market had the potential to pollute the bay (essentially modern-day Toronto's inner harbour), while the 'pestilential' odour emanating from hog pens was another irritant (Ontario Sessional Papers 1887: 82–3).

As the market had no on-site killing facilities, all of the animals sold for slaughter had to be driven to outlying butcher facilities: 'After being sold they are sent in droves through the heart of the city to slaughter-houses situated on every high-way [sic] leading into Toronto. These, being beyond the city, are scarcely, if at all, controlled; and hence suburban residence, throughout the summer and autumn months, becomes most undesirable' (Ontario Sessional Papers 1887: 84). Thus, the old Western Cattle Market (just west of what would become the Sky Dome a century later) was responsible for two different negative externalities: (1) odours and water pollution from animal excrement and (2) the need to drive animals on the hoof through the streets of the city to the slaughterhouse of whichever butcher finally purchased the animals.

These problems could be solved by following the model provided by Chicago Union Stock Yard, a large market on the edge of the city with sufficient land that slaughter facilities could be located nearby. Given Toronto's prevailing westerly winds, a location in the city's east end might have been preferable. But, induced by municipal tax exemptions as an industrial incentive from the town of Toronto Junction, northwest of the city of Toronto proper, the present-day intersection of Keele Street and St Clair Avenue was selected for the new market. The Union Stock Yards of Toronto was incorporated on 29 December 1900 and opened for business in 1903. Toronto Junction, which in 1909 was annexed by the city of Toronto, was ideally situated for a stockyard. It was on cheap land outside the densely built-up downtown area, and it was at the point where two competing railway lines came together: the Canadian Pacific Railway and the Grand Trunk. Initially, there were no packing plants at the stockyard; they remained scattered all over the city. William Davies was east of downtown on the Don River, while Park-Blackwell and the Harris Abattoir were both near the Western Cattle Market (Fancher 1999).

The first packing plant on the stockyards site was completed in 1905 and acquired by Swift Canadian in 1911. Gunns Limited constructed a second plant nearby which went into operation in 1907. In 1913, the Harris Abattoir expanded and built a brand new integrated packing plant across the street from the stockyards and adjacent to Gunns. As an incentive to invest and build in this suburban location, each of the three firms received land at low cost, provided that they agree to purchase all of their livestock at the new stockyards for a period of twenty-five years. Direct shipments were permitted, but in that case the firms agreed to pay the regular per head yardage fees just as if the cattle had first gone through the stockyards (McDonald 1985: 37–8).

Until the 1930s, both the Harris Abattoir and Swift Canadian held an ownership interest in the Union Stock Yards. In the United States, meat packers had been prevented from having any financial interest in stockyards with the packer consent decree of 1923 (Skaggs 1986: 106–7). The Swift Canadian and Harris interests in the stockyard were sold in the mid-1930s, and it came under U.S. control as the United Stockyards Corporation. In 1944, the Conservative government of George Drew made good on an election pledge and passed The Stock Yards Act to create the Ontario Stock Yards Board. The new board was composed of four representatives of livestock producers, one representative of the Meat Packers Council, and one member to represent the commission dealers who traded in livestock. By the end of the year, the Ontario Stock Yards had become a provincial utility and the balance of decision-making power on the board had shifted from the packers to the farmers (Archives of Ontario 1944; McDonald 1985).

Although it occupied only thirty-seven acres in land area, the Ontario Stock Yards was, in 1982, the largest five-day per week livestock market in North America. Winnipeg's market covered a larger land area, and some markets in the United States handled larger volumes, but they did not operate full-time or accommodate all classes of livestock (Toronto 1983: 9). Sales volume peaked in 1977 when the

Ontario Stock Yards handled 1.1 million head of livestock, including 580,000 cattle. Cattle numbers dwindled sharply thereafter as the kill-off of the 1980s reinforced the trend towards packer direct and auction mart sales.

It was becoming obsolete, but even so the Ontario Stock Yards remained the nucleus of one of Canada's most massive inner-city industrial complexes. In the early 1980s, the stockyards themselves only employed about sixty-five people directly. However, another 275 to 300 were employed by livestock dealers and commission firms associated with the livestock exchange. The seventeen meat and meat by-products businesses immediately adjacent to the yards employed about 3,900 people and shipped $1.5 billion annually in meats and animal by-products. None of these firms procured more than half their livestock from the yards, but synergies were generated by all those competing meat-oriented firms. The corner of Keele and St Clair had become a sort of wholesale meat hypermarket that served hundreds of small-scale butchers, meat processors, specialty stores, and restaurant and institutional buyers from all over the metropolitan Toronto area. The stockyard had triggered this localized meat-oriented agglomeration, but was later overtaken by it (Toronto 1983:4).

Employing 2,700 people and covering seventy-five acres the massive fully integrated Canada Packers meat-packing plant (a physical coupling of the Gunns and Harris Abattoir plants in 1930) dwarfed everything else in the stockyards' district (Figure 3.5). As well as the multispecies slaughter and packinghouse, the plant's departments included oils, pet foods, animal feeds, chemicals, feather industries, and a research centre. The Canada Packers plant was surrounded by five smaller plants: Swift-Eastern (successor to Swift Canadian), Canadian Dressed Meats (a dressed-beef plant owned by Burns Foods), Grace Meat Packers and Hunnisett Limited (dressed beef), and the Beef Terminal. The Beef Terminal was a custom slaughter facility which killed and dressed cattle for half a dozen smaller firms that cut and packaged fresh beef. These were surrounded by another ring of still smaller meat packers and firms that processed animal by-products, including Banner Rendering (heat reduction of fats and other carcass waste), Levine Brothers and Banks Brothers (hide curing), and Canadian Natural Casings which cleaned and cured intestines and colons for use as traditional sausage casings (Toronto 1983: 9–14).

The meat-packing complex was the core of a surrounding railway-oriented industrial district covering 241 acres, home to a total of 120

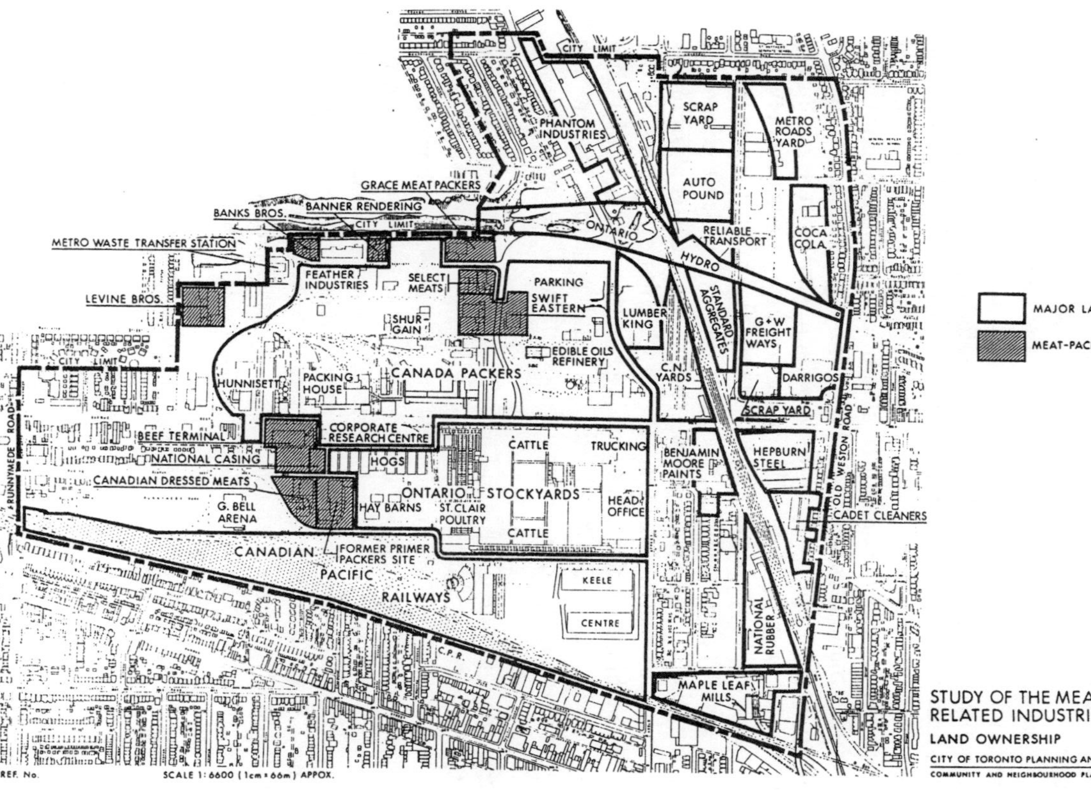

Figure 3.5. The Ontario Stock Yards industrial complex, 1983. Source: City of Toronto Planning and Development Department 1983, *Report on the Stockyards, Meat Packing and Related Industries in the Stockyards Industrial District*.

industrial and commercial enterprises which employed about 8,000 people. Surrounding firms benefited from the rail-and-road transportation facilities and industrial infrastructure. The meat processors, in turn, benefited because the industrial and commercial land uses constituted a buffer zone to separate residential land uses from some of the noxious aspects of the packing plants (Toronto 1983: 5).

The vitality of the industrial district surrounding the Ontario Stock Yards became an important component in the land use and economic planning of Toronto. The city was committed to the retention of high-wage industrial jobs such as those generated by meat-packing and allied industrial uses (Gardner 1983). Thus, the city would do nothing to discourage the operation of the yards, even though the generation of tonnes of manure and the daily arrival of truckloads of hay, straw and farm animals made little sense in the centre of a metropolitan region with a population approaching four million. Cattle were no longer being received or shipped by rail, and the road transportation network was so fragmented by the rail yards and topography that it was inefficient for semitrailer trucks to negotiate the narrow and congested streets. Yet, the stockyards were tolerated as the nucleus of Toronto's west-end manufacturing district: 'The Stockyards are pivotal to the continued stability of the meat-packing, manufacturing and heavy industry in the area. Their relocation would probably lead to the demise of substantial amounts of industry in West Toronto' (Toronto 1983: 3).

In the event, the stockyards did not relocate and abandon the meat-packing industry. Instead, the meat-packing industry abandoned the stockyards. With the closure of most of the large-scale horizontally integrated packing plants in the mid-1980s (described in Chapter 6), and the continuing trend towards packer direct sales for slaughter cattle and country auctions for stockers, the number of animals marketed through the Ontario Stock Yards dwindled. In 1993, it handled only 329,000 head of livestock. After running a deficit for ten straight years, the government of Ontario decided to close the yards in 1993.

Lethbridge Stockyard: Prototype of a Receiving Yard

A fairly typical example of the smaller Prairie receiving yards was located in Lethbridge, Alberta. The CPR had operated a livestock pen and cattle-loading facility at track-side just east of the town since about 1903. Amid agitation for mixed farming to reduce the dependence on specialized grain farms was a concern that there was insufficient livestock marketing infrastructure. Grain farmers had their system of country grain elevators on Prairie branch lines, but comparatively little investment had been made in the analogous system for the collection, purchase, storage, and transhipment of livestock. By taking a municipal initiative to establish its own stockyard, Calgary had consolidated its role as Alberta's livestock marketing capital, a position that Lethbridge boosters wanted to challenge.

Lethbridge was at the junction of five Canadian Pacific Railway lines leading in all directions, thus, Alberta's third largest city seemed to be ideally situated as a livestock collection and transhipment point. Unfortunately, the existing livestock pens were on dry land without access to water. This was a serious liability. Unless a farmer had ready access to a stockyard supplied with water, cattle marketing was a perilous undertaking. Livestock trains were often late, or had insufficient livestock cars for the cattle on hand, making it necessary to hold cattle overnight or longer.

In 1913, the CPR finally shifted the location of its livestock pens to a location at the city's fairgrounds with access to water from an irrigation canal. The fairgrounds facility was favoured as it made use of livestock infrastructure that was dormant for fifty-one weeks of the year. The fairgrounds site was replaced in 1931 by a still larger complex of holding pens and loading chutes for transferring livestock to railway cars on the east side of the city alongside the CPR's main line. But it was still just a scaled-up version of the hundreds of receiving yards found in every small Prairie town and on every branch line, for the temporary confinement and loading of cattle, hogs, and sheep. They were sometimes called stockyards, but they were not federally regulated, there was no veterinarial inspection available for export cattle, and they had no selling function.

After the Second World War, the Canadian embargo on cattle and sheep exports was lifted. Only 100 kilometres north of the U.S. border, the Lethbridge yard began to take on strategic significance as the centre of southern Alberta's cattle industry. With the completion of the St Mary River Dam and expansion of the land area under irrigation, the region was also poised for take-off as a cattle-feeding and -finishing specialist. The loading yards were operated directly by the CPR until 1950 when they were sold, together with the Calgary Stock Yards, to an operating subsidiary, the Alberta Stock Yards Company. The facility was expanded to become a full service public stockyard under federal regulation. To attain this status, an administration office, forty-two new pens, a livestock scale to weigh car-load lots of twenty-five to thirty cattle at a time, and an auction ring were added. The yard had separate holding pens equipped to provide food and water, and a squeeze for branding, dehorning, and vaccinating cattle. Loading facilities were available for single- or double-deck railcars, as well as transport trucks. Packer buyers, livestock commission agents, and livestock dealers established offices at the yard, along with the mandatory federal regulators, veterinarians, accredited weigh masters, and a provincial brand inspector. The initiative was trumpeted as the forerunner of a packing plant and nucleus of the southern Alberta cattle and beef industry (*Lethbridge Herald* 1950: 11–13).

In 1960, Canada's largest cattle processor and meat-packing firm, Canada Packers, established a beef plant on the edge of the Lethbridge Stock Yard. A specially built drive alley channelled slaughter cattle directly from the yard to the kill floor. A year later, a second beef plant was added by Canadian Dressed Meats, and in 1971 Swift Canadian, the second largest packer in Canada, built Lethbridge's third plant, just across the railway tracks from the first two. Together with the Lethbridge Western Stock Yards Company, a hide plant and nearby cattle feedlots, Lethbridge became the largest beef-producing industrial agglomeration in Canada in relation to its population size.

Cattle sales grew through the 1960s, as federally regulated stockyards reached their apogee, spurred in the case of Lethbridge, by new beef-packing plants (Figure 3.6). But numbers began to decline as direct-to-packer sales captured most of the slaughter cattle, community auctions ate into stocker and feeder cattle sales, and there were fewer cattle moving from west to east by rail. In contrast to the closure of the Toronto's Ontario Stock Yards, sixteen years later, Lethbridge's meat packers continued in operation after the Lethbridge Stock Yard was closed down in 1977. Its three adjacent packing plants no longer had any need for a centralized market. The Lethbridge Stock Yards had been instrumental in the development of the meat-packing industry in Lethbridge, but with changes in cattle transportation technology and marketing channels, federally regulated public stockyards had become obsolete.

Stasis and Change in the Interprovincial Flow of Slaughter Cattle

Origin–destination matrices for slaughter cattle reveal some interesting patterns in the flow of slaughter cattle between provinces (Tables 3.1 and 3.2). Interprovincial flows changed dramatically beginning in

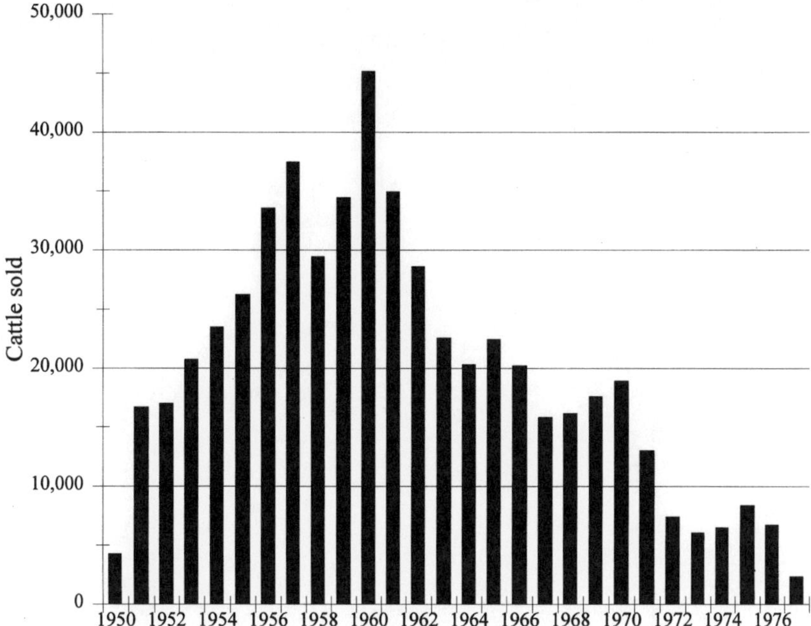

Figure 3.6. Lethbridge Stock Yard cattle sales, 1950–1977. Source: Agriculture Canada, *Livestock Market Review*, various years.

1960, yet underlying those flows is a constant. Beef packing is a raw material oriented industry and most cattle have always been killed in the province where they were fed to slaughter weight.

In 1959, the province of Quebec had a significant cattle deficit which was a result of the relatively small supply of feed grain produced in the province (Table 3.1). Local supplies of fat cattle were small, and cattle had to be shipped in for slaughter from every region of the country, especially from nearby Ontario. Even so, the kill per capita was less than one-third of the national average. Ontario, on the other hand, netted out as nearly self-sufficient in slaughter cattle. Manitoba had developed into a meat-packing specialist in 1959; it was killing 440.9 cattle per thousand capita, which was nearly four times the national average. It had a well-developed and strategically located cattle marketing and meat-packing complex at the Union Stock Yards in St-Boniface (Parliament 1974). Nearly half the cattle killed in Manitoba came from other

Table 3.1 Interprovincial flows of slaughter cattle, 1959

	Destination							
Origin	B.C.	Alberta	Sask.	Manitoba	Ontario	Quebec	Maritimes	Total shipments
B.C.	31,405	16,583			638	119		48,745
Alberta	10,158	643,445	1,537	24,042	5,559	5,253		689,994
Sask.	1,207	8,125	242,893	169,425	14,903	5,201		441,754
Manitoba				209,509	9,768	201		219,478
Ontario				3,408	582,557	58,765		644,730
Quebec					1,542	104,220	40	105,802
Maritimes					271	4,023	28,904	33,198
Total kill (receipts)	42,770	668,153	244,430	406,384	615,238	177,782	28,944	2,183,701
Self-sufficiency of cattle kill (%)	73.4	96.3	99.4	51.6	94.7	58.6	99.9	100.0
Kill per capita (000s)	26.3	501.6	264.2	440.9	98.7	33.8	20.1	123.1

Source: Raw data from Agriculture Canada, *Livestock Market Review*, 1959

Table 3.2 Interprovincial flows of slaughter cattle, 1997

Origin	Destination							Total shipments
	B.C.	Alberta	Sask.	Manitoba	Ontario	Quebec	Maritimes	
B.C.	49,010	3,003	19					52,032
Alberta	2,095	1,853,360	9,521		6,367			1,871,343
Sask.		48,947	160,224		10,518			219,689
Manitoba		8,055	6,456	31,003	9,291			54,805
Ontario					654,079		609	654,688
Quebec					21,236	223,483	11,599	256,318
Maritimes							67,762	67,762
Total kill (receipts)	51,105	1,913,365	176,220	31,003	701,491	223,483	79,970	3,176,637
Self-sufficiency of cattle kill (%)	95.9	96.9	90.9	100.0	93.2	100.0	84.7	100.0
Kill per capita (000s)	15.6	751.6	178.2	28.4	69.6	32.4	45.6	116.4

Source: Raw data from Agriculture Canada, *Livestock Market Review*, 1997

provinces, mainly Saskatchewan. Saskatchewan received very few cattle from outside the province; virtually all of the quarter of a million cattle killed there were raised within the province. But large volumes of Saskatchewan slaughter cattle were shipped out of province for processing, mainly in Manitoba, while many of its feeder cattle were destined for Alberta and Ontario (Regina Public Stockyards 1977), giving credence to long-standing concerns that Saskatchewan does not add enough value to its cattle (Rosaasen and Schmitz 1984: 74). Alberta had the highest per capita cattle slaughter thanks mainly to indigenous cattle supplies, with a small contribution from British Columbia.

Quebec and Manitoba had large cattle deficits in 1959, but every province obtained more than half of its slaughter cattle internally. The big numbers in Table 3.1 are on the main diagonal, indicating that slaughter cattle tended to be killed in their province of origin. Notwithstanding the long-distance west–east shipment of live cattle illustrated in Figure 3.2, the principal orientation of the beef-packing industry was always towards local slaughter cattle.

This local orientation persisted and strengthened over the next thirty-eight years (Table 3.2). The most notable change is in Manitoba, which neither produces nor receives anything like the number of slaughter cattle that it once did. Instead, Manitoba has a net outflow of cattle, both east and west. Alberta receives a sizeable volume of slaughter cattle from Saskatchewan, but 96.9 per cent of Alberta's cattle kill is shipped from within the province (although they may have been born and weaned in other provinces). The dramatic change between the two tables is in the column totals, which show that Alberta's receipts of slaughter cattle almost tripled while they fell in Saskatchewan and were decimated in Manitoba. Manitoba's receipts of slaughter cattle at packing plants (including local cattle) dropped from 406,384 in 1959 to only 31,003 in 1997.

In every region, cattle tend to be procured from local sources; in 1997 the provincial self-sufficiency of cattle slaughter ranged from 85 per cent to 100 per cent. Beef packing was even more raw material oriented in 1997 than it was in 1959, yet the subject matter of the following chapters will be the dramatic rationalization and locational change of the industry. The solution to this paradox is contained in Tables 1.1 and 1.2 which show that the spatial distribution of beef-cattle production was shifting from east to west at the very time that cattle and beef processing were similarly transformed. Cattle followed the grass and grain, and the beef-packing industry simply followed the cattle.

Part Two

PROCESSING BEEF

FOUR

Industrialization, Regulation, and Canada's Early Beef Packers

Canada is practically without abattoirs equipped for the slaughter of cattle except to a very limited extent for the home market; she has no system of refrigerator meat cars, and has, entering her ports, very few ships fitted for the carrying of chilled meats. In view of these facts, it is scarcely necessary to dwell on the risk which she is constantly carrying. At any time, in spite of the best efforts of her veterinary sanitary service, the appearance within her borders of one or other of the diseases scheduled by the British Board of Agriculture is within the range of possibility. As matters now stand, were such a thing to occur, especially during the short period in which our western cattle are shipped, or at the time when our winter fed steers are being marketed, the consequences to the producer would be disastrous, while the whole trade would receive a blow, from which it would require many years to recover. For this reason, if for no other, the establishment of a chilled meat trade on sound business lines and under proper control may fairly be termed a matter of national importance.

J.G. Rutherford, Livestock Commissioner (1909: 23)

The meat-packing industry began to industrialize in the 1860s and 1870s in the United States, but the first large-scale meat-packing plants did not appear in Canada until the 1890s. This chapter traces the technological and entrepreneurial beginnings of the earliest meat packers in Canada through to the end of the First World War and sets the stage for the emergence of the powerful meat-packing oligopoly in the 1920s and 1930s that is described in Chapter 6.

Pre-industrial Cattle Slaughter and Meat Packing

Until the 1890s, the production of meat from animals was a small-scale practice in Canada. The scale was limited because of the nature of the raw material, the process itself, and the finished product. First, the production of livestock was broadly dispersed through rural areas. The driving of livestock over any distance was costly in labour and in the shrinkage of cattle under the constant harassment of barking dogs and men brandishing goads and whips. In-transit losses of animals as a result of injury, drowning, or escape were significant. Once they arrived at the slaughterhouse, cattle were killed and dressed individually with two or three men carrying out the entire process, so volume was limited. Finally, because fresh meat was highly perishable, it was difficult to market large quantities in sufficient time to prevent putrefaction. Thus, preindustrial meat-packing was a small scale and seasonal activity.

Rural Cattle Slaughter

Prior to the turn of the century, farms were without any means of refrigeration in summer months and the carcass of a large animal would soon spoil. Pork was sometimes smoked on the farm and the carcass of a bacon hog was small enough that most of it could be consumed by a farm family before spoilage set in. But cattle were too big for family consumption and smoked or salted beef has never been widely accepted in Canada. In rural areas groups of sixteen to twenty-four neighbouring farmers formed cooperatives known as 'beef rings.' The terms were variable, but essentially each member in the beef ring was obliged to supply one beef animal each summer and to butcher it on the farm or pay a professional to do the job. The beef was distributed according to a chart, so that each member would receive a steak, roast, and boiling piece each week. From Alberta to Ontario, this type of reciprocity was a folk cultural institution to circumvent the problem of beef spoilage (*Alberta History* 1990; Spencer 1913: 106).

Traditional Meat Packing for Export

While much of the early nineteenth century demand for fresh beef and pork was satisfied through farm-killed livestock, export markets were served by specialized meat packers. Traditional meat packing, the pickling of pork or beef in wooden barrels for export using salt as a preservative, was a seasonal activity that required cool weather conditions to avoid spoilage. Meat packing was expensive and pickled beef was not received favourably by the British market, hence, barrelled pickled beef was used mainly for army rations and naval stores in circumstances where there was no alternative food source (Perren 1978: 72).

Prior to the development of integrated industrial meat-packing plants, slaughter and dressing of the carcass was a separate activity from packing the meat into barrels. The slaughterhouse and the packing house had different locational requirements, and therefore their operations were carried out separately. This spatial division of labour between slaughter and packing was especially marked in the case of hogs and pork. Pigs were difficult to drive any distance on the hoof, and so hog slaughter was typically located on the farm in the countryside. The eviscerated and decapitated carcass of a market hog was comparatively light and easy to transport from the country by sleigh. The packing plant was typically located near the wharves where it was prepared for shipment.

Integrated pork packing began when the slaughterhouse and packinghouse were first united under one roof in Cincinnati, Ohio, during the 1850s. The transportation of live hogs and salt pork in barrels was facilitated by Ohio River barge traffic. By the late 1860s, parts of the process were carried out with the hog carcass hanging from an overhead rail and the modern (dis)assembly line was born (Giedion 1948: 89). The integration of killing hogs, dressing carcasses, and packing pork by one firm in one location became the model, as pork packing industrialized in the United States.

Large-scale disassembly of cattle developed later. Beef was typically sold fresh, and until the advent of refrigeration, it had to be killed and dressed in smaller quantities close to the market. Cattle could be driven over longer distances than hogs and in all weather conditions, so they were typically walked to the point of slaughter, dressing, and retail sale. Montreal was one of the principal ports for packed meat exports in the 1820s, and it had facilities for the slaughter, packing, and shipment of beef in barrels (Moore 1820: 13).

Lower Canada began regulating the beef and pork trade in 1804 (Moore 1820: 14). Beef for export was restricted to fat cattle over three years of age. Oxen, cows, or steers were all acceptable provided they were well fattened and cut into pieces between four and twelve pounds in weight, 200 pounds to the barrel. The barrels themselves were to be made from seasoned white oak. Preservation of the beef was assured by requiring that each barrel should contain seventy-five pounds of high-quality salt and four ounces of saltpetre.

By 1838, beef and pork were also being exported from Upper Canada via Montreal at the head of navigation on the St Lawrence. But there was concern that the poor quality of Upper Canadian meat flowing through Montreal for export would adversely affect the reputation of Montreal-based meat packers in Lower Canada. The cuts were too large or too small and body parts such as ears, snouts, tails, feet, and legs were sometimes improperly included in the pack. Barrels were of non-standard sizes and made with insufficient hoops or from green wood which permitted leakage of the pickle. But the most serious problem with packed meats was lack of salt in the pickle, leading to spoilage (Moore 1838).

Nineteenth-century meat-packing legislation regulated the barrels and the quality of packed meat itself, but there was no requirement for systematic inspection for sanitation or the presence of disease. As the cattle trade grew and cattle markets provided the opportunity for contact among cattle raised in different regions, the potential for the spread of contagious disease grew. By the 1840s, as much as 20 per cent of the meat eaten in the United Kingdom came from animals that were 'considerably diseased' (Perren 1978: 63).

Slaughterhouse Reform

The drive for slaughterhouse reform came from three sources in the 1890s: overseas trade barriers erected against uninspected livestock and meat, domestic concerns about the public nuisance created by unsanitary slaughterhouses, and developments in the United States and abroad.

In 1892, British authorities placed a 'schedule' on Canadian cattle which required that they be slaughtered within ten days of disembarkation. By preventing fattening of Canadian cattle prior to slaughter the schedule effectively closed the British market to live Canadian cattle. The immediate cause for the schedule was an alleged case of pleuropneumonia in a Canadian animal. The charge was later shown to be false, as the animal was merely suffering from shipping fever or 'transit-pneumonia' caused by the prolonged sea voyage (Canada 1895: xii; Evans 1979). Canada argued that the embargo was simply a non-tariff barrier to protect British livestock producers, but it was not until 1917 that British authorities finally conceded that the protectionist policy could not be justified on the grounds of animal health (Saskatchewan 1918: 25).

The second incentive for reform was the growing nuisance posed by unregulated urban slaughterhouses. The urban butcher shop or market stall had limited facilities to house and slaughter livestock. The butcher craftsmen tended to purchase farm-killed hogs while cattle were dispatched and dressed out in a separate slaughterhouse. In some cases cattle slaughter was located quite close to the shop, exposing surrounding urban land uses to the odours, wastes, and run-off from crudely constructed shambles. In other cases slaughterhouses were deliberately located in suburban areas outside the city proper and beyond the jurisdiction of municipal health and sanitation officials. In either case, the butcher's slaughterhouse of the nineteenth century was typically ill-designed, imperfectly drained, and insufficiently lighted and ventilated (Ontario Sessional Papers 1887: 84–5).

In 1896, Ontario brought in the first provincial legislation to provide for inspection of meat and milk in urban areas. Municipalities were authorized to establish public abattoirs while local boards of health were given responsibility to enforce health regulations and to inspect live animals, carcasses, and meat. The regulations covering municipal abattoirs were extended to all private meat-packing establishments within the limits of any municipality in the province. The regulations provided for ante mortem inspection of animals for human consumption, post mortem inspection of organs for evidence of disease, sterilization of knives used on diseased animals, disposal of diseased tissues, and detailed construction standards covering drainage of blood and kill floor wash water and construction materials. Slaughter facilities required refrigeration, a barrow to contain and dispose of offal, an overhead rail to keep carcasses off the floor, a knocking box, and pens supplied with water troughs for animals awaiting slaughter. Leaky wooden gutters were replaced by floor drains and an underground system of piped drainage.

In 1904, Canada's first veterinary director, J.G. Rutherford, began to investigate meat inspection regulations in various municipalities across the country. There was enormous inconsistency from place to place. Some municipalities had a veterinary inspector while others used the chief of police (Goldberg 1989: 30–2). As late as 1906, there was not, outside of Montreal and Toronto, any systematic ante mortem or post mortem inspection of animals slaughtered in Canada. Even in Canada's two largest cities, inspection was incomplete and irregular. In Montreal there were meat inspectors at the two public abattoirs but no regular inspection of the private packing plants beyond occasional visits from the city's food inspectors. In Toronto there was ante mortem inspection of cattle received at the city stockyards but almost none at the privately operated packinghouses (Moore 1906: 9–10).

The pressures for federal meat inspection of large-scale export-oriented packing plants in Canada were similar to those experienced in the United States which had also lost its European export markets for meat and cattle because of alleged quality problems (Clemen 1923: 320–1; Skaggs 1986: 81–5). The large-scale U.S. meat exporters lobbied for federal meat inspection. Responding to pressure from the big packinghouses, the Congress passed the first meat inspection act in 1891 which governed only meat destined for export. Smaller packers serving local markets were not affected, giving them a competitive advantage over the large-scale packers in domestic markets. Livestock which was condemned, or likely to be condemned, for export went to uninspected plants and was sold for domestic consumption. Thus, it was in the best interests of the large-scale packers, the so-called beef trust, and in the best interest of U.S. consumers that federal inspection be extended as widely as possible.

While the British schedule on cattle exported from Canada, land use conflicts caused by small slaughterhouses in the built-up area of urban areas, and events in the United States put slaughterhouse reform on the policy agenda, the catalyst for meat inspection was a novel about working life in the city known as 'hog butcher for the world.'

The Jungle *and Sanitary Conditions in Canadian Packinghouses*

Set in Chicago's packinghouse district, Upton Sinclair's novel *The Jungle* (1906) was intended to illustrate the plight of immigrant labourers in the manufacturing cities of the United States in the early twentieth century. It was an exposé of ruthless exploitation and corruption in a wide range of businesses: the housing, real estate, and financial services industry, working people's restaurants and bars, railways and employers such as meat-packing plants. Sinclair stated, 'I aimed at the public's heart, and by accident I hit it in the stomach' (Sinclair 1962: 118). The furor caused by *The Jungle* led to two inquiries in the United States. The initial investigation by the U.S. Department of Agriculture (USDA) was a whitewash, implying that *The Jungle* had misrepresented the meat-packing industry. This conclusion was rejected by President Theodore Roosevelt, and a second committee made up of independent investigators was appointed to investigate conditions in Chicago stockyards.

The Neill-Reynolds report presented evidence confirming most of the novel's imputations about adulteration and contamination of meat products: 'As an extreme example of the entire disregard on the part of employees of any notion of cleanliness in handling dressed meat, we saw a hog that had just been killed cleansed, washed, and started on its way to the cooling room fall from the sliding rail to a dirty wooden floor and slide part way into a filthy men's privy. It was picked up by two employees, placed upon a truck, carried into the cooling room and hung up with other carcasses, no effort being made to clean it' (U.S. Congress, House of Representatives 1906: 19). Only one of Sinclair's claims was not substantiated: whether an employee fell into a rendering tank and was processed into lard will never be known with certainty (Dickstein 1981: xiv; Skaggs 1986: 124).

In June of 1906, the United States Meat Inspection Act extended jurisdiction of federal meat inspection to cover all species of livestock and red meats in interstate commerce as well as for export. The federal law did not apply to plants killing and dressing cattle and hogs for local, in-state markets. Ironically, Upton Sinclair's socialist novel prompted the passage of a law that reinforced the market position of the beef trust, and limited the operations of small-scale, meat packers to local markets. It was not until 1967 that the Wholesome Meat Act required that the states develop meat inspection programs with standards at least as rigorous as those administered by the USDA (Lesser 1993: 237; Skaggs 1986: 209).

Canada reacted swiftly to developments south of the border. A study was commissioned by the Department of Agriculture in the summer of 1906 to make thirty-five unannounced visits to packinghouses from the Maritimes to Alberta. The ensuing report found that conditions were 'reasonably satisfactory' and that the majority of plants were clean and well ventilated. Both the Montreal and Toronto plants of William Davies, Canada's largest pork packer were 'scrupulously clean' and well equipped. The relatively new Harris Abattoir in Toronto had on-site laundry facilities and flush toilets in separate washrooms on each floor. A few plants were unsanitary in some respects. For example, Fowler's Canadian Company of Hamilton (wholly owned by Swift Canadian since 1902) occupied a building that was 'old and out of repair.' The floor of the killing room was 'old, water-soaked, uneven and dirty,' the walls were discoloured and bespattered, while the hog-killing equipment was 'far from clean.' The door to the single unsanitary toilet room was nailed shut because of a sewer blockage, thus there were no hand-washing or toilet facilities for the 125 men employed at the plant. But Fowler's was an aberration, Canadian meat-packing plants were considered clean, bright, well-ventilated, and relatively sanitary by the standards of the day (Moore 1906).

Nevertheless, the public outcry in the wake of *The Jungle* was a significant factor in Canada's decision to introduce federal meat inspection. In Canada, as in the United States, the principal concern was to maintain export markets in Europe. To safeguard these markets, there were livestock and meat problems that extended far beyond the industrial hygiene conditions examined by Moore in his 1906 report. Both ante mortem and post mortem inspection were required to safeguard overseas consumers from diseases that the livestock could be carrying, especially tuberculosis. And there were serious grounds for concern: Canadian bacon showing distinct signs of tuberculosis had been seized in Britain in 1906. The Danish and Dutch governments had established meat inspection standards for exported meats which, in effect, set the minimum standards for British meat consumers. Using informal channels, the British government and city of London suggested to Canada's minister of agriculture that nothing less would be required of the Canadian government if British markets were to remain open to Canadian meat products (Watson 1906).

In its Livestock commissioner and veterinarian, Dr J.G. Rutherford, Canada had long had active inspection of live cattle shipments for export, thus there was a champion of the cause and a sentiment in favour of regulating the ante mortem treatment of food animals. Rutherford drafted legislation in late 1906 and all of the major Canadian packing companies were given an opportunity to review it. The largest packers seemed to be in favour of the act, however, they were also aware that the legislation would reinforce the duality between large-scale export-oriented packers and small-scale locally oriented butchers. Federal meat inspection legislation would regulate 'operations which because of the large business interests at stake, are well officered and presumably directed with care, while it excludes the small, cheaply operated, unsanitary slaughter houses because they do not technically qualify under your description of an export house .... None the less, however, these are the real offenders against public health, and their cheaply handled product often is a troublesome and unfair competitor' (Flavelle 1907).

For their part, the small-scale butchers who slaughtered on the farm or at their own slaughterhouse and sold fresh meat from market stalls were concerned that ante mortem inspection would drive them out of business. For example, the clerk of the Hamilton market wrote the minister of agriculture in 1907: 'We all concede the point that the meat should be inspected but after it is killed and offered for sale on the market as otherwise would simply drive the butchers out of business and place the trade and the consumer at the mercy of the Trusts which have become the curse of the United States from which the people over there are trying so hard to free themselves' (Hill 1907). The butchers were placated when the federal inspection legislation specifically excluded farm slaughter, local butchers, and the intraprovincial meat trade from its provisions. Naturally, this had the effect of reserving the higher quality cattle and hogs for export markets and keeping the lowest quality cattle for domestic consumption.

The Meat and Canned Foods Act was finally passed in 1907 and the Meat Inspection Service was born as an agency of the Department of Agriculture. Any plant wishing to ship its products across provincial or international boundaries was obliged to meet federal standards and submit to ante mortem veterinarial inspection of animals and post mortem examination of meat and organs. From 1907 until the 1960s about 100 slaughter plants in Canada operated under federal legislation while hundreds more locally oriented plants were subject to a variety of different regulations depending on the rigour of municipal regulation: 'At present inspection operates only in those plants which do an interprovincial business, though it covers all products of such establishments, whether sold locally or outside. The consequence is that the worst stuff is reserved for local killing and consumption. Some districts notorious for bad stock are avoided by inspected plants, only to find an outlet locally' (Saskatchewan 1918: 20).

The Saskatchewan Livestock Commission recognized the regulatory paradox identified by Sir Joseph Flavelle. As soon as federal inspection was brought in, the large-scale corporate packers would qualify to ship their meats across provincial boundaries, while the smallest plants would continue to operate under little or no regulation to supply local consumers.

The Public Abattoir Movement

The public abattoir movement was the second component of the slaughterhouse reform issue in the first decade of the twentieth century. The movement united urban residents suffering the public nuisance of small-scale slaughterhouses near residential areas and farm-based producers seeking improved access to overseas markets for their livestock. Public abattoirs would be located apart from residential areas and would have specialized sanitation facilities such as floor drains, effective ventilation, and ceramic tile walls. Farm groups from Quebec to Alberta called for the establishment of a federally regulated and financed system of cattle- and hog-killing establishments to foster meat exports. At the turn of the century, animal processing in Canada seemed to develop from a very different model than obtained in the United States where the private sector had already developed integrated meat-packing concerns that had come to dominate the industry.

The public abattoir had been a municipal institution in Europe since the Middle Ages. In the early nineteenth century, a Napoleonic system of public abattoirs was planned for suburban precincts, outside the city walls of Paris, and in every town in France. Butchers were required to slaughter and dress out livestock in these public abattoirs under government supervision. Animal by-products were retained by the abattoir to offset the cost of slaughter. (Heiss 1907: 85–7; Giedion 1948; Schwarz 1901: 8). By the 1860s, the system of small suburban abattoirs had become obsolete as Paris grew beyond its walls. A centralized public abattoir was conceived by George Eugène Haussman, prefect of the Seine and master planner of Paris. Abattoir La Villette was served by railway sidings and just across a navigable canal from a large cattle market. Both market and abattoir were bounded by major roadways at the outermost edge of the fortified belt of Paris. The massive steel and glass abattoir was opened in 1867, just in time for the International Exhibition: 'It became *the* abattoir, a prototype for the rest of the century, just as the boulevards and public parks of Haussman's Paris became models from which every growing metropolis of the continent took pattern' (Giedion 1948: 210). Hundreds of new abattoirs in elaborate and graceful designs with large windows and state-of-the-art equipment appeared all over western Europe (Cash 1907: 58; Ayling 1908: 70). In Britain organizations such as the Model Abattoir Society crusaded to eradicate the evils of small-scale privately owned slaughterhouses in favour of humane, hygienic, and above all, inspected public facilities. By 1908, 136 public abattoirs were scattered throughout the United Kingdom (Ayling 1908; Perren 1978: 91, 155).

Proposals to build municipal abattoirs in Canada coincided with calls for slaughterhouse reform in Britain. But the very fact that they were called 'abattoirs,' a word that did not come into English language usage until the nineteenth century, suggests that the French abattoir system also had some influence. The exotic term 'abattoir' made it clear that the institution of publicly financed slaughter would share nothing with the rude 'shambles' about which there had been so many scandalous accounts of unsanitary conditions and adulteration: 'The American meat factory is in no sense an abattoir. The abattoir has, indeed, for its essential object the prevention of those very abuses which have made the American meat-factory a byword in the civilized world' (Cash 1907: ix).

The advent of public abattoirs was not entirely the product of growing health concerns on the part of consumers. By 1890, Toronto butchers were supporting the construction of a municipal abattoir to centralize slaughter (MacDougall 1982: 6). Public abattoirs were also favoured by farmers to increase Canadian penetration of British meat markets. By the 1890s, mixed farms in eastern Canada were ready, willing, and able to supply greater numbers of cattle for export. The British schedule on Canadian cattle had curtailed live cattle exports but an opportunity in the British beef trade was perceived to exist for the farmers of Quebec: 'The demands of the British market are so enormous as to be almost inexhaustible, while there is also the certainty that they will increase rather than decrease in the future. At present [c. 1885] Canada has an insignificant share of this great and lucrative trade owing to the absence of the organization and facilities which are essential to put the Canadian producer in more direct communication with the British consumer' (Abattoir Question n.d.).

In spite of the manifest successes of Canadian bacon processors such as William Davies, there were no full-scale, export-oriented, beef-killing and -processing plants in Canada until 1896. The opportunities certainly appeared attractive. Quebec City's all-season port was only 2,600 miles (eight days) by transatlantic liner service from the London and Liverpool markets, while Chicago was 4,000 miles by rail and ship. Chilled beef from Canada would transit the cool North Atlantic while the growing beef shipments from Australia and Argentina had to cross the breadth of the tropics. Thus, Quebec farmers argued that their province was ideally situated for the export of both meat and livestock. Every year some 460,000 calves – mainly bull calves – were being slaughtered soon after birth because there was no domestic market for them. In the absence of any action from the private sector, farmers of the mid-1890s advocated that the federal government take the initiative and build a public abattoir to compete with U.S. meat exports and to provide an outlet for the surplus calves of eastern Canadian farmers (Abattoir Question n.d.).

Some fifteen years later, the very same arguments were reiterated by a group of western stock growers who formed the Chilled Meat Committee (CMC). Canada's live cattle trade had been effectively suspended by British import regulations but Canadian beef exports had not arisen to take its place. Yet the beef trade was a lucrative source of earnings for the United States, Argentina, and Australia. The committee proposed a system of thirty small 'feeder abattoirs' from Alberta to Quebec, each with a capacity of twenty-five cattle and 250 hogs per day and equipped to handle kill floor by-products. These feeder abattoirs were to be linked with five 'central depots' which were envisioned as modern industrial-scale packing plants to process all of the carcasses generated by the feeder plants and to kill a further hundred cattle and 1,000 hogs per day a day on their own account from local sources. The central depots were to communicate directly with two export depots, one at Montreal and the other, an open winter port with all-season access to tidewater. The hierarchical killing and shipping system proposed by the CMC was a little reminiscent of the grain handling and marketing system that was emerging at the same time, with one significant exception: it was to be operated by the federal government (CMC 1909: 26–9). The proposed system of public abattoirs was to handle both cattle and hogs: 'It would be practically impossible to build up a packinghouse industry within the Dominion, unless both cattle and hogs were treated at the same establishment' (CMC 1909: 31). The desirability of multispecies public abattoirs was justified by the need for a continuous stream of raw material on the hoof to keep industrial-scale kill plants operating cost-effectively and to build up the scale to keep a system of railway reefer cars operating at full capacity.

While rural-based producer concerns were one motive for the creation of a public abattoir, another stimulus came from urban residents. In 1910, some twenty slaughterhouses scattered around the city of Toronto were causing growing concern about sanitary conditions, meat quality, and the public nuisance imposed on neighbouring land uses. Individual federal inspection of each of these small slaughterhouses was impractical and in any case, none would have met the required standards. Sanitation and public nuisance were the primary motivations to provide a federally inspected central facility to do custom slaughter and provide facilities to chill carcasses for butchers all over the city and shut down the small private slaughter operations (Toronto n.d.).

A further motivation for the creation of a public abattoir was a scandal in 1912 over the provision of free land in the stockyards to Swift Canadian, Gunns, and later to the Harris Abattoir and concerns that an oligopoly was controlling the market. By encouraging small-scale butchers it was thought that the abattoir would help to break the monopoly of big packers in the Union Stock Yards (Lemon 1985: 14–17; McDonald 1985: 31).

The $400,000 Toronto Municipal Abattoir was opened in 1914 in Toronto's Western Cattle Market, charging 75 cents per head of cattle for its custom slaughter services. As a public institution, it was a conspicuous failure. The Western Cattle Market was no match for the Union Stock Yards as a source of livestock. So many small firms had withdrawn from the wholesale butcher business that by 1916 the plant was operating at less than 19 per cent of its designed capacity of 2,000 head per day. While the private sector packers earned windfall profits through the First World War, the public abattoir lost money in every single year of the war (Toronto 1919). Toronto's Municipal Abattoir struggled unsuccessfully for over forty years, continually subject to complaints that it was competing unfairly as it was exempt from taxation. Accumulated deficits of over half a million dollars were being paid by city taxpayers in what was characterized as a misguided vendetta against a non-existent 'beef trust' (Canada Packers, *Annual Report* 1932: 2–3). Closure of the money-losing Municipal Abattoir was considered for many years, but it remained in operation until 1960 when it was sold to Quality Packers, an independent pork packer that remains in operation to the present day, among the last federally inspected meat packers to survive in a downtown metropolitan location.

The establishment of government-owned and -operated animal slaughter facilities was widely advocated at the beginning of the twentieth century. Public ownership was thought to be desirable in the interests of livestock producers, to encourage meat exports, to challenge the dominant market position of the meat-packing oligopoly, and to safeguard consumers from uninspected meat. But Toronto's Municipal Abattoir was one of the few examples of direct government intervention in the slaughter of livestock in Canada. While the primary motive for its construction was to get cattle off the streets and consolidate small butcher slaughter into one federally inspected facility, it would never have been built if private sector industrial-scale meat-packing in Canada had kept pace with demand from domestic and export markets.

Industrialization of Meat Packing

Meat packing industrialized in the late nineteenth century. Technological development of the North American kill floor was entirely dependent on large-scale production based on an infrastructural and organizational triad:

1 Railway transportation of livestock in cattle cars together with trackside water, feeding, and confinement facilities to provide for the sustenance of living cargo and procure raw material from a vast hinterland
2 Rail-based carcass disassembly, staffed by semiskilled workers organized into a minute division of labour
3 Railway transportation to distribute chilled meat in reefer cars together with trackside icing stations to preserve a perishable finished product.

By developing and refining the railway refrigerator car, George Hammond and Gustavus Swift established the feasibility of large-scale centralized production of meat in Chicago (MacLachlan 1998a; 1998c). The railway networks, cattle cars for livestock, and ice-cooled reefer cars were crucial ingredients for the large-scale disassembly of cattle and hogs. But the U.S. system of slaughter and carcass dressing on the rail was not the only way that cattle could be disassembled, just as the extensive grazing of unimproved cattle on the open range was not the only way that cattle could be produced. In Paris, La Villette provides an interesting contemporary counterpoint to the methods pioneered in Cincinnati and Chicago. The European method of cattle production saw each beast treated with greater care, closer human handling, and a higher quality diet based on root crops as well as forage. Consistent with this more labour-intensive production technology was a more labour-intensive disassembly technology. Each animal was housed in its own individual stall and each was killed and dressed in situ by a single butcher without the aid of conveyors or division of labour, a 'curious symbiosis of handicraft with centralization' (Giedion 1948: 211).

While the industrialization of meat packing in Canada shared more in common with the U.S. model than it did with La Villette, there were also some pronounced contrasts. Canada's small population and its huge extent encouraged small-scale locally oriented slaughter long after Armour and Swift had wrought their industrial miracles in Chicago of the 1870s. Canada's first large-scale meat-packing plant was oriented primarily to the British bacon market. The first industrial-scale beef plants in Canada were built at a time when meat inspection and the public abattoir movement threatened to pre-empt the private sector from processing cattle. In the main, industrial scale meat-packing postdated government regulation in Canada while in the United States, the reverse was the case.

As nineteenth-century industrialization took hold, the disassembly of hogs on the rail and conveyed by a moving chain became the model for mechanization of every conceivable manufacturing process. The hog's sparse coat of hair was comparatively simple to remove by scalding and scraping, and the pink carcass was dressed with the skin still on. However, the thick and hairy hide of cattle had to be carefully removed by hand, which was not possible on a moving line. Hide removal was a skilled and labour-intensive process that stymied mechanization for many years. As late as 1948 mechanized hide removal was considered to be 'impossible.' A nineteenth-century invention to mechanize this phase of beef dressing was denigrated as American folk art (Giedion 1948: 239). Only one year later Canada Packers developed an innovative mechanical hide remover at its St-Boniface packing plant which revolutionized the technology of cattle dressing.

Technological Change on the Kill Floor

Through most of the nineteenth century there were only two sources of motive power on the kill floor: brute force (to swing a hammer, hoist carcasses, cut tissues, and manhandle swinging meat along the rail) and gravity (to propel hides and offal to the plant cellar). By 1910, powered material handling equipment and conveyor systems had made their first appearance. Machine-driven chains clanked around the kill floor, pulling carcasses along a rail positioned five metres above the floor. Mechanical rail stops at each work station halted the movement of the carcass until the task was complete. By the 1930s, photoelectric cells were used to detect the presence of a carcass and stop the line. Moving-top viscera inspection tables were introduced about the same time as rail conveyors (Rennie 1969: 23) to carry pluck, stomach, intestines, and heads through the kill floor area in tandem with the carcass from which they were extracted. The meat-packing industry was one of the first to adopt moving chains as motive power for conveying products on rails through a sequence of processing operations. Kill floor conveyors became the inspiration for Henry Ford's automobile assembly line (*Canadian Food Packer* 1942; Harding 1937: 20).

Electrical power was first used in the Chicago plant of Armour and

Company in 1893, and was installed in Gunn's Union Stock Yards plant in Toronto in 1906. Electricity provided an inexpensive and reliable source of light and motive power for conveyors and power tools, and the use of electrical machinery increased rapidly between 1915 and 1930 (Harding 1937: 28). By the 1920s, the first really effective electrical reciprocating power saws came into use for splitting the carcass, and many of the jobs formerly done with a cleaver were mechanized from then on. Earlier experiments with powered saws in the nineteenth century had, like many other attempts to mechanize slaughter, proven impractical, given the organic origins and the carcass-to-carcass idiosyncrasy of cattle anatomy. Eventually, however, technical innovations became flexible enough to surmount the problems of a non-standard and organic raw material. Powered knives and saws improved the cut quality of the carcass, and they greatly reduced both the skill and strength required of a butcher equipped with a cleaver (Rennie 1969: 46).

Stunning and Exsanguination

In the nineteenth century cattle were sometimes stunned by shooting. However, this was considered undesirable because of the high cost of ammunition and the damage done to saleable tissues. Bullets occasionally go wide of the mark and may destroy brain tissue or cheek meat for human consumption. Thus, it was more typical for cattle to have a rope placed around the neck and looped behind the horns which was then threaded through a ring securely anchored in the floor to cinch down and immobilize the head (Harrap and Douglas 1901: 89). The most common method of inducing unconsciousness was to apply a pole-axe or four-pound knocking hammer to the centre of the forehead about three inches below the horns. Figure 4.1 shows a pole-axe in use to stun the animal, not for decapitation. Once insensible, cattle were killed by 'sticking,' that is by stabbing the neck and slicing vertically to sever the carotid arteries and jugular veins, causing complete exsanguination in a matter of seconds (Harding 1937: 19). The practice of bleeding an animal to cause death and simultaneously exsanguinate the carcass appears to have its roots in Judaic dietary laws. The Greeks and Romans, by contrast, avoided spilling precious blood from the carcass and used strangulation or spearing to cause death yet minimize blood loss (Giedion 1948: 243).

During the 1880s, the stunning pen or 'knocking box' was developed. Animals would move through a drive alley into a closely confined pen

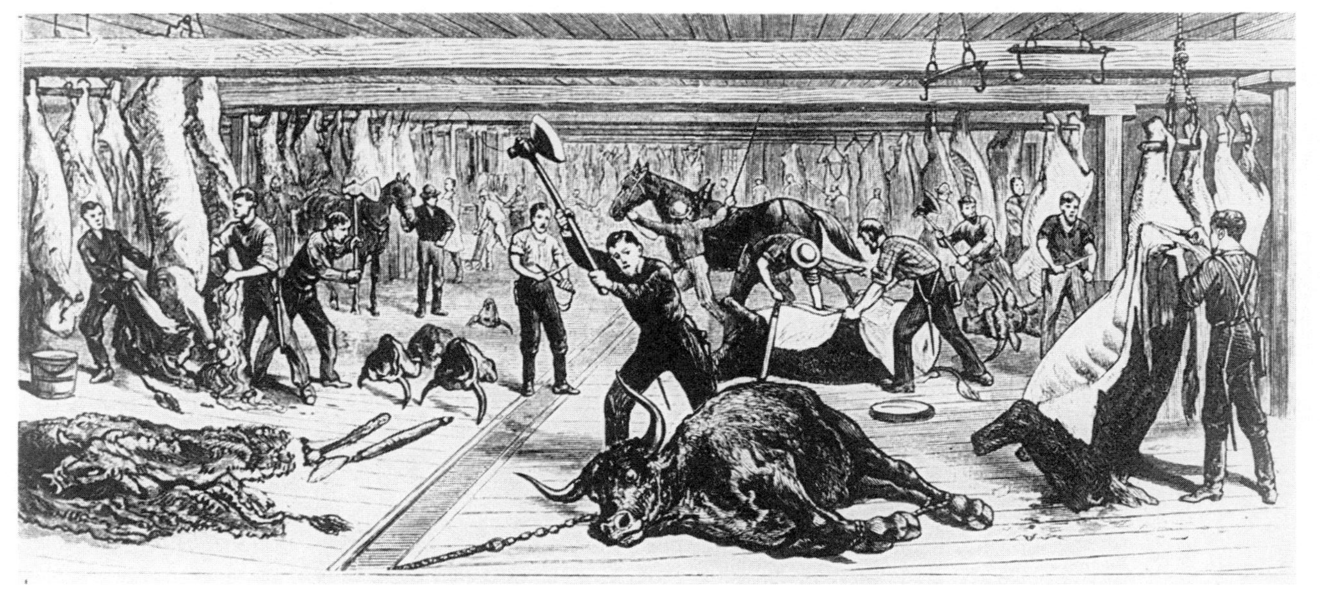

Figure 4.1. Cattle kill floor c. 1880. Source: *Frank Leslie's Illustrated Newspaper*, 67(1202), 12 October 1878, 92.

which exposed the head to the 'knocker' (a worker equipped with a long-handled hammer). After knocking, the animal would collapse, and the side of the knocking box would be opened to allow the unconscious animal to slide out and onto the floor. The animal would then be shackled with a short chain just above the hock joint on both hind legs and hoisted to a short bleeding rail some five metres above the floor.

Bed Dressing of Beef

Bed dressing was the standard beef carcass dressing procedure from the 1880s until 1950. After stunning, the carcass was hoist for bleeding and removal of the head and then lowered on corrugated 'siding beds' (also called 'skinning beds' or 'pritch plates') on the floor. Pritch bars were used to prop and brace the carcass on its back. Floorsmen worked in a stooped position around the prone carcass to detach the legs at the knee joint, partially remove the hide, bisect the sternum, and open the body cavity (Figure 4.1, centre). 'Siders' would continue to flay the hide from the brisket, ribs, belly, and down to the hind legs. Flooring and siding occupations were strenuous and physically exhausting.

A gambrel was inserted between the tendons of the hind legs and the partially skinned carcass was then raised to 'half hoist' with its rump about one metre above the floor. In this position the 'rump sawyer' would cut the aitch bone with a hand saw. The 'rumper' would cut the anus free of the hide and then skin out the hind legs. On the right side of Figure 4.1, a carcass is shown at half hoist while the rumper delicately removes the hide from rump. A paunch truck was pushed under the carcass to receive the offal when the 'gutter' finally eviscerated the carcass. With the completion of rumping, backing, and eviscerating, the carcass was finally hoisted all the way up to the dressing rail, suspended by the gambrel.

Once at full hoist on the dressing rail (left side of Figure 4.1), the removal of the hide continued, the 'backer' being careful to avoid peeling the delicate loin fat, while the 'hide dropper' would remove the hide from neck and shoulders and send it through a hide chute down to the hide cellar. The 'splitter' carefully divided the carcass into two halves using a cleaver to bisect the vertebrae. Dressing was concluded with a final trimming before the carcass was pushed into the chilling room. The dressed carcasses hanging in the far background on Figure 4.1 are a reminder that the age of mechanical refrigeration did not begin until the 1890s, one of the most significant changes in meatpacking technology in the late nineteenth century.

The bed dressing of the bovine carcass used an awkward mixture of batch and continuous disassembly processes. This stood in sharp contrast to hog processing, which used a more nearly continuous chain-driven process once the carcass was removed from the scalding vat:

> Because of its size and character the beef carcass does not lend itself completely to the endless chain system of dressing, which proves so advantageous in the case of dressing hogs. Numerous attempts to bring beef dressing closer to the endless chain method of handling have been made, such as the moving platform which was extensively tried, but it has been found that the generally used method of shackling, hoisting, bleeding, then dropping for skinning, half hoisting, and, finally, elevating for the final dressing operations, appears to be most practical. There still remains a doubt among packers as to the practicability of properly splitting cattle while moving, and it is reasonable to expect important changes in operating methods within the next decade. (Institute of American Meat Packers 1925: 12)

The 'important changes' expected by the Institute of American Meat Packers in the 1930s were, in fact, pioneered by Canada Packers' St-Boniface packing plant in 1950 and will be described in Chapter 5.

Everything but the Moo: Processing By-products

The traditional two sides of beef from the average beef carcass constitute about 60 per cent of the original live weight of the animal. The remainder of the weight is taken up by the hide (the most valuable single by-product), head, feet, viscera, fats, blood, and contents of the alimentary tract. The paunch manure has no value, as it costs as much to transport as it is worth as fertilizer. But the return on other cattle by-products is considerably higher than for any other species of livestock because of the value of the hide. In 1915, a carcass of beef could be sold for less than the price of the live steer, yet the packer would still make a profit (Clemen 1927: 9–10; Canada Packers 1943: 141–6; Rennie 1969: 24).

One of the chief advantages to large-scale processing in the late nineteenth century was the opportunity for enhanced by-product utilization. The processing of many by-products, which was simply not economic in small-scale butcher shops, could be very profitable in industrial-scale plants. One nineteenth-century commentator observed: 'A small butcher in the East cannot kill his meat and market it in competition with the stock-yards packers because he must waste what they save and sell' (Ralph 1892). Looking at the need for economies of scale from another perspective, the price for beef carcasses was so low in a competitive industry that packers had to have large production runs so that by-products could be harvested economically to offset low prices.

Industrial meat packing required a detailed division of labour. Specialization of workers, especially those with a knack for finicky occupations requiring a high degree of manual dexterity helped to enhance the quality of by-products, which is especially important in hide removal. With large-scale production, by-products can be more finely segregated to cater to specific markets or processes. For example, the various stomach linings can be separated into mountain chain tripe and honeycomb tripe. Visceral fats were suitable for making oleomargarine which had a higher value than tallow which was made from common back fat and trimmings.

The packing industry differs from most manufacturing operations in that it deals with *disassembly* instead of fabrication or assembly. Traditionally the live animal was purchased on a live-weight basis. The full weight and value of the carcass and by-products were unknown until after disassembly and sale. Cost accounting in traditional meat packing totalled the cost of live cattle, expenses for killing, dressing, and chilling, together with an allowance for the average amount of trimming of damaged product and condemnations. The total cost outlay was then reduced by the value of by-products produced which were credited to the account and deducted from costs to arrive at the total plant cost of the carcass in the cooler (Clemen 1927: 383–4). To the present day, packinghouse by-products are known as 'credits.'

By-products were crucial to the profitability of large-scale packers in the late nineteenth century. Packers could not earn a profit on the sale of beef alone. In 1889, for example, Philip Armour and Company would have lost $10.21 on every fresh dressed beef carcass it sold. Only when the value of the hide and other by-products was included did the packer make a profit of 59 cents per head, a sales margin of 1.2 per cent (Cronon 1991: 251). Sales of by-products gave the large-scale packers an enormous competitive advantage over small-scale butchers. In 1909, a very profitable year for the Harris Abattoir, then Eastern Canada's largest beef packer, only 55 per cent of the net earnings from the beef business or $1.70 per head was derived from the sale of fresh and cured beef itself (Table 4.1). The other 45 per cent of the firm's profits from beef operations, $1.41 per head, came from the sale of fats, casings for sausage, edible and non-edible offal, and fertilizer. This is still

Table 4.1 Net earnings per carcass: Harris Abattoir, 1909

Account	Earnings	Per carcass
Primary beef	$ 71,696	$1.51
Cured beef	1,674	0.04
Beef cuts	7,280	0.15
Subtotal	80,650	1.70
Animal fats	37,802	0.80
Casings	6,680	0.14
Offal	18,497	0.39
Fertilizer	4,000	0.08
Subtotal	66,979	1.41
Total	$147,629	$3.11

Source: Raw data from A.J.E. Child, 1960. 'The Predecessor Companies of Canada Packers Limited: A Study of Entrepreneurial Achievement and Entrepreneurial Failure.' Master's thesis, University of Toronto, 130.

the case in the contemporary fresh beef industry. And the larger the scale of the operation, the more efficiently by-products can be harvested.

The importance of by-products to beef processing has grown in recent years. In the late 1960s, the value of by-products were roughly equal to what it cost to kill and dress the carcass. The cost of custom slaughter is traditionally covered by the value of the hide and other by-products. By 1988, by-products were worth approximately four times the cost of the cattle kill. In part, this increase is a result of the ever more efficient harvesting procedures and in part it stems from adding value to by-products and seeking markets for them which becomes economical at very large scales of production (Grier 1988: 20). Hides are cured in the hide cellar of large packinghouses or in a central hide plant and then shipped to the United States or Asia for tanning into leather. Western Canadian cattle-branding practices are detrimental to the production of leather and branded hides are discounted for this reason (Horner 1981: 126). Once discarded, cattle blood is now used in many pharmaceutical products. Since animals are stuck and the blood is drawn before post mortem inspection is complete, the blood from any condemned animals will contaminate the blood contributed by other animals that pass inspection. For this reason, a separate hollow knife and plastic bag is used for each carcass. The most recent technology uses a vacuum extraction machine to draw blood from the circulatory system. The blood drains into a small tank which is changed frequently. Should a carcass be condemned, the entire contents of the tank must also be consigned to rendering with other inedible offal.

Canada's Nineteenth-Century Meat-Packing Firms

The emergence and most rapid growth of the corporate giants of the meat-packing industry occurred in periods of buoyant demand driven by rapid domestic growth and settlement, and during wartime when export market opportunities were especially attractive. In the late nineteenth-century cattle prices in the United States were driven up at the end of the Civil War, and Canadian beef was in great demand in western Canada to meet dietary needs of the great railway gangs, to feed Indians confined on reserves, and to satisfy the changing food preferences of a fast-growing urban market. At this time Pat Burns launched one of western Canada's largest domestically controlled agribusiness firms from his base in Calgary. In Winnipeg, Gordon and Ironside and Fares got their start as frontier dealers in lumber, grain, and cattle, and like Burns, they supplied beef to railway gangs and later invested in large-scale ranches in Alberta and Saskatchewan. In eastern Canada, the British market for bacon ('bacon' was used to refer to all cured pork products) provided terrific export opportunities for small-scale pork packers such as Laing Packing and Provision Company of Montreal, William Davies and Donald Gunn of Toronto, F.W. Fearman of Hamilton, and George Matthews of Peterborough to increase their volumes far beyond the limits imposed by local retail meat markets.

Great Britain required meat far in excess of its domestic production capacity and in peacetime the cheapest and highest quality source of pork lay across the North Sea in Denmark. Much of its beef was procured in Argentina. When Germany interdicted the coastal trade in cured pork products during the two world wars, Canadian meat packers had a lucrative opportunity to supply the British bacon market. Thus, it was bacon, not beef, that propelled the growth of the packing industry in eastern Canada. The manufacture of cured and smoked pork products (known as 'provisions') was a value added process that lent itself to industrial scale. Provisions had become the province of the larger packers because of the improved quality and low unit costs of large-scale brine curing and smoking operations. Throughout the late nineteenth century and during the First World War, 'Wiltshire sides' were promoted as the 'ambassadors of the Canadian bacon industry' and 'creators or destroyers' of an exporter's reputation on the British market (Metcalfe 1939: 17). The production of Wiltshire sides, cut and smoked to the precise specifications and preferences of the British consumer, imposed the first standards on industrial-scale pork packing. Wiltshire sides were specially cut, and required the most meticulous butchering to attain the uniformly high quality necessary for the discriminating British market (Canada Packers 1943: Chapter 7; Kenney 1945). Bacon was the foundation of the Canadian meat-packing industry.

Beef, on the other hand, was rarely subject to any value added processing. It was typically consumed fresh with minimal processing beyond slaughter, hide removal, evisceration, and disassembly. Most Canadian beef was dressed by local butchers or slaughtered on the farm. The scale of operations was limited by Canada's tiny domestic market and the difficulty of distributing fresh meats over the great distance between small cities and towns. Large-scale slaughter and sale of fresh beef in eastern Canada did not begin until 1896 (Child 1960: 43–5; Willis [1964]: 38), some twenty-five years after the industrialization of cattle slaughter in Chicago.

Harris Abattoir Company

William Harris was a British-born butcher craftsman who gained experience as a livestock dealer when he immigrated to Canada, where he eventually became the head livestock buyer for the William Davies Company in Toronto – the largest pork packer in the British Empire (Bliss 1978; Child 1960; Willis [1964]). With support from Davies's principals, Harris left the pork-packing and retail firm to open a beef slaughterhouse which would supply fresh beef to Davies's chain of retail stores. The Harris Abattoir was established in late 1896 at the foot of Strachan Avenue, adjacent to Toronto's Western Cattle Market. With a slaughter capacity of 500 cattle per week, the Harris Abattoir was, as its name implies, a plant for slaughtering and dressing carcasses which would then be sold to butchers for fabrication into portions which were cut to order. It was not a true packinghouse as the finished product was a freshly dressed side of hanging beef. The Harris Abattoir was quite a bold innovation: it was a beef specialist at a time when abattoirs were designed to kill all species. The firm entered the market in the very same year that Ontario legislation was brought in to provide for the establishment of municipally owned public abattoirs (Ontario Provincial Board of Health 1896). Thus, the establishment of the Harris Abattoir seems to have been motivated to pre-empt the creation of public abattoirs following the British model and to keep the slaughter and dressing of cattle in private hands.

Building on its success in the export of bacon to Britain, and perhaps with an eye to the increasingly diversified slaughterhouses of the Chicago-based packers, the William Davies company wanted a more active role in the beef business. After considering establishing its own slaughterhouse adjacent to its existing hog operations on the Don River, William Davies took a 50 per cent interest in the cattle-killing and beef-dressing operation which was reorganized; and incorporated as the Harris Abattoir Company Ltd. in 1901. Joseph Flavelle was appointed president, while William Harris and his sons undertook day-to-day management. The primary goal of the reorganized firm was to export fresh beef to Britain, a belated response to the British schedule on live cattle exports from Canada, introduced in 1892. A substantial export trade in canned meat, chiefly corned beef, had developed but there were as yet no significant exports of fresh Canadian beef (Bliss 1978: 115; Moore 1904: 26).

Thus, the Harris Abattoir aspired to emulate the large-scale exports of fresh beef by U.S. packers such as Swift which installed refrigeration equipment on twenty freighters for the transatlantic shipment of beef (Skaggs 1986: 96). The scheme seemed equally feasible in Canada. Finished fat cattle would be slaughtered in Canada in peak condition, there would be no shipboard shrink, no charges for loading and unloading live cattle, and no personnel required to provide on-board feeding and care. Freight charges would be based only on marketable carcasses excluding the unproductive weight of hides, heads, bones viscera, and blood which make up over 40 per cent of the weight of live cattle.

But the bold experiment to export fresh beef from Canada was a failure. In 1901, the Harris Abattoir exported 513 cattle, 7,832 live sheep, and 4,451 carcasses of beef, sustaining a loss of $25,451 on the transaction – a far cry from the very profitable beef export experience of New York meat wholesalers (Child 1960: 124; Yeager 1981: 54). Poor refrigeration at sea, irregular shipping schedules, and conservatism on the part of British butchers who were unaccustomed to merely cutting beef that was slaughtered elsewhere, combined to defeat the best efforts of the nascent Harris Abattoir (Canada Packers 1943: 26). Having equipped the plant for large-scale beef slaughter, Harris turned to local markets for fresh beef. While there was a small urban market in Toronto, and a demand for beef in peripheral regions such as northern Ontario, it was generally thought that markets in smaller centres and rural areas would be closed to fresh beef from Toronto given the cost of shipping live cattle into the city and of shipping fresh dressed carcasses out again. The large-scale urban slaughter of cattle and the large-scale marketing of fresh beef was considered a rash and risky venture (Canada Packers 1943: 26–7).

However, the Harris Abattoir benefited from economies of scale, an exceptionally lean production system, and from processing by-products. The reorganized firm became a success even though its principal goal to become a beef exporter had failed. Rapid growth in Canada's urban population, remote from rural farm sources of fresh beef was a further stimulus to the fresh dressed beef business. In 1900, over 75 per cent of the beef consumed in Toronto was slaughtered by small plants and butchers with a capacity of less than 200 cattle per week; but by 1920, 95 per cent came from large-scale packinghouse slaughter (Rennie 1969: 23). Markets for by-products were strong. Finally, there was growing demand for fresh beef to feed the railway construction gangs required to build two additional transcontinental railway lines through the bush of the Canadian Shield and over the top of Lake Superior. The Harris Abattoir operated sales branches in Sudbury, Timmins, and Haileybury as silver and gold fever swept northern Ontario.

The Harris Abattoir outgrew its first plant and looked towards a location in Toronto's new meat-packing centre: the Union Stock Yards district. Gunns Limited, a Toronto-based pork packer, and Swift Canadian had benefited from industrial incentives offered by the newly established Union Stock Yards and the town of Toronto Junction. The Harris Abattoir accepted a similar inducement and built a new packing plant with a weekly capacity of 5,000 cattle, 5,000 hogs, 1,500 calves, and 5,000 sheep. The plant employed 750 workers when it opened in November of 1913 (McDonald 1985: 37).

The new plant was a necessary component of the Harris Abattoir's new strategy to diversify as a fully integrated meat packer and to serve the domestic market. In adding 5,000 hogs per week to its kill when the new plant was opened in 1913, it was challenging its partner, William Davies. In 1916, Davies delivered a counter-punch when it completed a half-million dollar expansion of its own Don River plant which included a beef-processing facility so that it could begin to slaughter cattle as well as hogs (Child 1960: 113). Thus, the intercorporate division of labour and strategic alliance that made Davies the pork specialist and Harris Abattoir the beef specialist had been abrogated. Both the parent and the subsidiary had become horizontally integrated meat packers and were competing head-to-head in the Ontario market. Making matters worse, Davies had been implicated in a profiteering scandal which had not yet affected Harris. The Harris Abattoir bought out Davies's interests and severed its ties with the beleaguered firm in 1917.

As Harris became more committed to the Canadian domestic market, it began to look to the new hinterland provinces of Saskatchewan and Alberta for assured sources of cattle and hogs (Bronson 1973: 26). It was recognized even then that it made more sense to ship fresh beef and pork from the Prairies to the heartland than it did to move animals on the hoof. In 1918, Harris entered into a joint venture agreement with Gordon, Ironside, and Fares, the oldest meat-packing company in western Canada with plants in Winnipeg and Moose Jaw. But the venture was unsuccessful, and Harris sustained a loss of $1.1 million in 1921. Harris Abattoir abandoned its western partner and built an entirely new plant at the Union Stock Yards of St-Boniface in 1925 (Child 1960: 161). Gordon, Ironside, and Fares went out of business in the 1920s, eclipsed by an Ontario farm boy who made good in Alberta.

P. Burns and Company

Pat Burns was western Canada's 'cattle king' in the first three decades of the twentieth century. A semiliterate labourer in Ontario's bushland in the 1870s, Burns became a cattle trader and self-taught butcher in the 1880s, selling beef to the railway gangs building the CPR. His beef sales supported the construction of the CPR 'short line' joining Montreal to Portland, Maine, in 1887, the Calgary and Edmonton Railway in 1891, and the CPR's southern line through the Crowsnest Pass in 1897. P. Burns and Company also found a growing demand for beef in the mining and lumber camps of the Kootenay and Crowsnest Pass during the coal mining boom of the 1890s. The firm supplied beef to the agents of Indian reserves administered under Treaty 7. And at the height of the Yukon gold rush, Burns shipped beef to the Klondike to exploit the exorbitant market price of $1 per pound. Cattle were slaughtered in butcher camps, wherever fresh beef was needed, for example, on the bank of the South Saskatchewan River near the present day Saskatoon Exhibition grounds (Rennie 1969: 21). Unlike the founders of Canada

Packers, Burns was primarily a cattle dealer and fresh beef purveyor to institutional buyers. He was not a butcher craftsman or exporter.

Having followed railway construction westward, Pat Burns finally established his headquarters in Calgary where he built his first substantial slaughterhouse in 1890. Despite two major fires, his Calgary-based cattle and meat business prospered in the growing western market, and in 1914 Burns built his third Calgary packinghouse adjacent to the Calgary Stock Yards. The plant killed both cattle and hogs until 1984, when it was finally closed and later demolished. He expanded into Vancouver with a new abattoir in 1907. In exchange for agreeing to perform custom slaughter for rival firms (50 cents a head for cattle and sheep, 25 cents a head for lambs and calves) and building a stock yard for public use, P. Burns and Company received a subsidy on water and relief from taxes on improvements for ten years (MacEwan 1979: 105). Burns was accepting municipal subsidies to establish a plant in Vancouver at almost the same time as William Harris was receiving inducements from the town of Toronto Junction.

P. Burns and Company grew by acquiring competing meat packers in lieu of building new plants from scratch. They bought out William Roper Hull's meat-processing operations in Calgary in 1902 (Klassen 1999: 152); Williamson Brothers of Edmonton and took over their slaughter plant in 1912 (Rennie 1969: 25); in 1917, they purchased both the Russel Baker Packing Company of Prince Albert and the Armour and Company plant in Regina (Bronson 1973: 25). In 1926, P. Burns and Company bought the Winnipeg packinghouse of Gallagher, Holman and Co. which was immediately rebuilt to become a part of the growing chain of packing plants (MacEwan 1979: 106). While Pat Burns was Canada's 'cattle king,' his beef-packing enterprise took off when western farmers began to raise hogs on a large scale and the British bacon market opened to western Canadian pork during the First World War. Burns and Co. entered hog processing to became a horizontally integrated multispecies packing firm.

In addition to his slaughterhouse empire, Pat Burns became an active rancher and cattle dealer, integrating backwards to control the price, quantity, and quality of livestock inputs (Klassen 1999: 151). By 1900, purebred Herefords grazed his Bow Valley Ranch in what is now the south end of Calgary. The ranch occupied 9,000 acres of deeded land and included a 5,000-head feedlot (MacEwan 1979: 140), surely the first in Alberta. Burns survived the heavy cattle losses of the winter of 1906–7, and by 1912 he operated half a dozen large ranches in

Alberta from the Red Deer River south to the international border (MacEwan 1979: 142–3).

Like most other meat packers, Burns held diversified interests to help smooth the vicissitudes of the meat business. It added value to dressed meats with its 'Shamrock' and later 'Pride of Canada' brands of processed, canned, and smoked meats and sausage. Burns operated its first creamery in Calgary by 1909, and in 1924 it acquired Edmonton City Dairy. These interests were brought together under the Palm Dairies subsidiary umbrella. By 1928, the firm controlled sixty-five dairy plants and claimed to be the largest manufacturer of creamery butter in Canada (MacEwan 1979: 126–7). Burns was operating retail butcher shops by the 1890s and added a western Canadian chain of meat stores in 1902 (MacEwan 1979: 140). At its peak the firm operated a chain of ninety-five P. Burns and Company grocery stores and a large grocery wholesale operation across western Canada which survives as Scott National.

In 1928, Pat Burns sold his meat-packing interests for $9.7 million to Dominion Securities, and P. Burns and Company was reorganized as Burns and Company (Canada 1934: 2549–53). He retained his extensive ranch properties, but lost interest in the meat-packing firm he had created, especially after he was appointed a senator in 1931.

Like the Harris Abattoir, P. Burns and Company was primarily a supplier of fresh beef geared to domestic markets, especially those connected with staple extraction on the resource frontier. At the same time as Burns was supplying beef to the coal-mining towns of Alberta's Crowsnest Pass and British Columbia's Kootenay, the Harris Abattoir was operating wholesale branches in the mining towns of northern Ontario, riding the precious metals boom on the Canadian Shield. But while William Harris was a butcher first and a cattle buyer second, Burns was a rancher and cattle dealer first and slaughtered the beasts simply because that was the best way to sell them. For many years, Burns in Calgary and Harris in Toronto seemed content to divide the Canadian market along the Ontario–Manitoba border in their common goal to keep the Americans at bay.

The American Challenge to Canadian Meat Packers

Until the 1990s, meat packing was one of the few Canadian manufacturing industries to remain largely under domestic control. With the exception of some protectionist interludes such as the Fordney-McCumber Tariff of 1922 and the Smoot-Hawley Tariff of 1930, the market for cattle and beef has been continental in scope (Canada 1982: 38–9; Foran 1998: 14). Tariff avoidance was not the incentive for foreign-owned meat packers to locate in Canada that it was in other industries such as automobile assembly. In any case, the Canadian market was too small to be taken very seriously by the giants of the U.S. packing industry. The leading U.S. packers did establish some small Canadian packing operations in the early years of the twentieth century. Armour established a bacon plant in Hamilton and acquired a small slaughterhouse in Regina. Morris and Company acquired an equity interest in Gunns in Toronto. Wilson and Company operated out of a small plant in Chatham, deep in southwestern Ontario.

In the fall of 1920, the buoyant wartime markets broke for many different commodities and prices plummeted as currency devaluations swept postwar Europe. The big North American meat packers, which had been accustomed to producing full tilt for the previous six war years, suddenly found themselves with huge quantities of their output on consignment abroad, in transit, and in domestic inventory. As soon as the market broke there was a rush to sell off inventory which made prices drop even further. There were enormous losses throughout the industry in 1920 and 1921, and suddenly the meat packers found themselves with production capacity far in excess of demand.

This recessionary period had two important effects on the Canadian meat-packing industry. First, many of the big Chicago-based packers were on the brink of insolvency, and to cope with calamitous conditions, the U.S. packers quickly shed their smallest operations and most peripheral markets. In 1920, two of the U.S. firms, Armour and Company in Hamilton and Wilson and Company in Chatham, sold their Canadian subsidiaries and exited the Canadian market, never to return.

By the mid-1920s, Ontario's pork packers were in dire financial straits, as well. Gunns Limited became insolvent in 1926 and Armour and Company of Chicago was a minority shareholder. Gunns might have become a wholly owned subsidiary of Armour had not P. Burns and Company of Calgary then come to the rescue, loaning Gunns the money needed to pay off its U.S. creditors and acquiring a majority equity interest in the firm (Child 1960: 226–42). Burns's only plausible motive was to keep the industry in Canadian hands, Alberta ranchers have never been known for their philanthropy to Toronto-based industrialists! Burns sold its controlling interest to the Harris Abattoir in 1927, and Gunns passed out of existence. By selling Gunns to the Harris Abattoir, Pat Burns was creating a formidable eastern competitor that would become Canada Packers. But in dividing the Canadian market between two powerful Canadian firms which could dominate eastern and western markets, Burns was instrumental in keeping U.S. interests at bay.

The Canadian Packing Company was formed through a complex series of acquisitions affecting half a dozen different Ontario and Montreal-based meat packers which were ultimately taken over by Allied Packers of Chicago in 1919 (Clemen 1923: 801–2). However, the company lost a total of $1.7 million over six consecutive years of losses from 1921 to 1927 (Child 1960: 247–51), and it was clearly available for takeover by any firm wanting to establish its competitive position in the Canadian market.

As Canada's first and largest scale pork packer, William Davies and Company had thrived as a bacon exporter during the halcyon days of the First World War. But the firm was caught flat-footed at war's end and by the mid-1920s it was in massive financial difficulty. So it, too, was ripe for takeover, possibly by a U.S. firm.

While the Harris Abattoir had failed at its primary mandate, to export fresh dressed beef to Britain, it suffered less in the 1920s than the pork packers because it was not as exposed to the export market. J.S. McLean of the Harris Abattoir saw that if the beleaguered Canadian meat packers went on the auction block, U.S. interests could snap them up at 10 cents on the dollar and become invincible competitors in his own backyard. In masterminding the creation of Canada Packers from four smaller meat packers (Harris Abattoir, Gunns and Company, William Davies, and the Canadian Packing Company), J.S. McLean blocked entry by the U.S. packers and retrieved the Canadian Packing Company from the hands of U.S.-based Allied Packers. Thus, the merger of 1927 pre-empted the entry of U.S. packers by acquisition, keeping most of the industry in Canadian hands for over sixty years (A.J. Child Interview).

Swift Canadian

Chicago-based Swift and Company was the only big U.S. meat packer to make a successful assault on the Canadian market. It accomplished much of its rapid growth in Canada by acquisition. Swift entered the Canadian market in 1902 by purchasing two existing packing firms: Fowler Canadian, a bacon producer in Hamilton, and J.Y. Griffin and Company with its head office in Winnipeg. In 1908, Swift Canadian opened a brand new packing plant in Edmonton, a city of 18,000 and newly established as the provincial capital (*Food in Canada* 1958). In 1911 Swift and Company of Chicago expanded by acquiring D.B. Martin and Company of Philadelphia, and the Canadian subsidiary of the acquired firm, the first packing plant to have been built in Toronto's Union Stock Yards, fell into the hands of Swift Canadian. In a space of only nine years, Swift's had made a three-pronged attack on the Canadian market and established beachheads in the heartland of southern Ontario, the *entrepôt* of Canada's fast growing west, and the gateway to Peace River country and the north, easily the broadest market penetration of any meat-packing enterprise in Canada and arguably, of any foreign-owned manufacturing subsidiary at that time.

But access to the Canadian market was not the only consideration. Swift used its Hamilton plant to launch an attack on the British market in competition with William Davies. To enter this lucrative market it appears that the firm was prepared to absorb substantial losses through discount pricing. Joseph Flavelle, the managing director of Davies wondered: Why would Swift work with such 'feverish haste' to lose money? By 1903 he had his answer. Swift Canadian had successfully broken into the bacon market of northern England, a regional niche market that Davies agents had allowed to slip away (Bliss 1978: 131). Thus, Swift Canadian got its start by using a Canadian export platform to invade a prime overseas market.

The U.S.-based firm continued its expansion by acquisition strategy and moved rapidly to exploit the financial difficulties experienced by many small Canadian meat packers during and after the First World War. It acquired the Prince Rupert Meat Company in New Westminster in 1917, a packing plant in Moncton, New Brunswick, in 1925, and a year later, Gordon, Ironside and Fares's plant in Moose Jaw which had been closed since 1921. Moose Jaw offered a reduction in the price of water and electricity and a fixed rate of tax for the next eleven years as inducements to Swift Canadian to make the acquisition. In 1926 Swift Canadian reached its maximum spatial extent and operated plants from the Atlantic to the Pacific, becoming the first meat-packing firm to operate in Canada on a continental scale (*Saturday Night* 1926).

The Price of Prosperity

Few industries have been as embroiled in as many scandalous charges of product adulteration, unsanitary procedures, and accusations of price fixing as meat packing. In few other industries is there as much potential for morbid sensationalism, and in few other industries are the stakes as high. The industry produces meat, one of the most intimate of all commodities: flesh that is placed in the mouth, chewed, and swallowed. The large-scale meat packers were ideal targets for a popular press driven by consumer appetite for sensationalist journalism. To some extent the big packers were misunderstood and abused by a rabid media more interested in yellow journalism than in the dissection of arcane accounting procedures in a technically complex industry. But when times were good, the packing business was outrageously profitable.

Scandals or merely unfounded allegations against the packers were often linked closely in time to events taking place south of the border. The embalmed beef scandal of 1898 alleged that the tinned 'bully beef' provided to U.S. troops during the Spanish-American War was preserved with formaldehyde, the same carcinogenic preservative used for human cadavers. Analysis by the USDA's Bureau of Chemistry failed to detect any formaldehyde, and over 90 per cent of the allegations of adulteration were without foundation (Kolko 1963: 98–100; Skaggs 1986: 81–5, 122). In 1902, only two years after the embalmed beef scandal broke in the United States, there were allegations that the tinned beef (manufactured by 'a leading Canadian firm') sent to feed Canadian troops in the Boer War in South Africa had been processed with boracic acid (*Canadian Grocer* 1902: 40). A government inquiry failed to unearth any evidence to support claims of adulteration.

Time and again allegations against the meat-packing industry were investigated in exhaustive detail by government commissions or tribunals. In no case did the charges stand up to scientific or legal scrutiny, and all were later repudiated. But Canadian packers took the brunt of the bad press and the damage was done by the charges themselves.

Although sanitation and adulteration issues came to the fore more than once, it was market dominance and the incredible profitability of the meat-packing industry that earned most of the public opprobrium in Canada. This was the price of prosperity for the early twentieth-century meat-packing scions.

Profiteering in Ontario: William Davies and Company

William Davies's Toronto facilities had been exonerated by the Moore report of 1906; indeed, sanitation in its Toronto plant was beyond reproach. It even had troughs for washing boots before entering the curing cellars, a safeguard found only in the most up-to-date packing plants of the 1990s. However, the firm was the subject of a steadily worsening series of scandals from 1907 through to the end of the First World War. These exposés sullied the name of William Davies as a profiteering monopoly which made a great deal of money at the expense of both livestock producers and consumers.

Just as Moore was completing his report in Canada and as sanitary problems in the Chicago plants were becoming widely recognized, the full dividend payment record of William Davies was accidentally publicized (Bliss 1978: 183). That the largest pork packer in the British Empire had been paying annual dividends averaging 51 per cent of the paid up share capital between 1892 and 1906 should have been the cause for a major scandal, especially among Ontario's hard-pressed hog farmers. The reaction to the profit record was actually quite mild: 'Still, the emperor had been shown to be wearing fine silk under his simple workingman's coat; Flavelle thought the disclosure was a crippling blow to his company's influence in the industry' (Bliss 1978: 183).

Four years later, in September 1911, Flavelle was once again defending the profitability of his firm and the industry. In a theme that would be repeated in years to come, Flavelle argued that abattoirs producing commodity fresh meat in large volumes turned over their capital from twenty-five to forty times per year. Rapid turnover made meat packing unique among manufacturing industries, permitting an extraordinarily low sales margin of 1 to 2 per cent on fresh meats and 2 to 2.5 per cent on cured meats. Thus, even if the packer made no money at all, the extra revenue accruing to the producer or the price savings to the consumer would be an almost imperceptible 1 to 1.5 per cent (Flavelle 1911). The high-volume, low-margin argument did not convince the media. Days later, and only one week before the federal election that was to defeat Laurier's Liberals and repudiate the Reciprocity Agreement, the *Toronto Daily Star* turned its display window into a meat display case to demonstrate the differences in retail meat prices between William Davies stores in Toronto and stores in Buffalo, New York. Davies responded with angry letters, full-page advertisements, and a Davies store display which purported to show that the original comparison was unfair and that U.S.–Canadian comparisons actually favoured Canadian consumers (Bliss 1978: 217; the *Toronto Daily Star* 1911).

Thus, before the First World War, mistrust of the monopoly market power of meat packers was clearly manifest among both livestock pro-

Figure 4.2. 'The way it is played.' Profiteering scandals painted the meat-packing concerns as exploitive monopolists in the first decade of the twentieth century. Source: *Toronto Daily Star*, 15 September 1911.

ducers and household consumers of meat (Figure 4.2). Although the grossly unsanitary conditions found in U.S. meat-packing plants had not been detected in Canada, the media pointed to price gouging when William Davies, Canada's largest pork packer, cracked its whip.

Davies increased its exports of Wiltshire sides to Great Britain dur-

Table 4.2 Profit and loss statement of William Davies Company Limited, 1913–1917

Item	1913	1914	1915	1916	1917
Profits from operations exclusive of retail stores but net of bonuses	5,010	15,521	484,631	1,335,454	1,634,161
Profits from retail stores	98,552	75,350	100,969	60,326	48,610
Total	103,562	90,871	585,600	1,395,780	1,682,771
Profits from operations net of retail stores as a percentage of sales	n/a	0.14	2.87	5.32	3.99
Profit after deduction of interest expense as a percentage of capital	n/a	6.89	43.32	80.02	57.48

Note: All data for fiscal year ending 31 March.
Source: Henderson Commission, 1918. 'Report of the Henderson Commission on Canadian Packers' Profits.' Reprinted in Saskatchewan, 1918. *Final Report of the Live Stock Commission of the Province of Saskatchewan 1918*. Printed by order of the Legislative Assembly (Regina: King's Printer), 48.

ing the First World War. Consumer prices inflated rapidly, and this was blamed on alleged profiteering by 'cold storage' companies which were hoarding and even destroying food to drive up prices. Davies was caught up in the net that had been spread for cold storage firms since it required coolers to chill carcasses coming off the kill floor, and as one inquiry led to another, it was then accused of adulterating its premium quality bacon with excess salt water. In fact, William Davies had been the victim of sloppy investigation by accountants who did not understand the meat-packing business (Bliss 1978: Chapter 14). But it also became clear that the firm earned grotesque profits throughout the war years. Its traditionally modest sales margin of about 1 cent for each dollar of revenues jumped to 5.3 per cent in 1916. The firm's profits on operations increased exponentially from $5,010 in 1913 to $484,631 in 1915 to $1,634,161 in 1917. Driven primarily by export sales to the British War Office to feed soldiers fighting and dying in Flanders, these profits (net of interest expense) amounted to 43.3, 80.0 and 57.5 per cent of invested capital from 1915 to 1917 (Table 4.2), and the dividends added to Flavelle's multimillions. The popular press revelled in exposing the larcenous pork packers of central Canada

(*Saturday Night* 1917). The purity of Davies's premium quality pork products had been questioned, and the seeds of distrust in the meat-packing industry had been sown. The fabulous financial success of Davies was exposed for all to see. Sir Joseph Flavelle, the newly titled baronet, became 'his lardship,' Canada's most infamous wartime profiteer (Bliss 1978).

Monopoly Power on the Prairies: P. Burns and Company

One of the problems disaffecting the agricultural electorate of the new province of Alberta was the deterioration of the income that could be earned in the livestock industry. Part of the problem lay in the disastrous winter of 1906–7 and the gradual shrinkage of free range, forcing mixed farmers to employ more labour- and capital-intensive methods. At the same time as the *Toronto Daily Star* was complaining about the poor prices for livestock, and the high price of meat in Ontario, 'the beef commission' was struck jointly by the provinces of Alberta and Manitoba to inquire into all aspects of the marketing of livestock and meat, and to determine whether an illegal combine was manipulating livestock and meat prices (Alberta 1908).

The commission interviewed thirty-five retail butchers and a P. Burns and Company manager, but found it impossible to arrive at consistent estimates of the average profit made on each carcass. Their detailed calculations of the cost of cattle, and the selling price of each one of the primal beef cuts gave gross margins that ranged from 100 per cent to less than 10 per cent. Part of the difficulty was that cattle and beef prices varied over time and between regions. And in some cases it seems that the butchers did not really know how much money they were making. Small butchers incurred considerable costs in the procurement of individual animals. They operated under the credit system in the days before cash and carry sales came to be the rule in retail sales, and their revenues were difficult to determine because of the problem of bad debts (Alberta 1908: 35–7).

Turning to the large packers, it was clear that P. Burns and Company was close to being in a monopoly position in Alberta as it controlled much of the retail trade. It also had enormous influence over livestock prices, thus, it was close to being a monopsony as well. Pat Burns defended the meat-packing establishment without apology:

> There are a lot of people in this country who think it is the right thing to knock the C.P.R., Gordon and Ironside [predecessors of Gordon, Ironside

> and Fares, Winnipeg's largest meat packer] and Burns, but I want to say that we three have made this country, and it is a pity that there are not more Burns and Ironsides in this country. Why if I were to close down tomorrow, in ten days the people in this country would be starving.
>
> Q. Do you not think, Mr Burns, that there would be somebody found to take your place if you went out of business?
>
> A. Not much. They could not do it. This business of mine has taken years to build up. (Quoted in Alberta 1908: 37)

The commission concluded that the retail monopoly enjoyed by P. Burns and Company was a 'very undesirable condition of affairs.' Despite all of the innuendo and the weight of public opinion, the commission admitted that it was unable to present evidence to prove its case and that many of the accusations against Burns could not be substantiated under oath (Alberta 1908: 37). The commission concluded that it had *not* found any irrefutable evidence that a combination existed in restraint of trade in either livestock or meat (Alberta 1908: 46).

Conclusion

Industrial-scale beef packing in Canada lagged behind events south of the border. Large-scale Chicago-based meat packers began killing large volumes of cattle in the 1870s, once railway reefer cars were perfected to ship swinging beef from the Midwest to the eastern seaboard. By the 1880s, the United States was exporting chilled beef to Europe. In Canada there was some movement towards the European public abattoir system before three private sector firms adapted U.S. methods to Canadian conditions and pre-empted calls for a system of publicly owned and operated abattoirs. Canada's earliest large-scale plants to kill cattle and chill beef were significant because their construction was an integral part of a locational shift. With the new plants, slaughter moved away from the public market, the back door of the city butcher shop and the rude shambles on the edge of the city. Large investments in industrial-scale meat packing were attracted towards stockyards or public cattle markets with railway access. The earliest cattle slaughter plants were established, not by the traditional butcher craftsmen and exporters of cured bacon, but by entrepreneurial cattle dealers and ranchers: P. Burns and Company (Calgary 1890), Harris Abattoir (Toronto 1896), and Gallagher-Holman and Gordon, Ironside and Fares (Winnipeg 1902–3).

Four large firms had emerged in Chicago to create a U.S. meat-packing oligopoly (Swift, Armour, Morris, and Hammond) by the mid-1880s. Only one of these early U.S. meat packers (Swift) made a concerted and ultimately successful effort to operate in Canada, leaving the ground open to Canadian firms. Yet it would not be until the late 1920s that the many smaller firms in Canada which functioned as meat packers, retailers, and cattle dealers emerged as truly national firms to create a national industry.

While Canadian meat packers trailed U.S. firms in the scale and scope of their operations, the public distrust of the packers and scandalous allegations about profiteering, adulteration of meat products, collusion on livestock prices and unsanitary conditions were felt in Canada at almost the same time as in the United States. But that is where the parallel ends. In the United States, government commissions looked for and found evidence of all these things, and then the government took regulatory action against them. Canada looked for evidence against its meat packers, but failed to uncover clear and irrefutable evidence to support any of the allegations. Federal meat inspection was established in Canada, but it had more to do with equivalent legislation in the United States than it did with sanitation problems in Canada.

The goal of establishing a dressed beef export trade with Britain never succeeded. In relation to the huge economies of scale and agricultural land resources of the United States, Argentina, and Australia, Canada could not compete in the production of beef cattle, the slaughter and dressing of beef carcasses, or the infrastructure to move chilled beef to tidewater for export.

FIVE

The Kill Floor at Mid-century: From the Knocking Box to the Hot Box

The kill floor at Valley Meats (a pseudonym) is a white-painted room about 18 metres square with a 4-metre ceiling. They only kill on Wednesdays. Other days are devoted to cutting and boning carcasses, stuffing sausages, tending the smoke house, and waiting on customers. On this Wednesday morning, the kill floor has two full-time workers, one part-timer, a provincial inspector, and a visitor from the university. They killed nine market hogs and four big sows from 8:00 to 10:15 before stopping for coffee. The beef kill started at 10:45. Let's follow the second of the seven cattle to be slaughtered today, a two-year-old light brown heifer. At this time of year it is likely that she was culled after failing to reproduce successfully.

11:03 *She enters the knocking box. The knocker loads a single shot .22 rifle and aims it carefully at her forehead from a range of about one metre. The first bullet has little effect, so the knocker reloads and fires again. She collapses, insensible.*

11:04 *A chain is attached to her right hind leg, and she is raised by an electric hoist until her head just clears the floor. The left hind leg kicks feebly.*

11:05 *The knocker sticks the heifer and some twenty litres of blood pour out onto the floor in about forty-five seconds. He skins the face and head of the carcass.*

11:07 *The skinned head is cut off and taken across the room to the inspector.*

The inspector bones out the cheek meat ('It's really not my job but I don't mind doing it') and examines the lymph nodes and the jaw muscles for lesions. The skinned and boned-out head (still containing the eyeballs) is hung on a hook through the jawbone on the head-inspection rack. Because of neuro-muscular activity, the disembodied head continues to twitch and the jaws chew very gently, until the head cools and brain activity finally stops.

11:08 *The carcass is swung up and over to a second worker on a high platform about ten feet off the floor.*
11:09 *Using a knife, he cuts off the fore legs at the carpal joint.*
11:10 *The lower abdomen of the carcass is sliced open terminating with a circular cut around the anus. The rectum is tied off, and the bung is pushed down into the pelvic cavity, known as 'dropping the bung.' (In packinghouse parlance, 'dropping' means to cut off and remove any part of the carcass). The tail is skinned, out and cut off.*
11:11 *The free left leg is skinned, and the heifer's small udder is cut off. Using a knife, the leg is cut off at the hock, about ten centimetres above the hoof.*
11:16 *The delicate process of skinning the hind legs, known as 'legging' continues. When the left leg is completely skinned, the weight of the carcass is transferred from the chain-wrapped right leg to a stainless steel gambrel which is inserted through the 'gam cord' (equivalent to the human Achilles tendon). The gambrel itself is hooked to a traveller hanging from the overhead rail.*
11:22 *Both legs are now skinned, and the hide is skinned off the hips and down to the flanks. This is as low as the 'legger' can reach from his raised platform.*
11:23 *Work stops to assist in knocking and hoisting the next beef to enter the kill floor.*
11:30 *The carcass is slid along the rail to the skinner-eviscerator on a movable hydraulic platform equipped with an air knife. The air knife has a circular blade – imagine a large stainless steel pizza cutter powered by compressed air. The air knife helps to peel back the hide around the loin, ribs, and shoulders.*
11:35 *The hide is completely free of the carcass from rump to shoulders and is draped, inside out, over the neck and onto the floor.*
11:40 *The fore legs are skinned out by hand, the hide is cut away from the neck, and it falls to the floor.*
11:42 *The hide is dragged over to a dumpster. It will be shipped to a hide plant in Cochrane, Alberta, tomorrow where it will be cured prior to export to Asia for tanning.*
11:44 *The abdomen is cut open and twenty kilograms of viscera slump out of the cavity in one membranous package, landing on a stainless steel table. The gutter separates the 'pluck' (heart, liver, and trachea) from the rest of the viscera.*
11:47 *The viscera are pushed off the table into the paunch truck.*
11:50 *The gutter hands the pluck to the provincial inspector who slices open the liver and heart to search for abscesses, lesions, and other symptoms of disease.*
11:51 *Using a large band saw that hangs from the ceiling, the entire carcass is split in half along the back bone.*

11:52 *Minor imperfections are trimmed away from the carcass. The gutter hoses down the carcass and turns the hose on himself to remove blood and bits of hair. The gut bucket is wheeled over to a dumpster destined for the rendering plant.*
11:58 *The hanging carcass is weighed on the overhead track scale, and a warm carcass weight of 667 pounds is recorded.*
11:59 *The carcass is pushed into the chiller or 'hot box,' ending the disassembly process.*

The focus of this chapter is the organization and technology of contemporary cattle killing and dressing of the beef carcass. The overview describes the wide range of slaughter plant production scales from farm slaughter to small provincially inspected plants such as Valley Meats to very large-scale beef plants that kill up to 4,000 cattle per day. Technological change in the postwar period is outlined, highlighting the revolutionary Can-Pak system for on-the-rail dressing of beef carcasses and the adoption of the principle of humane slaughter. The chapter concludes with the inauguration of provincial meat inspection and its impact on the smaller packinghouses.

Valley Meats is typical of hundreds of small provincially inspected packing plants that operate from coast to coast. It operates in a small agricultural service centre of about 5,000 people. It kills only one or two days a week, when a provincial inspector is present, and although it will handle all species, it is geared mainly to hogs and cattle. Valley Meats is proud of the quality of its sausage and smoked meat products. It sells retail from a delicatessen counter at the 'front end' of the plant. The proprietor believes that his competitive edge is individualized service and detailed knowledge of customer preferences; most of the customers are greeted by name.

But in scale and technology Valley Meats is not at all typical of the way most cattle are slaughtered and most beef is dressed. Less than 10 per cent of Canada's total cattle slaughter takes place in provincially inspected plants, and Canada's largest four plants account for 75 per cent of the entire federally inspected cattle kill. It took two hours to kill and dress seven cattle at Valley Meats, while a very large-scale plant would kill and dress about 600 in the same time frame. On a modern mass production kill floor, each of the individual tasks described in the opening vignette would be done by a separate worker in a fixed location on only one species of livestock. With a variety of different jobs performed on different days of the week, these workers are not really proficient at any one of them. They are a pleasant, hard-working, and cooperative team of three. But they also appear a little ham-fisted in a small facility that is less than state-of-the-art.

Alberta regulations permit the use of a rifle for stunning in provincially inspected slaughter plants. On the day of observation, one big steer was subjected to six separate rifle shots in the forehead before it finally collapsed. And after all that, no one was surprised when the inspector condemned the hemorrhaging cheek meat to the paunch truck for rendering. The multi-purpose knocking box serves both hogs and cattle. However, it is really too small for cattle, and the gate mechanism is poorly designed. Waiting cattle clearly see the fate of the animal in front of them, but this does not appear to cause any anxiety. The skinner-eviscerator on the hydraulic platform left several black eyes (circular patches of meat created when the air knife bit too deeply and removed the outer fat covering) and cuts in the hide (where the knife cut too shallowly). He is awkwardly positioned and, as a trainee, he has not yet mastered this difficult job.

Small plants such as these do not often see the cream of the feedlot crop. One four-year-old Holstein cow was apparently culled because she had mastitis. Lying on the floor, her udder was swollen and hard as a soccer ball. The skein of white scar tissue on one of the beef hearts suggested that the animal was not very healthy, perhaps because of a nutritional deficiency. The livers of several of the pigs killed before coffee break showed the tell-tale white spots of a nematode infestation; nematodes are intestinal parasites that thrive when pigs live among an excess of manure.

Although some are of low quality because of inept skinning, the cattle hides will be sold to a hide plant for $60 to 80. All of the other by-products (blood, offal, paunch manure, lower legs, ears, udders, skulls, tails, and trimmings) are destined for rendering. In a small plant such as this, there are insufficient by-products from thirteen hogs and seven cattle to make it economical to sort, clean, and market the fancy meats and edible offal. For example, the cattle feet are invariably rendered in small plants. But in larger-scale packing plants, cattle feet may be specially processed and packed for niche markets such as the West Indies where they are esteemed as a low cost source of beef.

In scale and scope, Valley Meats is similar to small-scale slaughterhouses found in almost every Canadian town and city during the nineteenth century. While the plant lags far behind state-of-the-art methods used in large-scale specialized beef plants, it also uses methods and equipment not yet developed in the nineteenth century. The plant uses an electric chain hoist (in place of a block and tackle), an air-powered knife (instead of a straight butcher's knife), and a band saw (that replaced the hand saw and cleaver). The entire process takes place on the rail; there are no siding beds as described in Chapter 4. A provincial meat inspector is present throughout the kill.

Overview of Cattle Slaughter

Until the 1960s, the scale, technology, and organization of cattle slaughter may be considered in three categories: unregulated farm slaughter, small- and medium-scale packing plants, and large-scale horizontally integrated meat packers. A new category, very large-scale vertically integrated beef specialists, which first began to appear on the scene in the 1960s, will be discussed in Chapter 8.

Farm Slaughter

Stock farmers and ranchers have always had to do some slaughter. Slaughter was an integral part of farm work and subsistence in the nineteenth century and well into the twentieth. In 1934, J.S. McLean, president of Canada Packers, commented, 'Half of the beef sold in Canada never sees the packing house, it is killed in the farmer's yard, or in the villages' (Canada 1934: 2536). As late as 1951, the Census of Agriculture reported 181,000 farm-slaughtered cattle in the previous year, about 16 per cent of the total kill in federally inspected plants in 1950. Animals may break a leg in a gopher hole late on Saturday afternoon, cows may hemorrhage uncontrollably after calving, cattle may gorge themselves on green alfalfa and suffer such severe bloat that euthanasia is the only treatment. This problem is less often confronted by contemporary stock farmers who call in a veterinarian for sick animals and can truck 'cripples' from the most rugged and distant pastures directly to the local abattoir.

Among the many skills possessed by nineteenth-century farmers and ranchers was the ability to kill and dress almost any kind of carcass. Fewer farmers have the skills and inclination for farm slaughter today; however there is still a significant level of farm slaughter and butchering in Canada by farmers who have the facilities to do the job and who derive great satisfaction from being self-reliant. A big chest freezer is essential, as not even the largest farm family can consume a fresh beef before spoilage sets in. In some cases farm-killed beef is used to barter informally with neighbours for the use of pasture land or equipment.

Almost everyone in the country knows someone who will kill or dress out a farm-killed carcass. Such operators may work on an informal and part-time basis and are completely uninspected. In some cases their cutting rooms are well equipped and their butchering skills are a matter of considerable pride. Cutting rooms invariably specialize in custom slaughter in which the owner of the live animal retains ownership and pays an informal fee for converting a live animal into a chilled carcass (typically paid in kind as the custom slaughterhouse takes the hide and by-products in trade for the service of killing) and an additional fee for cutting, grinding, wrapping, and freezing of the carcass. As cutting rooms are not inspected, they may not legally sell meat. In emergencies they may euthanize injured or sick animals for consumption by the owner and dress out game during the hunting season. Cutting rooms are little larger than a single-car garage, and the best equipped have a one-tonne chain hoist, walk-in cooler, and an electric band saw.

Small- and Medium-Scale Meat Packers

Despite the importance of economies of scale in meat packing, the industry remains heterogeneous. Canada has hundreds of small- and medium-scale slaughter and packing plants serving local or niche markets with a proud tradition of quality and service. Most small- and medium-scale packers are provincially inspected and many sell retail. The provincially inspected cattle kill in Canada amounted to 165,400 head in 1999 or 5.0 per cent of the total reported cattle slaughter (Agriculture Canada 2000). Small and mid-sized packers typically kill a mixture of species and combine custom killing with livestock purchased on their own account through a local auction mart or directly from farmers. Small packers such as Valley Meats might kill and dress twenty to fifty animals per week, with a handful of employees. Retail sales are typically a significant part of the firm's revenues. Medium-scale packers operate in a true factory setting with up to 100 employees, a kill capacity of up to 2,000 per week, and sell to both wholesale and retail markets. Small- and medium-sized packers are often family businesses, and employees seem to share many social and family ties, especially in rural Quebec and eastern Ontario.

In spite of the closure of the majority of Canada's larger meat-packing plants during the 1980s because they were too old and too small to compete in a continental meat market, hundreds of small-scale abattoirs and meat processors remain in operation. How have they been able to survive in the face of vigorous competition from large-scale processing plants with lower cost structures? Flexibility is built into small multispecies plants. Workers may be switched from the hog line to the cattle line in a matter of minutes, and the kill floor can respond quickly to changes in the livestock on hand. A worker might be on the kill floor on Mondays, drive the truck for deliveries on Tuesdays and do counter service on Wednesdays. Many of the small packers are found in smaller communities with lower wage rates, especially for family members.

Small- and medium-scale meat packers are traditionally diversified and they kill all species of livestock. One of the common complaints of large-scale packers is the seasonal fluctuation in the supply of livestock. Seasonal variation in hog and cattle slaughter can be easily accommodated in smaller operations by devoting more days of the week to hogs in spring, cull stock in fall, and cattle in winter. The ability to kill all species is a distinct advantage to keep fixed capital equipment in constant operation. A visit to a small packer's cooler reveals an astonishing variety of carcasses. On a typical day one might find sides of local beef with a mixture of lean old cows for grinding and prime steer carcasses for a farmer's freezer; young market hogs for premium hams and huge old sows for grinding into sausage; some tiny calf carcasses which are still dressed with the hide on to prevent the veal from drying out, and occasionally some more exotic carcasses such as llama, ostrich, or even wild boar.

Small provincially inspected plants tend to require large quantities of lean ungraded boneless beef for sale as hamburger and for processing into local specialty products such as sausage. Yet they cannot sell large quantities of the more expensive cuts which find their main markets in the chain stores which will not deal in provincially inspected beef. Thus, provincially inspected plants often require larger quantities of boneless beef for grinding than they can afford to produce in-house, given the mix of cuts on a typical beef carcass. To fill this need, small-scale provincial packers often buy large quantities of boneless 'boxed beef' originating from large-scale federally inspected plants in Canada, the United States, or Australia. Visitors to the cooler of a small meat plant in a rural area may be bemused to see cartons of 85 per cent lean Australian beef sitting beside a steer carcass that was born and raised only a few kilometres away – one of the many ironies of a globalized commodity food chain.

From the producer's point of view, the small packer provides 'one stop shopping' and full service. They will kill, chill, cut, and wrap any form of livestock except poultry. Beef is usually slaughtered on a custom basis, while hogs are more often purchased for processing into specialized processed meat products such as sausage, hams, and cooked or smoked meats. Medium-sized plants typically have a single kill floor with one line dedicated to cattle, which because of the length of carcass, requires a high rail with raised work stations. A lower rail serves for both hogs (which require post mortem immersion in a scalding tank to loosen hair and bristles) and small stock (calves, sheep, lambs, and goats) which must be kept dry. Small-scale livestock producers seem to favour doing business with small provincial packers that have the flexibility to respond to their specialized needs.

Small- and medium-scale packers do not compete in the same markets as large firms. The small-scale packer is able to sell within a regional market of about 200 kilometres. Beyond that distance it is at a disadvantage relative to the large-scale packer whose service is based on buying livestock in meat surplus regions and shipping meat to livestock-deficit regions (Clemen 1923: 797). Small packers sell to consumers who prefer to buy their meats fresh at the point of slaughter, to patronize a small-scale operation, and to pay a small premium for the satisfaction of consuming locally produced livestock. Through a retail front-end, provincially inspected plants may derive as much or more income from retailing as they do from custom slaughter and meat processing. They are invariably locally renowned for some processing specialty such as Black Forest ham or Italian sausage. Snack foods such as pepper sticks or jerky often contribute significantly to revenues. The limitation is that they cannot sell meat wholesale to clients that are across provincial borders. Large chain supermarkets typically advertise themselves as selling only federally inspected meat, thus, provincially inspected packers are unable to penetrate national markets. Instead, they concentrate on small independent meat retailers and some local hotel, restaurant, and institutional (HRI) clients. As institutional clients (e.g., hospitals, retirement homes, and universities) turn to large-scale multinational food service suppliers, and as national chains supplant locally owned restaurants, the HRI market for provincially inspected meat is dwindling.

The medium-scale meat packer was a traditional part of the commercial and industrial infrastructure of virtually every Canadian city. The local packer was the source for fresh and processed meats and the principal market for local livestock producers up to the 1920s. After that time, the market power and the lower cost structure of the big three began to force small and medium packers out of business. Nevertheless, many medium-sized packers have turned their flexibility and the loyalty of niche markets into a powerful competitive advantage. They have managed to adapt and survive the structural changes in the industry, while many of the larger scale integrated packers perished, in spite of their superior cost efficiency.

Large Horizontally Integrated Meat Packers

Once at the top of the meat-packing hierarchy, large-scale integrated meat packers have disappeared, like the dinosaurs. They were horizontally integrated in the sense that they killed all species and all types of livestock (cattle, hogs, and sheep) except poultry. For example, the cattle dressing line would accommodate choice fat cattle, emaciated dairy cows, aging bulls, and any other bovine that might come along. But there was a striking asymmetry in the value that was added to different species. Cattle were killed, chilled, and shipped to retail stores as sides of swinging beef, suspended from a rail. Hogs, on the other hand, were killed, chilled, fabricated into smaller cuts, and much of the meat was cured and smoked or cooked to manufacture a broad line of prepared and packaged meat products. The horizontally integrated packers were organized into separate departments which typically included beef, provisions (hog killing and curing and smoking of bacon), small stock (sheep, lambs, and calves), cooked meats and sausage, rendering and edible oils, soap, fertilizer, and feed. The large horizontally integrated packers were federally inspected, thus, they could sell across both provincial and international borders, as well as to the supermarket chain stores.

While the traditional horizontally integrated packinghouse killed all species, many of them started out killing only hogs as that was the input for their principal line of business in smoked ham and bacon products for export. In western Canada some small firms specialized in fresh dressed beef. But as small firms grew large, they eventually added other species to their product line, to act as a hedge against low prices and to gain flexibility. For example, Calgary Packers was built adjacent to the Calgary Stock Yards in 1938 as a dedicated beef plant. The firm grew during the Second World War, and it added a hog killing line in 1951 before it was acquired by Canada Packers in 1955 (Canada 1961: 360–1). Twenty years later the plant reverted to its specialized beef processing mandate, as the trend to dedicated single species plants took hold. J.M. Schneider got its start in pork sausages, and its competitive edge was always its branded pork products. But it diversified into processed beef products in 1932 and began to slaughter cattle in 1933. Schneider's continued killing cattle until 1989 when it reverted to its original specialty in hog killing and pork processing (J.M. Schneider 1989). While a few small multispecies federally inspected packers remain in operation, the clear trend is towards specialization in a single species, age, and grade. Thus, the large-scale horizontally integrated plant has become obsolete, and most have been closed although a few have been converted to specialize in a single species.

Most of Canada's metropolitan centres had at least one packinghouse of substantial size, and many had a packinghouse district linked directly to a stockyards and livestock exchange. The large-scale horizontally integrated plants were invariably sited adjacent to a railway line. In fact, large plants required three separate rail spurs: one for livestock adjacent to pens and the kill floor, one for chilled edible products adjacent to a loading dock and the coolers, and one with access to the rendering plant for inedibles such as hides, paunch manure, bone and blood meal from rendering, inedible tallow, and brown grease. Packinghouses that were located on the edge of the city in the first decade of the twentieth century were hemmed in by other urban land uses by the 1980s.

Most of the large-scale horizontally integrated plants in Canada were built between 1910 and 1940, and as they became obsolete in the 1980s, the redevelopment value of their large central land parcels made closure and demolition an attractive proposition. This is a pity, as the older packing plants were fascinating industrial structures. They were multi-story plants in which the main direction of flow was up and then down, and unlike modern-day plants, as little as possible was moved horizontally. Livestock generated potential energy by walking up long inclined ramps to reach the kill floor at the top level of the plant. This was converted to kinetic energy as gravity powered the downward flow of products and by-products created in the disassembly process. Swift Canadian completed a new six-storey plant in St-Boniface in 1939 which was typical of the multilevel packinghouse. The top story was devoted to sausage, cooked meats, and canning. Cattle and hogs walked up long, inclined ramps from the livestock pens to the fifth-level kill floor where carcasses were dressed. Holding coolers, smoke ovens, and the fancy meat department were immediately below on the fourth floor. Pork cutting took place on the third floor, while rendering tanks and the lard refinery were on the second. Curing vats for ham and bacon and the hide cellars were on the lowest level.

Virtually all of these old buildings include a series of extensions that seem to reach in all directions, each with a slightly different architectural style. The J.M. Schneider plant in Kitchener marches up Courtland Street with a series of visible expansions since it was first built in 1924. Demolished in 1996, the central portion of Canada Packers' plant in Toronto's stockyards district dated from 1930, clearly newer than the turn of the century structures at either end that had formerly housed the Harris Abattoir and Gunns Limited. The Peterborough plant of Canada Packers (previously operated by Matthews-Blackwell Packers) was a classic industrial abattoir built of brick and masonry complete with its own water tower before demolition in 1964. Completed in 1936, the Edmonton plant of Canada Packers was built of reinforced concrete with stark red brick curtain walls which won the gold medal at the Toronto Chapter Exhibition of Architecture and Allied Arts in the Bauhaus period which presaged the minimalism of the international style (Arthur 1937).

Technological Change on the Kill Floor

Beginning in the late 1940s, technological changes led to significant kill-floor developments. Canada Packers developed its Can-Pak beef kill methods which spread throughout Canada and the United States, introducing continuous flow technology from the knocking box to the hot box. In the 1950s, more humane slaughter methods were adopted and regulations prohibited sticking conscious or semiconscious animals. Finally, a tainted beef scandal in 1962 and the growing desire for greater quality control in chain supermarkets made federal inspection status a necessity for most industrial-scale packinghouses.

In the early twentieth century technological change on the kill floor was slow and incremental. U.S. meat packing had been at the forefront of the mass-production revolution in the late nineteenth century, but only modest productivity gains and technological developments took place in the first half of the twentieth century. Between 1890 and 1954, output per person-hour grew slowly at an average 0.5 per cent per year in meat packing compared with 2.2 per cent for all manufacturing (Brody 1964: 241–2). The source of this productivity improvement was partially from reduced capital inputs and partially from increased output from a unit volume of livestock. The increased efficiency in the use of livestock resulted from more complete use of the carcass and by-products and production of more value added items in the meat-packing plants which had formally been the preserve of the retail butcher (Ruttan 1954).

After the Second World War a variety of new methods and machinery such as captive bolt stunners, mechanical air-powered knives, mechanical hide skinners, electronic slicers, and weigh scales began to appear. Labour productivity in U.S. meat packing jumped by 24 per cent between 1947 and 1954 and by nearly 15 per cent between 1954 and 1958 (Page 1998: 281). As demand for meat lagged behind productivity growth, meat-packing employment began to fall, and postwar technological change became the impetus for the decentralization of the U.S. meat-packing industry, a trend not felt in Canada until some twenty years later.

Continuous On-the-Rail Dressing of Beef: The Can-Pak System

One of the principal sources of these productivity improvements was the development of 'on-the-rail-dressing,' a Canadian innovation. The essence of on-the-rail dressing, or the Can-Pak system, as it came to be known in Canada, was to hoist the animal immediately after it was stunned and keep it moving continuously on an overhead rail past stationary workers positioned at the height most advantageous to their particular task in a highly specialized division of labour. The exhausting stooping over prone carcasses by floorsmen, time lost in walking around carcasses on blood-slick floors, the danger of falling overhead trolleys, and the time loss and expense of raising, lowering, and reraising carcasses were eliminated. In one small-scale combination hog–beef kill floor in Burlington, Ontario, production per person-hour using the Can-Pak system was twice that of the older floor and hoist technology. Production could be doubled from fifteen to thirty cattle per hour simply by adding more labour and work platforms and running the line faster; no additional floor area was required (*Food in Canada* 1964). The Can-Pak system reduced the time elapsed from the knocking box to the cooler from fifty minutes to thirty minutes (Canada 1961: 379). Finally, the Can-Pak apparatus took up less space in the plant for a given carcass throughput.

The system was developed with considerable experimentation after an extensive time and motion study of the carcass dressing process at Canada Packers' St-Boniface plant, among the newest plants in the corporate chain. In 1951, the St-Boniface plant was acclaimed as the first packing plant anywhere with a complete and operational on-the-rail dressing system (Force 1951; Rowe 1952). By 1952, Canada Packers had installed on-the-rail dressing systems in its large-scale Toronto and Montreal plants as well. Continuous on-the-rail dressing was also retrofitted at Swift Canadian plants in St-Boniface, Edmonton, and Calgary by 1964. As late as 1962, Can-Pak was one of only two on-the-rail dressing systems in use in the United States (*Canadian Food Industries* 1962: 59; Logan and King 1962: 25). But the Can-Pak technology was not as economically efficient at production scales of less than 600 to 700 cattle per week (Canada 1961: 379) It was not installed in Canada Packers' smaller-capacity plants such as Charlottetown, Hull, Peterborough, or Vancouver which were among the first to be closed when production capacity was rationalized.

The knocking box was essentially unchanged except that by the 1950s captive bolt stunners were replacing the knocking hammer. Instead of shackling both legs above the ankle prior to hoisting and sticking, only the left leg was shackled above the knee. Thus, the right hind leg was unencumbered and immediately available for skinning by a 'legger,' an operative equipped with a power saw to remove the hind foot (in place of a knife or cleaver). The legger stood on the 'high bench,' raised six feet above the floor, the most comfortable and efficient position for this task. At the same time, the front feet were removed with power shears by a worker down at floor level. Once the right hind leg was skinned, a hook was inserted through the gam cord and the weight of the carcass was power hoisted to a heavy-duty trolley attached to the overhead dressing rail. The weight now shifted to the right leg and the left leg could be unshackled as the carcass was detached from the bleeding rail. A second legger skinned out the left leg and removed its hoof. 'Dropping the bung' was accomplished by cutting a circle around the anus, freeing the sphincter from the surrounding hide. A snug elastic o-ring, the size of a Cheerio, was used to cinch the rectum and avoid contamination of the carcass by intestinal contents.

Opening and rimming the front was done by a worker on a hydraulic platform that could be raised or lowered to accommodate cattle of different sizes, while maintaining an upright position for the worker. A 'weasand hook' was used to tie off the weasand (esophagus) to prevent contamination by stomach contents. The aitch bone was cut with power shears which were faster than the hand saw and made a cleaner-looking carcass. Once the hide was partially skinned away from the legs and rimmed around the abdomen and belly, a mechanical hide puller was used to peel off the rest of the hide. The mechanical hide puller was a critical part of the Can-Pak system and many different designs were used. The early models required hand skinning and removal of the head before the hide was pulled up, risking contamination of the carcass from 'tag' (clumps of sticky wet manure clinging to the hide). Later models pulled the hide down from the rump all the way down to the nose which reduced contamination.

After removal of the head, the sawing of the brisket bone (formerly done on the floor with a hand saw or cleaver) was accomplished by a worker on a low platform using a reciprocating saw with guard to avoid piercing the paunch. Once the carcass had been opened, evisceration or 'dropping the gut' was accomplished with one deft knife stroke to fully open the carcass yet avoid piercing the viscera and contamination of the carcass by stomach and intestinal contents. After a few more knife cuts of the mesentery, the weight of the viscera itself was sufficient for the internal organs to slump out of the body cavity in one large intact mass. The viscera and pluck were placed on a moving viscera table to be examined as they passed government inspectors. The moving table was synchronized with the movement of the carcass on the evisceration rail, so that if a carcass were condemned during post mortem inspection, the corresponding head and viscera could be condemned as well.

The carcass was then split into two sides using a band saw to bisect the vertebrae precisely down the centre line. The two halves of the spinal cord were removed and the fins of the vertebrae were scribed with a hand saw and pounded back. Urogenital organs were carefully removed during hide removal and went into the rendering tank with other inedible offal (pizzles and testicles are now recovered for sale in export markets).

The dressing process concluded with a final trimming to remove residual bits of hide, bruises, blood clots, and any contaminated material that might cling to the carcass. A skilled trimmer could correct many minor imperfections in dressing and improve the appearance of a carcass by pulling the fell over bare places and setting it with skewers. The carcass was hosed down to remove blood and bone dust. The two sides of the carcass would then be shifted to a beam scale that measured the combined hanging weight on the rail. Each of the sides was then covered in a hot wet muslin shroud which was wrapped tightly around the rump and loin and held in place with half a dozen stainless steel pins on each side. Finally, the carcass was then pushed into the cooler to begin a twelve- to fifteen-hour period of chilling from approximately 100 degrees Fahrenheit to 34 degrees. The next day the shroud would be removed and the side transferred from the hot box to the sales cooler which was painted white and brightly lighted to show off the beef to best advantage.

Until the advent of boxed beef, the appearance of the carcass was extremely important as the dressed side of beef was the finished product. It was vital that the manual removal of the hide not take off any fat especially in areas such as the lower back where the fat tends to be quite soft and may adhere to the hide and tear away from the carcass giving rise to 'peeled loins' which lowered the value of the side. Similarly the scribing and pounding down of the fins (spinous processes of the thoracic vertebrae) was a purely cosmetic process to give a broader appearance to the rib and chuck and improve the marketability of the side. Shrouding of the finished carcass came into general use in the 1920s. The subcutaneous fat covering on an unshrouded carcass becomes knobby and uneven as it cools, making the side less visually attractive. The tightly wrapped muslin shroud forced the fat to cool in a smooth, almost creamy layer and helped to bleach the fell, giving it a bright white colour.

Other than the ingenious design and engineering of the mechanical hide puller and the increased use of mechanized butchering tools, the Can-Pak system was innovative as an application of the principles of time and motion study to simplify a complex and dangerous series of tasks. With continuous rail dressing the work became less arduous and less hazardous. By presenting the carcass to each worker at the most convenient and comfortable height for the task to be performed, the Can-Pak system resulted in a higher quality carcass. By holding the workers stationary while the carcass was mechanically moved, the amount of walking on wet and slippery floors was reduced.

While the conventional bed dressing technology using siding beds had gone out of use in large-scale beef plants by 1960, it remains in operation in some small-scale plants up to the present day. In the 1960s, the conventional method using two or three siding beds side-by-side, offered lower unit costs up to about fifty head per hour. At higher scales of output, completely conveyorized rail systems had declining unit costs up to a scale of 120 head per hour (Hammons 1961; Logan and King 1962: 104).

Regulatory Developments in Slaughter Technology

In Chapter 4 the role of slaughterhouse reform was highlighted to show its importance in the development of industrial-scale meat packing, especially for export markets. The potential entry of a network of publicly owned and federally inspected abattoirs was pre-empted by the rapid development of private sector industrial-scale meat packing at the turn of the century. Fifty years later new concerns prompted calls for further regulation, encouraging the packers to adopt new practices, and motivating the smallest to invest and expand or shut down, further concentrating the industry in the hands of the largest federally inspected plants.

Humane Handling and Slaughter

Public concern regarding the humane handling of livestock has roots that go back to the early nineteenth-century animal protection movement in Britain. Humanitarian concerns were bolstered by the clear link between ante mortem animal abuse and financial losses through spoiled meat. Ante mortem abuse was costing money.

The humane slaughter principle requires all food animals to be stunned into unconsciousness before any blood is drawn. The animal should die of exsanguination without ever regaining consciousness. This principle was being advocated in Britain, following the lead of many European countries, in the late 1890s (Cash 1907; Harrap and Douglas 1901: 134). A long-handled hammer was in general use in nineteenth-century Britain, while Germans favoured a pole-axe. By the first decade of the twentieth century several different types of captive bolt pistols and specialized firearms for stunning confined animals were commonly used in Europe.

But humane slaughter in Canada lagged behind developments in Europe. In 1907, the beef commission examined slaughterhouse conditions in Alberta and Manitoba. The commission was quite satisfied with cleanliness, but it was appalled by the methods then used for stunning cattle:

> We desire to draw the attention of the government particularly to the cruel treatment to which the animals are subjected while being stunned. The animals are run into cages holding one to each cage, and after the doors are properly secured, a man with an instrument resembling an axe, except that it is pointed where the axe is blunt, walks on a beam above the

> animals and administers the fatal blow. In this operation the treatment which many an animal receives before losing its senses is simply appalling. If the animals be struck in the proper place one light blow is sufficient to relieve it from all further pain, but we were present when it took as many as seven or eight blows on different portions of the head to bring the animal off its feet. After this a chain was attached to the hind feet of the animal, and when it had been strung to the ceiling the final blow was administered by a man slightly more expert at his business. Such treatment as this can be attributed to no other source than carelessness on the part of the employers who have the work in hand. We have given a description of what happened in the case of one animal, but hundreds of innocent beasts which go to our slaughter houses are doomed to a similar fate. (Alberta 1908: 37)

The commission argued for legislation to regulate slaughter methods for two reasons: the cruelty to animals that they had witnessed had no place in a 'civilized' society, and it was recognized even then that brutal treatment has a detrimental impact on meat quality.

Bruising of cattle may be caused by trampling after animals fall down on slippery floors in trucks and stock cars, from overcrowding in loading and unloading chutes, and from goring by cattle which have not been dehorned prior to shipment. Whipping and beating by animal handlers is another source of contusions. Bruises have to be trimmed off the carcass, reducing their weight and value. According to one survey, 15 per cent of hogs showed symptoms of rough treatment. The monetary loss from the cutting out of bruised tissue and scarring of cattle carcasses was estimated at $1.5 million in 1925 (Canada Minister of Agriculture 1925). In 1933, Canada Packers observed that only a small percentage of hogs marketed were of a quality eligible for the British Wiltshire market, but of those, a considerable proportion were disqualified because of the bruising from mishandling (Gibbons 1951). Cattle were treated no better according to a former supervisor of the Edmonton livestock market: 'In one particular case, a trucker was engaged to load and transport two cows to an Edmonton plant. The farmer failed to provide suitable loading facilities and one animal was badly beaten in an effort to make it jump into the truck. Its condition was evident and the plant accepted it only "subject to inspection," ... I checked the carcass in the killing floor; it was a mass of jellied bruises and the entire carcass was condemned. Both the farmer and trucker were convicted and fined for cruelty' (Quoted in Kenney 1949: 23).

The development of more humane cattle slaughter in Canada was a long time coming and it followed developments in hog slaughter. Mechanical stunning devices for hogs are not very practical because of the anatomy of the porcine skull. Up to the 1950s, the universal killing method for hogs in Canada was to shackle the fully conscious animal by the hind feet, hoist it, and stick the thrashing and squealing pig while it hung upside down. This was dangerous, dirty, and noisy work. In the United States, a system for carbon dioxide anesthetization was developed in 1952, ensuring that hogs were unconscious prior to sticking (Manning 1956; Murphy 1952).

Canadian packers were slow to adopt this innovative system, until the mistreatment of hogs in the 1950s became the focus of media attention and a test case in the courts (Leckie and Morris 1980: 73–4). A public inquiry concerning cruelty to animals in Toronto's Municipal Abattoir provided a further incentive for the regulation of slaughter. Allegations that kill-floor workers used meat hooks to drive cattle and allowed shackled cattle to hang for several minutes before kosher kills were completed, and trampling of cattle in the knocking box provided gruesome testimony and created great public opprobrium (Toronto 1958). A joint committee of the Meat Packers Council of Canada and the Ontario Society for the Prevention of Cruelty to Animals (OSPCA) was struck in 1957, and it submitted its final report late that year. The committee arrived at the principle that had been advocated in Britain fifty years earlier: 'That no animal being slaughtered for food purposes (excepting ritual slaughter) should be shackled, hoisted, hung, cut bled, or scalded without first being rendered unconscious and insensible to pain in a humane manner' (Cash 1907; *Food in Canada* 1957: 27).

Just as Cash had discovered in Britain, in 1907, the committee found that captive bolt pistols, already in use in about two-thirds of the Canadian plants it visited, were the simplest and least expensive means of stunning cattle prior to slaughter. Canada Packers had been among the first to experiment with captive bolt pistols in 1954. Captive bolt pistols remain in use in most cattle plants today. The captive bolt pistol (commonly called a stunner) uses a 0.22 cap or a blast of compressed air to propel a steel bolt. In the most commonly used pneumatically powered penetrating bolt stunners, the bolt is a steel cylinder 1.5 centimetres in diameter which breaks through the cranium and penetrates about 10 centimetres into the skull.

In 1959, the Canadian government passed the Humane Slaughter of Food Animals Act which required compliance with slaughter regulations by December 1960. The legislation, applying to both federally and provincially inspected slaughter plants, was motivated by the Meat Packers Council/OSPCA committee report and many of its provisions were taken directly from its recommendations. (Leckie and Morris 1980: 73). The Canadian legislation also reflected similar legislation passed only six months previously in the United States. Among other provisions, the act prohibited hanging an animal by the leg for slaughter before being stunned into unconsciousness using electric current or carbon dioxide gas (principally for hogs), a mechanical device such as a captive bolt pistol or rifle, or a manual blow to the head (typically using a hammer) for lambs and calves. By December 1959, Canada Packers had installed carbon dioxide stunning facilities on its three largest hog kill floors: Toronto, Winnipeg, and Edmonton. Compliance with the 1959 legislation for cattle slaughter was more straightforward, since captive bolt pistols were inexpensive and no other modifications were required if the plant already had a knocking box. By 1960, Canada Packers was using captive bolt stunners for cattle in all but one of its plants. Ammunition costs varied since some animals required as many as three shots (costing 1.5 cents each) before becoming unconscious with an average of 1.25 shots per animal (*Food in Canada* 1960a). Manual stunning (using a hammer) was permissible for small stock (calves and lambs) until 1993.

Kosher Slaughter

Most Jewish dietary laws are set out in the biblical books of Leviticus and Deuteronomy. Prohibited foods include any four-footed animal that does not chew its cud (e.g., pigs) or that does not have cloven hooves (e.g., horses or rabbits); blood, fat, and sinew; diseased animals; and any animal that has not been killed in accordance with Jewish laws of slaughter. The laws of slaughter are spelled out in detail in the Talmud. *Shechitah* (ritual slaughter) must be performed by a trained *shochet* (ritual slaughter craftsman). The shochet uses a knife with a straight blade about eighteen inches long. The blade must be razor sharp and without the slightest nick. Both carotid arteries and the windpipe must be severed in a single slicing stroke, without any downward pressure and without the wound closing back over the blade during the cut.

After slaughter and drainage, the shochet conducts a *bedikah* (examination) to verify that the animal was healthy and rejects any animal with a discoloured brain, ulcerated stomach, or diseased lungs. The butcher performs *porshen* (separation) in which all of the arteries and sinews are removed. As its sinews are difficult to remove, the hindquarter is not normally used by the kosher trade. Koshering refers to the removal of blood. This is accomplished by soaking the meat in water, coating it with salt, and allowing the blood to drain and then washing to remove all traces of salt. Kosher beef has to be chilled more rapidly than conventional beef so that it may be cut the day of slaughter and delivered for retail sale within twenty-four hours (Institute of American Meat Packers 1925: 46–8; Trepp 1980: 58).

Until The Humane Slaughter of Food Animals Act took effect in 1960, kosher slaughter was performed on cattle which were hobbled and immobilized with ropes and rolled onto their sides on the ground or were shackled and suspended by the hind legs. Needless to say, the cattle thrashed violently, making it difficult to consistently administer the ritual cut in exactly the right position across the throat and slowing exsanguination. But in 1960, Canada Packers developed a new type of slaughter pen and procedure to comply with Canadian humane slaughter and meat inspection legislation, and simultaneously fulfil all of the Talmudic requirements of shechitah. The Can-Pak kosher restraining pen confined the animal on its feet, but forced its head up and forwards so that the throat was exposed and fully extended. The shochet could then deliver a swift, clean, and true ritual cut through the neck from ear to ear, instantly severing all blood vessels and causing rapid death. The new method was safer for the schochet since the animal was confined and suffered no ante mortem distress prior to exsanguination. In addition, the probability of a misplaced and ineffective ritual cut was greatly reduced (Barrat 1958; *Canadian Food Industries* 1960; *Food in Canada* 1960a: 1960b).

If kosher slaughter is properly executed, cattle display little or no reaction after their throats are cut, and sensibility is lost within two minutes (Daly 1988; Grandin and Regenstein 1994b). Calm cattle collapse within ten to fifteen seconds, especially when the knife stroke is rapid and decisive. A slow knife stroke is more likely to stretch the arteries, slowing the rate of exsanguination. Excited cattle tend to remain conscious for a longer period, underlining the need for gentle treatment and carefully designed cattle handling facilities up to and including the restraining device.

The killing area in and around a restraining pen used for kosher slaughter becomes quite bloody. Provided the previously slaughtered cattle were calm at the time of the cut, this in itself does not appear to upset subsequent animals. Cattle will voluntarily enter a restraint device that is covered with blood and some may even lick or drink it (Grandin 1993b: 292). But severely agitated cattle emit a fear pheromone, a social hormone which communicates fear to other cattle. This induces a chain reaction and all subsequent animals in the restraining device also become fearful. Thus, the design of slaughter facilities and calm, quiet handling seems to be more important to humane slaughter than the actual method of dispatch.

Tainted Meat and Inauguration of Provincial Inspection

The popular press has never been reticent about covering tainted meat exposés in gruesome detail. A series of meat scandals hit the Canadian popular press in 1962, prompting new standards for meat in the plant and at the retail counter. In February 1962, at the height of the annual convention of the Meat Packers Council of Canada, the Consumers' Association of Canada presented its concerns about the illegal sale of 'tainted meat.' For instance, a Peterborough County man was charged with selling meat from dead animals, ostensibly presented for use as pet food (*Globe and Mail* 1962a: 9). Seven days later, an eighteen-year-old in Walkerton, in Bruce County, Ontario, was charged under the Food and Drug Act and convicted of selling dead animals as food (*Globe and Mail* 1962b: 8). The Consumers' Association of Canada alleged that the Meat Packers Council had not done enough to bring the problem of uninspected and tainted meat to the attention of government. Many of the people in the industry were aware of these practices, yet took no action until the issue was publicized by whistle-blowing consumers. Later in 1962, a small Ontario meat processor was accused of combining and grinding uninspected cow and horse meat, while a Victoria butcher was accused of selling ten pounds of abscessed beef liver (*Canadian Labour* 1962). Although some 80 per cent of the meat sold in Canada was produced in federally inspected plants, only 5 per cent of Canada's 2,149 slaughter plants in 1959 were inspected. The source of tainted meat problems was the large majority of small uninspected plants that produced a small fraction of the total meat supply (Canada 1961: 97; *Winnipeg Free Press* 1962: 11).

All of the major chain stores and major retail meat markets began to advertise that they bought only federally inspected meat bearing the 'Canada Approved' stamp. Uninspected local suppliers to the major chain stores were suddenly cut off from their high-volume markets, and dozens of plants were obliged to meet federal standards or go out of business. The tainted meat scandal disrupted meat marketing and was responsible for a rush to meet federal meat standards. Fifty new meat plants became federally inspected in 1962. Hoffman Meats of Kitchener was one among many smaller packing plants which had only been inspected by a city veterinarian. It absorbed substantial losses as sales volume dropped and capital spending projects were rushed through to raise the plant to federal standards. For example, the finish and slope on the plant's floors required upgrading, new floor drains were required, walls were refinished, and wooden trolleys and shelves were replaced with stainless steel. By meeting federal inspection standards Hoffman Meats was able to expand its hog-processing operation, and it remained a force in Ontario markets until its acquisition by Canada Packers in 1983. But for many smaller plants, the demand for federal standards was the impetus to go out of business or to withdraw from slaughter and meat-processing operations (*Food in Canada* 1962a, 1962b).

In 1964, Ontario announced that it would prohibit the sale of uninspected meat by all except small farmers effective January 1965. There were some 400 uninspected plants in Ontario in 1964, and few could qualify for inspection without substantial renovation or, in most cases, building entirely new plants (*Food in Canada* 1964). In 1967, Quebec implemented a meat inspection system that subjected all meat for sale in the province to provincial inspection requirements. In 1965, there were 1,100 abattoirs in Quebec. About 20 per cent of these had closed by 1967, while eighty new plants were designed and built to satisfy provincial meat inspection standards (Cosh 1967).

In Alberta local kill plants were not regulated until the advent of the Alberta Meat Inspection Act in 1973. Unlike federally inspected plants, provincially inspected facilities in Alberta may accept the carcasses of animals slaughtered on the farm in emergency situations, and portions of farm-slaughtered hogs for curing and smoking. As in other provinces, retail meat sales are permitted from a provincially inspected plant.

Beef Inspection in Federally Inspected Slaughter Plants

An ante mortem inspection within twenty-four hours of slaughter is mandatory under present federal meat inspection regulations. The visual inspection is designed to identify animals which might be afflicted with a disease making them unfit for human consumption, which pose a threat to the health of plant workers, which have been recently treated with a pharmaceutical, or which will require special handling for humane reasons. Among many obvious symptoms, inspectors look for animals which are unable to stand up ('downers'), crippling deformities of limbs or lesions in the hide, abnormal secretions from the eyes, nose, or mouth, and ocular squamous cell carcinoma ('cancer eye').

Based on this inspection, animals may proceed for normal slaughter, be set aside for rest or treatment prior to reinspection, be set aside for separate slaughter (typically at the end of the day's kill to avoid contamination), or in rare cases, they may be tagged 'condemned.' Condemned animals are immediately slaughtered in situ in the animal receiving pens and, together with 'found deads,' removed directly to the inedible section of the plant where the entire carcass goes to rendering ('into the tank'). If animals are so crippled that they cannot be humanely moved, permission may be given to stun animals in the holding pens so that they may be transferred painlessly into the plant for bleeding.

A strain of brucellosis found in cattle may be passed on to humans. The disease is positively diagnosed when an agglutinization test causes a blood reaction; thus, the afflicted cattle are typically described as 'reactors.' Bovine tuberculosis is detected, as in humans, by a reaction to tuberculin injection. Bovine tuberculosis may also be detected post mortem upon inspection of the mesenteric and lymph nodes and organs such as the lungs, liver, and spleen. Canadian cattle have been free of both brucellosis and tuberculosis since the mid-1980s. In the unlikely event that either disease were detected ante mortem, the animal would be separated from other cattle, slaughtered outside the plant, and the carcass destroyed.

Post mortem inspection begins with the head. Lymph nodes are examined and incised (sliced) to identify any irregularities, and the jaw muscles are dissected to detect parasitic lesions. Virtually every organ of the thoracic and abdominal cavity is visually examined and palpated to detect abscesses, tumours, or other signs of disease. The liver is incised and carefully examined for parasitic liver flukes. At least four deep incisions are made into the heart to inspect for parasitic lesions. The carcass itself and especially the joints and outer muscular surfaces are also inspected for signs of disease, tumours, lesions, or arthritis.

The decision tree for the many conditions that may affect animals ante mortem or carcasses post mortem is complex. The ultimate decision is whether to approve or condemn the entire carcass or parts of it. Depending on the nature of the condition, condemned material is either sent for rendering or, perhaps, used for pet food. However, many slaughter plants are not close enough to a pet food processor to make this worthwhile, and in such cases condemned materials and carcasses go straight into the tank for rendering.

Conclusion

In terms of both size and livestock specialization, meat packing is a heterogeneous sector. Competitive forces and technological changes such as the Can-Pak system of continuous on-the-rail dressing of the beef carcass favoured the construction of ever larger plants to take advantage of economies of scale, yet a considerable number of small-scale packers remain in operation thanks to their flexibility and ability to serve niche markets such as custom slaughter.

Government regulation transformed the Canadian kill floor, most notably in the requirement for captive bolt pistols, but not before public awareness and concerns about animal welfare became the driving force in changing the way the packers treated their living raw material. Commissions of inquiry and ensuing legislation caused packinghouses to adopt humane handling and slaughter practices by the 1960s. When a minority of small-scale packers and butchers were caught misrepresenting and adulterating meats, the large-scale packers were no doubt delighted to see the advent of provincial meat inspection. Many of their small-scale competitors were obliged to comply or exit the market. While this certainly improved sanitation standards and the public image of meat quality, it also contributed to a further increase in the concentration of the industry, limiting the choices available to both consumers and producers, and thus, the modern kill floor remained in the hands of a meat-processing oligopoly and oligopsony.

SIX

Canada's Beef Trust: The Rise and Fall of the Big Three

The two largest packing companies in the United States, Swift and Company and Armour and Company, do not together account for as high a proportion of the packing business in that country, as Canada Packers, Ltd. alone accounts for in Canada. This dominating position of the company emphasizes the natural disparity in bargaining power between the packer and the primary producer and facilitates unfair competition in the distribution of packing house products by encouraging price discrimination and other uneconomic competitive practices.

Canada 1935, *Report of the Royal Commission on Price Spreads:* 59–60

The contemporary oligopolistic structure of the Canadian meat-packing industry and the significance of the structural changes in the industry cannot be fully appreciated without understanding the background of the big three: Canada Packers, Burns and Company, and Swift Canadian. These three companies emerged in the late 1920s as a national oligopoly with powerful influence in the cattle commodity markets, beef retail markets, and industrial labour markets until the 1980s. They were referred to as the 'big three,' imitating the terminology used to refer to the big five meat packers in the United States (Perry and Kegley 1989) and sometimes as the 'beef trust,' the epithet coined by Upton Sinclair (1904) to compare the market dominance of the big meat packers with John D. Rockefeller's nineteenth-century monopoly over oil refining and distribution.

Canadians have been wary of the meat-packing oligopoly ever since the early twentieth-century revelations about the manipulation of livestock and meat prices in western Canada (Alberta 1908) and profiteering by William Davies in Toronto (Bliss 1978). Although based in the United States, polemics such as in the book *Prime Rip* (Swanson and Schultz 1982) and allegations by investigative television journalism programs such as *Sixty Minutes* (CBS) or *Dateline* (NBC) add to the public relations problem of meat packing on both sides of the border. The Canadian government and judiciary made attempts to curb the big three's market power, but none of their attempts at competitive regulation was very successful. Powerful agroindustrialists are obvious targets for both producer and consumer groups, but they have been almost invincible to a barrage of bad press and a long succession of government commissions. Yet they appear as hapless victims in the face of changes in consumer dietary preferences, technological change, and the aggressive strategies of entrepreneurial competitors.

Beginning in 1976, per capita beef consumption began to decline in Canada, creating overcapacity in the industry. Only one year earlier the cattle cycle entered a steeply declining phase. These two factors triggered a shake-out in the packing industry in the mid-1980s that saw the disintegration and collapse of the big three. Although technological change and developments in the labour market for the meat-packing sector should not be gainsaid, the fortunes of the industry have always depended on exogenous market developments: wartime demand, cattle supplies and commodity prices, and consumer tastes for red meat.

By 1990, Canada's big three had contracted dramatically and by 2000 all vestige of the original firms had disappeared. Swift Canadian divested its holdings from 1970 to 1980, and all of its former plants have been shut down leaving the Swift brands and trademarks as the only asset of lasting value. With Swift Canadian out of the picture, meat packing became one of the few manufacturing industries in Canada with foreign controlled firms accounting for less than 5 per cent of the industry's sales in 1980 (Ruston 1983: 23). Canada Packers closed all of its eastern slaughter plants and was taken over and merged to form Maple Leaf Foods in 1992 which then sold the remaining western beef plants. Only the newest of fourteen former Canada Packers' meat-packing plants remains in operation, under new ownership. Burns Foods went through several changes in ownership, and closed all but two of its kill plants before divesting the remaining assets to Maple Leaf Foods in 1996. None of the eight former Burns Meats plants remains in operation as a beef plant. The decline and fall of the once mighty big three forms the backdrop for the changing geography of meat packing in Canada.

Historical Geography of the Big Three

This chapter picks up the corporate history of Canadian meat packing in the late 1920s, just after the merger that created Canada Packers and Pat Burns's divestiture of his firm which was renamed Burns and Company. It was an inauspicious time for meat packing, as international markets had collapsed almost overnight and every meat-packing firm was in some financial difficulty. In the midst of the Great Depression, the meat packers received a reprieve in the form of access to the British market, the very same source that had given birth to the industry in the 1890s and renewed hope during the Great War. The Ottawa Agreements of 1932, in which Britain granted Canadian packers a very favourable quota for their exports, was a beacon for pork processors in the darkest days of the Great Depression. In the midst of generalized unemployment and industrial retrenchment, the meat-packing sector enjoyed a boom. Closed plants were re-opened, and small domestic-scale packers reoriented themselves to export markets by investing and upgrading provincially or municipally inspected plants to become federally inspected. For example, J.M. Schneider's in Kitchener became federally inspected in 1933, while Canada Packers and Swift Canadian built new plants in western Canada.

Canadian meat packers benefited from the British bacon trade during the Second World War just as they had during the First World War. And just when the traditional bacon trade pattern between Britain and Denmark resumed, shutting out Canadian pork exports, Canada lifted its wartime embargo on meat exports to the United States in 1948. Cattle and beef exports skyrocketed until Saskatchewan's aftosa epidemic shut the trade down almost overnight in 1952. Shipments of canned meats to the most devastated parts of Europe through the United Nations Relief and Rehabilitation Agency was a further source of post-war growth. The domestic market was also growing rapidly, as the level of beef consumption in the Canadian diet grew rapidly to reach a peak in 1976, while the Canadian cattle herd peaked in 1975. Thus, the first thirty years of the post–Second World War era were dominated by market growth and relatively profitable operations, as Canadian meat packers acquired their competitors, built new plants, and steadily increased their market penetration.

Canada Packers: Merger, Rationalization, and Expansion

In August of 1927, the Harris Abattoir and William Davies, Canada's first and largest meat packer, merged into a holding company, Canada Packers Limited, which went on to purchase the Canadian Packing Company. James S. McLean, sometime schoolteacher and insurance salesman, and husband to Sir Joseph Flavelle's niece, was the architect of the merger and first president of Canada Packers.

Sir Joseph Flavelle had forged the early alliances between competing members of Toronto's meat packing establishment that eventually became Canada Packers. Flavelle proved to be an exacting accountant and shrewd financial manager, as he rose to become managing director of William Davies, which was for many years Canada's largest and oldest meat-packing concern. In offering young J.S. McLean a bookkeeping position at the Harris Abattoir in 1902 (Bliss 1978: 115), Flavelle proved himself as a good judge of management capacity as well. Flavelle trained J.S. McLean and passed on his financial acumen and meticulous accounting practices, a legacy that would last sixty years in Canada Packers.

For several years after its incorporation, Canada Packers attempted to operate as a true holding company for the four meat-packing concerns it had merged. But as the Depression took hold, a new policy to rationalize and consolidate the firm's holdings was adopted. In Toronto, the Gunns and Harris Abattoir plants, which by happenstance were adjacent and directly across St Clair Avenue from Toronto's Union Stock Yards, were joined by a second-story overpass and converted into a single integrated plant. A third Toronto plant (the old William Davies slaughter plant on the Don River) was converted into a cold storage facility and soap works, while the fourth (Canadian Packing Company) was closed, sold, and later demolished. The two Montreal plants (previously William Davies and Canadian Packing Company) were also adjacent, and these too were physically joined to form one large plant. The plants remaining in operation were able to increase volumes, spread fixed costs over larger production runs, and devote more space in each plant to specialized departments such as rendering (Canada 1934: 2289).

By 1933, nine plants had been rationalized into five and head office staff was reduced by 50 per cent, while the plant-floor workforce was reduced by a third. The merged network of 'branch houses' (wholesale warehouses with cold storage facilities) that distributed meats and produce to retail stores contained considerable redundancy. With rationalization, the newest and largest branch house in each city was retained, while the older and smaller operations were closed and sold. The 'Maple Leaf' logo replaced each of the constituent firms' name brands, so that Canada Packers would benefit from national advertising. In total the savings effected by amalgamation and rationalization amounted to $7 million per year (Canada Packers 1943, *Annual Report*: 2).

Just as Canada Packers had restructured and consolidated its Toronto and Montreal operations, the Ottawa Agreements were signed in 1932, creating virtually limitless pork-exporting opportunities to Great Britain. Hitherto, the firm's westernmost plant had been in Winnipeg, and it was unable to penetrate livestock markets west of Saskatchewan. Thus, in the depths of the Depression an entirely new plant was opened in Edmonton in 1936 to exploit northern Alberta's hog production potential both for export and domestic markets. Another new plant in Vancouver was opened in 1938 to serve the isolated British Columbia market. In 1940, Canada Packers bought Hunnisett Limited, a small independent packing plant located adjacent to its Toronto Stock Yards complex. Hunnisett's was virtually in the shadow of the largest packing plant in Canada, yet it was kept in operation for many years to give the colossus a window on the competitive world of small-scale packers. In this way, Canada Packers transformed a group of firms that started out as butcher retailers in nineteenth-century Toronto into a multiprovincial enterprise with a market presence from Quebec to British Columbia and with important markets in Britain by the eve of the Second World War.

As an amalgam of four diversified meat-packing businesses Canada Packers remained highly diversified. It processed packinghouse by-products to produce edible oils such as lard and tallow, soap, and casings, it maintained a network of rural creameries throughout central Ontario, and the produce business established originally by Sir Joseph Flavelle expanded as the 'York Farms' line of canned fruits and frozen vegetables. These products would be bought by the same customers who purchased meat products, sold by the same sales force, and shipped in the same refrigerated trucks to make up full loads to remote markets.

Canada Packers integrated backwards as it converted rendering products such as bone, blood, and meat meal into fertilizers and its 'Shur-Gain' animal feeds. It integrated forwards by acquiring two of Ontario's largest leather tanneries to provide an internal market for calf skins and cattle hides. In the postwar era it built a gelatine factory to use pork rind, added detergents to its line of soaps, and a department to produce glycerine from the by-product of soap manufacture.

The expertise and plant used to refine animal oils was also used to refine vegetable oils into shortening and margarine. Entry into each of these product markets was an incremental step in a rational, if convoluted, pattern of vertical and horizontal integration. Canada Packers became the most diversified of Canada's meat-packing firms. But the livestock-based commodity chain remained the core business and it provided a powerful logic to the direction of growth.

In the aftermath of the Second World War, Canada Packers moved to consolidate itself as a truly national-scale packinghouse. Beginning in the Maritimes, it acquired and rebuilt a fire-gutted packing plant in Charlottetown from Davis and Fraser Limited in 1947, and in 1954 it leased a small municipal abattoir in Saint John to serve the New Brunswick market. Upon the death of J.S. McLean in 1954, his son, William Flavelle McLean, became chief executive officer, a position he would occupy until 1980.

To secure a larger share of cattle from southern Alberta, Canada Packers acquired Calgary Packers in 1955, at that time the tenth largest packing firm in Canada. Wilsil Limited of Montreal (with roots dating to the Montreal Abattoir which was founded in the 1880s) had become Canada's fourth-largest meat packer in 1955, when it too was acquired (Canada 1961: 13–14) as Canada Packers' second Montreal area slaughter plant. Canada Packers also invested heavily in renovating and expanding its existing plants. The old Montreal and Hull, Quebec, plants were extensively renovated while the St-Boniface, Edmonton, and Vancouver plants were expanded. Capital was invested in new equipment to implement the Can-Pak system in all of the plants that killed significant numbers of cattle.

While Canada Packers expanded its network of plants to span Canada from coast to coast, the core of its packing operations was still in Toronto. Over a ten-year period, from 1946 to 1955, the flagship plant at what had become the Ontario Stock Yards earned a greater gross profit than all of the other meat-packing plants combined (Table 6.1). The St-Boniface plant, with the same cattle slaughter capacity, and the second-largest hog slaughter capacity, was a distant second and all of the other plants made only modest contributions to the firm's income statement. In general, the rate of return as a percentage of capital employed was higher in the plants with greater slaughter capacity and lower in the smaller plants. Profitability was thus sensitive to volume, a clear demonstration of the economies of scale in meat packing. The glaring exception was the relatively small Hull plant which had the

Table 6.1 Slaughter capacity and profitability: Canada Packers' plants, 1946–1955

Plant location	Weekly slaughter capacity		Ten-year-average plant results, 1946–55		
	Cattle	Hogs	Trading profit[a] 000s	Interest[b] 000s	Rate of return[c] %
Charlottetown	300	2,500	150	431	8.1
Montreal (Davies)	1,500	8,000	2,464	4,606	9.2
Peterborough	600	3,000	323	749	3.4
Toronto	4,500	18,000	16,716	13,843	13.2
Hull	800	4,500	2,141	1,188	16.9
St-Boniface	4,500	12,000	5,606	4,995	12.7
Edmonton	2,000	8,000	2,632	2,111	13.5
Vancouver	750	1,800	1,406	1,671	1.0

[a]Gross operating profit before interest and taxes
[b]In essence this is an opportunity cost as calculated by Canada Packers' accounting system. It is the interest income that would have been earned on the fixed and working capital invested in each plant assuming a 6 per cent rate of interest.
[c]Trading profit as a percentage of capital employed, that is, fixed plus working capital.
Source: Canada, 1961 *Report of the Restrictive Trade Practices Commission Concerning the Meat Packing Industry and the Acquisitions of Wilsil Limited and Calgary Packers Limited by Canada Packers Limited* (Ottawa: Queen's Printer), 84, 381

highest rate of return, likely because it was the oldest and most depreciated of Canada Packers' assets and because its labour force had lower wages than most other operations.

Table 6.1 also illustrates an accounting framework that was unique to Canada Packers and that had roots in the management philosophy of J.S. McLean, a mathematician turned bookkeeper, secretary-treasurer, president of the Harris Abattoir, and finally president of Canada Packers. Doubtless McLean's methods had their ultimate origins with Sir Joseph Flavelle. The theory was that any capital that was invested in fixed plant in any particular corporate activity could have been invested elsewhere, risk free at 6 per cent. Thus, no department of the firm could truly be said to earn a profit until it had first paid the hypothetical 6 per cent charge on capital employed in the department. This system gave autonomy to the various department managers, but held them accountable for their true profit performance in relation to the opportunity cost of the capital invested in the department. The opportunity cost metric also helped the firm to make better pricing decisions in the very competitive meat-packing environment (Child 1960: 174).

Canada Packers' Gradual Exit from Fresh Beef

The geography of Canada Packers plants began to shift in the 1960s as it closed its smallest and oldest plants in eastern Canada and built specialized beef plants in western Canada. The oldest and smallest plants were typically multi-species, multi-level plants which in some cases dated back to the nineteenth century. The Peterborough plant, which dated back to 1884, was closed in 1962, the Saint John, New Brunswick, plant was gradually wound down during the late 1970s, and the Wilsil plant in Montreal was over sixty years old when it, too, was closed in 1981. The Hull plant, which included a large limestone structure dating back to 1898, stopped producing meat products in 1977, but wholesale distribution operations were not finally wound up until 1982. The Charlottetown plant which had been rebuilt in 1947 was finally shut down in 1984. In western Canada, the beef slaughter operation in the small Vancouver plant was closed in 1970, the larger Edmonton plant killed its last cattle in 1979 and stopped killing hogs in 1984.

While cattle processing was terminated in many of the older multi-species plants, Canada Packers began to invest in new beef plants in western Canada: two in Lethbridge, one in Red Deer, and two in Moose Jaw. The existing Calgary plant was reconfigured to operate as a large-scale carcass breaking and beef-cutting department to produce boxed beef (described in more detail in Chapter 8). At the same time as Canada Packers was developing its new western beef plants, its largest and oldest plant in Toronto was becoming progressively more obsolete. Markets for cattle were becoming so competitive that the price of beef and by-products was not covering the cost of the cattle used to produce them (Canada Packers 1978, *Annual Report*: 5). This was further complicated by a seven-week strike in 1978 that cost the firm some $10 million (Canada Packers 1979, *Annual Report*: 6). By 1980, the firm was complaining about a 21.5 per cent decline in cattle marketings and the existence of considerable idle capacity in the industry (Canada Packers 1980, *Annual Report*: 4). In 1984, Canada Packers acquired Hoffman Meats from Gainers which operated a hog-kill plant in Kitchener, and it took over Burlington-based Tender-Lean Beef Ltd. Tender-Lean was a ten-year-old, single-story, 4,000-head per week cattle plant which used the Can-Pak continuous on-the-rail dressing technology and included a modern cutting room to ship boxed beef (Beatty 1994; Canada Packers 1984, *Annual Report*: 1984: 4). But the new state-of-the-art plants could not staunch the losses in Canada Packers' packing-house division, and in January 1984 the cattle and hog-slaughter operations in its flagship plant at the Ontario Stock Yards were permanently closed.

The St-Boniface plant which was opened as the Harris Abattoir (Western) in 1925 went out of production in 1987. The firm's fresh meats segment began to hemorrhage, as its income slipped from $15.7 million in 1988 to break-even in 1989, to a loss of $3.5 million in 1990. In fact, the whole firm was performing poorly but among all its diversified holdings, the beef business was Canada Packers' most severe problem. The Tender-Lean plant in Burlington, acquired so recently to replace the flagship plant on the edge of the Ontario Stock Yards, was itself closed in 1990, and all of Canada Packers remaining beef operations were concentrated in Alberta and Saskatchewan.

On 2 October 1989, William Flavelle McLean retired from his position as chairman of the board. He was still the family patriarch and controlled 30 per cent of Canada Packers' equity, but the firm was up for sale. While the firm was not performing well, its real estate holdings, especially the sites of abandoned meat-packing plants across the country, had considerable value (Enchin 1989). In 1990, Canada Packers was the subject of a complex takeover involving Maple Leaf Mills, a diversified Canadian flour-milling company, and Hillsdown Holdings PLC, a British-based agroindustrial conglomerate.

On 28 June 1990, Canada Packers acquired 100 per cent of the shares of Maple Leaf Mills from its owner, Hillsdown Holdings. Canada Packers paid for the acquisition with 29.5 million of its own shares valued at $12 each for a total of $354 million. With those shares in hand, Hillsdown owned 45 per cent of Canada Packers. Second, Hillsdown Holdings purchased an additional 7.2 million shares in Canada Packers at $16.50 per share, giving Hillsdown Holdings a controlling 56 per cent interest in the firm (Canada Packers 1990, *Annual Report*: 35) The name was changed to Maple Leaf Foods on 22 May 1991, which was remarkably appropriate since Canada Packers' brand name for packaged meats had been 'Maple Leaf' since the early 1930s and its CP logo featured a maple leaf.

Under new management, the new firm moved swiftly to divest some of the key businesses that had anchored Canada Packers over the years. Following unsuccessful attempts to sell all four of the western beef plants en bloc, the remaining beef plants in Calgary, Red Deer, and Lethbridge were shut down in 1991, while the newest plant in Moose Jaw was sold to Intercontinental Packers of Saskatoon in 1991 and acquired by Calgary-based XL Foods in 2000. In its first year in operation Maple Leaf laid off 2,500 workers and closed twelve plants (Evans 1991).

While it had abandoned fresh beef, the firm moved to strengthen its position in prepared meats with the acquisition of Unox Meats from Unilever Canada, giving it brands such as Shopsy's, Hygrade, and La Belle Fermiere. Maple Leaf purchased Fearman's Fresh Meats of Burlington and the Mary Miles bacon brand for $14 million in 1991. Thus, Maple Leaf Foods consolidated and strengthened its position in fresh pork and value added processing of national brand name packaged meats. Maple Leaf operated under Hillsdown Holdings for less than five years before it was acquired by Wallace McCain (formerly of McCain Foods) and the Ontario Teachers' Pension Plan in April of 1995.

Swift Canadian and Gainers

For nearly eighty years Swift Canadian was the exception, the only U.S.-owned subsidiary to enter the Canadian market for meat in a serious way or to challenge the Canadian firms that dominated the industry. Like its domestically controlled competitors, Swift Canadian also operated grain mills, dairies, poultry plants, and a soap company – all in some way integrated into the growth and processing of animal products. But the Chicago-based parent kept its Canadian subsidiary on a very short leash, and Swift Canadian never had much autonomy. Union correspondence was contemptuous of the subsidiary's inability to take any initiatives without first securing authority from the parent firm in Chicago. For example, a letter from the United Packinghouse Workers of American (UPWA) assistant director responsible for the Swift Canadian chain to the president of a Winnipeg local union described the relationship with Stewart Wylie, then superintendent of Swift Canadian:

> I got in touch with Mr Wylie and asked him what progress he had made with regard to [a medical plan]. He said he was sorry but he had got simply nowhere. At this time, I told him I had lost my patience and was thoroughly disgusted with the manner in which Swift's had carried on negotiations this year. I said that the committee were completely frustrated during negotiations and felt that he and Mr Summerell [superintendent, Winnipeg plant] were acting as mere stooges and were sent into negotiations by the [parent firm] with their hands tied behind their backs. I also told him

> that our people, meaning the delegates to negotiations, were going back into the plants and saying that Canada Packers, and particularly, Mr Carroll [vice-president and manager of industrial relations] of Canada Packers, was negotiating for the Swift Company. (UPWA 1956)

Swift Canadian allowed, and even encouraged, Canada Packers to set the standard for wages and benefits and despite the parent's size and financial depth, it never exercised much industry leadership.

Following a period of rapid growth from 1900 to 1925, Swift Canadian coasted on its existing plant and infrastructure until the start of the Second World War. In 1939, Swift Canadian closed its aging Winnipeg plant and replaced it with a massive horizontally integrated packing plant in St-Boniface. The St-Boniface facility permitted Swift to take advantage of Canada's preferential access to the British bacon market gained through the Ottawa Agreements, a trade preference not available to plants in the United States. Thus, Swift's motive for investment in the Canadian meat-packing sector in 1939 was exactly the same as it had been in 1903, to use a Canadian platform to exploit the privileged position of Canadian bacon in the British market. Swift Canadian acquired Union Packers in Calgary in 1946, the Alberta Meat Company in Vancouver in 1958, and Presswood Brothers' Toronto plant in 1967.

In 1971, with assistance through the Regional Development Incentives Act under the Department of Regional Economic Expansion, Swift Canadian opened what was destined to be its last plant in Lethbridge. It was a single story dedicated beef plant that distributed its fresh dressed beef in carcass form (Johnston and den Otter 1991: 196). But even as Swift Canadian was inaugurating its new beef plant in Lethbridge, its U.S. parent was contemplating radical restructuring, as would be the case for all of the old-line U.S. meat packers.

In 1967, Swift and Company was the world's largest meat packer and the thirteenth-largest firm in the United States, but its profitability was slipping and sales margins of 0.7 per cent were not very attractive in an era dominated by conglomeration, diversification, and the divestment of unprofitable business units (*Dun's Review* 1967: 36; *Nation's Business* 1976: 39). In 1973, Swift and Company restructured itself as a conglomerate holding company called 'Esmark' (from the 'S' in Swift's). Following the conglomerate model, strategic decision-making was decentralized in autonomous and typically unrelated business units.

Swift diversified into a wide range of products from petroleum to women's undergarments, reducing the role played by the cyclical meat-packing industry in corporate operations and positioning itself for the divestiture of its traditional core line of business (Tamarkin 1980: 34). Inspired by the effective consumer brand-name performance of its Playtex subsidiary, the firm began to focus its diversification efforts on differentiated products and proceeded to divest its cyclical commodity businesses, beginning with fresh meats which had been its core line of business since 1875 (*Business Week* 1979: 168). Continuing financial difficulties were the catalyst for Esmark to begin closing packing plants in the late 1970s, and it finally spun off its U.S. fresh meats business as Swift Independent Packing Company (SIPCO) with a public share offering in 1981 (*Business Week* 1980: 100–1; Perry and Kegley 1989: 86–7; Skaggs 1986: 197–8).

Divestment of the fresh meat business in its Canadian operations was problematic because the dressing of fresh meats and processing of branded meat products were closely integrated under one roof in the subsidiary's smaller general purpose plants. It was difficult to divest commodity-type meat operations yet retain the name-brand meat products. Swift Canadian began its gradual divestment strategy in 1967 by acquiring Presswoods Brothers, a small family-owned pork packer close to its Toronto plant. With the small meat-processing plant to keep its brand name in the Toronto market, Swift Canadian proceeded to close its flagship plant on the edge of the Ontario Stock Yards in 1967. Other plant closings by Swift Canadian included Calgary in 1968, New Westminster and Moncton in 1971, and the massive St-Boniface plant in late 1979. With these properties gone, Swift Canadian had sculpted itself into a more saleable organization, and it was finally divested to Gainers in 1981.

Gainers Limited had roots in Edmonton going back to 1891, when the railway arrived and John Gainer opened a home-based butcher shop. Diversifying into livestock dealing and meat wholesaling, the firm remained in family hands through three generations. Expanding to take advantage of wartime demand for meat products, Gainers built a new slaughterhouse on Edmonton's south side in 1940 with a capacity of 10,000 hogs and approximately 250 cattle per week, and it acquired a second plant in Vancouver in 1945. The firm expanded its marketing and distribution system in the 1950s and 1960s to become a key competitor in the fresh and processed-meats industry of western Canada with a workforce that peaked at 650 (Klassen 1999: 133–4;

McIntyre 1941). Although remote from Edmonton's stockyard, the centrally located Edmonton plant site gained in real estate value making the firm doubly attractive as a takeover target. In September 1978, Gainers was acquired by the Patrician Land Corporation, a private firm owned by Peter Pocklington, the flamboyant Edmonton-based entrepreneur and owner of the Edmonton Oilers hockey franchise.

Gainers, in turn, bought Swift Canadian in early 1981 but Gainers never became one of the big three, as it began to sell off or close the meat-packing plants almost as soon as it bought them. The Vancouver and Toronto plants were closed, while the Lethbridge plant was sold to Canada Packers in 1984. Gainers' original plant on Edmonton's south side was closed and its operations were consolidated in the former Swift's plant near the Edmonton Stock Yards. While the motive for acquisition by the Pocklington group of companies is difficult to discern, it appears that the principal goal was not to enter meat packing at all, but to gain control over the valuable parcels of real estate owned by Swift Canadian and Gainers in the heart of metropolitan areas. All but one of Swift Canadian's remaining plants were closed and their assets divested. By 1989, Gainers was once again a single-plant firm operating in Edmonton, although it continued to operate Swift Canadian's old network of sales branches in Western Canada.

Gainers was seized by the Alberta government in October 1989, when the firm failed to repay a government-secured loans package totalling $67 million. By 1993, Gainers was losing $20 million per year, and Alberta had accumulated a further deficit of $107 million in one of the province's most embarrassing economic development failures. The plant was up for sale for several years. A.J. Child summed up the problem in 1993: 'Gainers of course isn't worth anything. The government puts out press releases that they want to sell something but they don't have anything to sell ... An obsolete meat-packing plant has no value' (MacDonald 1993: C3). Gainers shut down its 2,000-head per week beef kill line in 1993, along with the last of the wholesale branches originally owned by Swift Canadian. The Edmonton plant with a 20,000-hog per week kill line and pork-processing facilities was finally sold to Burns Foods in November 1993, and the provincial government absorbed a $173 million loss as Gainers passed out of existence.

Burns Foods

Like Swift Canadian, Burns and Company did not add to its network of slaughter plants from 1926 until 1942. It became comfortably established as a western meat packer that posed no serious threat to eastern markets. However, Harris Abattoir and its successor, Canada Packers began to expand in western Canada with new plants in St-Boniface (1925), Edmonton (1936), and Vancouver (1938). This competitive challenge to the territory that had been dominated by Burns and Swift Canadian did not go unanswered. Burns began to expand and diversify in eastern Canada. It acquired Dumart's Limited (Canada's fifth-largest meat packer) in Kitchener in 1942, and in 1955 it purchased Montreal-based Modern Packers and its kill plant subsidiary, Dominion Packers (Canada 1934: 2532).

From the time it was sold by Senator Pat Burns in 1928, Burns and Company had suffered from mediocre management and lacklustre performance. Shares were trading well below book value when the firm was taken over by eastern interests in 1964 and renamed Burns Foods. In the same year, the obsolete Winnipeg plant was closed and production was relocated to a large new facility in St-Boniface in 1964. A major reinvestment was committed to the Kitchener plant to cement the firm's position in eastern Canada. But in spite of reinvestment, new management and half a dozen consultants' reports, attempts to reverse the firm's slide were unsuccessful.

By 1966, Burns Foods was in dire straits; it suffered the death of its president in 1965 and revenues were in decline. A last minute reprieve arrived in the form of A.J. Child, formerly vice-president of Canada Packers, and president of Intercontinental Packers of Saskatoon. Child took over as president and chief executive officer of Burns Foods in 1966. With Howard Webster of Montreal initially taking a majority interest, Child eventually purchased a controlling interest in the firm and succeeded in turning it around.

But it was a near-run thing. An eleven-week strike at Canada Packers began on 18 July 1966, three months after Child was given a chance to rescue his new firm. Canada Packers was out of the marketplace and off store shelves for almost three months. Burns seized this golden opportunity and re-established its name-brand meat products in the retail marketplace. The meat-packing division enjoyed a sales increase of $15 million, while profits from meat packing turned around from a loss of $1 million in the first half of the year to a profit of $1.5 million in the second half of the year.

Much of the credit for the turn around must go to A.J. Child, an accountant and financier who learned his craft at the knee of J.S. McLean in Canada Packers beginning in 1930. At the Harris Abattoir,

McLean had employed a system of 'weekly results' which he, in turn, had learned from Joseph Flavelle who implemented the system in the 1870s. Weekly results provided more timely information than the monthly statements used by competitors. This was especially important in the meat-packing industry which buys a volatile commodity and converts it into a variety of consumer goods which also have erratic prices: 'A typical [meat-packing] plant sells hundreds, perhaps thousands, of different items each week and the pattern of sales is never the same for any two weeks. Selling prices and costs are the reverse of stable; they may change each day' (Child 1960: 121).

Within weeks of taking over, Child swept aside many of the middle managers and administrators that had clogged the Burns hierarchy. For example, the head office staff of the meat division was reduced from eighty to thirty in the first month. And he installed financial control systems inspired by those used at Canada Packers to dissect the firm's operating performance, and to identify the sources of profit and loss with precision:

> On the accounting side, I scrapped everything that had been instituted, the profit and loss statements and the ancillary statements that had been 'dreamed up,' if that's the right word, by Peat, Marwick Mitchell – they were just a lot of paper that accomplished very little. The first week I was here, I threw out all the accounting systems pertaining to profit and loss, accounting systems pertaining towards expense analysis, and so on. I constructed a profit and loss statement that was weekly, that was on one page. And I constructed an expense analysis that was monthly on one page. And that, of course, not only simplified the system, but when I would hold a weekly management meeting of the key people we could look at one page and get the whole picture of what had happened the previous week. And we developed those statements very, very quickly so that nothing could get away from us. If we saw that there were certain flaws revealed by the weekly P&L we were able to get at them very quickly. (A.J. Child Interview)

Consistent with Sir Joseph Flavelle's and Canada Packers' practice, Child restored operating autonomy and responsibility for weekly and monthly results to individual plant and branch managers.

The results of Child's turn-around strategy were stunning. A corporate-wide loss after-tax of $94,000 on $228 million in sales in 1966 became an after-tax profit of $908,000 on $224 million in sales in 1967.

By 1976, when Howard Webster and Arthur Child took the firm private, after-tax profits had reached $5.7 million on $722 million in sales.

Under Child's leadership a major reinvestment was committed to the Calgary plant in 1966. The firm continued to expand by acquisition: Pool Packers in 1969 (Brandon); Canadian Dressed Meats in 1970 (Toronto and Lethbridge); Kitchener Packers in 1972; and Alberta Western Beef in 1973 (Medicine Hat). In the early 1970s Burns reached its broadest span of control with plants from Vancouver to Montreal. In June 1973, it acquired a 28 per cent interest in Western Canadian Seed Processors (renamed Canbra Foods), a Lethbridge-based canola crusher and edible-oil processor. The firm maintained its stellar performance under Child but at a price: the gradual diminution of meat packing as the core line of business.

Meat packers, like all commodity processors, are dealing with markets which are constantly changing. The annual reports of packing companies are a litany of month-to-month price fluctuations. Packing plants alternate from months of hugely profitable operations to losing streaks as, for example, when Burns's western cattle plants were losing some $40 on every beast they dispatched in the late spring of 1975 (Burns 1976, *Annual Report*: 3). Thus, meat packers cannot afford to 'stick to their knitting' and specialize in the activity they know best.

Burns's earliest diversification took the form of vertical integration to process and add value to by-products, the essence of the competitive advantage of industrial-scale meat packing. Second, diversification was motivated to employ the branch-house system more fully and carry perishable food products which had similar cold storage and refrigerated transportation requirements as fresh meats. Third, diversification was motivated to spread and attenuate the risk inherent in a cyclical commodity: 'Certain segments of the food industry, such as meatpacking are exceptionally vulnerable to losses resulting from market and cyclical factors. These losses, when they occur, must be offset by gains from other activities' (Burns Foods 1976, *Annual Report*: 1).

The implications of the diversification strategies pursued by all of the old-line packers were twofold. First, meat packing played a diminishing role in total corporate revenues and profitability. By 1975, meat-packing operations contributed only 12 per cent of Burns Foods' earnings before tax. Thus, the strategic emphasis of the meat-packing firms was no longer focused on livestock and meat products. Second, once other opportunities were available, it became clear in the 1980s that the capital invested in meat-packing assets did not earn as high a return as it did in other business segments: 'The future of the meatpacking industry in Canada is clouded. There are two reasons: the return on investment in meat packing is far too low, and the industry is labour-intensive. With a high rate of obsolescence, meat packing plants often require more cash for capital expenditures than they generate. They do not return as much for the investor's dollar as many other industries. With wages and salaries constituting a very high proportion of total costs, any increases that exceed increases in productivity have a major effect on profits' (Burns Foods, 1976, *Annual Report*: 7).

Burns Foods' Gradual Exit from Fresh Beef

Through the 1970s and 1980s Burns Foods became a holding company, gradually withdrawing from its traditional core line of business in meats. Packing-plant closures included a hog plant in Regina in 1974 which had been a part of the firm for fifty-seven years since it had been acquired by Pat Burns in 1917. The closure was attributed primarily to the creation of the Saskatchewan Hog Marketing Commission and its livestock sale and pricing procedures.

On the other hand, the Medicine Hat cattle plant was closed on 31 December 1977, only four years after its acquisition. Attempts to run this slaughter plant profitably by two other firms had ended in failure in the 1960s, but Child thought that Burns Foods had the acumen to operate profitably where others had failed:

> I bought that plant and it was a mistake. I don't hesitate at all to tell you I've made lots of mistakes. That was one of them. I bought that plant because I thought it would be close to our source of raw material namely beef, of course it was solely beef. But as it turned out we didn't need that source of raw material, there was plenty available elsewhere. And also the cattle people in that area let us down very badly. They said if you acquire this plant we'll bring you our cattle. Which they didn't do, because the plants in Lethbridge paid them the same amount as they would have got delivering to Medicine Hat, so we ended up with no advantage. I partly blame the cattle people for that but I should have known better. Cattle owners look for the best dollar they can get. Which is the essence of the business. (A.J. Child Interview)

The closure of the Medicine Hat and Regina plants illustrates the importance of livestock supply to the viability of kill plants. Over-capacity in the slaughter industry and a shortage of livestock are the most common rationales for slaughterhouse closures. Of course, the complaint of a 'shortage of livestock' must always be qualified, 'at a price the processor is willing to pay.' But this is a relatively new phenomenon. When the majority of livestock were killed in metropolitan regions with livestock deficits, plants often brought livestock in from a considerable distance; cattle could come from anywhere by rail and were marketed through large livestock exchanges. In recent years, raw material oriented slaughter plants have come to depend more on local sources of livestock. Thus, it is more likely that those regional livestock markets will not be able to supply livestock of the quality that is required at the steady volume that a kill plant needs to fully employ the capital that has been sunk into plant and machinery.

In other cases the plants selected for closure were becoming chronically unprofitable because of their inner-city stockyard locations which were no longer suitable for large-scale animal slaughter and processing (e.g., Modern Packers in Montreal, Canadian Dressed Meats in Toronto). The penultimate plant closures in Calgary and Kitchener were part of Burns's strategy to break the pattern bargaining system (described in Chapter 8).

By 1990, Burns was left with only two meat-packing plants. The large-scale integrated plant in St-Boniface which was built in 1964 became the company's principal meat-packing operation. Here Burns slaughtered hogs, produced its line of name-brand processed meat products, and ran a small beef-kill operation for the Manitoba market. In Lethbridge, Burns operated a dedicated beef plant built in 1960 as a one-story kill and chill operation to which was added a boxed beef department at a cost of $900,000 in 1976. At that time the firm asserted it was the most modern plant in Canada. But by the 1990s, in competition with other very large-scale packers, the plant typically operated at less than one-half its design capacity.

In November 1993, Burns Foods enlarged its meat-packing operations once again when it acquired Gainers from the Government of Alberta. In exchange for undertaking a $22 million capital investment in the sixty-one-year-old Edmonton plant, the provincial government sold the Gainers business (including its Canadian rights to Swift brands such as Swift's Premium Ham, Lazy Maple Bacon, Butterball Turkey, and Brown 'n Serve Sausages) to Burns Foods for $25 million. In essence, the business had to be given away after the provincial government had already lost $115 million in a vain attempt to recover its original $67 million loan. The deal included the business, the capital equipment, and a lease on the plant itself while the government retained ownership of the Edmonton real estate (*Western Report*, 1993).

Arthur Child died on 30 July 1996 at the age of eighty-six. Two months later Burns Foods sold off its Burns Meats subsidiary to Maple Leaf Foods on 16 September 1996. Thus, in 1996 the remnants of Canada's big three meat packers (Canada Packers, Swift Canadian, and Burns Meats) had all been brought under the Maple Leaf Foods corporate umbrella. The catch also included a number of smaller fish, independent packers that had first been regional competitors and were later acquired: Canadian Dressed Meats, Fearman's Meats, Gainers, Hoffman's Meats, and Presswoods Brothers to name only some of the more recent ones. It seems likely that Burns's two most modern plants, and the brand names of the various predecessor companies, were what Maple Leaf really wanted out of the bargain.

When striking workers did not respond favourably to a mediator's report advising them to accept an 86 cents an hour wage increase, Maple Leaf Foods made good on its ultimatum and closed the Edmonton plant in August 1997, eliminating some 850 jobs and erasing the last tangible evidence of Swift Canadian's coast-to-coast meat-packing empire.

Maple Leaf ended beef operations in the Lethbridge plant on 12 May 1998, and it was converted to hog slaughter, becoming the first hog plant in Canada to employ 'hot-skinning' to prepare skinless pork cuts specifically and exclusively for the Japanese export market. It seems ironic that the Maple Leaf Foods pedigree includes William Davies, the first Canadian packer to export Wiltshire sides of pork, specifically and exclusively for the British export market (Canada Packers 1943: Chapter 7; Kenney 1945).

Intercontinental Packers

The history of 'Intercon' is largely the story of one remarkable man, Frederick Mendel. Born in Westphalia in the newly unified Germany of 1888, the son of a wholesale butcher, Mendel's primary business was exporting canned Polish hams to the U.S. market, which seems paradoxical given his Jewish faith. The secret of Mendel's success was the purchase of the patent rights to the Biesser ham-curing process, known generically as artery pumping. The Biesser process injected brine through the existing vascular system in the pork muscle, ensuring a more uniform penetration of the pickle and reducing the curing process from two months to seven days. In improving the quality of ham and reducing production costs, the Biesser process was instrumental in establishing the premium quality reputation of Mendel's Polish hams in the 1930s (Mendel 1972: 56, 71).

Concerned by the Nazi threat, Mendel emigrated from Hitler's Germany to Hungary, and after a narrow escape from Europe after the outbreak of war, he resolved to immigrate to Canada, at the age of fifty-two. Late in 1939, he purchased an abandoned meat-packing plant in Saskatoon. The nearly empty building that Mendel took over had a chequered past. It had started out as an automobile assembly plant in 1911. The structure was converted to an abattoir by a Saskatoon cooperative, but was unsuccessful and closed down in 1938 (Bronson 1973). Locals felt the broken-down old plant was a losing proposition and were amused that Mendel would risk $5,000 on such a dubious venture. By June 1940, Mendel had invested $100,000, and the little plant was up and running under the name of Intercontinental Pork Packers.

In April 1941, Intercon was processing 1,500 hogs per week and after investing in a $150,000 extension, it reached 9,000-head per week in 1944 (Bentham 1941). The firm's primary mandate was to produce canned Polish-style hams for export to the United States, replicating the business that Mendel had operated in central Europe before the war. But Mendel was soon stymied by Canada's embargo on meat exports to the United States. Once again the war had put an end to his canned ham exports and once again he was nearly ruined. The federal government, which controlled the production of strategic meat products, awarded Intercon a weekly quota of 20,000 pounds of Wiltshire sides for export to Britain, a market that was 'not enough to live on, and not enough to die on' (Mendel 1972: 133). Intercontinental was on the brink of insolvency as working capital dried up, and Mendel nearly accepted an offer of acquisition from Swift Canadian. But he persevered, and like the big three Canadian meat packers, profited from wartime bacon exports to the United Kingdom.

At war's end, Intercon installed a beef-kill floor and by operating double shifts, reached 2,000 head of cattle per week by 1947. Mendel went on to purchase a smaller packing plant in Regina in 1950 to gain full coverage in the province of Saskatchewan (Matthews 1955: 14). In 1960 Mendel became chairman of the board, and A.J. Child, with thirty years of experience at Canada Packers and Harris Abattoir, became president. Under Child's direction, Intercon acquired Red Deer Packers as a kill plant to increase the supply of hog carcasses for processing at the Saskatoon and Regina plants. In 1964, Intercon acquired the

Pacific Meat Company in Vancouver and reached its maximal spatial extent. In each case, Intercontinental bought run-down old plants and invested substantial sums to renovate and modernize each one.

For a brief time Intercon was included with Canada Packers, Swift Canadian and Burns Foods to create Canada's 'big four' meat packers. When A.J. Child left the firm in 1966 to take over Burns Foods, Intercon returned to family control and it began to contract, closing three of its four plants by 1980. The original plant in Saskatoon closed its beef operations, resumed its wartime role as a pork specialist, and was renamed Mitchell's Gourmet Foods.

Smoke but No Fire: Inquiries into Price Fixing

In the first decade of the twentieth century, both William Davies in southern Ontario and Burns and Company in Alberta and Saskatchewan were pilloried as profiteers, monopolists, and monopsonists who used their market power to exploit hapless farmers and to bilk naive consumers. The bad press had little impact on their profitability: it was the collapse of world meat prices after the First World War that did the most serious damage. Between 1935 and 1987, the market power of Canada's big three meat packers continued under scrutiny as they faced a royal commission, a Restrictive Trade Practices Commission, and a three-year court case under the federal Combines Investigation Act. Once again, allegations of collusion and price fixing were not punished with much more than a slap on the wrist; however, the constant preoccupation with charges that they had an unfair degree of market concentration may have prevented the big three from expanding as they would have liked. In the event, the big three were challenged and ultimately defeated by a new generation of meat packers, not by government regulation. If monopoly power had conferred such invincibility, how was it possible for a handful of new entrants to muscle in and defeat the big three in little more than a decade? Three sets of proceedings, about twenty-five years apart, provide evidence of the market clout of the big three, even though all efforts to limit their power were in vain.

Royal Commission on Price Spreads, 1934–1935

At the height of the Depression the Conservative government of R.B. Bennett struck a royal commission (Canada 1935) to investigate the effect of corporate concentration on consumer prices. The commission earned headlines, and by targeting powerful department stores and grocery chains such as Eaton's and Dominion Stores, they were applauded by populists on both the right and the left (Bliss 1987: 425). The marketing of livestock was singled out as an area in which large firms were allied against ostensibly hapless farmers. According to one member of Parliament: 'My firm conviction is that packinghouses in West Toronto [implying Canada Packers and Swift Canadian] have a combine, and farmers going there don't get a square deal' (*Globe* 1934a: A1).

On the second day that the commission began to collect evidence, it interviewed A.W. Laver, commissioner of public welfare for the city of Toronto, who described specific examples of the working poor, people with full-time jobs whose wages were so low that they still needed relief payments. In essence, the commissioners believed that the city of Toronto was subsidizing firms that were paying wages which were not sufficient to meet the basic needs of workers and their families. One of those included on the list was a shipper employed by Canada Packers for seven years (Canada 1934: 54, 60, 69). This broke in the Toronto newspapers on 28 February (*Globe* 1934b) and by 7 March, J.S. McLean, president of Canada Packers, was in Ottawa as a commission witness to protest that his firm had been named publicly. He explained the circumstances under which the man was put on short-time before being laid off following which he applied for relief (Canada 1934: 224–6). But the damage had already been done; the newly renovated Canada Packers' head office plant was painted as a sweatshop, and the seven-year-old firm had failed to escape the bad press that had dogged its predecessor, William Davies.

It seems that the commission was well briefed on meat-packing industry working conditions. They used McLean's voluntary appearance to set the record straight on the misleading charges of paying 'starvation wages' to begin questioning McLean about other employment practices in the meat-packing industry. Workers punched in at the normal start time of 7:00 a.m., but in the event that no work was available (commonly because livestock had not yet reached the plant) the workers might be left 'standing by' for several hours without working and without being paid (Canada 1934: 227–34; Grover 1996: 28). This was common practice in all of the packing companies until plants were unionized but, once again, Canada Packers bore the brunt of the disgrace.

The commission's findings on the meat-packing industry itself came as no surprise, but it was the first time that the industry had been carefully assessed in a report that had the weight and authority of a royal commission. In outline form, and based on data current to 1932, the commission established:

1 The industry was highly concentrated, that is, a very small number of firms accounted for a large proportion of sales. Of the 135 federally inspected establishments in the industry, twenty-four plants (18 per cent), most operated by the big three, accounted for 84.7 per cent of total output. Canada Packers accounted for 59 per cent of total industry revenues, while Swift Canadian had 26 per cent; thus, two firms controlled 85 per cent of the industry's output by value (Canada 1935: 55). However, this measure of market concentration did not include the large proportion of livestock that were killed on the farm or in uninspected slaughter plants.
2 The meat-packing industry fared well over the Depression years relative to manufacturing as a whole. Meat production declined much less than total manufacturing output. While industry-wide economic data are imperfect indicators of performance, taken at face value they suggested that the packinghouse industry was able to insulate its sales margins from Depression conditions more effectively than could the livestock producers. The reason for the superior performance of the packers relative to livestock producers was attributed to the market control exercised by the Canada Packers and Swift Canadian meat-packing duopoly: 'While there is no direct evidence of a combination between these companies, we are not persuaded that prices have been subject to the same fluctuations as might be expected in a more generally competitive field' (Canada 1935: 56).
3 Just as William Davies was pilloried for its outstanding profit performance during the First World War, Canada Packers received the same treatment for its above average performance during the Depression years. In 1931 and 1932, both Swift Canadian and Burns and Company experienced losses, while Canada Packers earned returns on invested capital of 3.9 and 6.3 per cent respectively. However, comparative financial analysis is perilous because of the subjective nature of depreciation and the question of whether reserves should be treated as profit. The commission asserted that 'the true profits of Canada Packers, Limited, are probably greater than disclosed by the records' (Canada 1935: 57).
4 Finally the commission alleged that Canada Packers practised price

discrimination by charging lower prices and more favourable payment terms to large-scale chain retailers and higher prices to small local butcher shops (Canada 1935: 58). In condemning discriminatory discounts, advertising allowances and loss leaders, the report was as critical of the market control exercised by the meat packers as it was of the large retail chain stores (Bliss 1987: 425).

The Royal Commission on Price Spreads report concluded that the market concentration of meat packing in Canada was higher than in the United States as argued in the vignette that opened the chapter. But by the time the commission's report finally appeared, Canada was emerging from the Depression. The Second World War provided a further distraction, and no action was ever taken on the commission's findings.

Restrictive Trade Practices Commission, 1959–1961

In 1959, the Restrictive Trade Practices Commission investigated Canada Packers' 1955 takeover of two formerly independent meat packers: Wilsil in Montreal and Calgary Packers (the fourth- and tenth-largest packers in Canada in 1954). Once again, it was alleged that by controlling a large proportion of total industry sales, Canada Packers was able to use its market power unfairly. The allegations took ten pages to frame, but in essence they resolved into four assertions:

1 Corporate concentration in the meat-packing industry had increased with the acquisition of Wilsil and Calgary Packers. Canada Packers controlled more than one-third of total inspected slaughter which understated its true retail market power because it supplemented its hog kill with carcasses purchased on the wholesale market.
2 The dominance of Canada Packers varied among regional livestock markets, and differences between regional market prices differed by more than simple costs of transportation. The acquisitions of Calgary Packers and Wilsil enhanced Canada Packers' ability to control livestock prices in the Calgary and Montreal markets.
3 Canada Packers was formed by merger, was growing by merger, and had a corporate policy to make further acquisitions as the foundation for growth; thus, there was potential for it to gain even greater market power.
4 Aside from the exercise of greater market power, the commission argued that Canada Packers' increased size did not improve its efficiency since 'there are no significant economies available from multi-

> ple plant operations in the meat-packing industry.' Indeed, the firm actually suffered higher administrative costs and was more cumbersome as a consequence of its large size (Canada 1961: 16). The allegations concluded: 'Canada Packers is a combine because it is a merger, trust or monopoly, in that it has acquired control over or interest in the businesses of others, to wit: Wilsil Limited, Calgary Packers Limited, Dominion Stores Limited and Thrift Stores Limited and because such merger, trust or monopoly has operated and is likely to operate to the detriment or against the interest of the public.' (Canada 1961: 17)

After an exhaustive study of corporate documents and hearings over a span of two years, the commission questioned whether Canada Packers' minority equity position and seat on the board of directors of Dominion Stores might interfere with fair bargaining between buyer and seller or limit the opportunities for other suppliers to gain equal access to consumers. It found that the acquisition of Wilsil and Calgary Packers removed two independent buyers from important livestock markets in Montreal and Calgary which 'significantly lessened the competition previously existing in the trade in livestock' (Canada 1961: 427).

The commission made two recommendations. First, that the government explore the possibility of seeking a court order under the Combines Investigation Act to dissolve the mergers with Wilsil and Calgary Packers, which by then had been consummated some six years previously. If this were not possible, it might be possible to seek a court order enjoining Canada Packers from making any further mergers which would lessen competition in the meat-packing industry. In the end, the government did not act on either of these recommendations.

While the Restrictive Trade Practices Commission meted out a slap on the wrist to Canada Packers, no concrete action was taken to prevent further concentration. Yet the commission may have had some effect. It was the first time that any thorough study had actually found a Canadian meat packer guilty of attempting to eliminate competition. Canada Packers did not attempt any further acquisitions of Canadian firms in the fresh meats industry for the next twenty-five years. It appears that the firm decided that it could not risk further growth in the Canadian market and turned to overseas investment to expand its meat-packing operations. Sales offices were established in Britain and West Germany, and meat-packing and -processing plants were acquired in Australia and Europe. Canada Packers' foreign investments in fresh and processed meats were ultimately unsuccessful, and these problems may have distracted the firm from giving full attention to its Canadian packinghouse system.

Conspiracy to Reduce Competition, 1984–1987

In 1984, a series of charges were laid under the Combines Investigation Act against Canada Packers; Intercontinental Packers and its subsidiary, Red Deer Packers, Burns Foods and its subsidiary, Burns Meats, Eschem Canada (successor to Swift Canadian), and Gainers. Burns, Swift Canadian, and Gainers reached an out-of-court settlement, paying $700,000 and costs to seven Alberta hog producers (*Globe and Mail* 1983: 10). Canada Packers and Intercontinental Packers were indicted under the Combines Investigation Act of having conspired to lessen competition in the trade of hogs and pork products on the Dutch auction system operated by the Alberta Pork Producers Board. Unindicted co-conspirators included Burns, Eschem Canada, Gainers Limited, and some forty-six employees of these firms (*Regina* v *Canada Packers Inc. et al.* 1988). Intercontinental Packers pleaded guilty on two of the charges, and Canada Packers was once again thrust into the leadership position of defending the industry at large. The indictment alleged that over a period of eleven years, from 1965 to 1976, there had been conspiracy to set prices on slaughter hogs, to share the available slaughter hogs on a mutually agreed basis, and collusion to offer high-volume pork cuts at a mutually agreed price.

Canada Packers' defence was based in significant measure on the expert testimony of three agricultural economists. Dr Larry Martin of the University of Guelph argued: (1) The relevant market for hogs and pork is continental and is not limited to local markets such as the Alberta Pork Producers Board electronic auction. (2) The Alberta Pork Producers could sell in other regional markets, and the chain stores need not purchase pork cuts and products from Alberta-based packers if their prices were too high. (3) Analysis of regional price differences revealed no evidence that Alberta livestock prices differed from prices in other regions by more than the cost of transportation.

Dr Bruce Benson at Florida State University and Dr Merle Faminow at the University of Manitoba emphasized the interdependence of regional markets: 'Hog prices in Alberta are clearly linked with those in other Canadian cities. Given these results, it is our opinion that the *geographic market encompassing the forces which determine the price of hogs in Canada is at least national in scope*. It is inappropriate to define Alberta (or even Alberta and its immediate neighbours) as a separate market for hogs during the time defined by our study period' (Quoted in *Regina* v *Canada Packers et al.* 1988: 185).

The trial lasted one-and-one-half years, but the Crown failed to prove, beyond a reasonable doubt, that Canada Packers was guilty of conspiracy. There were many possible explanations for the price behaviour that had been observed. An 'exchange of views as to the value of hogs' was not in itself evidence of promises to set prices (*Regina* v *Canada Packers* 1988: 134). Once again, there had been a great deal of smoke, but no fire. Suspicions of price fixing and collusion among the big three had not been proven with the certainty required under the penal provisions of the Combines Investigation Act.

Canada's meat-packing industry has endured charges of oligopoly price fixing for nearly a century. Corporate concentration in this industry is very high, but that in itself is not a sufficient condition to demonstrate collusive or anticompetitive behaviour. A highly concentrated industry can be just as competitive as an industry with a low concentration ratio (Grier 1988: 22). The turnover of meat-packing firms and plant-scale rationalization of cattle slaughter over the past two decades is evidence that production costs are still vital to survival in a competitive industry dominated by a handful of packinghouse titans.

Conclusion: The Essence of Meat Packing

During the 1980s, no one spoke more eloquently or at greater length about the 'plight' of the corporate meat packers than A.J. Child, president of Burns Foods. In many respects he was arguing along the very same lines as Sir Joseph Flavelle, the mentor of J.S. McLean, who in turn, was Child's role model. In good years meat-packing operations may have very large profits in absolute terms, but expressed as a percentage of revenues, they are minute. For example, Burns Foods' meat-packing division earned $1.5 million after tax in 1971 (a good year), but these earnings were what was left from $227 million in sales less $225.5 million in costs (largely livestock) and taxes. Thus, the sales margin (net profits divided by sales) was 0.6 per cent. Assuming a 50 per cent retail mark-up from the packinghouse door to the checkout counter, consumers pay $340.5 million, and the packer's share of this is only $1.5 million. This is 0.4 per cent or 2 cents on a $5 steak. The meat packer's profit is virtually imperceptible to the consumer. This is the argument that Sir Joseph Flavelle was making in 1917 when he described making 'a great deal of money out of a small return upon a big turnover' (Bliss 1978: 357).

J.S. McLean, the president of Canada Packers, patiently and repeatedly explained how the meat-packing industry was a very high-volume and very-low margin business. His remarks at a company sales conference in 1953 provide a good example:

> On the surface it may seem the narrow margin of profit makes the business a hazardous one. In fact, just the opposite is the case.
>
> The narrow margin on sales is sufficient, because the turnover is so rapid. A successful packing company turns over its capital seven or eight times within a year ... What does turnover mean? It means this: we buy the live animals today, process them into meats within three or four days, deliver them to our customers within another six or seven days, and get our money back within another eight or nine days. On average the interval between the day we pay for the live stock and the day we get the money back into the bank is, perhaps, 25 days.
>
> There are 365 days in the year. In other words, on Fresh Meats we turn over our money approximately 14 times within a year. In the case of Cured Meats and Cooked Meats the processing period is longer. Average turnover is perhaps ten times a year. On other important lines such as Fertilizer and Canned Goods, turnover is only once per year.
>
> On all products which it handles, Canada Packers actually turns over its capital between seven and eight times each year. This means that if we make a net profit of 1% on sales, it works out to a net profit of 7 or 8% on capital. (J.S. McLean, quoted in Canada 1961: 390)

The math teacher from Lindsay was still teaching some very important lessons only a year before his death in 1954. In a high turnover business based on a perishable product, sales margin becomes the universal comparator of efficiency. McLean showed the connection between sales margin and return on invested capital, the vital performance measure of enterprise under capitalism. And taking the packers' annual reports at face value, the returns on meat packing became so low in the 1980s that there was no justification for committing further capital to the enterprise.

Meat packers sometimes make huge profits, not because of their sales margin, but because of their huge volumes. Thus, we come full circle to the essence of the genius of meat-packing giants such as Philip Armour and Gustavus Swift. They industrialized cattle slaughter and meat packing and discovered that the economies of scale were sufficient to pay for all of the added costs of refrigerated transportation that their huge volumes required. And just as the big three Canadian meat packers put most of the small-scale packers out of business with plant production volumes on the order of 5,000 head of cattle per week, they, too, vanished from the scene in the face of an aggressive new generation of packinghouse titans processing 20,000 head per week and more.

SEVEN

Organizing Kill-Floor Workers and Pattern Bargaining

In May 1995, when I first met Mr Child, he was 85, a little too elderly for his ruddy brown toupee to be very plausible. His eyesight had so deteriorated that he could no longer read normal print or enjoy the spectacular view from his 42nd floor office in Calgary's Petro-Canada Building. But he was still a powerful personality and one of Canada's most successful industrialists. He was fond of asserting: 'This is a very, very demanding business and of course, I'm a very, very demanding person. You have to be.'

> *In the United States meat packers found out that they could take on the unions and win, either by holding firm, or by closing plants. And the union understands only one thing and that's power and the only weapon that is effective against unions is plant closures. On the other side of the coin, the only weapon that unions had used up to that point was the strike weapon. So now the tables were turned. Meat-packing companies in the United States first found out that rather than submit to union demands they could profitably close plants, which they did. That extended over here to this country. I told the union that if you people go on strike, our plants at Calgary and Kitchener will be closed the next morning and that's what happened and that happened with a number of other plants across the country. And it was that fear of plant closures that broke the spirit of the union. I don't think that's too extreme a statement ... The ability of the Canadian meat packers ... to close plants was a weapon that the unions were not able to combat and as a result ... the major meat-packing companies went off on their own. Canada Packers was able to negotiate agreements without looking over their shoulder at what we would do or somebody else would do. We did the same and the whole system of more or less so-called joint bargaining disappeared. And now*

when we negotiate a contract in the meat-packing industry we don't pay the slightest attention to what our competitors may have done. A crucial item in this situation was Lakeside Packers at Brooks which defied the union, got rid of the union and have been without a union ever since. The ramifications of that are very interesting.

A.J. Child, Chairman of the Board, Burns Foods, 8 May 1995

In the mid-1940s total labour costs approximated less than 10 per cent of revenues in the packinghouse industry (Canada Packers, *Annual Reports*, various years), thus wages and labour relations might appear to be of minor impact to the overall profitability of the industry. However, the profit margin on sales was only about 1 per cent, and livestock costs, some 80 per cent of revenues, varied little among the large meat packers. For these reasons, wages were a critical component of competitiveness and overall profit margins.

Given the present anemic condition of industrial unionism in general and in packing plants in particular, it seems remarkable that at one time the sector was one of the most heavily unionized in both Canada and the United States. One wonders, considering the difficulty that unions are having organizing plants and maintaining collective bargaining, how did they ever become organized in the first place? Canada's packing plants were organized during the Second World War for the same reasons that automobile assembly, steel works, mines, and lumber mills were organized: the demand for war material, virtually zero unemployment, and government policies that became favourable to organized labour. With the erosion of all of these conditions by the mid-1980s, the fortunes of unionized packinghouse workers went into decline.

Meat Cutters: Aristocrats and Outcasts

The internal division of labour was key to the industrial age, and in the nineteenth century it was epitomized in large-scale meat packing. Professor John Common's discussion of labor conditions in the turn-of-the-century Chicago packing industry provides some vivid and apposite examples of the detailed nature of the division of labour in cattle slaughter which illustrate how deskilling was manifest on the nineteenth-century disassembly line (Braverman 1974). The internal division of labour on the kill floor was minutely detailed. The most highly skilled jobs were scarce, and most workers, especially those with the least seniority, specialized in less skilled and less remunerative vocations:

> It would be difficult to find another industry where the division of labor has been so ingeniously and microscopically worked out. The animal has been surveyed and laid off like a map; and the men have been classified in over thirty specialties and twenty rates of pay, from 16 cents to 50 cents an hour. The 50 cent man is restricted to using the knife on the most delicate parts of the hide (floorsman) or to use the axe in splitting the backbone (splitter); and, wherever a less skilled man can be slipped in at 18 cents, 18½ cents, 20 cents, 21 cents, 22½ cents, 24 cents, 25 cents, and so on, a place is made for him, and an occupation mapped out. In working on the hide alone there are nine positions at eight different rates of pay. A 20-cent man pulls off the tail, a 22½-cent man pounds off another part where the hide separates readily, and the knife of the 40-cent man cuts a different texture and has a different 'feel' from that of the 50-cent man. Skill has been specialized to fit the anatomy. (Commons 1904: 3–4)

This is a classic statement of the Marxian alienation of labour under industrial capitalism. The essential humanity of workers almost disappears when they are reduced to a monetary value: 'a 20-cent man.' The worker's minute task had no intrinsic meaning, it was dictated by the anatomy of the beast, and designed to minimize the waste of paying a more highly skilled worker to do what was judged to be less valuable work: 'In this way, in a gang of 230 men, killing 105 cattle an hour, there are but 11 men paid 50 cents an hour, 3 men paid 45 cents, while the number getting 20 cents and over is 86, and the number getting under 20 cents is 144' (Commons 1904: 4). Some forty years later little had changed. The specialization principle in meat packing is as relevant in a contemporary Canadian context as it was in the United States at the turn of the century. During the Second World War, when Canadian meat-packing output reached all-time highs, the need for a small cadre of highly skilled workers and a much larger number of unskilled luggers and cleaners was attributed to an 'elaborate specialization of functions and the development of many workmen who because of repetitive practice have become intensely skilled. There are probably few industries where workers become more skilled and where the efficiency gains resulting are as marked. Since it takes a very considerable time to acquire such skill, those who already possess it tend to be regarded and to regard themselves as key men. Not all jobs require equal skill, however, and quite a percentage of the employees may properly be classed as unskilled' (Drummond n.d. 21).

Skilled Work

Of all the butcher trades in Chicago in the early twentieth century, those who dressed cattle were the 'butcher aristocracy,' the most highly skilled of all the knife workers in the slaughter and packing industry:

> Their strategic position is explained by the character and expensiveness of the material they work on. The cattle butcher can do more damage than any other workman; for a cut in the hide depreciates its value 70 cents and a spotted or rough carcass will be the last to sell, with the risk of depreciation of a perishable product. The sheep butcher merely 'pulls off' three quarters of the hide, but the cattle butcher can pull off only 2 per cent. The entire hide must be neatly cut off, leaving the 'fell' or mucous covering, intact on the carcass to give it a good appearance. The 'splitter' too, must make a neat and smooth cut straight down the middle of the ivory-like 'fins' of the backbone, or the wholesaler cannot easily dispose of the piece. (Commons 1904: 3)

Twenty years later the Institute of American Meat Packers (IAMP) codified state-of-the-art packinghouse practice, emphasizing the differences between dressing hog and cattle carcasses. The hide of the hog is so embedded in fat that, until recently, it was impractical to remove it unless the market for pig skin was extraordinarily strong. Only the hair is removed by scalding, scraping, and singeing. The cattle hide is a valuable by-product, and it is more loosely attached to the carcass by an elastic tissue or fascia known in the packinghouse as the 'fell.' If the carcass were skinned carelessly, the fell could be stripped away from the carcass leaving an unsightly 'black eye,' a round patch of exposed muscle that appears dark against the white fat covering. The value of a side of beef with such an imperfection had to be discounted. The integrity of the hide was also important; cuts and scores discounted the value of a hide, requiring precision and dexterity on the part of the 'butcher aristocrats.' Similarly, cattle were stunned with knocking hammers, while hogs were shackled and bled while still fully conscious. Until the use of captive bolt stunners became widespread, knocking required great precision. Too strong a blow would crush the skull, driving bone splinters into the brain, preventing its sale as fancy meat. Too light a blow would fail to induce unconsciousness and cause such distress that the quality of the meat would suffer: 'Present [1925] operating methods entail a great amount of exacting individual work, dealing with products of great value, which are ... easily depreciated through improper or inefficient handling. Operating supervisors are confronted with the necessity of speeding up operations so as to turn out the maximum amount of work for the labor outlay; yet this must be tempered by the fact that overcrowding of labor may easily lead to very serious losses in product' (Institute of American Meat Packers 1925: 13). The IAMP echoed the observations made by John Commons. The beef-dressing labour process made speed-up problematic, not because of its dehumanizing effect on labour, but because of its detrimental effect on product quality and the bottom line.

Only a minority of jobs on the kill floor were truly skilled occupations such as journeyman electrician or stationary engineer. Most of the line workers are semiskilled; it takes a few weeks to learn the knack and become proficient at a carcass-dressing job. Until the advent of mechanical hide-removing machines, 'floorsmen' were the highest paid of the beef butchers. The floorsman used a knife to loosen the hide of a beef carcass, and it was important to avoid cutting too shallowly, slicing the hide itself yet not cutting too deeply, severing the fell between skin and fat: 'My knife knows where to go even when my eye can't see it' (Purcell 1953: 26). The critical and strenuous job of floorsman has been eliminated in most plants, especially in large-scale plants that operate with on-the-rail dressing systems. Meat cutting has become so minutely subdivided in the packinghouse that few butchers are competent in every phase of the process from the knocking box to the cooler.

Gendered Work

The use of a knife traditionally marked the critical division between men's and women's work in the packinghouse, just as it did in the dining room when it came time to carve the joint. The skilful use of a knife set the butcher aristocracy apart as a male bastion:

> A skilled meat cutter could move his knife quickly and smoothly along the contours of a carcass, feeling precisely where to sever ligaments and sinews so that the separate cuts of meat emerged quickly and in good form. If a worker did not have the right touch, the job would become slow and messy. In addition to knowing how to make the proper cuts, a skilled

> worker honed his knife constantly to keep the cutting edge razor sharp. This involved drawing the knife over the sharpening steel at exactly the right angle with exactly the right pressure. The steel, which each knife worker hung on a chain around his waist, had to be prepared with sandpaper of varying textures so that its minute striations were precisely suited to the blade's edge. (Fink 1995: 252)

Although the kill-floor workers in industrial-scale packing plants were not journeymen butchers, knife work required great skill to do tasks repetitively, quickly, and with a minimum of physical force. Knife work, was traditionally men's work, and with the exception of true tradesmen, such as electricians, was the highest paid occupation in meat packing. In the British view, butchery had such a brutalizing influence on its practitioners that the occupation was suitable only for adult males (Ayling 1908: 75).

While there have always been some women workers in Canadian packing plants, the division of labour was sharply gendered. Women's jobs tended to be in the fancy meats department where edible offal is cleaned and packed, stuffing sausages, slicing bacon, and on a packaging line where meat products are weighed, wrapped, boxed, and labelled. The kill floor was a masculine domain. But as packinghouse labour requirements increased during the Second World War, women began to enter the industry in greater numbers and the 'feminine touch' made its way to the kill floor (Grover 1996: 69). Women were confronted by resentment, their 'decency' was called into question, and those who accepted the challenge, were stigmatized. Deborah Fink (1995) captures the prevailing attitude in Iowa meat-packing plants with the title of her essay: 'What Kind of Woman Would Work in Meatpacking, Anyway?' After the Second World War Canada's packinghouse labour force remasculinized, but this has changed rapidly since the 1980s. One human resources manager in an Alberta beef-packing plant recalled hiring the very first woman for a kill-floor position in 1984. The kill floor in that plant is now 20 per cent female, and 40 per cent of the workers staffing the fabrication lines are women.

Dangerous Work

Packing-plant work is dangerous, even at the best of times. After the stress of handling, transportation, and crowding with unfamiliar animals, live cattle may be cantankerous and unpredictable. They pose a threat to drivers, knockers, shacklers, and stickers. They are stronger and quicker than any other livestock except horses. Beef carcasses weighing over half a tonne have been known to fall off their gambrels, imperiling anyone working below. In all meat-packing plants, the floors are wet and slick, causing slip and fall injuries. Meat hooks of a size, length, and position that is convenient for holding meat also pose an impalement hazard. Knives slip, causing injury, traumatic amputation of fingers, and sometimes even death when critical arteries are severed. Steel-mesh gloves and chain-mail body armour have been in use for many years to prevent knife cuts. But adjacent co-workers on the line are still vulnerable to errant blades, especially when work stations are located close together, and workers must move about to keep up with a moving chain. Clothing and then limbs can get caught and pulled into heavy machinery, causing the grimmest of human injuries and mortality on the kill floor (Shilliday 1991). Less spectacular than dismemberment, but more chronically debilitating, repetitive stress disorders such as carpal tunnel syndrome disable joints while heavy lifting takes its toll on the human back. The high rate and specific nature of meat-packing injuries has changed little in the past fifty years (Reed 1942).

While packinghouse work has always been both arduous and dangerous, there was a distinct spike in the rate of injuries during the mid-1980s. The number of workers in Canadian meat-packing plants had declined, yet the number of reported injuries rose. The rate of injuries increased from 28.0 to 34.4 per 100 workers between 1982 and 1986. In part, the increased risk of injury has been attributed to the growing scale and specialization of the work (Novek 1992: 22–4). But the period from 1982 to 1986 was also marked by corporate restructuring, rationalization, wage concessions, job action, and a flood of replacement workers in some plants which may also have had some influence on lost time injuries. Injuries also became more severe. In Ontario, with 40 per cent of total employment in the meat industries in the 1980s, days lost to injury per 100 employees rose from 439 to 643 between 1983 and 1986 (Novek et al. 1990: 284).

In Alberta, the meat, hide and pelt processing (MHP) subsector has among the highest lost time claim rates within the manufacturing and processing industries. In 1998, for example, there were 7.8 lost-time claims per 100 person-years worked in MHP processing, compared with only 5.0 in manufacturing and processing taken as a whole. The rate of lost-time injuries in MHP was only exceeded by two other subsectors in 1998: furniture and allied products and masonry construction trades. The risk of workplace injuries is quite strongly influenced by age and job tenure (the length of time worked at a particular occupation), the two serving as proxies for experience. The youthful workforce in the new generation of meat-packing plants, and their rapid labour turnover, offer a partial explanation for the high lost-time claim rates in MHP, but the inherently dangerous nature of meat-packing work should not be gainsaid (Alberta Human Resources and Employment 1999).

Ethnicity and Occupational Status

While men dominate the kill-floor labour force, meat-packing occupations have traditionally been low in status, and for many decades they attracted large numbers of recent immigrants and visible minorities. In the United States, the pattern of ethnic succession in meat packing parallelled the succession of immigrants to the Midwest. The first large group was Irish immigrants in the 1870s. For a short period in the early 1880s, German immigrants were the largest single group. They were succeeded by Poles and later by Lithuanians, Czechs, and Slovaks. By 1911, the U.S. Immigration Commission estimated that some 60 per cent of the meat industry's workers were foreign-born (Purcell 1953: 29). Towards the end of the First World War, the great northward migration by African Americans was under way from the rural poverty of the deep south to the urban industrial jobs of the Midwest, notably in the packinghouses. Black workers were used as strike breakers at first, and then they became permanent workers, albeit at the bottom of the skill, pay, and job status hierarchy. During the Second World War the northerly migration of blacks accelerated so that by 1942, Chicago's meat-packing sector was probably the first basic manufacturing industry to count African Americans as a majority of its workforce (Purcell 1953: 30). Ethnically diverse packinghouse workers shared a common trait; they were industrial outcasts with limited economic opportunities compounded by a lack of education. The low status of slaughter and meat-cutting occupations is not unique to the United States.

The *burakumin* are the definitive pariah class of Japanese society. They are principally employed in occupations dealing with dead flesh such as the slaughter and butchering of animals and tanning leather. These are perceived as 'polluting acts' under Buddhist and Shintoist ideology. The traditional foods of the *burakumin* include jellied tendon, smoked horse meat, and fried intestine, by-products of the slaughterhouse and considered inedible by most Japanese (Suzuki and Oiwa 1996: 133–41). It is interesting to note that ethnic foods associated with African-American and Hispanic-American culture include chitlins (fried intestines), tripe (lining of the rumen or first stomach of cattle), cattle and pig feet, and oxtails. These are the low value by-products of meat packing that many North Americans view as abhorrent and even nauseating. British meat-packing cities such as Leeds, Edinburgh, and Glasgow were advantaged by having large working-class populations to consume edible offal and other slaughter by-products (Perren 1978: 46).

In early nineteenth-century Britain, the disembowelling and dismemberment of carcasses was thought to be so dehumanizing that it inevitably caused a reduction in the moral standards of both the worker and the precincts of the city where slaughter took place: 'The persons who are employed to slaughter in those underground cellars appeared to me just of the same description of characters that you can see upon the dusthills, the most filthy, low, disgusting characters that can possibly be mentioned' (quoted in Philo 1995: 675). Packinghouse work was similarly disdained, and even in Chicago of the 1950s, there was a certain prejudice towards those who worked in the 'yards' (Purcell 1953: 21). As might be imagined, modern-day kill-floor workers take umbrage to such characterizations. They are quick to point out that they play a vital role in the provision of an important source of protein for the large majority of the population that eats meat, however, the work remains stigmatized.

On top of this prejudice, working conditions in a packinghouse are seldom pleasant. Workers on the kill floor and dressing line labour in a hot steamy atmosphere, exposed to blood, offal, and a certain amount of excrement and mud attached as 'tag' to the hide of some animals, especially in late winter and early spring. The coolers are damp, an inevitable result of the chilling of steamy hot carcasses, the fabrication floor is deliberately kept a few degrees above freezing to prevent spoilage, and workers are issued knitted gloves. The kill-floor odour is a pervasive sweet smell of meat, blood, and organs, and one quickly gets accustomed to it. But when tank rooms and rendering apparatus are opened up for maintenance, they stink abominably. The processing of some viscera products involves the handling of bodily fluids and alimentary contents that would otherwise be untouchable filth. Butcher smocks start out each day freshly laundered, but at many work stations on the kill floor they are spattered with blood for much of the work day.

Early Packinghouse Labour Relations

The Amalgamated Meat Cutters and Butcher Workmen of North America (the Amalgamated) was chartered on 26 January 1897. As its name suggests, the union sought to represent a combination of journeyman meat cutters operating primarily in retail trade and butcher workmen in large-scale packinghouses. As an American Federation of Labour (AFL) affiliate, the Amalgamated was geared to the craft of cutting meat and embraced 'all men who use a knife.' In an age when unions were organized by craft rather than industry, they laid claim over overlapping jurisdictions. Retail butchers came under the auspices of the Retail Clerks, cattle drivers were claimed by the Teamsters, meat cutters were claimed by the Amalgamated, while meat packing itself might be claimed by the Coopers. Within an integrated plant, many separate unions might lay claim over different phases in the value added process of industrial meat packing. Thus, a large city and packing centre such as Chicago had separate locals to represent Hog Butchers, Sheep Butchers, Beef Boners, Beef Casing Workers, Beef Carriers, Sausage Makers, Hide Cellar Men, and Oleo Workers (Commons 1904: 2).

In eastern Canada the Amalgamated began organizing meat-packing workers towards the end of the First World War. When commodity meat prices crashed in 1921, and a 12.5 per cent wage cut was applied across the industry, the workers represented by the Amalgamated went on strike in Montreal, Toronto, and Chatham, Ontario. However, support from the American-based international union was weak, and the employers quickly turned to replacement workers. The strike failed, and the Amalgamated passed from the Canadian scene (Montague 1950: 37).

The United Packinghouse Workers of America

Attempts to organize meat-packing workers did not succeed until legislation more sympathetic to organized labour was passed, and until unions became structured along industry lines instead of by craft. This was achieved first in the United States and later diffused into Canada. The National Labor Relations Act (Wagner Act) become effective in 1937 when its constitutionality was established by the U.S. Supreme Court. An integral component of Franklin Roosevelt's 'New Deal' presidency, the new legislation gave workers the right to organize into trade unions independent of the company of employment for the purpose of collective bargaining, and required employers to 'bargain in good faith.' By fostering union security, and outlawing discrimination or discharge of employees who organized or joined unions, the act fostered industrial unionism in the United States. Equivalent rights were not conferred in Canada until Order in Council P.C. 1003 was promulgated in 1944, setting out wartime labour relations regulations and creating Canada's National War Labour Board (NWLB). While P.C. 1003 was in effect between 1944 and 1946, unions structured along industrial lines enjoyed rapid growth in Canada.

Shortly after the Wagner Act came into effect, the Congress of Industrial Organizations (CIO) was established to encourage industrial unionism as an alternative to craft unions. Bargaining power would be based on the sheer numbers of unskilled workers on which mass production depended, rather than the monopoly on scarce skills that had characterized the craft unions. The newly formed CIO was instrumental in the creation and rapid growth of powerful industrial unions such as the United Auto Workers, United Steel Workers, and eventually United Packinghouse Workers of America (UPWA).

The Packinghouse Workers Organizing Committee (PWOC) was created in October of 1937 and by the middle of the Second World War, the PWOC had organized about 60 per cent of U.S. packinghouse workers (Perry and Kegley 1989: 103). Since the Amalgamated had made little headway in Canada, the PWOC had a relatively clear field to organize Canadian packing plants as well (Brody 1964: 195–6), and it began organizing in Canada in 1939. By 1940, Canada Packers' and Swift-Canadian's Toronto plants had received PWOC charters (Montague 1950: 75). Some of the western Canadian plants were organized as federal locals of the Trades and Labour Congress of Canada (TLC), the umbrella group for craft unions in Canada. But the TLC showed little interest in its packinghouse locals, and beginning in 1942, the PWOC began to take its place (Grover 1996: 64).

The PWOC was chartered by the CIO as the UPWA in 1943, and a Canadian district was created at its founding convention. Aided by P.C. 1003, the Canadian district of the UPWA organized most of the major meat-packing plants. By 1945, the union had forty-two locals in Canada representing some 10,500 workers and it enjoyed near unanimous support among its members.

In 1943, the UPWA targeted Canada Packers' St-Boniface plant and organized it with the help of local 'communist sympathizers.' Following the model that served it so well in the United States, the union used the successful unionization of the Canada Packers plant as a lever to certify the neighbouring Burns and Swift Canadian plants. Having organized the big three, the UPWA then went after smaller independents such as Winnipeg's Public Abattoir. Most of Manitoba's meat-packing workers were organized by the end of the war, a remarkable feat considering that, as late as 1942, none of the province's packinghouses were unionized (Grover 1996: 88–96).

The earliest wartime collective agreements in the Canadian meat-packing industry were negotiated on a plant-by-plant basis. Beyond recognition of collective bargaining, the first agreements achieved very little. For example, the first agreement at Canada Packers' flagship plant between the 'Toronto Employees Plant Council' and Canada Packers, dated 3 March 1942 stated: 'The Company agrees to pay and the employees agree to accept the presently existing wage scale of wage rates during the life of this agreement, subject to modifications permitted from time to time by the National War Labour Board' (UPWA, 1942). The company reserved the right to adjust wage rates of individual employees within the existing wage scale, opening the door to allegations of favouritism or discrimination. At the end of the 1943 fiscal year, Canada Packers granted its workers a 'full cost of living bonus' of $4.25 per week and individual wage adjustments that averaged 4 cents per hour (Canada Packers 1943, *Annual Report*: 6).

In Alberta, a number of plants had local unions chartered directly by the AFL. In Edmonton, for example, Packing Employees Federal Union No. 78 represented employees of Canada Packers Limited, Burns and Company, and Swift Canadian in 1943. Following a union appeal to the NWLB, each of the three companies was directed to pay the same wage schedule to its Edmonton workers based on a six-tier occupational classification (Table 7.1). During the Second World War the workers on the beef kill were still the packinghouse aristocrats, as described by John Commons forty years earlier.

In imposing such a regional wage standard on three competing firms, Canada's NWLB established the principle of regional wage equality before the UPWA came to dominate the industry. It would be twenty years before the big three were paying the same wages within all regional labour markets. Yet there was clearly an incentive for the companies to take wages out of competition as shown by the following letter written by Burns and Company to the associate minister of the federal Department of Labour: 'It is essential in order that employees may not

Table 7.1 Selected wage rates in Edmonton packing plants of Canada Packers, Burns & Co., and Swift Canadian, 1943

Occupational classification	Hourly wage ($)
Beef kill	
Floorsman	.80–.85
Rumping	.70–.75
Head skinner	.65–.70
Beef sticker	.60–.65
Beef knocker & hang on	.55–.60
All other jobs	.50–.55
Hog kill	
Splitting	.65–.70
Hog header	.60–.65
Belly shavers	.55–.60
All other jobs	.50–.55

Note: Occupations were selected to represent each different wage range. Cattle butchers had 22 different occupational classes while hog butchers had 28.
Source: National War Labour Board, Finding and Direction, Case File A-2, 24 November 1943

be persuaded to move from one company to another that packing house wages, hours of work, holidays with pay, etc. should be the same in each packing centre, and that any packer whose present arrangements respecting wages, holidays, with his employees do not compare favourably with the others or even the one paying the highest rates of wages, should be permitted to adjust his rates of wages etc. so as to conform with the highest paid in each packing centre' (Burns 1942).

Taking wages out of competition within local labour markets was as desirable for employers as it was for unionized employees. The crux of the issue between employers and their unions was that the companies were content with industry-wide standards within regionally segmented labour markets, while the employees were dedicated to the principle of uniform compensation from coast to coast.

Collective Bargaining in Meat Packing

The three most distinctive features of industrial relations in the meat-packing industry can be traced to the middle 1940s: industry-wide pattern bargaining in which a master agreement negotiated with one firm was applied uniformly across the industry by most of its competitors; the gradual elimination of geographic wage differentials within the industry; and a labour grade system that assigned premium rates over the base wage to more highly skilled jobs. These features were an artifact of wartime labour relations in the United States, and they all entered the Canadian industry in the late 1940s as the UPWA came to dominate meat-packing unionism in Canada.

Pattern bargaining is the negotiation of a 'key bargain' which provides the model for collective agreements between a union and a group of employers who follow the pattern. Typically, the union targets one firm and negotiates a company-wide contract known as a 'master agreement.' Once the key bargain is struck, the union demands identical terms from all of the other firms that follow the pattern. Pattern bargaining is the process and the master agreement is the vehicle for standardizing wages and working conditions across an industry (Perry and Kegley 1989: 123).

Pattern bargaining was not unique to meat packing; it was a feature of the steel and auto industries as well. But the meat-packing industry was less localized in the traditional manufacturing belt, and packinghouses were spatially distributed on a truly continental scale. Unionized meat-packing plants spanned North America from the eastern Seaboard and Maritime provinces to the West Coast and from a major meat-packing and stockyards complex in Fort Worth, Texas, to a miniature replica in Prince Albert in central Saskatchewan. In comparison with other manufacturing industries, meat packing had one of the most geographically uniform systems of industrial relations on the continent. The issue of a national wage for a national industry, irrespective of regional productivity, and cost-of-living differences was a distinctive feature of pattern bargaining in meat packing.

Wage negotiations were made more complex by the requirement for a premium to compensate packing-plant workers doing jobs with higher levels of skill, importance to carcass value, and tactile delicacy. During the Second World War, a labour grade system was formulated by the National War Labor Board of the United States which had twenty-five separate job groupings, each paying 2.5 cents an hour more than the grade immediately below it. The highest job classification would therefore carry a premium of 60 cents an hour above the lowest. These labour grades became known as 'brackets.' Each job in the packing plant would be assigned a set number of brackets. The number of brackets was multiplied by the bracket rate and added to the unskilled labour rate to arrive at the hourly wage for the task. The ultimate goal of the packinghouse labour movement was to reward the same job with the same number of brackets no matter where in the country the job was performed or what firm actually employed the worker.

From its inception, the UPWA was committed to an industry-wide, multi-company bargaining process. In a sense there already was some basis for industry-wide collective bargaining as the meat-packing firms clearly wanted to take wages out of competition within regional labour markets. But the packing firms did everything in their power to resist national bargaining and the negotiation of master agreements with the Packinghouse Workers.

The 1944 Negotiations: Recognition and Precedent

By 1944, many of the big three plants had been organized by the UPWA including Canada Packers in Toronto, Peterborough, Edmonton, and Vancouver; Swift Canadian in Moncton, Toronto, Winnipeg, Moose Jaw, and New Westminster; and Burns in Winnipeg, Regina, Prince Albert, Edmonton, and Vancouver. The primary goal of the UPWA was to hold national negotiations with the Canadian big three. From the union's point of view, national bargaining was necessary because of the national scale of the industry and national scope of the big three firms. Accordingly, the Canadian District of the UPWA initiated negotiations with Canada Packers for the first time in the summer of 1944. The union reasoned that once it signed a master agreement with the largest firm in the sector, Swift Canadian and Burns would be sure to follow (Craig 1964: 97). When Canada Packers demurred on the question of a nationwide master agreement, the union went on to make the same request of Swift and Burns with the same result. The firms never made their objections to national bargaining clear except to state that it was a departure from past practice. Apparently they were unwilling to submit themselves to the uncertainties attendant on an untried system of wage determination. Perhaps the multilocational firms were unwilling to surrender the flexibility of bargaining with one plant at a time; if one plant were to strike they could shift production and continue to serve the market from other plants.

The union demonstrated its resolve by holding strike votes in all of the plants it represented in Canada with over 99 per cent of workers voting in favour. The threat was not designed to get the attention of the firms themselves (their intransigence was already well established), but to alert the government that the operation of a crucial wartime industry was being threatened. The strike vote strategy had the desired effect, as the federal government appointed Justice S.E. Richards as an industrial disputes inquiry commissioner in October of 1944. Thus, the first national labour negotiations in the meat-packing industry were held under the auspices of wartime legislation by the federal government.

The Richards Report of 1944 (Canada, *Labour Gazette* 1944) failed to establish any agreement on wages and working conditions, and the union's goal of establishing a system of national negotiations was not achieved. Wages and working conditions were gradually settled on a plant-by-plant basis over the course of the next year. However, the UPWA and the big three did reach agreement on three important prerequisites for pattern bargaining: settlement of future differences by collective bargaining, mechanisms to deduct union dues from wages at source and ensure union security, and the coordination of expiry dates for the various collective agreements.

The 1945–1946 Negotiations: Towards National Bargaining

Progress on national wage standards and working conditions became the critical issues in 1945 negotiations. Burns and Company was the first to be approached in June of 1945. The principal demand was a forty-hour, five-day work week (down from the prevailing forty-eight hour, six-day week) with no decrease in total weekly pay. As in 1944, the union threatened an early strike vote if the companies would not consent to company-wide bargaining. But the federal government intervened more actively than expected.

Under the War Measures Act, orders in council put Burns and Company, Swift Canadian Company Limited, and Canada Packers Limited under the custody of a government-appointed controller in October of 1945 (Canada, Privy Council 1945). This extreme and unusual measure was justified by the risk of disruption in the flow of food to civilians and the military in Canada and Europe and the potential impact on agriculture. The same device was later used in the United States during a Swift and Company strike in January of 1946. Acting under the War Labor Disputes Act, President Truman, ordered the secretary of agriculture to seize and operate the plants affected which brought an early end to the strike, as well as a substantial wage increase (Purcell 1953: 60).

While under the management of the controller appointed by the Canadian government (James Gordon Taggart, chairman of the Meat Board), the union and the firms were directed to negotiate in good faith to settle the dispute, while some 12,000 unionized employees were enjoined from strike action under the War Measures Act. Government action freed the companies of the strike threat while forcing them to negotiate nationally in the context of a new inquiry commission. The union's strike strategy had been undermined, but it achieved its goal of national company-wide negotiations (Craig 1964: 112). The report of the second inquiry commission formed, in essence, a nationwide, company-wide template for local collective agreements. The work week was reduced from forty-eight to forty-five hours (except for Quebec which was reduced from fifty-four to forty-eight hours) and wage rates were increased by 6.8 per cent. Although the 1945 negotiations left the key issue of national bargaining unresolved, it was construed as a union victory simply because there was a precedent for determining wages and working conditions at the national level. On the other hand, the union fell short of its 30 per cent wage increase and forty-hour work week demands.

Surprisingly, the final step in achieving national bargaining was attained not under federal government pressure but as matter of free choice by Canada Packers and Burns and Company. Two reasons have been offered for this reversal of what had previously been an intransigent position. By 1946, the big three had gained a healthy respect for the UPWA leadership and understood the strength of their resolve to achieve national bargaining. The firms became convinced that unionism could no longer be avoided; the time had come to accept the new industrial relations regime and make the best of it. Second, it was simply more efficient to have corporate-level industrial relations professionals conduct one set of national negotiations every two years than to contend with a never-ending stream of local plant negotiations at various locations around the country (Craig 1964: 127). This was supported by a former executive officer of Burns Foods: 'The advantage [of national negotiations] was definitely the fact that you got a monkey off your back in one fell swoop. As opposed to having to go from branch to branch and be left up to the vagaries of what might happen as a result. You take a [militant] plant like Prince Albert; I doubt that if we hadn't had pattern bargaining whether we would have ever got away without a strike each time we negotiated in Prince Albert. But they were pulled along by the national bargain' (William Goetz, Interview). By the summer of 1946, national-scale company-wide bargaining had become a reality in the Canadian meat-packing industry. The three master agreements still had significant differences, but they contained uniform provisions for wages and for some working conditions.

The 1947 Negotiations: National Strike Action and Arbitration

At the end of March 1947, the federal government relinquished its wartime control over labour relations within the designated war industries, and the provinces resumed their role in regulating collective bargaining in most industries, including meat packing. The UPWA could no longer expect federal government intervention to assist in their negotiations.

In June 1947, the national office of the union tendered identical bargaining proposals to each of the big three: a general wage increase of 15 cents per hour, elimination of geographic wage differentials, union shop and compulsory check-off, a forty-hour work week, and improved vacation provisions. In contravention of all of the provincial labour relations statutes, the union held illegal strike votes in Swift Canadian plants across the country. Swift Canadian may have been the target of the first set of strike votes because, as the only U.S.-based packer, the union hoped that it would benefit from the progress it had made south of the border. Swift Canadian already tended to pay higher wages than Canada Packers or Burns, so it offered the greatest potential for wage increases in other chains. Some 98 per cent of Swift Canadian workers voted in favour of strike action. When negotiations deadlocked, illegal strikes began to spread across the country through the early days of September 1947. The strike extended to independent plants as well, so that at its peak, the 1947 strike affected 14,150 workers in forty-seven meat-packing plants across Canada (McTague 1947: 1791).

Facing pressures to join in arbitration proceedings with the other companies (Swift Canadian had always avoided any type of third-party intervention in its affairs) and the possibility that its plants might be seized and placed under another government-appointed controller in Manitoba and Saskatchewan, Swift Canadian settled for a general wage increase of 10 cents an hour across the board plus increases of 1.5 to 3 cents an hour in some plants to bring regional wage rates closer to a national standard (Craig 1964: 190–1). Strikers at Burns and Canada Packers returned to work on 22 October 1947 based on an interim 7 cents per hour increase with all other matters at issue to be settled by binding arbitration. In essence, the decision of the arbitrator C.P. McTague (chairman of the Ontario Securities Commission and formerly chairman of the NWLB), treated the Swift Canadian settlement as the key bargain: 'If I did not have before me very much in evidence the settlement between the Union and Swift Canadian Co. Limited, I might have reached a different conclusion from the one I have reached ... I think that it must be concluded on balance that the Union and the Swift Company in that settlement arrived at a figure generally considered just to the worker and within the ability of the Swift Company to pay and carry on competitively with Canada Packers and Burns and Company' (McTague 1947: 1792). Burns and Canada Packers' employees received an additional 3 cents per hour to bring their total general increase to 10 cents per hour, identical to the Swift settlement. McTague's remarks suggest that Swift Canadian blinked first and had it not settled so fast and so high, Canada Packers and Burns would not have had to pay so much. From that time on, it was left to Canada Packers to lead the way in national negotiations!

In addition to the general wage increase, the wages in the lower paid plants were increased as much as 5 cents per hour to reduce geographic differentials. For example, workers in Canada Packers' lowest paid plant in Charlottetown received an increase of 5 cents per hour, while employees in the more highly paid Toronto and Vancouver plants received nothing more than the general wage increase. Thus, the McTague arbitration reduced geographic wage differentials, the first step along the road to national wage uniformity. The agreement also brought stability to labour relations in meat packing by preventing the union from exercising the strike vote strategy, which had worked so effectively from 1944 until 1947. Henceforth, the union was required to attempt to settle differences through conciliation, mediation, or arbitration before it resorted to the ballot box (McTague 1947: 1794). This provision remained in the industry's collective agreements until 1982.

The 1947 agreement established a number of precedents for national bargaining in the meat-packing industry. First, the national bargaining that had first taken place under federal government auspices in wartime continued in a markedly different peacetime regulatory environment amid eight different provincial jurisdictions. Second, a key bargain was reached, albeit unwittingly, by Swift Canadian which served as the pattern for the other two members of the big three. Third, the first steps had been taken towards a reduction in geographic differentials and the development of a uniform national wage rate.

Technological Change and Unionization

Just as the United Packinghouse Workers were in their ascendency in Canada and the United States, new technologies such as continuous on-the-rail dressing and mechanical hide-pullers were developed in 1950 to make the cattle kill less arduous and less dependent on the highly paid 'butcher aristocracy' which was required for bed dressing. After many decades during which technological change had languished in meat packing, there was an abrupt burst of innovation that coincided neatly with the emergence of a new landscape of unionism: 'The correlation between technological changes and the solidification of unionism in meat packing is exact ... Through a pervasive rationalization of production, meat packers began to reduce their dependence on an increasingly expensive and problematic labour force ... Thus, although meat packers may have accepted the new reality of organized labour in the context of higher meat prices and expanding sales of high-value processed meats, they moved quickly to undermine the base of union power by further mechanizing and de-skilling packinghouse work' (Page 1998: 283).

The introduction of technological change in Swift Canadian's western plants provides a case in point. In 1964, Swift Canadian introduced on-the-rail beef dressing in conjunction with a Johnson mechanical hide-puller in its Edmonton, Calgary, and St-Boniface slaughter plants. By 1965, the UPWA was concerned with its impact on the packinghouse labour force. The mechanical hide-puller eliminated the highly paid jobs of hide dropping, backing, and rumping that had previously been necessary using the bed dressing technology. Second, Swift proposed a labour grade classification for the new occupation of 'Johnson hide puller operator' of eight brackets. The union opened its negotiations with an offer of ten as had been negotiated with Burns and later raised it to twelve as had been negotiated with Canada Packers. Swift Canadian was prepared to pay twelve brackets if Canada Packers was paying twelve, but it was unwilling to go to seventeen brackets, the rate formerly paid to backers (made redundant by the technological change) and which the UPWA had succeeded in negotiating with Swift's home country plants in the United States (UPWA 1965).

A second example of technological change was the installation of chain-driven loading facilities, in 1964, to convey sides of beef directly from the coolers to the rails of special purpose reefer cars in Canada Packers' new Lethbridge kill and chill plant. Mechanizing the transfer of half carcasses did away with the job of the beef luggers, an unskilled but strenuous job rated at nine brackets (UPWA 1964). In short, technological change on the kill floor reduced the packers' dependence on both the specialized butcher skills for removing hides and the brawn demanded of luggers. By deskilling kill-floor operations, the packinghouses gradually reduced their reliance on a labour force that was growing increasingly militant and well paid.

Progress in Wages and Working Conditions after 1947

The pattern bargaining system matured in 1948, and traditions were established that would not change for the next thirty-six years. Two-year agreements became the norm, and a bargaining protocol became established. Long before collective bargaining began, delegates from all of the meat-packing locals of the UPWA would meet at a national bargaining conference to formulate their demands. The union formed bargaining teams for each of the three 'chains,' one for each of the companies. Each union bargaining team was composed of delegates from each company's local unions and was led by an assistant director of the Canadian district. The three chain committees would form the union's national bargaining committee. Heads of labour relations in each of the big three would also meet beforehand to discuss their bargaining positions. The bargaining team from each firm was composed of its head of labour relations and the general manager of each of its packing plants. After these preliminaries, the big three and the UPWA would meet at a Toronto hotel. The bargaining team from each firm and its corresponding chain of the union met separately (Craig 1964: 84).

In 1948, and most subsequent years, pattern bargaining was generally led by Canada Packers, the largest firm in the Canadian meat-packing industry and the price leader in the consumer marketplace. It also paid relatively high wages. In 1948, the average wage at Canada Packers was $1.01 compared with $0.95 in the meat industry as a whole and $0.91 for all manufacturing industries (Canada Packers 1948, *Annual Report*: 14). Since it had the most plants, the union's Canada Packers' delegates tended to control union policy (Bain 1964: 147; Downie 1972: 54). The procedure for the other two members of the big three, Swift and Burns, together with their union representatives, would be to wait for Canada Packers to reach a settlement before then agreeing on virtually identical terms. The union's press release at the conclusion of the 1958 negotiations gives a vivid sense of the conformity of the pattern:

> The twenty-one cent per hour wage and fringe pattern established by the United Packinghouse Workers of America with Canada Packers Limited for its 6,000 employees in 10 plants has been agreed to by Swift Canadian Co. Ltd. for its 3,000 employees in 6 plants and with Burns & Co. for its 3,000 employees in 9 plants across Canada.
>
> The terms of the price setting package are subject to ratification by the union's 12,000 members covered by the three master agreements across Canada ... It is expected that the terms of settlement will also spread to the 2,500 union members employed by the small or independent meatpacking companies throughout the country. (UPWA 1958)

In the event that an agreement was not forthcoming, one firm would be targeted for strike action (usually Canada Packers) while the other firms and their unions went back to work and waited for a settlement (Forrest 1989: 394).

As the meat-packing companies expanded their operations by acquiring existing meat-packing companies or by building new plants, they attempted to leave the new operations outside of the master agreement and the big three wage pattern. The union, on the other hand, was committed to bringing these new establishments under the master agreement. For instance, Canada Packers acquired Calgary Packers and Wilsil Limited of Montreal in 1955. Both acquisitions retained their corporate identity after the merger and operated under their own names in an ultimately futile attempt to avoid the collective bargaining umbrella of the UPWA. One of the issues in Canada Packers' 1966 strike was the question of extending the master agreement to cover the firm's new kill and chill beef plant in Lethbridge and in branch houses scattered across the country (Figure 7.1). The union prevailed in the case of the Lethbridge plant while most of the smaller branch houses were eventually closed.

By pattern bargaining, the UPWA and its successor unions made semiskilled, meat-packing workers among the highest paid manual workers in Canada in the 1950s, 1960s, and 1970s (Forrest 1989: 398). Between 1956 and 1966, Canada Packers' wage rates (under the master agreement) increased by fifty-nine per cent compared with a 21.6 per cent increase in the cost of living index and a 47 per cent average wage increase for all manufacturing industries. By 1966, Canada Packers wage rates were 20 per cent higher than the average for all manufacturing industries (Canada Packers Limited Annual Report 1967: 6). In 1983, when compensation reached its peak, the master

Figure 7.1. 'Divide they conquer – United we stand.' The importance of bringing all plants in the chain under the master agreement and the pattern bargaining umbrella. Source: Negotiation Bulletin No. 17, United Packinghouse, Food and Allied Workers. Archives of Ontario C262-7-7CPG5.

agreement looked very attractive indeed. The base wage was $11.99 an hour and job class increments reached 8 cents per hour meaning an additional $1.20 an hour for a typical job rated at fifteen brackets. Morning and afternoon rest periods were increased to fifteen minutes in length and there were 11 paid holidays in the calendar. Vacation time was generous with three to five weeks for those with five to twenty years of service and early retirement was available by age sixty-one. Life insurance, sick benefits, long-term disability, and pension benefits improved in much the same way (Taylor and Dow 1988: Appendix A).

This was a far cry from working conditions in 1942 when the work week was set at fifty-six hours with a time-and-a-half wage premium only payable after ten hours work on weekdays and after six hours on

Saturdays. A two-week vacation was provided to male employees with five to twenty years of service; there were eight statutory holidays a year; there were no benefits; the nominal grievance procedure did not provide for arbitration, and there was no provision for union security or recognition of union officers. There was no formal job grade system, and when the collective agreements finally formalized a minimum base wage rate, unskilled women were paid 88 per cent of the wages paid to their male counterparts, a difference of 11.5 cents per hour in 1949. By 1966, women's starting rates were 94 per cent of their male counterparts, and the sex differential finally disappeared from the wage scale in 1971 (Taylor and Dow 1988).

U.S. Influence on Working Conditions

One of the earliest attempts of the UPWA to improve working conditions dealt with practices that were unique to meat packing. In 1945, the union wanted employers to provide specialized apparel (e.g., rubber boots, rubber and oilskin aprons, and warm clothes for use in the cooler), as well as knives and other small tools required for work. It also wanted the companies to pay for the time workers spent sharpening knives and changing into working clothes: 'If a worker in the fertilizer department were to go home without changing clothes, he would probably have the signal honour of being the sole occupant of the street car, perhaps even to the exclusion of the motorman and the conductor' (UPWA 1945: 3).

The justification for these demands was the precedent set in the United States which originated ultimately with wartime labour directives from the U.S. government to the U.S. big four meat packers. As a foreign-owned company, Swift Canadian functioned as a conduit of U.S. reforms in working conditions, and the UPWA was quick to point out the absurdity of any inconsistencies between the two countries. For example, Swift Canadian agreed to pay for a meal if an employee had to work more than five consecutive hours after the first meal period (typically after nine hours of work), but it would not pay workers for the mealtime itself: 'Whereas Swift & Co. in the United States furnish a free meal and pay for twenty minutes time spent eating it, they refuse the same privilege to the Canadian workers. The workers are at a loss to understand the dual policy of Swift and Co. and feel that they are being discriminated against because they are Canadian workers' (UPWA 1945: 4). By drawing attention to inequities such as these, the international union liberalized the meat-packing work environment in Canada and transmitted progress in working conditions from the United States to Canada.

Pattern Bargaining: Towards National Standards

As the UPWA gained strength and contracts specified wages in black and white for the first time, it became apparent that there were enormous differences in compensation between companies and regions. The first goal of pattern bargaining was to establish a key bargain with a geographic wage schedule and to impose that same schedule on all the firms who followed the pattern. The second goal of pattern bargaining was to eliminate the geographic wage differential between places.

Intraregional Standardization of Wages

By 1947, each of the big three had collective agreements covering plants from the Atlantic to the Pacific (in the case of Canada Packers and Swift Canadian) and from Ontario to the Pacific (in the case of Burns). In every region where it operated a plant, Swift Canadian paid the highest wages in the region (Figure 7.2). For example, in Vancouver Swift Canadian paid male employees 89 cents an hour, while Burns and Canada Packers paid 86 cents an hour – 3.4 per cent less. By 1969, the intercompany differentials had finally disappeared and each of the big three was paying the same regional base rate (Figure 7.3). Wages had been taken out of competition within regional labour markets. Vancouver had the highest base wage at $3.02 per hour, the Prairie plants paid $2.945, Toronto and Montreal area plants paid $2.975, and Canada Packers' Charlottetown plant trailed the pack at $2.89 per hour. (In the 1980 contract Charlottetown received a special one-time increase to bring it up to national wage levels; however, the plant was closed in 1984.)

As well as bargaining for a standard base rate between firms within regions, the UPWA was committed to standardizing job rates in different plants. The differences in the reward attached to various jobs among companies became an important bargaining issue. For example, in 1946 the job of beef boning in Winnipeg area slaughter plants was rated at 84 cents per hour at Burns, 97.5 cents per hour at Swift Canadian and $1.10 at Canada Packers. With the advent of a common regional base rate, and the creation of a system of brackets, a certain degree of standardization in job grades was achieved. Inequities remained, however, not only between firms within regions but also

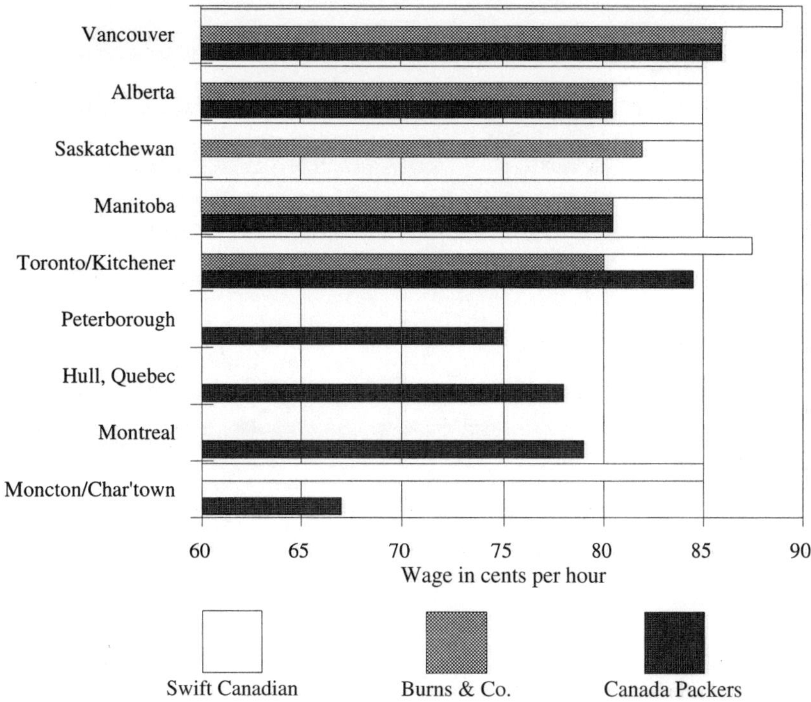

Figure 7.2. Wage differentials in Canadian packinghouses, 1947. Unskilled male base rates at the big three meat packers. Source: Collective Agreements of United Packinghouse Workers of America.

between regions within firms. Figure 7.4 shows examples of individual kill-floor jobs at Burns and Company that received different levels of compensation in different cities. In 1948, the UPWA and the big three agreed to work towards a consistent premium for different labour grades across the country, a goal that was finally achieved in 1956.

Interregional Standardization and Wage Convergence

The second goal of pattern bargaining was to attain a single nationwide base wage and eliminate differences among regions. The goal was clearly articulated in the 1940s but took nearly forty years to come very close to fruition. Why was this such an important issue for the United Packinghouse Workers?

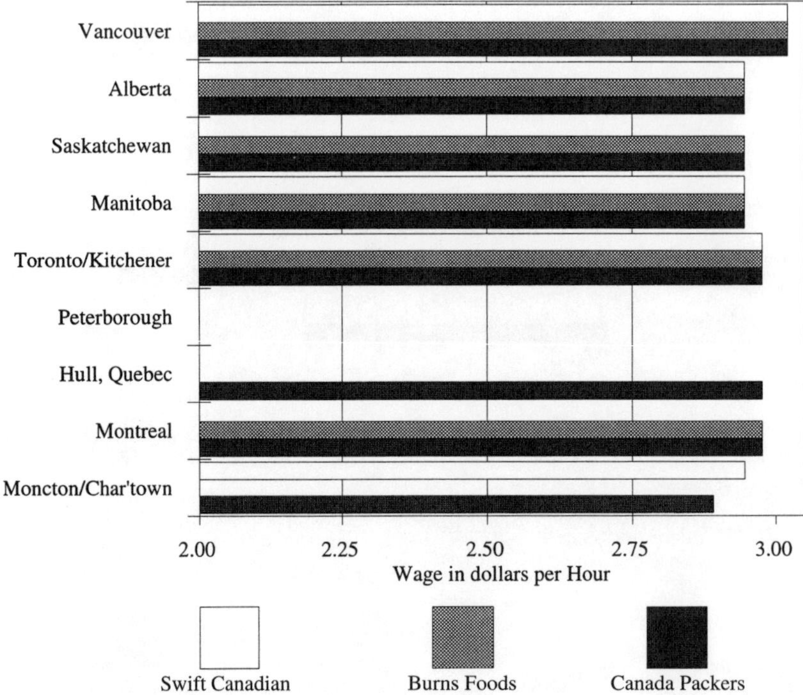

Figure 7.3. Wage differentials in Canadian packinghouses, 1969. Unskilled male base rates at the big three meat packers. Source: Collective Agreements of United Packinghouse Workers of America.

The foundation of the union's case for the elimination of regional wage differentials rested on three footings: to meet the basic needs of the lowest income groups in the packinghouse labour force, to recognize a national wage in a national industry, and to follow the precedent of gradual elimination of regional differentials in the U.S. packinghouses. For these reasons, a uniform national wage was the ultimate goal and principal justification for the national bargaining process. The most clearly reasoned justification for a national wage was presented in the union's submission to the McTague arbitration (UPWA, 1947).

Until the early years of the twentieth century, meat packing was localized in geographically isolated markets. Thus, local conditions and the idiosyncrasies of isolated urban labour markets permitted a

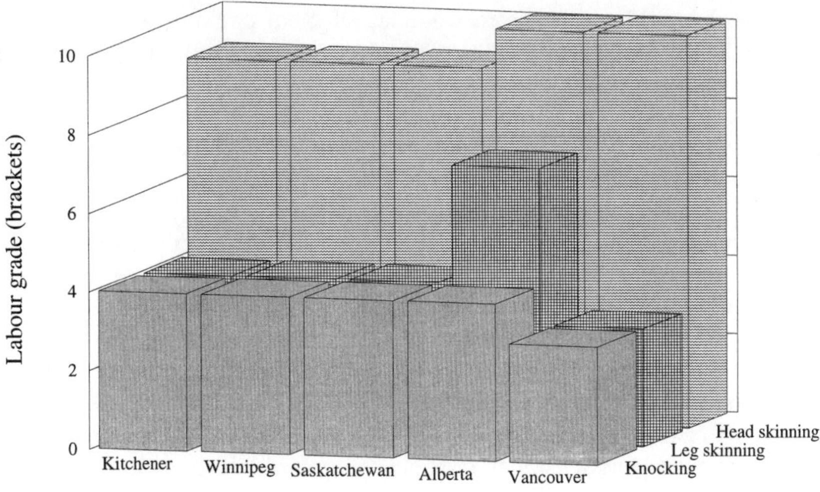

Figure 7.4. Labour grades at Burns and Company, 1955. Source: 'Job Rate Comparison,' National Archives of Canada, United Food and Commercial Workers, MG 28 I186 Vol 7.

wide range of different wage scales in firms which were typically small, family owned, and operated by journeyman butchers. With the creation of national-scale firms and national product markets there also came an impetus to unionize on a national scale in precisely the way theorized by John Commons. However, wages tended to be driven down by the weak financial condition of most of the big meat-packing firms in the post–First World War period. Management economized on labour costs by hiring unskilled packinghouse workers at the lowest possible rates.

In 1947 base wages in big three packing plants ranged from a low of 67 cents per hour in Charlottetown to a high of 89 cents per hour in Vancouver. The companies often cited regional cost-of-living differences to justify their wage differentials. The union argued that the economies of small city living were exaggerated and in any case the wage differentials had not been scientifically calculated to compensate for these variations. Examples such as centrally distributed foodstuffs, coal for home heating, and housing were presented to show that consumer goods were often more costly in smaller centres, further disadvantaging packinghouse workers outside Toronto and Vancouver. The union argued that the real problem was the inadequacy of meat-packing wages and the chronically depressed living conditions of meat-packing workers. All those who earned the base rate, no matter what their location, would have difficulty in attaining a decent standard of living.

The second union argument in favour of eliminating geographic wage differentials concerned the national character of the industry. First, the technology and nature of packinghouse work was the same everywhere; there were no geographic differentials in working conditions, work place hazards, or the strenuous character of the work. Also, by the late 1940s, a truly national livestock and meat market had emerged. The only difference in costs of livestock between the Atlantic and the Pacific coast was the cost of transportation. Meat and meat by-products flowed from surplus areas to deficit areas to equalize prices so that ceteris paribus, fresh western beef sold for the same price as eastern beef. Finally, meat products were sold in a national market, promoted by national brand-name advertising, and produced by national-scale corporate packinghouse systems. The union argued that when regional variations in labour rates were eliminated, the firms would have a better comparison of their true costs and any tendency to inefficiency in plants benefiting from lower wages would be eliminated. The union did not want to see any incentive for production shifting to exploit regional differentials in wage costs, concluding: 'Low [wage] rates in some localities potentially provide an entering wedge to destroy gains in living standards so far won by the union. The economically sound and enlightened course is to wipe out altogether the existing geographical wage rate differentials' (UPWA 1947: 37). It seems ironic that after years of progress, these fears would be realized in precisely the way that the union foresaw and wanted to avoid in 1947.

The third union argument in favour of eliminating regional differentials was the precedent being set in the United States. By 1947, there had been some progress in achieving a uniform wage floor in the United States north of the Mason–Dixon line (Brody 1964: 213). From the Atlantic to the Rocky mountains, the Chicago-based 'metropolitan wage rate' had gradually become the norm: $1.02 for male workers and $0.915 for females. The metropolitan rate applied as equally in Ottumwa and Mason City, Iowa, as it did in Chicago or St Louis. The southern rate was still markedly lower than the metropolitan rate, but it too was converging on the national average.

In the view of the UPWA, meat packing was a national industry

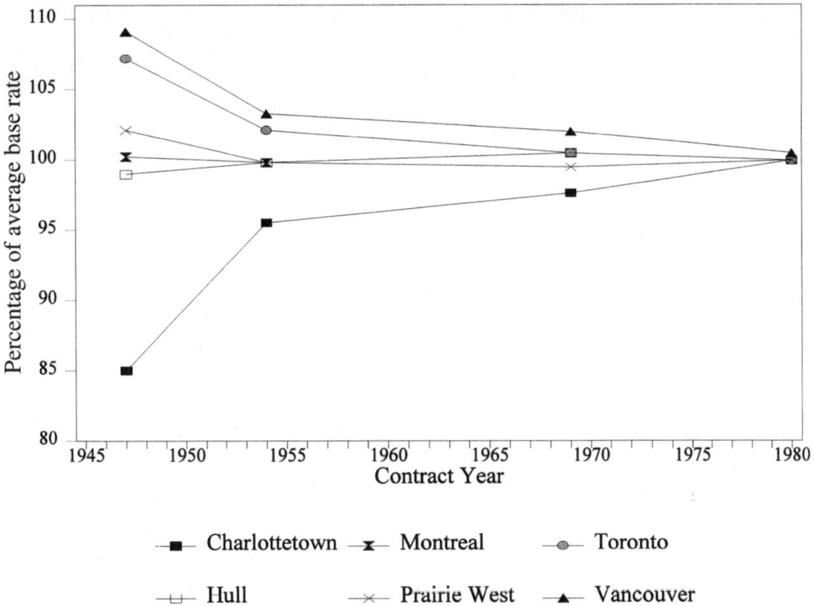

Figure 7.5. National wage convergence at Canada Packers, 1947–1980. Regional wages as a percentage of Canada Packers' average male base wage. Source: Collective Agreements of United Packinghouse Workers of America.

dominated by national firms operating in national markets. The union noted that there were uniform base wage rates in both of Canada's national railway systems, in basic steel production, and in the post office. Thus, the union argued that meat packing, too, should have a national wage floor without regard for where a plant was located or its workers lived.

The easiest way to portray interregional wage differences is to focus on one multilocational firm, Canada Packers, which had the most geographically extensive plant network (Figure 7.5). The wide variation among the six packing regions in 1947 gradually converged until 1980 when a nationally standardized base wage rate was in effect everywhere but Vancouver (Taylor and Dow 1988: Appendix A). Convergence in regional wage differentials was accomplished in two ways: (1) when wages increased by a fixed number of cents per hour, the relative difference between packing centres diminished and (2) the lowest paying plants sometimes received higher wage increases than plants with higher base rates.

By 1980, the packinghouse union's goal had been reached. It had secured a standardized compensation package among the big three within regions and was pennies an hour from a national wage standard.

Conclusion

The meat-packing industry in both Canada and the United States has been an oligopoly since the early years of the twentieth century, although controlled by different firms. Aided by the Wagner Act in the United States and P.C. 1003 in Canada, wartime labour regulations in both countries, one international union was able to organize most of the meat-packing plants on the continent. Following the CIO tradition of industrial unionism, the UPWA had prevailed over the meat packers: first, in securing recognition of their union; second, in establishing a system of national bargaining; and third, in achieving a level of regional wage equity seen in few other industries. A system of pattern bargaining modelled on one first developed in the United States was imported into Canada. It persisted long after wartime labour relations were liberalized since it was in the interests of both employers and labour to take wages out of competition. Regional wage differentials converged gradually over some thirty years in spite of geography. But, as we shall see, the principle of a 'national wage' for a 'national industry' did not stand the test of time or of geography.

In assessing the results of a meat-packing strike in 1904 that saw the Amalgamated Butcher Workmen badly beaten by the Chicago-based packing companies, Clemen (1923: 703) argued against the butcher aristocracy thesis of John Commons (1904): 'Indeed, the division of labour had gone so far in the industry that it made the skilled workers no more indispensable than the unskilled; e.g., cattle butchers, who were thought to be the aristocrats of the trade, were the easiest men to replace. The second reason, following closely on the first, was that the technique of the industry allowed the use of hordes of unskilled negroes and non-English-speaking laborers offering themselves at the gates.' Technological change in the late 1940s and 1950s permitted even further deskilling as beef-dressing technology adapted conveyorized on-the-rail systems to move the work, while the meat cutters stood at their stations, tended their machines, and performed their minute tasks – over and over again.

EIGHT

An Industry Transformed: Meat-Packing Metamorphosis

Norm Leclaire entered the meat-packing industry in 1966 as one of Canada Packers' 'beef luggers,' the husky young fellows who manhandled 200-pound quarters of beef from the cooler to the reefer cars. When I met him he was the business agent for Local 401 of the United Food and Commercial Workers.

> *'We struck that plant [Lakeside Packers in Brooks, Alberta] on the first of June 1984. That strike lasted 44 months. At some time, what the hell was it, 1988? The international union told us: 'Look, try one more round of negotiations. If you're not going to get an agreement there, we're not going to fund your strike anymore.' I maintained a picket line out there for almost four years. When that strike was over, we probably still had forty people that were picketing there. Yeah.*
>
> *Uh oh Jesus, I'll tell you! I spent four years raising money to keep that strike going. I was paying probably on the average of more than $300 a week strike pay out there. We had one more try at bargaining and then they dried the money up so we ended the strike. We have gone back out there several times, the last time being last September [1994], to try to reorganize a membership there ... That plant has always had a mega turnover ... every time we went out there to reorganize, we'd get a committee organized, there would be interest, in a month you'd have fifteen guys working that had been on the committee for your plant, and then they'd be gone. And we just couldn't do it.*
>
> Norm Leclaire, Agent, United Food and Commercial Workers, Local 401, March 2, 1995

On July 23, 1999, yet another certification vote was held by the UFCW: 71 per cent of Lakeside's hourly workers voted against the union.

Since the 1960s, the trend in meat-packing plants has been away from multistorey multispecies plants and towards specialization in one livestock species and often only one grade and sex. The new generation of very large-scale vertically integrated beef specialists is also distinctive for their rapid processing speed and very large scale of output. The minimum economic scale for a beef kill plant has increased continuously. In the mid-1980s, the minimum efficient plant size for a modern beef plant in the United States had been fixed at 300 to 350 head per hour or 600,000 to 700,000 cattle per year (Ward 1988: 24–31). With up to twelve shifts per week, and maximum chain speeds of over 400 head of cattle per hour, the largest plants killed over 1,000,000 head in 1999.

Very large-scale beef plants are typically found in small cities and towns close to large concentrations of cattle feedlots, in regions well suited to the production of feed grain. In North America these regions have coincided with a rural populist political culture that has never been supportive of the labour movement. Some of the very large North American cattle-killing plants are not unionized, a change from the postwar decades when the United Packinghouse Workers of America were at their apogee. In 1999, the three top cattle-feeding states are also the top cattle-killing states. Kansas, Nebraska, and Texas accounted for 61.4 percent of commercial cattle slaughter in the United States (USDA 2000b). They are also 'right-to-work states' which sharply limit union security and the ability of unions to organize workers. Alberta, with 68.7 per cent of Canada's federally inspected cattle kill in 1999, has the lowest union density of any province (Akyeampong 1999). Alberta labour legislation makes it relatively difficult to certify new unions while Alberta Labour Relations Board decisions have been less than accommodating for collective bargaining from a union perspective (Reshef 1989).

Very large-scale beef plants often specialize in choice grain-fed cattle (fat cattle or 'fats') that are anticipated to yield a carcass grading A or better. These plants are more vertically integrated than the first-generation kill and chill plants of the 1960s. After twenty-four hours in the cooler, the sides are broken into the five primal cuts (hip, sirloin, short loin, rib, and chuck) and some of these are further broken into subprimal cuts. The primals or subprimals are then vacuum packaged and placed in boxes for shipment. Other plants specialize in killing cows, typically older, thinner dairy cows culled from the dairy herd. After twenty-four hours in the cooler, the inspected but ungraded dairy carcasses are boned out by hand and the bones themselves are further processed to produce mechanically separated meat. Most cow meat is then ground, formed into patties of specified fat content, and shipped to fast-food restaurant chains.

The larger scale federally inspected beef packers operate two eight-hour shifts to increase capital utilization and further reduce costs (Grier 1988: 20). While double shifts impose added costs (for doing all cleaning and maintenance in the small hours of the morning), sixteen-hour per day operations have become the norm to recoup the enormous capital investment in a very large-scale beef plant. These plants tend to buy directly from only the largest feedlots and sell their product to the larger retail and food service chains.

Contemporary Developments on the Cattle Kill Floor

While the Can-Pak system marked an important milestone in the mechanization of cattle slaughter in 1950, technological change has continued into the new millennium. But compared with other mass production industries, packing plants still rely heavily on a manual labour process using conventional knives and hand-operated power tools. Despite feedlot efforts to standardize slaughter cattle, the great variety in the conformation of carcasses and fragility of animal tissue has stymied the transition from mechanization to full automation. Enormous increases in production scale have been accomplished by increased chain speeds, an ever more detailed division of labour, and to some extent, by intensifying the labour process. Like other assembly processes, human work on the kill floor is growing increasingly machine-paced with workers performing repetitive manual operations at ever greater speeds (Novek 1992: 27).

Improvements in Cattle Handling

The most visible technological development on the outside of Canadian livestock plants is the new style of animal confinement and handling facilities associated with the work of Dr Temple Grandin. An animal scientist at Colorado State University in Fort Collins, Grandin has been an important influence on kill-floor technology and the welfare of food animals. Her work includes surveys of the treatment of animals in Canadian and U.S. meat-packing plants, measurement of livestock welfare, and the conditions of confinement, handling, and transportation that induce stress in livestock. She has applied her research findings to the design and development of confinement and handling systems to reduce stress in livestock. She has advocated and designed the construction of sinuously curved cattle races with solid walls to channel cattle smoothly from their holding pens to the kill floor. In the three largest kill plants in Canada, Grandin's distinctive designs have replaced the slatted orthogonal drive alleys in common usage until the 1980s. Cattle tend to balk at shadows, reflections, and upon seeing people directly in front of them. Ninety-degree corners and the contrast between light and dark created by slatted fencing are especially problematic. Through her consulting firm, Grandin Livestock Handling Systems, she has designed pens and drive alleys for Cargill in High River, IBP in Brooks, and Better Beef in Guelph, Canada's three largest cattle-processing plants.

Animal welfare is important to packing plants because there is a marked decline in meat quality from animals that are stressed just before slaughter. Even mild stress in hogs because of excessive heat, rough treatment, or excitement just prior to stunning causes a rapid decline in the pH of the meat, leading to a condition known as pale, soft, exudative (PSE) pork. The beef from cattle which suffer stress immediately prior to slaughter becomes dark, firm, and dry (DFD), known colloquially as a 'dark cutter.' DFD affects some 1 to 2 per cent of all cattle slaughtered. The immediate cause is the reduction of glycogen reserves normally stored in muscle at the time of slaughter. Glycogen depletion results from preslaughter stress which includes aggressive behaviour and mounting among unfamiliar cattle, exposure to new environmental conditions including cattle liners and holding pens in abattoirs, electric prodding by inexperienced or impatient cattle handlers, lack of food and water, and shipment in extreme cold or heat exacerbated by overcrowding. The proportion of dark cutters can be reduced with some very modest design features to reduce preslaughter stress: non-slip floors in drive alleys; avoidance of loud noise such as hissing air from pneumatic tools, high-pitched saws, and banging of heavy doors; provision of bedding and water in pens; and training cattle handlers so that electric cattle prods are seldom required to coax cattle into the knocking box.

There is no way of detecting DFD ante mortem. Post mortem, the port wine colour of a DFD carcass is the conspicuous evidence of a 'dark cutter.' A dark cutter is downgraded to a B4 even though it might be eligible for an A grade based on other criteria. Blind taste tests have shown that consumers are unable to distinguish DFD beef by taste and smell alone from cooked bright red beef. Taste and smell are immaterial, however, as consumers reject dark-coloured beef at the retail showcase. In the United States, the DFD beef from dark cutters was typically discounted by 35 cents per pound on the rail in 1995. Assuming an average 756-pound steer carcass, this amounts to a discount of $264.60 to the producer (Grandin 1993a; 1993b; Schmidt 1995: 21).

Downers, Cripples, and the Regulatory Paradox

A 'downer' is an animal that is so sick or so badly injured that it cannot stand up by itself. The decision to cull elderly cows is often precipitated by a walking disability caused by a fracture or joint disease. Euthanasia and use of such animals for food seems to be the only option, yet most slaughter plants are not well designed to handle crippled livestock. In her survey of mainly federally inspected plants in Canada, Grandin (1995) did not observe any sick, debilitated, or emaciated animals. She went on to argue that downers and cripples have not been miraculously healed; they are simply being diverted to smaller plants which are not federally inspected.

The regulatory paradox is that as standards in federally inspected plants rise and plants are more stringently regulated to meet demands for humane animal handling, an underclass of small provincially inspected plants is left to handle livestock so crippled and sick that they are unable to walk into the livestock trailer or into the stunning box. The more stringently the big federal plants are regulated, the greater will be the demand for less regulated facilities. While standards appear to have risen in the large federally inspected plants, many small-scale and less closely monitored plants remain in operation to kill and process the less seemly animals. According to Grandin (1995: 13): 'There is a need to review practices in provincial plants that are not federally inspected or members of the Canadian Meat Council. It is likely that bad things are going on in some small provincial plants. I have learned from experience that very small plants come in two basic types. They are either excellent or disgusting.'

For many years consumers have expressed concern about the high levels of market concentration by the oligopoly that dominates the industry. Yet the large-scale plants which buy high quality cattle from large feedlots and sell to the national chain stores have relatively high standards of performance on humane slaughter and sanitation. The smaller provincially inspected plants, which come closer to the model of atomistic sellers in perfect competition assumed by classical economics, tend to process the older livestock and are less likely to have the state-of-the-art machinery and equipment for humane slaughter and reduction of carcass contamination.

Slaughter Technology

As the chain speed in cattle plants has increased, one of the chief bottlenecks has been the stunning process. Multiple knocking boxes are required to achieve production scales in excess of 800 head per day. To solve this problem Grandin was instrumental in the development and application of a double-rail restrainer system which is now found in many large-scale cattle slaughter operations (Figure 8.1). Animals walk into a chute and down a ramp leaving them calmly straddled on a pair of smoothly moving rails separated by a broad groove to accommodate the brisket and reduce pressure on the sternum. As soon as they emerge from a hold-down rack, they are stunned by a worker standing comfortably above the restrainer, while another down on the floor shackles each left hind foot as it moves by. The inert carcass gradually rises off the moving rails on a moving overhead chain, and it goes into a short queue before exsanguination. Such a smoothly operating and mechanized killing device seems diabolical, but it is far less stressful than the older knocking box technology (Grandin 1991; 1993b: 302–4).

With the exception of ritual slaughter, mechanical stunning for cattle and calves is now universal. A pneumatically powered captive bolt pistol is the tool of choice, although for mature bulls with exceptionally thick skulls, large bore rifles or a special stunner powered by an explosive cartridge may be used. Bulls may also be pithed by inserting a flexible rod into the stunner hole and forcing it all the way to the back of the skull to destroy the brain stem (Grandin 1995: 15).

In the 1990s, the animal rights movement became more influential, and once again, humane slaughter practices have become an issue in Canada. Headlines such as 'Animals butchered alive former USDA inspectors say' (*Globe and Mail* 1998b), and polemical books such as *Slaughterhouse* (Eisnitz 1997), reflect and provoke growing public concern with animal welfare and the visceral shock effect of apparently barbaric practices in slaughter plants. In a survey of handling and stunning practices in twenty-one medium and small Canadian slaughter plants, Grandin (1995) found better livestock handling in Canadian packing plants than in the United States. Only one of the six beef plants visited was not in compliance with humane slaughter practices, as it made a practice of jamming two cattle into a knocking box designed to hold only a single animal.

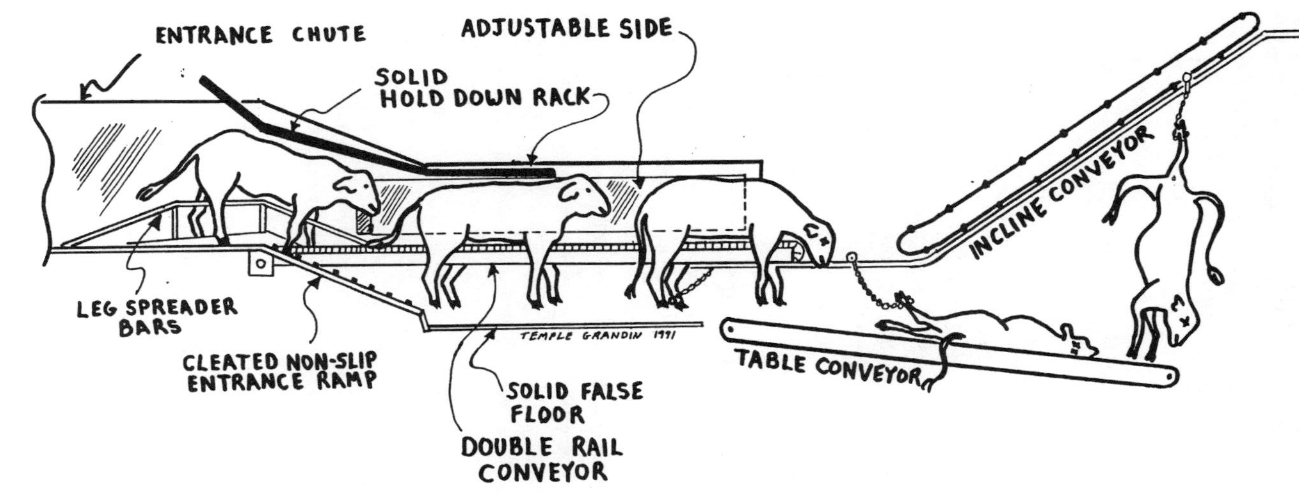

Figure 8.1. Twin rail restraining and stunning system. Source: Temple Grandin, Grandin Livestock Handling Systems, Fort Collins, Colorado.

The results of a follow-up study were disappointing (Grandin 1999). Only three of five federally inspected beef plants passed the stunning audit (i.e., stunned 95 per cent or more of the cattle successfully with the first shot). In one plant an animal was hoist to the bleeding rail while still sensible. In the United States, marked improvements in stunning efficiency have been credited to McDonald's Restaurants, which includes animal welfare as part of their food safety evaluation of ground-beef suppliers (Grandin 1999).

Halal Beef

While Kosher beef has become a declining niche market, halal has taken its place as the most common form of ritual slaughter in Canada. With the growth of the Muslim community, and the growing importance of export markets in Islamic countries, the market for halal (literally, 'the permissible') beef has grown rapidly. Muslim dietary rules are set out in the Koran. Pork, blood, and animals dying as a result of beating, strangulation, or goring may not be consumed by Muslim adherents (Grandin and Regenstein 1994).

Traditional halal and kosher slaughter are similar in that both require that the animal be conscious before the throat is cut. Kosher slaughter is invariably performed by a highly trained Jewish shochet while halal may be performed by any adult Muslim, provided that just prior to slaughter, a prayer is recited: '*Bismillah-e-Allah-o-Akbar*' ('with the name of Allah who is great'). If a Muslim is not available, animals may be killed by any person 'of the book' (a Christian or Jew). In some plants where Muslim workers are not available, it is sufficient for the person bleeding the animal to simply read the prayer in Arabic. Perhaps because of the lack of training required of halal slaughterers, Grandin (1994b) observed that halal cattle slaughter done with short, hacking cuts with a short, eight-inch skinning knife caused vigorous reaction and obvious distress. However, mechanical stunning has been approved by Muslim authorities such as the Islamic Food and Nutrition Council of America (IFANCA) for halal, provided that it is used only to desensitize the animal and that the animal does not die prior to the ritual slaughter (Green 1997).

Beginning in 1991, MGI Packers in Kitchener carved out a niche market by converting all of its cattle kill to halal, and by 1997 it had become the second-largest beef-kill plant in Ontario (Rose 1997). Halal beef is entering the mass market. In the United States, McDonald's Restaurants and the U.S. military require halal products. Ironically, perhaps, some meats are sold bearing both the K for kosher and the crescent M, a registered halal trademark of IFANCA (Green 1997). But most consumers seem quite unaware that the federally inspected beef they buy in the supermarket may also meet the strictures of the Koran.

Dressing the Carcass

Contemporary packing plants are invariably single-story structures although most have a lower level for the hide cellar where hides are cured for export and for the fancy meats department where edible offal is cleaned and trimmed. However, most of the operations that were on as many as six different floors in old-fashioned, horizontally integrated packing plants are located on the same floor at ground level in very large-scale beef plants.

In the reduction of contamination, hide pulling is the Achilles heel of the whole beef-dressing process. As carcasses move along the rail, the carcass that is having its hide removed is adjacent to a carcass that has just had it removed. The hide is pulled from the carcass quite rapidly and a certain amount of manure spatter is inevitable, especially in spring when conditions are wet and an animal may have 15 to 20 kilograms of tag clinging to its hide (Allen 1999: 38). No matter how painstaking the cattle-dressing process is, mechanical hide pulling is bound to cause some contamination which can be reduced but never eliminated completely. To cope with line speeds of 350 head of cattle per hour or more, three different hide-pullers may be applied to different parts of the carcass to gain greater control of the hide with less spatter (Grier 1988: 18; Bjerklie 1997). Spatter affects mainly the outer surfaces of the carcass which often end up as trimmings used in ground beef. Great care is taken to prevent contamination from one carcass to the next on the line, but zero tolerance is an almost impossible goal (Schmidt 1998: 38).

To segregate different processes and help prevent cross-contamination, plants are divided into separate sections, and traffic between sections is discouraged. Carcass dressing is separated into a hide-on area that begins with knocking live cattle and ends when the hide is completely detached. The hide-off area where the carcass is dressed, eviscerated, split, and trimmed extends from the hide-puller to the beef cooler. The boning and fabricating lines are separated from the kill floor by the coolers for chilling hot carcasses. To avoid the contamination of packaged case-ready products by effluvium from the kill floor, nothing but the sides of beef themselves moves between the kill floor and the fabricating department. At Better Beef in Guelph the two sections of the plant even have separate washrooms and cafeterias. 'Pack-off,' where beef cuts are vacuum packed and placed in boxes for shipment, is similarly segregated from carcass fabrication.

No one gets into an up-to-date kill plant without changing footwear to prevent the entry of contaminants from outside. Everyone, workers and visitors, wears steel-toed rubber boots, a freshly laundered smock, hair net, beard net, ear protection, helmet, and gloves. In many plants there is an elaborate code of helmet colours to indicate one's position in the plant hierarchy from beginners on probation to senior management. Where possible, visitors go through the plant in the reverse direction to product flow to prevent contamination of the finished product with material from the livestock pens or kill floor. Floor-mounted boot washers which spray and rinse off all foreign material are strategically located at every entry point to prevent contamination being tracked from one area to another. Hand washing, perfunctory though it may sometimes be, is enforced when moving between different parts of the plant. Positive air pressure may also be used to exclude airborne contaminants from meat-cutting areas.

The beef-dressing line is carefully designed to avoid the potential for contamination by adjacent carcasses on the rail. All cutting tools must be immersed in scalding water between each animal on the line. At some work stations and for some tasks, direct contact with blood and viscera is unavoidable. For these workers, there are long rubber aprons and special boots. Between each animal on the line, the worker steps into a clear plastic shower booth equipped with water jets at different levels to remove all trace of the previous carcass.

Computer assisted manufacturing (CAM) has made its way into almost every secondary industry. Its strength is in transforming a precisely standardized input such as steel bar stock into a precisely machined shape. The organic variability of the raw material in meat packing and the complexity of its finished product would seem to stymy applications of CAM to meat packing in the near future, just as it was thought to prevent continuous rail dressing until the 1940s. As if the size, variability, and weight of the material were not enough, the sanitation requirements of a meat-packing plant pose a further obstacle. Until recently, sophisticated electronics could not long survive carcass-to-carcass tool sterilization or the end of shift wash-down, in which every surface of the plant is subject to a blast of scalding water (Aylward and Murphy 1991). An important first was registered in

1997, however, when a packinghouse robot was developed in Quebec to automate the removal of ribs from pork bellies (Burn 1999). This successful innovation suggests the potential for future applications of robotics in beef carcass fabrication, especially to replace manual tasks having high rates of repetitive strain injuries and for cuts which must meet very fine tolerances.

Inventory control is an integral part of CAM, and Cargill's High River plant was the first in Canada to incorporate an electronic carcass-tracking system. Each trolley hook travelling on the overhead rail has a machine-readable pattern of holes that gives each carcass an identification number. Every time a carcass is weighed, or moves from one part of the plant to another, the trolley hook is scanned and its location recorded. Thus, the plant is able to automatically update a database that matches the carcass with the name of the feedlot which delivered the animal, date and time of slaughter, live weight, hot carcass weight, cold carcass weight, name of the intended customer, and any other information that may be required (Bjerklie 1990: 30–1). Carcass tracking has the potential to become a routine packinghouse activity should consumers be willing to pay the premium required. Beef could eventually be traced all the way back to the producer to certify that it is free of diseases such as bovine spongiform encephalopathy or to guarantee that it has not been treated with artificial growth promoters (Fearne 1998).

Electrical carcass stimulation is becoming standard practice in large-scale beef plants. After evisceration and splitting, each side of beef on the moving line comes into contact with electrodes which apply high-voltage electrical current as the side of beef slides along the rail. Electrical stimulation helps to tenderize and improve the overall palatability of beef, especially for steer carcasses (Jeremiah et al. 1997a).

The most recent development to reduce contamination on dressed beef carcasses is steam pasteurization. Steam pasteurization is a patented process developed in 1995 and has entered service in several large-scale Canadian beef plants to reduce pathogenic contamination on the exterior of the carcass (Langman and Bacon 1999; Gill 1998; Smith 1996). Sides of beef on a moving chain move through a blast of air to blow any excess water off the side and then, four sides at a time, they enter a chamber about the size of a city bus in which they are subject to scalding steam at high pressure to kill pathogens anywhere on the exterior of the sides. After seconds in the hot steam the surface of the carcass rises to about 90° Celsius before it is shifted into a second chamber and sprayed with cold water to reduce the exterior temperature to close to the freezing point. In this way the carcass exterior is pasteurized yet does not have time to cook.

Several other technologies to reduce contamination are in use on an experimental basis. High pressure air or water may be applied to freshly stunned animals to remove tag before exsanguination, and before any part of the carcass is opened, steam vacuums may be used during hide removal to remove foreign matter, and the carcass may be washed with an organic acid before or after evisceration (Allen 1999). Irradiation (electronic pasteurization) is being actively considered as an additional means of eliminating bacterial contamination from fresh beef but it faces consumer resistance (*Lethbridge Herald* 2000a: A4).

Fabrication and Boxed Beef

Fabrication refers to the practice of disassembling (breaking, fabricating, or even 'fabbing') a beef carcass into its five primal cuts which are then sorted and packaged into corrugated cardboard cartons for shipment.

The fabrication floor of a large-scale beef plant has a very different feel from the kill floor. The kill floor has a hot, almost steamy atmosphere the year round, and workers typically wear only a light, short-sleeved, white cotton shirt under chain mail and perhaps a rubber apron. The fabrication floor is maintained at a temperature just above the freezing point the year round; workers are warmly dressed with a quilted coat under the white butcher's smock. Every day the workers are supplied with three freshly laundered knitted gloves: one for the right hand that holds the knife, and two for the left with a steel-mesh glove worn in between them. The fabrication floor is brightly lit with an abbreviated colour palette, stainless steel machines and tables, white plastic conveyor belts, white-coated workers, and of course, the red-and-white primal cuts of beef.

Sides of beef are transferred back onto a moving chain after twenty-four to thirty-six hours of hanging motionless on a cooler rail where they were graded. The sides move past meat cutters who each cut off a different large primal cut, gradually disassembling the side until the last piece, the hip and hind leg, is lifted off the hook and the carcass is completely disassembled. This is heavy and skilled work, as the chain never stops moving and the workers must walk and cut at the same time and then return to their original position, being careful not to stab one of their fellows in passing. After removal from the carcass, each of the different primals goes on to a separate moving table, some twenty to thirty metres long, which runs perpendicular to the chain from which the side was dissembled. Thus, there are half a dozen parallel moving table disassembly lines, each one dedicated to a different primal, each staffed by about twenty workers, although the number may increase depending on the throughput that day.

Primals are carried along on the table's central belt. Workers lean forward and snag a primal with a meat hook held by one hand, while the other wields a knife to make a complex series of deft and well-practised cuts. Fat goes on the trim belt, bones go on the bone belt, and the primal itself goes back on the centre belt for the next manual operation. At first, one red-and-white piece of chilled muscle looks much like another, and the neophyte could be forgiven for perceiving little method to fabrication; it appears that workers are slicing off pieces at random. But after one watches this process for a few minutes it becomes clear that each worker is, in fact, working on the same piece of anatomy making precisely the same cuts and separating the same tissues over and over again. In fabrication the knife work looks effortless. For many tasks the knife is held in a stabbing position with the blade extending down from the bottom of the fist, and the cutting action appears to be done with an artful finesse, the sort of dexterity that comes with constant repetition. A white plastic scabbard hangs from a white plastic chain around the worker's waist, the meat cutter's badge of office. It contains several knives and a steel. Whenever there are a few seconds of 'slack time' between primals, the knife is drawn over the steel with a few fluid strokes to realign and set the cutting edge. By touching up their blades after every few cuts, experienced meat cutters reduce the cutting force that is required and so avoid repetitive stress disorders such as carpal tunnel syndrome. As cycle times increase, however, workers have less and less time to sharpen their tools (Grey 1999: 22–3; Langman 2000a).

At the far end of the table the primals and subprimals are ready for pack-off, where they are placed in clear plastic bags which are evacuated and sealed shut by a Cryovac machine and then placed in cartons. When a carton is fully packed it is sealed and identified with bar-coded labels to indicate the date and time and the precise weight and specification of its contents; then it is moved by conveyor belt to the shipping coolers where it is held until loading on a semitrailer reefer.

Centralized beef breaking began in the 1950s, when the U.S. supermarkets began disassembling sides and quarters in their distribution centres, eliminating carcass breaking from the back room of the retail store. By the 1970s, retail supermarket chains such as Canada Safeway, Steinberg's Miracle Foods, and the Oshawa Group all had established their own central meat-cutting plants. They received sides and quarters of beef from kill and chill plants, broke and boxed the beef, and shipped it to the various stores in the chain. By centralizing all of these disassembly and meat fabrication operations in one, high-volume and specialized plant, the chain stores benefited from economies of scale and were able to allocate a different mix of cuts to each store in a way that was no longer dictated by the number and mix of cuts that come on a side of beef (Friend 1957: 14; Brody 1964: 242–3).

Initially, the primal cuts were simply placed in boxes 'naked' – exposed to the air and protected only by cardboard – which limited their shelf-life. By the late 1940s, the patented Cryovac process had been developed to evacuate and hermetically seal a transparent moisture resistant bag which would shrink and cling tightly to the contours of the meat it enclosed. The key technological element in the boxed beef revolution was neither the box, nor centralized carcass breaking; it was Cryovac packaging which was responsible for greatly extending the shelf-life of fresh beef. By 1977, 62 per cent of the boxed beef in Canada was vacuum packed (*Canadian Grocer* 1978a: 5).

In the United States, beef fabrication began to shift from the retailer's central-processing facilities to the packinghouse in the 1960s. In Canada, the major food retailers were loath to relinquish any element of control over the quality of product that they sold; thus, beef was still merchandised in carcass form long after boxed beef had made inroads in the United States (Canada 1976: 92). In 1976, 83 per cent of the tonnage of the beef fabrication in Canada took place in supermarket chain central-processing plants and only 17 per cent was in the hands of the packers (Huff and Mehr 1976: 3). In 1973, for example, Canada Safeway's wholly owned subsidiary, Lucerne Foods, established a central beef-processing plant in Calgary to purchase truckload lots of hanging beef of specified grade and yield. The central plant produced boxed beef for all of Canada Safeway's stores in western Canada.

But as the proportion of cattle slaughter in Alberta increased, the cost of shipping sides of beef to central-processing plants in Ontario and Quebec became prohibitive, prompting Canadian packers to integrate forwards and establish their own carcass breaking and boxed beef facilities. In 1976, the Lethbridge cattle-processing plant of Burns Foods was the first packinghouse in Canada to add a boxed beef line, and Canada Packers was second when it opened a beef fabrication line at its Calgary slaughter plant in 1977. Canada Packers went on to systematize a triangular boxed beef production system in southern Alberta which linked Calgary to feeder plants in Lethbridge and Red Deer. This spatial division of labour in which slaughter and carcass dressing took place in kill and chill plants closest to the source of cattle and beef fabrication was situated in a metropolitan beef market persisted from 1977 until the plants were closed in 1991. The division of killing and cutting in separate plants made the best use of existing infrastructure, but it imposed high transportation costs. XL Beef in Calgary is one of the few remaining Canadian plants that still kills its cattle in one plant and fabricates the carcasses in a separate plant, fifteen minutes away by truck. But these older facilities are dwarfed by newer and much larger fabrication and boxed beef operations directly integrated with large-scale kill plants such as Cargill Foods, Better Beef, and IBP's Lakeside Packers.

From the point of view of the packer, boxed beef offers several advantages. By disassembling the carcass at the point of slaughter, the packer can direct each primal or subprimal cut to wherever the greatest demand and highest price may be found. By eliminating an average of 120 kilograms of hide, bone, fat, and connective tissue, only the highest value portions of the carcass are shipped to the market, reducing transportation costs. This leaves by-products at the packing plant where they are most efficiently processed. Boxes weighing twenty to thirty kilograms are easy to palletize, containerize or even move by hand, unlike a side of swinging beef weighing 150 to 200 kilograms which is extremely difficult to move and, in large volumes, requires the installation of overhead rails in the truck and in the store. Finally, with the advent of boxed beef, the side of beef was no longer the finished product, and the finer points of its appearance were no longer a competitive advantage. Thus, the kill floor supplying beef that will go to retail as primal cuts in a carton need not smooth the fat cover by shrouding the carcass.

Boxed beef also contributes to faster turn-over in the packinghouse, in keeping with the just-in-time principle. When beef was shipped as hanging carcass sides, it was aged in holding coolers for as long as twenty-one days. Aging in a cooler permitted the slow breakdown of collagen and elastin, the proteins that bind meat fibres together. Enzymes occurring naturally in the beef break down these fibres making it more tender and palatable. The enzymatic action is slowed in a cold environment, but this is necessary if tenderizing is to take place before the action of bacteria, moulds, and other organisms cause the meat to deteriorate and become unfit for human consumption (Schweisheimer 1957).

Aging beef by traditional methods is an expensive process for two reasons. First, the working capital invested in the cattle is left locked up in cold storage for three weeks, reducing the speed with which capital can be turned over. When interest rates and inflation are high, the speed with which the finished product can be sold is even more crucial to profitability. Second, aging of beef in holding coolers is costly simply because of the expense of cooling large volumes of air and beef for such a long period. Cold storage is especially sensitive to energy costs. It is little wonder, then, that boxed beef began to replace hanging beef in the 1970s and early 1980s, a period of high energy prices and double-digit interest rates. Boxed beef is ideally shipped the day after slaughter. It ages in a box, in a semitrailer, en route to the marketplace, and because it is sealed in a Cryovac bag, with less dehydration. Thus, boxed beef minimizes the time that beef is stored in plant coolers, complementing the just-in-time strategy of minimizing the time that cattle are kept in pens awaiting slaughter.

Coupled with the growth of cattle feeding and slaughter in Alberta, boxed beef has made an important contribution towards the diversification of the Alberta economy, adding more value to a resource product that used to go east in railway cars as a weaned calf. Boxing beef adds about 10 cents per pound to the value of beef. In 1984, this would have represented $40 million annually (11,800 carcasses per week × 650 pounds per carcass × 0.10 × 52 weeks) if all of the carcasses then moving from west to east were in boxed form (Kerr and Ulmer 1984: 35).

The New Generation of Meat Packers

The new generation of meat packers entered the U.S. meat-packing industry in the 1960s and 1970s. With lean production systems and a low wage structure they drove most of the old-line packers out of the business in less than twenty years. Unlike traditional meat packers, they were not diversified into branded consumer products or integrated forward to process carcass by-products. Instead, they entered the market as specialized cattle and hog slaughter operations and integrated backwards into feed grains, cattle feeding, and in the United States, farrow to finish hog production. By 1988, the new big three beef packers in the United States were composed of IBP with 27 per cent of the total national cattle slaughter; ConAgra with 21.1 per cent; and Excel (Cargill) with 17.1 per cent. In terms of steer and heifer slaughter alone, the four largest firms account for 81 per cent of the revenues. By the 1990s, the U.S. meat-packing industry was more concentrated than it had been when concerns about the 'beef trust' first surfaced over a century ago (Azzam 1998: 107, 120). Two of the largest U.S.-owned meat packers entered the Canadian beef-processing market in 1989 and 1994, speeding the withdrawal of Canada's big three from the beef market and profoundly changing the industry's market structure. By 1999, Kevin Grier, a noted Canadian cattle-marketing analyst would comment: 'The Canadian meat industry is really an American industry. Especially in beef. Consolidation in the beef sector in Alberta has only strengthened the American presence in Canada' (Bjerklie 1999a: 56).

Cargill Foods

Established in Minnesota as a grain trading enterprise by William Cargill in the 1860s, Cargill Foods has developed into a diversified global-scale agribusiness. Cargill remains privately owned and closely held. Cargill began trading grain in Montreal in 1928, and it now operates a number of large-scale inland grain terminals in Alberta and Saskatchewan and dockside grain terminals in Prince Rupert, Thunder Bay, and Baie-Comeau. The firm is one of Canada's largest suppliers of seed grain, animal feed, and fertilizer (Broehl 1998; Cargill Foods n.d.; Kneen 1994; Ontario Ministry of Agriculture and Food 1987).

In 1978, Cargill entered meat packing by acquiring MBPXL Corporation which was itself the product of the merger of Missouri Beef Processors and Excel. The new subsidiary was renamed Excel Corporation, and it began an ambitious investment program to build new slaughter plants and beef-fabricating facilities. In 1982, the firm added a new fabricating plant in Dodge City, Kansas, with a capacity of 17,500 carcasses per week, roughly five times the largest boxed beef operation then existing in Canada. By then Excel had become the sixth-largest beef packer in the United States, accounting for 12.5 per cent of the total output of boxed beef (Skaggs 1986: 198–9; 215–16).

With annual sales of $9 billion and a daily cattle slaughter capacity of 21,800, Cargill's Excel subsidiary is ranked the third-largest meat and poultry firm and the third-largest in cattle slaughter in the United States, after IBP and ConAgra. Its five U.S. cattle plants are raw material oriented in the feedlot states from eastern Nebraska to the Texas

Panhandle. In 1992, Excel plants killed an estimated 6.25 million head of cattle, roughly 20 per cent of all the cattle killed in the United States (Bjerklie 1999a; *Meat Processing* 1990 and 1993; Excel Meats 2000).

Cargill announced construction of its first Canadian meat-packing plant in October 1987. The $55 million state-of-the-art kill plant was opened in May 1989 in High River, just 40 kilometres south of Calgary. High River was an attractive location because of its proximity to southern Alberta feedlots and to Calgary's metropolitan labour market. The plant kills only grain-finished steers and heifers that are expected to attain a carcass grade of A or better (Thomas 1989). It was designed with a single-shift capacity of 6,000 head of cattle per week at a chain speed of 160 per hour based on one shift per day. The plant was planned from the outset to include a boxed beef production line, hide-curing facilities, and rendering. By the summer of 1999 the High River plant had accelerated to a chain speed of 260 head per hour, or 3,850 head per day based on two shifts. Although Cargill Foods markets its beef under the 'Excel' trademark, it is unrelated to XL Foods, an independent Calgary-based beef packer with links to a nineteenth-century Alberta ranch that used 'XL' as its cattle brand.

Financing for Cargill's new plant was aided by a $4 million grant from Alberta's Processing and Marketing Agreement, a $50 million regional development program designed to encourage secondary manufacturing firms and add value to crude agricultural products. By processing cattle, second only to wheat in Alberta's agricultural revenue, the Cargill plant was exactly the type of investment that the provincial government program had been designed to attract and encourage. But as soon as plans for the new plant became public, the provincial funding was denounced by Alberta's existing meat packers. They observed that Alberta's cattle kill was only 21,000 cattle per week in 1987, yet the province's existing plants had slaughter capacity sufficient to dispatch 30,000 per week. It was suggested that the subsidy would enable Cargill's new plant to operate at a loss just long enough to drive all of the existing competitors out of the market (Byfield and Johnson 1987: 29). The counter-argument from the provincial government and Alberta feedlot operators was that some 200,000 finished cattle were being exported from Alberta each week at that time, and a new kill plant would add value to more cattle in Alberta. In addition, the creation of a big new market for cattle and low prices for grain would provide an incentive to increase the production of finished slaughter cattle in southern Alberta feedlots. In 1992, Cargill Foods acquired Trillium Meats of Rexdale, Ontario, which receives boxed primal cuts from its kill and fabricating plant in High River and produces case-ready beef as its finished product. Thus, Trillium functions as a 'middle point' between the region of beef surplus in Southern Alberta and the region of beef deficit in southern Ontario (*Globe and Mail* 1992).

IBP and Lakeside Packers

In 1960, IBP was founded as Iowa Beef Processors in Denison, Iowa. With a $300,000 loan from the U.S. Small Business Administration, the firm pioneered several innovative strategies. Their new plant in Denison was far from metropolitan packing centres such as Chicago, Kansas City, or St Louis. In common with Canada Packers' new plant in Lethbridge, which was built at the same time, Iowa Beef Processors' first plant was a highly mechanized single-story operation dedicated to beef. IBP was acquired by Occidental Petroleum in 1981 and went public in 1987 as 'IBP Corporation' with a 49.5 per cent stock offering (Perry and Kegley 1989: 90–2; Tinstman and Peterson 1981).

While some of its plants are represented by the United Food and Commercial Workers or the Teamsters, collective bargaining has never been cordial at IBP. Until 1989, there had never been a negotiation without a strike and the company became skilled in the use of replacement workers and other tactics designed to break strikes (Perry and Kegley 1989: 92; Skaggs 1986: 205).

While IBP was not the first to fabricate beef for shipment in cartons, it began breaking beef carcasses into primal cuts in 1967 and did more than any other packer to perfect and popularize the boxed beef concept. It has also been a leader in achieving large volumes at great efficiency using state-of-the-art technology in highly specialized kill plants. IBP became a formidable low cost competitor because of the lower transportation costs for boxed beef and a wage structure estimated to be as much as 40 per cent lower than its competitors (*Business Week* 1980: 101). To keep labour costs down, IBP selected plant locations in small communities in rural areas (Ruston 1983: 19). Although the firm entered the industry as a beef specialist, controlling 25 per cent of the market in 1980, it built its first hog plant in 1982 and became the largest hog processor in the United States in 1990 (*Business Week* 1980: 100–1; IBP 2000; Meat Processing 1990).

With sales of $14.1 billion in 1999, IBP is the largest red-meat processor in the world. On 1 January 2001, IBP announced a definitive merger agreement with Tyson Foods of Springdale, Arkansas, for $4.7 billion. In this transaction, the world's leading producer of fresh beef and pork was taken over by Tyson Foods, the world's largest fully integrated producer, processor, and marketer of chicken and chicken-based convenience foods. Horizontal integration of red and white meat processing on this scale is unprecedented in North America or, indeed, anywhere else in the world.

IBP has a daily slaughter capacity of 40,100 head of cattle, nearly double the capacity of second-place ConAgra Beef which kills 23,500 cattle per day (Langman 2000b). It operates nine cattle-slaughter plants in the United States which are tightly concentrated in Iowa, eastern Nebraska, and Kansas, with one huge outlier at Amarillo in the Texas Panhandle and a smaller one in Pasco, Washington. IBP's Amarillo beef complex has the greatest beef-slaughter and -processing capacity, and the fastest chain speed in the world; it also includes an on-site leather tannery to add value to its cattle hides. The competitive edge for IBP has always been its low cost leadership in commodity beef and pork which enabled it to triumph over the old-line packers such as Armour and Swift. Beginning in 1996 the firm began to diversify away from its reliance on commodity meats to include value added segments of the meat industry. In 1997, it acquired firms producing a variety of brand-name processed meats and prepared food products from burritos to pepperoni sausage (Bjerklie 1999b). Diversification has also included expansion into Canada. In 1994, Lakeside Packers of Brooks, Alberta, became IBP's first foreign acquisition.

Lakeside Farm Industries Limited began in 1966 as a cattle feedlot on the western edge of Brooks, Alberta, an agricultural service centre about 150 kilometres east of Calgary on the Trans-Canada Highway, with a population at that time of only 3,400. The firm was incorporated with the merger of some local feedlot and feed-mill operators and grew very rapidly. Lakeside Farm Industries Limited was structured as a miniature agribusiness conglomerate, growing grain for silage which was then fed to cattle in a corporate feedlot. Lakeside operated separate divisions producing hogs and poultry, milling feed grain, and distributing fertilizer. When new sources of capital were required in 1973, Mitsubishi became a partner with the Alberta-based business, and a small beef-slaughter plant was opened in 1974 as Lakeside Packers.

The original plant was expanded twice from 2,800 head of cattle per week in 1989 to 11,000 per week in 1994 when the firm was acquired by IBP. By 1997, its maximum chain speed had reached 370 head per hour compared with 400 head per hour in IBP's fastest plant in Amarillo. In scale of output, Lakeside Packers is now the largest in Canada. In the summer of 1999, it was killing over 2,300 cattle per shift with twelve shifts per week, a capacity of 28,000 head per week or 1.4 million per year. As well as being Canada's largest cattle-slaughter plant, Lakeside Packers is unique as the only Canadian kill plant directly adjacent to its own feedlot. It is integrated from the acquisition of feeder cattle all the way to the shipment of boxed beef.

Until 1997, Lakeside Packers produced only sides of beef, most of which were shipped directly to Lucerne Foods in Calgary, the meat fabrication arm and central distribution centre for Canada Safeway stores. At Lucerne Foods the sides of beef from Lakeside were fabricated and packed in cartons for shipment to Safeway stores all over western Canada.

Once it became part of IBP, the Brooks plant completed a large-scale beef fabrication facility to break its beef carcasses down to subprimals and ship much of its product as boxed beef. At the same time as it was integrating forward into beef fabrication, Lakeside continued to integrate backward and expanded its feedlot from 40,000 to 75,000 head. The feedlot, which is directly across the Trans-Canada Highway from the plant, is the largest single feedlot in Canada and the only one that is integrated directly with a kill plant. Lakeside's feedlot is not yet large enough to supply more than about 20 per cent of the cattle slaughtered in the plant and the firm negotiates forward contracts all over southern Alberta (Manitoba Red Meat Forum 1993: 6).

Better Beef

Better Beef is a single-plant, family-controlled business adjacent to the Guelph Correctional Centre in Wellington County, near the heart of southern Ontario feedlot country. The establishment was built in 1975 by the Ontario Ministry of Correctional Services as a beef and pork plant (Irvine 1978). At that time the facility was part of a scheme intended to supply all the correctional facilities in Ontario with fresh meats, dairy products, and produce using inmate labour and facilities built on the grounds of correctional facilities. Providing inmates with knives, meat hooks, and other cutting tools was apparently never anticipated to be problematic. The plant operated for a short while under provincial control and was then leased by Essex Packers, a Hamilton-based firm with a plant in Windsor. When Essex Packers became insolvent, the de Jonge family took over the assets in 1976 and brought the Guelph plant back into operation.

The plant has been continuously expanded and modernized over the years. By 2000, it was killing 7,500 cattle per week on a one-shift basis, and it is Canada's third-largest cattle processor. Unlike most of the other beef plants in Ontario, Better Beef does not slaughter cows. Instead, it focuses on choice corn-fed steers and heifers, mainly from Ontario feeders. It has a fabrication floor and most product goes out as boxed primals. With the closure of all of the big three plants in Toronto and Montreal, Better Beef became the largest cattle slaughter plant east of Alberta.

The Collapse of Pattern Bargaining in Meat Packing

The collapse of pattern bargaining in meat packing was not an isolated event; it was a manifestation of the changing political climate and overall decline in industrial unionism throughout Canada and the United States during the 1970s and 1980s. The industrial employment base began to erode and the great 'united' industrial unions originally formed under the CIO umbrella (e.g., Auto Workers, Electrical Workers, Packinghouse Workers, Steel Workers) were unable to maintain their membership base in the manufacturing sector (Dawes 1987: 23). As its membership shrank, the United Packinghouse Workers of America gradually merged out of existence, becoming part of the United Food and Commercial Workers (UFCW) in 1979, reducing the influence and power of meat packing workers in the international union. The transformation of labour relations in the Canadian meat-packing sector followed close on the heels of the collapse of packinghouse unionism in the United States.

The sweeping changes in U.S. packinghouse labour relations had their roots in the corporate restructuring in each of the U.S. big four employers. As early as 1954, Cudahy closed four of its Chicago area plants and by 1960 most of the major meat processors had abandoned the corporate and logistical hearth of the packing industry (Brody 1964: 242). The old-line packers fell victim to the merger wave of the 1970s; most were spun off and later expired in the 1980s (Perry and Kegley 1989: Chapter 6).

With its innovative strategy and low cost structure, IBP had seized commanding market share in fresh beef and became the prime mover in the restructuring of the industry's old-line producers. In June 1982, the firm imposed a four-year wage freeze on its slaughter facility in Dakota City, Nebraska, which prompted 2,450 UFCW workers to walk off the job. Picket lines became violent, the National Guard was mobilized, and after weeks of impasse, IBP announced that it would reopen the plant with replacement workers (Skaggs 1986: 204–5). And it did. The packinghouse division of the UFCW had been beaten in the United States.

In the summer of 1984, Canada's forty-year-old pattern bargaining system began to unravel, two years after concessions had transformed the U.S. industry. Like an old rope, the system of labour relations began to fray in many different places at nearly the same time. There is no evidence of collusion on the part of the firms, nor was there any apparent national strategy on the part of the UFCW to defend itself. The pattern bargaining structure was no longer advantageous to the firms or appropriate to the changing spatial organization of the industry. While the UFCW did not capitulate immediately, the aging workforce lacked the aggressive and tenacious will that had characterized the old UPWA in a different industrial age.

Gainers

By 1984, Gainers had divested all of its meat-packing assets except for the large horizontally integrated plant in Edmonton that it had acquired from Swift Canadian. In July 1984, Gainers offered its UFCW workforce a two-year wage freeze, a two-tier wage structure with new employees starting 40 per cent below the base rate, and cuts to employment benefits. This concession package precipitated a strike vote. Just before the strike deadline the firm advertised for replacement workers. Because of the recession and high unemployment at that time, some 1,000 strike-breakers lined up on the street to apply for replacement positions. The impending strike was called off and wage concessions were accepted. Coupled with events south of the border, these events in a relatively small but defiant firm set the tone for retrenchment and concessionary wage demands in the larger firms.

Over the next two years, the plant's pork output tripled and as the contract deadline approached, the firm once again advertised for replacement workers. But this time the workers struck. The strike began on 1 June 1986, and replacement workers began crossing picket lines the next day. A nationwide boycott of Gainers products organized by the UFCW was somewhat successful, but the firm's export orientation prevented the boycott from having a crippling impact on the firm. Canada's most violent and bitter strike in recent memory lasted six-and-a-half months before the firm was charged with bargaining in bad faith and was persuaded to re-employ striking workers with wages frozen at rates well below other pork plants in the industry (Noël and Gardner 1990).

Lakeside Packers

Lakeside Packers followed the Gainers initiative by rejecting the pattern imposed by the UFCW. The union responded to the offer of a wage cut with a strike beginning 1 June 1984. Even after the wage cut, Lakeside was offering the highest wages in the town of Brooks which had been hit hard by recession in Alberta's oil patch. The company succeeded in hiring replacement workers at a wage 30 per cent below the union base rate and the strike was finally broken forty-four months after it had begun – an ignominious defeat for the UFCW. The company maintained its non-union replacement workforce and successfully opposed all subsequent efforts to restore collective bargaining. The defeat of the UFCW by Lakeside Packers was significant for two reasons. First, Lakeside was the first employer to successfully challenge the forty-year-old system of pattern bargaining. Second, although Lakeside was a modest-sized and little-known independent beef packer in 1984, it went on to become the largest fresh beef plant in Canada.

Canada Packers

In July 1984, Canada Packers entered into national negotiations with the UFCW. It offered a wage freeze and a two-tier wage system with a starting rate 15 per cent lower than the base rate that would increase to the base level after two years. The offer was rejected with about 60 per cent of the union membership voting for a nationwide strike in late July 1984. Once Gainers had succeeded in imposing its wage freeze, and Lakeside had hired replacement workers at two-thirds the price of its former workforce, Canada Packers imposed more severe concessions: a 25 per cent cut to the start rate, elimination of time and a half for scheduled weekend work, and cuts to benefits. A tentative settlement was rejected by the membership and moderation of the concessions demanded by the company came at a high price. The nationwide master agreement which had existed since 1947 was divided in two: an eastern agreement and a western agreement. Wage rates in the western beef plants were lower than in the eastern pork plants.

In its 1986 negotiations, Canada Packers dropped the other shoe. Collective bargaining was conducted at the plant level and separate agreements were concluded with each of the surviving plants. A wage differential was imposed with a smaller wage increase in the western beef plants and higher wage hike in the eastern plants. Hog butchers had become the new packinghouse aristocracy, while beef butchers received less.

By 1989, Canada Packers' western beef plants were threatened by the massive new Cargill beef-processing plant in High River. The former industry leader was forced into a reactive mode, and its last plant-specific collective agreements sought to restore regional wage standards with reference to competing plants. For example, the Lethbridge plant's collective agreement specified: 'Effective April 1, 1989, the base rate will be adjusted to the average base rate of the following competitors: Lakeside Packers Ltd. (Brooks), Cargill Limited (High River), XL Beef (Calgary), Dvorkin Meat Packers (Calgary), Burns Meats (Lethbridge).' The industry leader and the primary target of pattern bargaining for decades had become a follower. Canada Packers' Lethbridge beef plant would pay the average wage of its regional competitors.

Burns Foods

In the 1970s, Burns was growing increasingly aggressive towards its meat-packing labour force as a result of low wage competition and diminishing profitability. Its Prince Albert plant had been in operation since its acquisition in 1917, and in 1972, $471,000 was reinvested to upgrade and expand its facilities. But in March 1975, the firm discontinued everything except its hog kill and the entire plant was closed in December 1976. While reduced hog production in Saskatchewan was an important factor in the decision to reduce capacity, national wage and benefit standards were clearly the main issue:

> The average wage at the Prince Albert plant was $6.60 per hour. The average wage for all other businesses in Prince Albert is probably about $4.75 per hour. If the rate paid at the Burns plant had been $6.00 per hour, the plant would easily have been viable and remained fully in existence with some 400 employees. However, with a master contract covering all plants across Canada, the union does not consider individual plant situations. A further part of the story is labour productivity, or the amount of production per man per hour. The Prince Albert plant consistently had the lowest productivity of all the plants in the company. An improvement of 15 per cent in productivity would have kept the plant profitable and in full

> production. There was no appreciable improvement even after two-thirds of the operation were closed down. (Burns Foods 1977, *Annual Report*: 7)

While the inflation of packinghouse wages relative to other sectors was one problem, of far greater impact was the difference in wages paid by meat-packing plants within the same region.

By the 1980s, Burns had diversified into other food-processing businesses so that meat packing made only a modest contribution to revenues and had a negligible or even negative effect on profitability. Returns on invested capital were so low in meat packing that reinvestment would require more capital expenditure than it could generate. For example, Burns Meats' Kitchener plant was old, and obsolete and labour-management relations were poor; it lost $600,000 in 1982, $1.2 million in 1983, and $500,000 in the first half of 1984. The firm's multi-species slaughter- and meat-processing head office plant in Calgary had operated since 1914. By 1984, it too was technically obsolete and losing even more money than the Kitchener operation (William Goetz, Interview). The plant paid the industry standard base rate of $11.99 per hour and, when increments were included, it paid an average wage of $15.11, well above the $11.14 average for competing plants in the United States. Burns asked for a $5 per hour wage base wage reduction. Workers voted to reject the offer, knowing it meant certain plant closure, but they simply could not afford to accept a 40 per cent wage reduction (Best 1984).

Against the backdrop of wage concessions at Gainers and Lakeside Packers, Burns Meats insisted on local bargaining, while the UFCW opposed any change to the national negotiations that had been the practice for more than thirty years. This led to a charge of 'bargaining in bad faith' and 'unfair labour practices' brought by Burns against the union in Ontario, Alberta, and Manitoba. The Ontario case was heard in July 1984. The issue was whether the union could pursue to impasse its demands for nationwide negotiations and a single national collective agreement. The company argued that its Kitchener plant competed in a local market and that several of its regional competitors in southern Ontario enjoyed the advantage of paying lower wages and benefits. For example, Fearman's Meats in Hamilton and J.M. Schneider in Kitchener paid wages some 10 to 20 per cent lower than Burns' Kitchener plant.

The Ontario decision turned on the definition of the bargaining unit. Labour relations in meat packing fall under provincial jurisdiction; a bargaining unit could not extend beyond the bounds of the province. Burns operated only one plant in the province, hence, its Kitchener plant constituted the entire bargaining unit and the employees in that plant had an obligation to bargain in good faith. The union was instructed to go back to its local negotiating table to bargain with local management at the Kitchener plant (*Canadian Labour Relations Board Reports* 1985: 363). In early October, union members voted 6 to 1 to reject the concessionary contract offer: 'The members knew, as they voted, that rejection meant the butchering and meat processing plant would be closed and more than 600 jobs lost' (Hossie 1984: 1). Burns made good on its threat and immediately closed the Kitchener plant.

Scant weeks earlier, the same issue had been brought before the Alberta and Manitoba labour boards. Burns had also attempted to impose local bargaining on its St-Boniface plant. When the local union refused to enter into anything but a national agreement, the firm alleged and the board found that the union had failed to make every reasonable effort to conclude a collective agreement. The Manitoba Labour Board ordered the UFCW back to the table to bargain in good faith for a collective agreement with the Winnipeg plant of Burns Meats (*Manitoba Labour Relations Board Decisions* 1984). Alberta's Labour Relations Board ruled that the striking UFCW local union had committed an 'unfair labour practice' by insisting on national bargaining (Forrest 1989: 396). In both cases, the local unions were ordered to resume local bargaining to negotiate separate collective agreements for Burns' Winnipeg and Lethbridge plants. Thus, Burns Meats, which had never been an industry leader and never set the pace by negotiating the key bargain, was instrumental in demolishing the system of national negotiations and pattern agreements. With the Calgary and Kitchener packing-plant closings fresh in their minds, the remaining local unions accepted wage concessions on a plant-by-plant basis.

In 1984, the tradition of pattern bargaining and master agreements collapsed. The union preferred to call the system the 'institutional foundation' of collective bargaining, but the firms showed just how fragile the foundation was. Plant-level bargaining by the companies followed and concessions were demanded with plant closure as a credible threat. Union attempts to forestall concessions with strikes was futile as replacement workers could be hired with impunity. The profitability of the industry was sufficiently low that the companies were prepared to follow through with the threatened plant closures if local unions would not accept wage concessions. The standardization of wages across the country among all of the old-line meat packers that had finally been achieved in 1980 gave way rapidly. By 1988, the industry was once again characterized by wage differentials among regions and individual plants.

Explaining the Collapse of Pattern Bargaining

The companies could have attempted to dismantle the national bargaining system much earlier than they did. The big three seemed to be quite satisfied to deal with unions as certified bargaining agents and the industry-wide pattern helped to regulate product market competition and simplified bargaining: 'For employers and employees alike, unionization brought stability and higher living standards' (Forrest 1989: 399). One former Canada Packers plant manager observed: 'In terms of union versus non-union workers, I would prefer to work with unionized workers. I have had both type of workers, and I prefer the union people' (Ross Held, Interview). Why did the master agreement and pattern bargaining system come unstuck after nearly forty years of relatively harmonious labour relations?

In theory, two sets of conditions must be met for a union to have bargaining power (Craypo 1993; 1994: 68): firm conditions and union conditions. The firm must have the ability to pay higher wages by raising prices or increasing productivity. The union must organize all the plants in the industry, eliminate competing unions, and structure bargaining units so that the union may strike effectively. As these conditions began to erode, the structure of the industry changed, creating the conditions for a change in bargaining structure.

Firm Conditions

For many years the industry leader, Canada Packers, did have the ability to pay based initially on the very profitable war years and later on as a result of its market leadership and efficient scale of operations. The 1950s, 1960s, and 1970s were dominated by rapid population growth and rising per capita consumption of beef. The firm's only international competitors, the big U.S. meat packers, laboured under the same union and a similar pattern bargaining system; they posed little threat to the Canadian market. Canada Packers led the industry, set the key wage bargain, and was targeted by the union. It could afford comparatively generous wage settlements because, under the pattern bargaining system, all of its competitors played by the same rules. In an effort

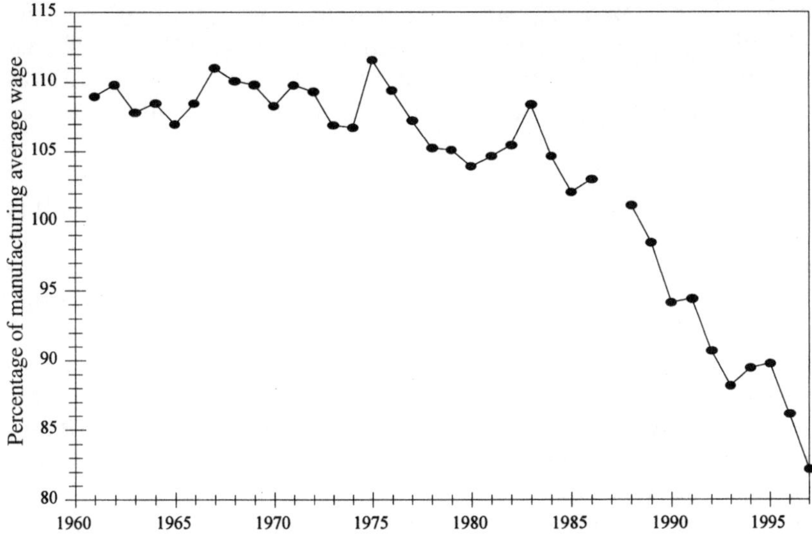

Figure 8.2. Wages in meat packing as a percentage of wages in manufacturing industries, 1961–1997. Census of Manufactures data not available for 1987. Wages are pretax, net of benefits for production and related workers. Source: Statistics Canada Manufacturing Industries of Canada cat. no. 31-203.

to avoid strikes, Canada Packers may have led the whole industry into an unstable situation in which collapse was inevitable. Wages in the meat-packing industry were 8 to 12 per cent higher than the average for all manufacturing industries until 1984 (Figure 8.2). Beginning in 1984 when the pattern bargaining system disintegrated, meat-packing wages began to fall in both real and relative terms, reaching 82 per cent of the average manufacturing wage in 1997.

Canada Packers was the most diversified meat-packing firm in Canada, producing both commodity beef and value added and differentiated consumer products. Paradoxically, diversification into commodity and value added products put diversified firms in an inferior bargaining position. If the firm had to take a strike to enforce wage restraint, it was at a disadvantage relative to firms which produced only commodity beef. In the event of a strike, consumers could buy fresh commodity meats imported from the United States or non-unionized plants and, when the strike was over, the firm could quickly regain its market share in fresh meats. But brand-name processed meat products were a different story. Brand loyalty, which is hard won through product advertising, retail discounting, packaging, and special promotional displays, can switch rapidly during a strike. Consumers turn to processed meats produced by U.S. and non-striking firms, and their new allegiance is difficult to break once the strike is over. Hence, Canada Packers was ill-positioned to withstand a strike because of the great damage that would be done to the market share of its branded product segment.

A debilitating eleven-week strike in 1966 had an enduring influence in Canada Packers labour relations strategy. The firm suffered a decline in sales and a $1.9 million loss on livestock products. Consumer products were off store shelves for three months, and it was difficult to regain its position as the market leader. To prevent a recurrence of this type of damage, it appears that the firm resolved not to be trapped into fighting any more battles on behalf of the whole industry. Canada Packers' loss was a shot in the arm for its smaller rivals. For example, Burns was in desperate straits at that time, and the strike at Canada Packers helped save the company from bankruptcy (William Goetz, Interview). Canada Packers' 1966 strike also benefited J.M. Schneider, its largest non-unionized competitor in pork and processed meat products. Competitors increased their production scale rapidly, while Canada Packers' products were out of the retail market, and inevitably some consumers developed new brand loyalties which had a serious impact on the market share of the larger firm:

> All of these strikes were in the summer. Everything was closed down. It was absolutely debilitating, especially in our consumer branded products. Once consumers get away from buying your product for thirteen weeks, it becomes very difficult to get them to come back. These strikes were very difficult for the company. And, because of that, the union had a great influence over the company. The company ended up with higher labour rates in the beef and pork plants than people like Lakeside and the other smaller packers in Winnipeg and Edmonton. Our labour rates were not unlike those in Burns and Swift though. When we did come back from one of these strikes, it took us six to nine months to get our volume and our market share back ...
>
> In fact, in the meat-packing industry you have to make sure that your plant is cleaned out the day before the strike happens. It is extremely vulnerable. Certainly we had a very high cost labour structure. It was mainly caused by our processed meats operation because of the market share. It

> is very easy to get your market share back in the beef and pork business in two or three weeks. It, however, is not easy to get the share back for wieners, bologna, and the other part of the market that is debilitating. (Lloyd Macleod, Interview)

After its bitter experience in 1966, Canada Packers avoided strikes and meat-packing wages rose ever higher. By the 1980s, meat packing had become a segmented industry. The special-purpose beef plants could take a strike but needed lower wages to compete with the new line of low cost producers of fresh dressed beef south of the border. The hog-slaughter and pork-processing operations in older integrated plants could not afford a strike but could afford to pay higher wages.

Union Conditions

Between 1941 and 1946, the UPWA had organized all of the big three packing plants and a good number of the smaller independents. While it succeeded in organizing most of the largest plants, the UPWA failed to organize them all. Its most notable failure was J.M. Schneider in Kitchener, whose employees chose an association in lieu of certification by the UPWA in 1944 and remained non-union ever after. Schneider's was able to avoid unionization with a generous compensation package that always came close to providing the same level of wages and benefits as the pattern negotiated by the UPWA with the big three.

Of greater concern to the big three were the many independent packers and processors that were certified by the UPWA, yet were able to negotiate wages and benefits lower than the pattern imposed on the majors. Regional firms could be formidable competitors within local market areas yet they paid less, arguing that their small size prohibited paying master agreement wages (MacDowell 1971). By not organizing all of the firms in the industry and not imposing the same wage costs on all firms, the union broke their pledge to 'take wages out of competition.' This was an important factor in the closure of Burns' Kitchener plant:

> There's no question, in Kitchener in particular, we suffered a tremendous disadvantage in our labour rates with all kinds of packers that operated down in [Southern Ontario] – big, small, and medium-sized. They all had a cost advantage over us, Fearman was two dollars below us. Well, then there was the succession of agreements that were signed after that. So instead of the union saying, 'Okay, you've got to come to parity,' they

> would only sign an agreement giving them the terms of the new 'Master' Agreement, added on to the prevailing lower base rates that they had in effect. So they didn't eliminate any of the differential. [Interviewer: 'You wanted Fearman's workers paid more?'] We wanted them paying what we were paying! (William Goetz, Interview)

The final straw came when the union failed to hold all of the competing firms that it had once organized. Lakeside Packers (later acquired by IBP) set the precedent and showed how a small, but determined independent in an unfavourable climate for organized labour could break a strike even though it was backed by a large international union.

Sweeping structural changes sometimes have their origins with the innovative strategic behaviour of a single firm – sometimes of a single individual. At the right time and place such an innovator can create and defend an entirely new competitive position in the industry based on a cost-cutting strategy (Broadway 1998). Clearly IBP's union avoidance strategy in the United States and Gainers' and Lakeside's successful challenges to unionization in Alberta are exemplars. However, these initiatives only succeeded after three successive union defeats before the labour boards of Ontario, Manitoba, and Alberta had transformed the institutional foundation of pattern bargaining.

The New Labour Geography of Meat Packing

With the demise of national bargaining and national wage standards, the labour geography of meat packing was transformed and species differentials, regional labour climates, and the characteristics of the labour force itself became the new determinants of wages and working conditions in the industry.

Species Differentials

Between 1904, when John Commons observed that the workers who dressed beef carcasses were the 'butcher aristocracy,' and 1950, when continuous on-the-rail dressing systems began to enter the largest plants, little had changed in the kill-floor labour process. Since that time, technological change extracted considerable skill from the removal of the hide that had made the dressing of beef so different from pork. Additionally, multi-species plants gave way to single-species plants. This provided the opportunity to introduce a segmented labour market into the industry. Notwithstanding the efforts to differentiate beef

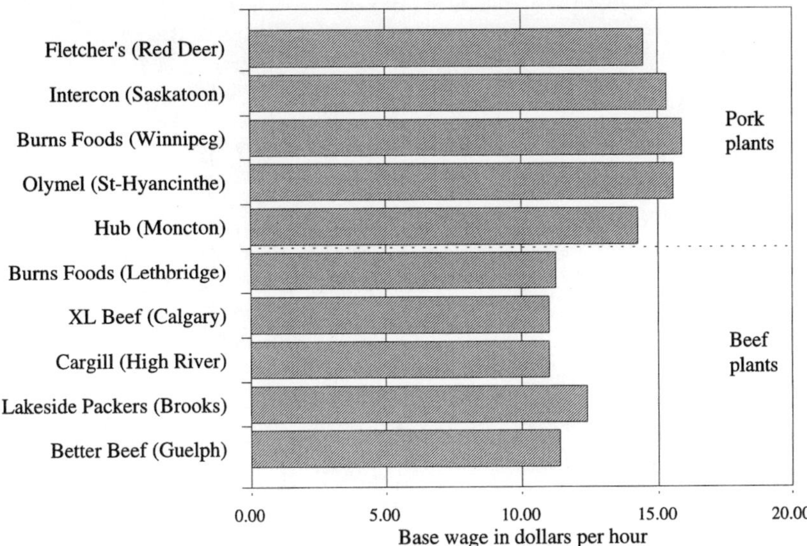

Figure 8.3. Base wages in selected large packing plants, 1993. Source: United Food and Commercial Workers, *Packinghouse Industry Reference Manual*, 1993.

(described in Chapter 9), much of the output of the modern beef-packing plant is still commodity beef in a carton, differentiated only by cut and grade. The meat cutter's skill has become less critical. Hog plants, on the other hand, were able to pay higher wages as they include a greater proportion of value added processing which is sold as a branded and differentiated product.

By the 1980s, a three-tiered wage structure had emerged in the United States. Beef plants averaged between $7 and $8 per hour, hog slaughter plants averaged $8 to $8.50 per hour, and pork processing plants which might also slaughter sufficient hogs to meet their raw material needs averaged $9 to $10.00 per hour (Perry and Kegley 1989: 164). As in the United States, the main determinant in the geography of Canadian meat-packing wages in the early 1990s was the species of livestock (Figure 8.3). In 1993, the average base wage at five of Canada's larger pork-processing plants (some processed small numbers of other species as well) was $15.09 per hour, while the average base wage at five of Canada's larger cattle and beef specialists was $11.41. The hog-processing sector was swept by labour strife in the late 1990s,

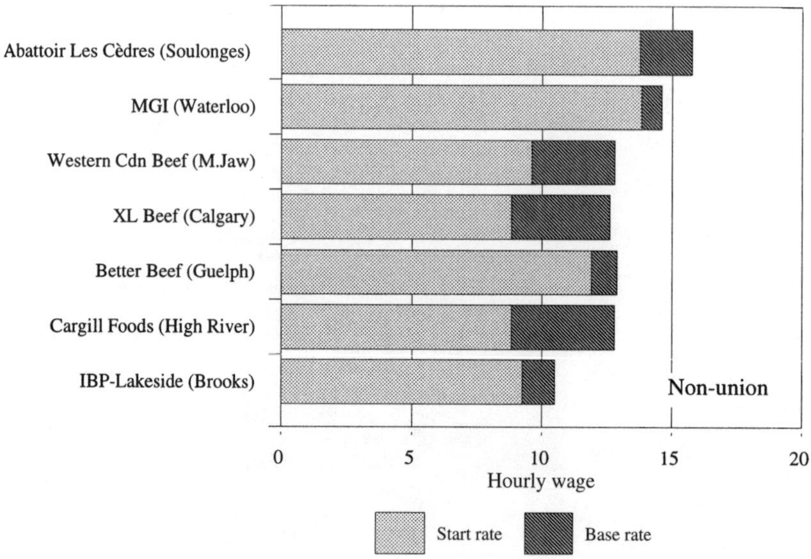

Figure 8.4. Base and starting wages in Canada's largest beef plants, 1998. Source: United Food and Commercial Workers, *Meat Packing Reference Guide*, 1999.

and three major hog processors and pork packers, Maple Leaf Foods in Edmonton, Fletcher's Fine Foods in Red Deer, and Quality Meat Packers which still occupies the Municipal Abattoir site on the edge of downtown Toronto, experienced lengthy strikes. The pork packers succeeded in imposing wage concessions in the late 1990s, just as the beef packers had done in the 1980s (Grier 1999).

By the late 1990s, the pattern of wages in beef plants (Figure 8.4) appears as regionally variegated as packinghouse wages were in 1947 (Figure 7.2). All of the major packing plants have a two-tier wage system, and in most plants it takes two years for compensation to rise to the base rate. Given the high level of turnover in most of these plants, many meat-packing workers are not employed long enough to attain the base rate. Alberta plants pay less than Ontario plants, but their workers have a lower cost of living, while the Alberta plants have higher distribution costs to serve distant markets in British Columbia and Ontario. Non-union IBP-Lakeside pays the lowest base wage anywhere in Canada, but its workers enjoy a lower cost of housing in small-town Alberta while the firm must absorb higher costs to manage and transport its commuter workforce. There is some tendency for the largest plants, which tend to be in the strongest bargaining position, to pay the lowest wages. The smaller players, with less clout at the negotiating table, tend to pay higher rates. The highest wage is found in Abattoir Les Cèdres, a small cow processor and boning plant in rural Soulonges County, just west of Montreal. In the absence of national negotiations, master agreements and pattern bargains, the geography of packinghouse wages has become idiosyncratic, and individual plant variation depends on the unique features of local labour markets and the bargaining position and skill of individual plant managers and local unions.

Alberta's Labour Climate

The United Packinghouse Workers got their start in the industrial heartland where industrial unionism was strongest. As meat packing shifted out of Chicago, Toronto, and Winnipeg and into the western Plains, it came under more conservative labour jurisdictions and a labour relations climate less conducive to the survival of organized labour. Thus, the union tended to be broken in the right-to-work states of the high plains and in Canada's case, in Alberta. The liberal climate for organizing and for securing a first collective agreement that existed under wartime labour relations boards became progressively less hospitable to organized labour, most notably in the province of Alberta.

In any ranking of Canadian provincial labour legislation, Alberta stands out as the least accommodating to collective bargaining, and organized labour has atrophied in Alberta since the early 1980s (Reshef and Murray 1991). The province has been governed by politically conservative parties for many decades (Social Credit followed by the Progressive Conservatives), and the provincial legislature is influenced by a disproportionately large rural constituency that has never been strongly supportive of the urban labour movement. Through most of the post–Second World War period, Alberta labour law has not had provisions to facilitate compulsory dues check-off by the employer or substantive provisions to cope with technological change in the workplace. Matters only got worse from labour's perspective with the passage of a new provincial Labour Relations Code (Bill 22) in 1988 which contained measures that weaken a union's ability to organize new bargaining units (Reshef 1989: 535; 1990: 26). Partly because of this labour legislation, Alberta is the least unionized province in Canada. In 1998, the province's level of unionization stood at 25.3 per cent, well below the national average of 33.3 per cent (Akyeampong 1999: Table 1). Employers have prevailed over labour at the negotiating table and on the picket line, and it is, therefore, little wonder that meat-packing wages in Brooks, High River, and Calgary are low in comparison with other locations. The new pattern for the industry is set, not by national negotiations but in a province with Canada's weakest labour legislation and lowest union density.

New Packinghouse Workers

Until about 1990, the meat-packing labour force was overwhelmingly male, middle-aged, and white. A sea change in the packinghouse labour force is one of the most conspicuous changes in the meat-packing revolution. Women still constitute a minority of the workers on the kill-floor workforce, but in some plants this minority is creeping up to 25 per cent of the workers on the carcass-dressing line. In the fabrication area women, mainly young women, approximate 40 per cent of the workforce, and women are entering both supervisory and training functions in significant numbers as well. A majority of the workers on packaging lines for prepared meats are female. Some work is still physically arduous, and these higher paying jobs tend to be done by the strongest and most experienced men.

Second, the workforce is younger. As recently as 1990, many of the workers were middle-aged and significant numbers were approaching retirement age. Many had worked in the same meat-packing plant for several decades. With rates of turnover that approach 100 per cent per year, the average meat-packing worker is aged somewhere in the middle twenties while many plant-floor supervisors are in their late twenties.

Third, the workforce has become more ethnically diverse than ever before. Packinghouse workers have always included a sizeable number of immigrants. But in the packinghouse of the late 1990s the diversity had become striking. Signs in packing plants are printed in Spanish and Vietnamese, as well as in English, but Slavic languages and Italian are also common. Workers from Somalia and southeast Asia are conspicuous by their presence in packing plants in small Alberta towns that until recently were notable for their lack of visible minority groups. At a shift change, the young and ethnically diverse workforce pours out of meat-packing plants looking for all the world like a typical group of university students escaping a particularly dry lecture. But the impression one gains of the age and sex composition of a packing plant depends on whether it is the afternoon or graveyard shift. The graveyard shift tends to have a younger and more ethnically diverse workforce, while the day shift is older and more experienced, having earned the seniority to work while the sun is up.

The new generation of packing plants is plagued by high levels of turnover that may approach 100 per cent per year when the workforce is growing. Only half an hour south of Calgary, Cargill's High River plant benefits from access to a large metropolitan labour market. Virtually all of its production workers commute to the plant from Calgary; those who live in the idyllic suburban environment of High River itself are drawn mainly from the management ranks (Broadway 1998). Lakeside Packers has more onerous labour problems, as Brooks is more distant from large labour markets; about one-third of its labour force rides one of twelve company buses that drive the 100 kilometres from Medicine Hat for the start of each shift. Lakeside pays a finder's fee of $500 for any production worker who stays on the job for three months, and it has recruited as far afield as Newfoundland to maintain a stream of new hires to replace those who cannot tolerate the working life of a career meat-cutter.

There are no easy jobs in a meat-packing plant. But even after the wage concessions exacted in the 1980s, a meat-packing job in Brooks pays a base rate of $9.25 per hour compared with $6.00 in the nearby McDonald's Restaurant. And with the high turnover, those who can tolerate the work may look forward to rapid advancement to supervisory and training positions. But for many workers meat-packing employment is viewed as a seasonal or temporary occupation, not a career. At the ballot box the new packinghouse workers at Lakeside Packers are not prepared to endure the extraordinary short-term costs of unionization for the uncertain benefits of collective bargaining over wages and working conditions.

Kill and Chill on the Prairie

Until 1960, cattle slaughter in Canada and the United States was oriented towards large metropolitan markets and stockyards at strategic nodes on the railway net. In general, the large horizontally integrated packing plants were in the largest metropolitan areas of each region in the country: there were two or more major federally inspected plants in each of Montreal, Toronto, Winnipeg, Edmonton, Calgary, and Vancouver (Figure 8.5).

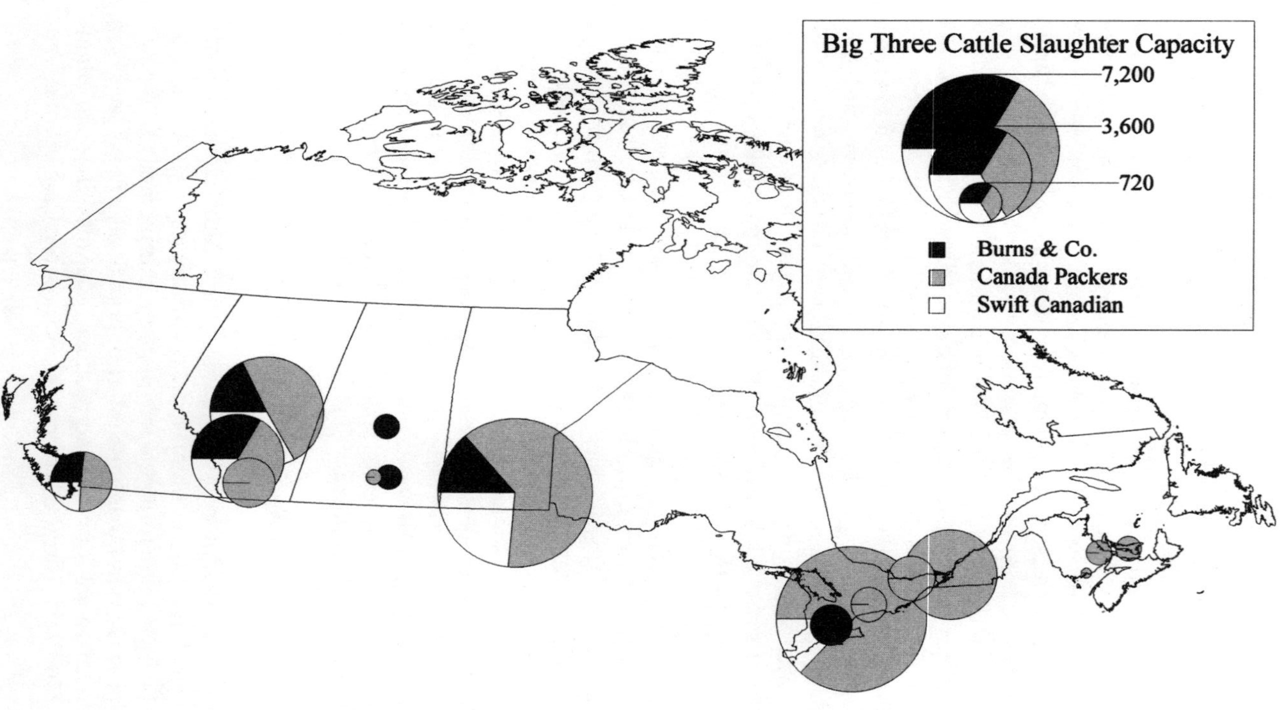

Figure 8.5. Big three slaughter capacity in Canada, 1960.

Locational change in Canadian cattle slaughter began in 1960, led by the big three meat packers. A new generation of dedicated beef plants was opened in smaller cities relatively close to supplies of grain-finished cattle. Canada Packers was the first to build a dedicated beef 'kill and chill' plant in Lethbridge, Alberta, in 1960. Between 1960 and 1975, Canada's big three ultimately built or acquired six middle-sized kill and chill plants in western Canada: three in Lethbridge and one each in Red Deer, Medicine Hat, and Moose Jaw. Most were gradually expanded in capacity to reach 3,000 to 5,000 head per week.

Two factors explain the incremental expansions in these specialized beef plants. There was great uncertainty attendant on the ability of specialized beef plants to obtain sufficient supplies of local cattle to keep them running at full volume the year round. The beef specialist plants had no other livestock species to fall back on if cattle supplies failed to materialize. Once the local cattle market had been tested through all the seasons over a period of years, expansion became a less risky proposition. Second, the plants were constantly pursuing the minimum efficient size threshold which climbed almost continuously through the 1970s and 1980s. In 1960, it was thought that a capacity of 1,000 head of cattle per week would exhaust virtually all the technical economies of scale that were then available to cattle-processing plants (McLean 1964: 4). Thus, each of the new generation of beef plants started out small and grew by expansion, mainly in their cooler space. Cooling capacity is always the binding constraint on the output of a kill and chill plant (Morris and Iler 1975). The plant labour force can work overtime, the line speed for dressing carcasses can be increased, more people can be brought in to do more minutely specialized jobs, and a second shift may always be added. But cooler space is vital and fixed – every carcass must cool for at least twenty-four hours before shipping, and the sides cannot be allowed to touch each other because the air will not circulate, leading to spoilage.

Like the all-beef plants in the Great Plains of the United States that were built at the same time by new meat companies such as Iowa Beef Processors, these new facilities were beef specialists. They were built in a single-storey configuration on the edge of small cities each with a population of less than 50,000. Like IBP, these plants were initially geared to sides of fresh dressed beef as the finished product. But the kill and chill concept was an innovative type of facility in Canada: it killed cattle and chilled carcasses but it did no meat-packing per se. It smoked no bacon, cooked no sausage, stuffed no wieners, and broke

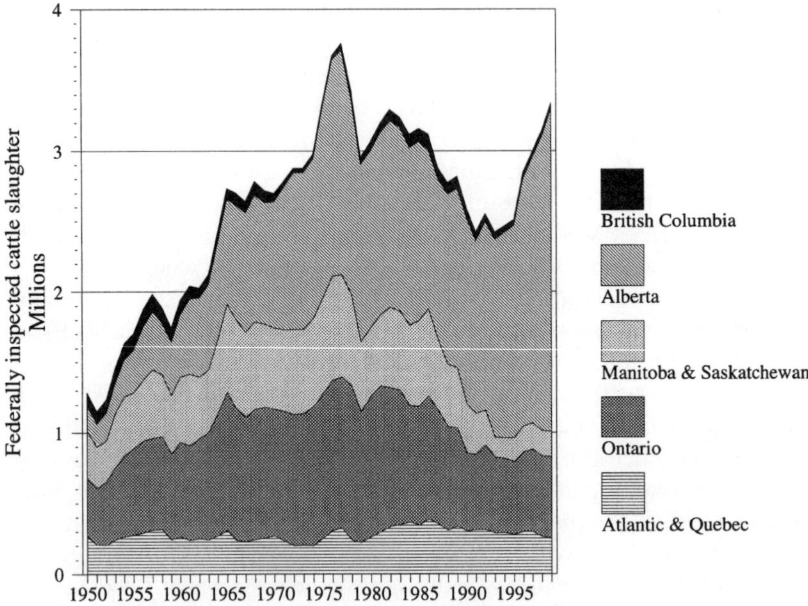

Figure 8.6. Federally inspected cattle slaughter by region, 1950–1999. Source: Agriculture Canada, *Livestock Market Review*, various years.

no carcasses. Kill and chill plants were cattle processors that shipped carcasses in their crudest form.

The western beef plants may have been innovative but the corporate structures remained unchanged. The big three retained their dominant position in the Canadian market; they simply began adding more value in western Canada, contributing to an agroindustrial complex that was articulated with the eastern Canadian heartland by ribbons of steel for the refrigerated shipment of swinging beef.

The construction of these new plants had no immediate impact on the existing packing-plant infrastructure. The beef cycle was enjoying a prolonged phase of growth. Canada's population was growing fast, and per capita beef consumption was increasing. As Figure 8.6 demonstrates, the federally inspected cattle kill more than doubled from 1.7 million in 1959 to 3.8 million in 1978. This was the apogee of the beef industry in Canada. After 1978, the federally inspected cattle slaughter began to decrease for a number of reasons. First, the cattle cycle entered a predictable downward phase and the herd began to shrink (Figure 1.1). While the herd was shrinking, so was per capita beef consumption and the growth rate of Canada's human population of consumers. Figure 8.6 shows how the federally inspected kill plummeted from 1977 to 1980, rallied until 1982, and then dropped even further. This created beef-processing overcapacity in Canada.

With no prospects for a resumption of market growth, the lagged corollary of the growth and expansion of low cost cattle-processing capacity in the 1960s was contraction and shutdown of the high cost cattle-processing capacity in the 1970s and 1980s. The highest-cost plants were typically the oldest market oriented plants. Canada Packers closed beef kill lines across the country: Saint John (1976), Montreal (1981), Hull (1971), Peterborough (1959), Toronto (1984), Edmonton (1979), and Vancouver (1970). Burns closed beef kill lines in Vancouver (1961), Prince Albert (1975) and Edmonton (1978). Swift Canadian closed beef plants in Calgary (1968) and New Westminster (1971). At the end of this first round of rationalization, most of the smaller multi-species market oriented plants had been taken out of production and beef processing shifted to the new-generation plants, principally in southern Alberta.

No sooner had the first wave of mainly intracorporate rationalization been completed than a second wave of rationalization completely restructured the industry in western Canada. While there was still overcapacity and the number of cattle slaughtered in federally inspected plants was still declining, the announcement of a massive new plant (Cargill) and the expansion of an independent (Lakeside Packers) served notice that the beef industry would be operating in an entirely new competitive environment. As the massive Cargill facility rose out of the ground in the ranch country north of High River, it was clear that the older and smaller players would be closing their doors; they simply could not compete in this new high speed, high volume cattle-killing regime. Figure 8.7 provides a snapshot of the spatial distribution of cattle slaughter at this moment. It catches the new Cargill plant in its first full year of production, still with only one shift per day, and just before Canada Packers' western beef plants had been closed.

The second round of rationalization, principally in the western beef plants, began almost as soon as construction plans for Cargill's new operation were confirmed. Table 8.1 summarizes the rationalization in slaughter capacity in Alberta over the ten-year period ending in 1998. Five plants operated by the big three or their successors and one inde-

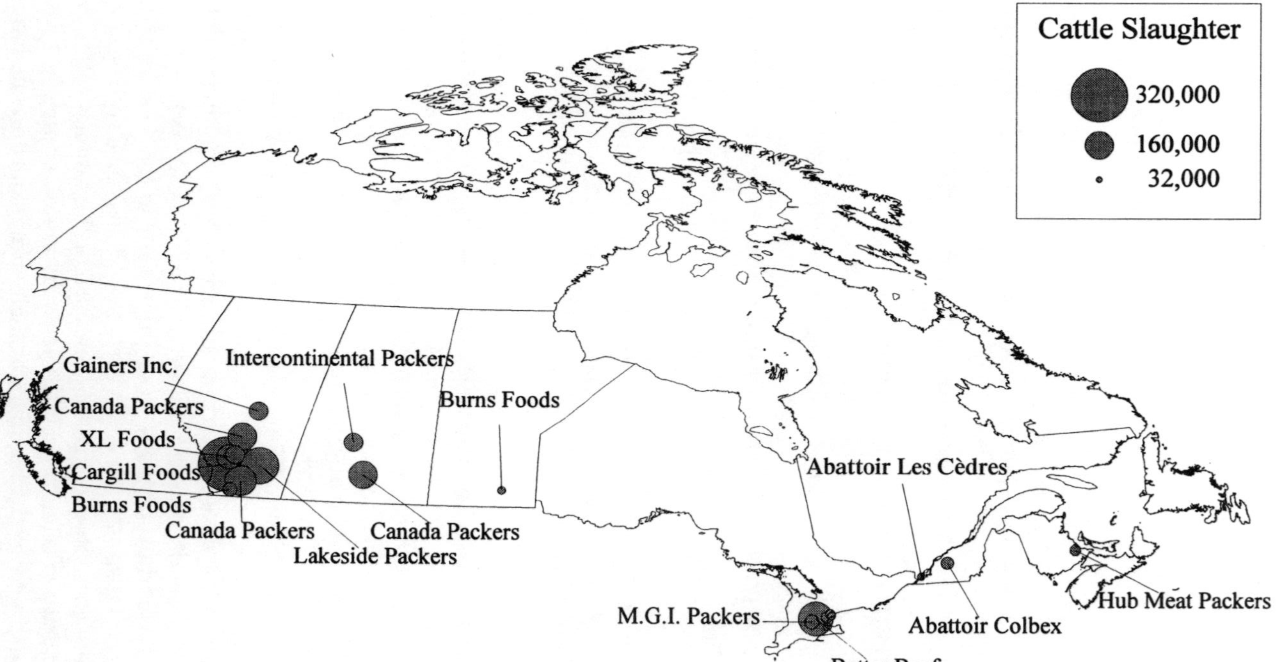

Figure 8.7. Selected large federally inspected slaughter plants in Canada, 1990. Source: Raw data from Agriculture Canada, *Livestock Market Review*. Retrieved from the World Wide Web 23 July 1999, http://www.agr.ca/misb/aisd/redmeat/redmsece.html, Table 26.

Table 8.1 Rationalization of cattle slaughter and processing in Alberta, 1987–1998

Firm	Location	1987 Average weekly slaughter	1998 Weekly slaughter capacity	Notes
Canada Packers	Red Deer	3,250	Closed	
Canada Packers	Lethbridge	3,600	Closed	
Canada Packers	Calgary		Closed	Fabrication only
XL Beef	Calgary	5,000	5,000	
Dvorkin Meat Packers	Calgary	3,100	Closed	
Gainers	Edmonton	2,500	Closed	
Burns Meats	Lethbridge	1,800	Closed	Sold to Maple Leaf, converted to hog slaughter
Lakeside Packers	Brooks	3,200	28,000	Sold to IBP 12 shifts/week
Cargill Foods	High River	Announced	23,100	12 shifts/week
Others		450	450	
Total		22,900	56,550	

pendent closed their doors, while Cargill opened and gradually expanded its massive new plant in High River and IBP acquired and enlarged the Lakeside plant in Brooks.

But the market dominance of these U.S. giants is not complete. In the second tier of beef production are two independent Canadian firms which succeeded in outlasting their much larger competitive rivals: Better Beef in Guelph and XL Foods with plants in Calgary, Edmonton, and Moose Jaw. Some medium-sized federally inspected beef plants survive because they specialize in the slaughter of dairy cows and boning of ungraded beef, they serve a distinctive ethnic market niche, or they enjoy a dominant position in a regional market: MGI Packers in Kitchener, Saint Helen's Meat Packers in Toronto, Abattoir Colbex in St Cyrille, just east of Drummondville, Abattoir Les Cèdres in Soulonges, outside of Montreal, and Hub Meat Packers in Moncton are representative.

Conclusion

One of the important themes in contemporary research on manufacturing has emphasized the importance of flexible specialization strategies

(Schoenberger 1988; Scott 1988). Driven by global product markets which are constantly changing, and facilitated by computer-integrated manufacturing, a crisis in Fordist production was transforming the spatial division of labour at a global scale. Economies of *scale* were no longer significant as economies of *scope* would increasingly reward the flexibility of multiskilled workers and the dense web of transactions among small innovative firms in new industrial districts. One implication was that the need for a vocationally trained and skilled workforce and proximity to specialist suppliers would keep at least some manufacturing activities in North America in the face of an exodus of jobs to the export platforms of Mexico and Asia.

As a crude resource processing industry, meat packing provides an interesting counter-example that has not conformed to the flexible specialization thesis. It is true that provincially inspected packers such as Valley Meats have survived in large measure because of their flexibility and ability to provide specialized services to livestock producers and meat consumers. But over 95 per cent of Canada's cattle slaughter takes place in federally inspected plants which are mainly large-scale, mass production facilities. Thus, the meat-packing industry seems to be a remarkably consistent extension of a nineteenth-century mass production process that was inaugurated in Cincinnati (Porkopolis) and refined in Chicago. 'Fordism' was born when the concept of chain-driven disassembly of hog and cattle carcasses was adapted and applied to the assembly of automobiles on a moving assembly line in Highland Park, Michigan, in 1913. The essence of the nineteenth-century industrial innovation was the unprecedented scale of production, the use of a mechanized chain to carry moving animal parts past stationary workers, a minutely specialized division of labour, and the use of the railways to integrate the industry over half a continent. By the 1990s, the scale was larger, the rail-based disassembly process was more continuous, the division of labour even more minutely specialized, and the semitrailer truck replaced the railway to knit the whole commodity chain together. In common with other food-processing industries, meat packing remains dependent on a bulky and perishable raw material that draws processing towards its source. Economies of scale remain vitally important, and while very large-scale beef packing has become more specialized, it is anything but flexible.

Part Three

MARKETING BEEF

NINE

Marketing Meat: From Branch House to Postmodern Retailing

Mr Steve was our Dominion Store butcher about 1957. Shoppers would take a number on a plastic card and wait patiently to be served. One-by-one, Mr Steve would holler out the numbers to make sure each customer was served in turn. He was the only store employee who discussed prospective purchases in any detail, and there was always time for an individual greeting, the occasional joke, comments on whatever was on special that week, and suggestions for cooking. But the missing digit on his stubby blood-stained hands was his most interesting feature. I have never been able to watch a butcher since without surreptitiously counting fingers.

Each item of fresh red meat was individually requested and individually cut to order. You could watch the roast – your roast – being cut just for you with a confident rolling slice; Mr Steve seemed to know the precise size required for a family of three. ('Watch your fingers,' I wanted to shout, 'Don't cut off any more of them!') The roast was placed on a piece of waxed paper, proffered for approval and weighed. Mr Steve would squint at the scale, and somehow determine exactly what it should cost, down to the last penny. It was then wrapped in brown paper and secured with a wide piece of red paper tape. The final step in the retail transaction was to scrawl the price of the item on the brown paper using an enormous black crayon.

Customers no longer have the time to take a number in the modern retail meat department. And the butcher is in the back; he has no time to chat with customers. All the meat available is out in the case, precut in individual portions on styrofoam trays, overwrapped with clear plastic and labelled by a computer showing the name of the cut, its weight, price, and date it was packaged. A separate label sometimes provides a recipe.

The great strength of the entrepreneurial agroindustrialists who created industrial meat packing was in marketing, not in the manufacturing process itself. Philip Armour once stated that he had never held a knife in his hand: 'If you showed me a piece of meat I could not tell you what part of the bullock it came from' (Wade 1987: 221). Gustavus Swift was a retail innovator at a time when traditional butchers cut each piece of meat to order. Swift recognized that sales would increase if meat was were cut and displayed ahead of time: 'The more you cut, the more you sell' (Swift and Van Vlissingen Jr 1927: 76.) Swift's injunction remains one of the guiding principles of meat-counter management.

Control over distribution, transportation, and retailing was vital to the success of nineteenth-century meat packing. Indeed, the industry depended as much on the marketing of meat and by-products as it did on processing itself. Small-scale butchers could afford to buy, produce, and sell when they guessed the time was auspicious and exit the market when it was not. But the large-scale packers had so much capital invested that they had to remain in constant production and depend on efficient distribution systems to make money even when markets were unfavourable. The big packers built up networks of 'branch houses' to distribute their full line of fresh and processed meats This is especially important in the production of an invariant mix of perishable products. From each animal the packer must accept and market two front quarters and two hind quarters. The nationwide scale of market penetration offered by the branch house system permitted packers to spread this anatomically fixed mixture in different directions, and so avoid having a glut of, say, stewing meat in one regional market and a surplus of fillet mignon in another. But these economies only became available when transportation and refrigeration technology made possible the large-scale distribution of a perishable product that had to be chilled at every step in the distribution chain.

Distributing Beef

Distribution of meat products was critical to the earliest meat packers because of the unprecedented volume of perishable product they produced. The branch house and the railway reefer were both revolutionary and prerequisite to the emergence of industrial-scale meat packing at the beginning of the twentieth century. The emergence of the new generation of meat packers in the 1960s was largely the result of a second revolution in meat distribution as boxed beef, central distribution centres, and highway reefers replaced the earlier distribution chain.

Overcoming Perishability at Wholesale: The Branch House System

Large-scale processing of a perishable product was inextricably bound up with an in-house system of distribution which was internalized through packer-owned branch houses. The branch house provided cold storage for perishable meat products distant from the location of the factory and close to retail markets. In addition to being a centre for product sales and distribution, branch houses were also the site for further value added processing. Branch houses processed pork into bacon, ham, and sausage for local retail markets. Branch houses provided an opportunity for the packers to integrate forwards, adding more value in-house through company-owned smoke-ovens, appropriating the profits that would otherwise flow to jobbers and consignees further down the commodity chain. This was especially important in an age when there were still distinctive regional food preferences that could not be met by plants operating on a national scale.

As the branch-house systems matured, they also began to integrate backwards and the largest branch houses did some slaughter in-house. They also integrated horizontally to handle other perishables such as eggs, dairy products, and poultry. Each branch was treated as an independent profit centre, but they were always a captive market. Branch houses never handled competitors' products.

The advantage of horizontal diversification was that the sales force for fresh and processed meat could also sell butter, eggs, and poultry to the same retailers who bought the meat. Delivery of butter, eggs, and poultry could be accomplished in the same refrigerated trucks that carried fresh meats. Horizontal diversification also permitted the expansion of the branch-house system into markets that would have been too small to support a wholesaler if fresh meats were the only product line (Clemen 1923: 407–9).

In an era when food retailers were small and had limited refrigeration, branch houses had the storage capacity to receive full railcar loads (at that time 21,000 pounds or about 10 tonnes) of packinghouse products. This saved freight costs for small and peripheral communities. Each branch-house had a staff of ten to twenty people and was invariably located on a railway siding near the centre of a small city.

The first meat-packing branch houses in the United States were established by Swift and Company in the 1880s. The branch-house marketing system diffused rapidly. The big five meat packers (Armour, Swift, Morris, Wilson, and Cudahy) operated 544 branch houses in 1889, 887 in 1908, and about 1,165 by 1917 (Clemen 1923: 386–9; Yeager 1981: 291). In establishing their own distribution infrastructure, the meat packers and breweries were among the first firms to internalize the physical distribution function and deliver directly to the retailer, cutting out the independent wholesaler. The need for refrigerated storage facilities accounts for this innovation and meat-packing branch houses became the model for the distribution of a wide range of food products (Chandler 1977: 299–302).

Canadian meat packers were slower to develop wholesale systems. Most had entered the industry as retailers and they continued to operate their own chain stores. At the time of its dissolution, William Davies operated only four branch houses per se; however, it also operated large-scale cold storage warehouses in Toronto, Montreal, and Winnipeg (Canada Packers 1943: 41). The objective of Toronto's Harris Abattoir was to export chilled beef overseas. When it was thwarted in this goal, it turned to the domestic market of eastern Canada. It began supplying its chilled beef to agents in Montreal, Sault Ste Marie, and Nova Scotia in 1903. These agents included a mixture of wholesalers and meat packers in their own right, all operating at arm's length. By 1904, the Harris Abattoir emulated the U.S. packers and internalized marketing, wholesaling, and cold storage by establishing five of its own branch houses in Montreal, Hamilton, Sydney, Ottawa, and Halifax (Child 1960: 126). By 1923, the Harris Abattoir operated fifteen branch houses from Sydney, Nova Scotia, to Windsor, Ontario. When it gained control over the assets of Gordon Ironside and Fares of Winnipeg, it added four more from Fort William to Moose Jaw. This was impressive Canadian market penetration at that time, but in relation to the branch-house networks south of the border, it was small indeed.

In keeping with its western orientation, Burns and Company operated nine branch houses in western Canada during the First World War. Its span of market penetration extended from Whitehorse in the Yukon to Victoria at the southern tip of Vancouver Island and east to Kenora and Fort William. In addition to its packinghouse wholesale branches, it also operated fruit distribution and dairy branches over the same western Canadian territory (Burns 1934, *Annual Report*).

Canada Packers had over forty branch houses at the time of its creation by merger, and twenty were still in operation as late as 1958 (Canada Packers 1943: 235; Canada Packers 1958, *Annual Report*). But with the advent of refrigerated truck transport and the growth of supermarket chains, its network of branch houses became obsolete and began to shrink, a process which accelerated in the 1960s. The branches that survived longest tended to be those in large metropolitan centres not already served by a local packinghouse (Quebec City) or in peripheral locations (Thunder Bay).

Two factors accounted for the demise of the meat-packing branch house: the replacement of rail transportation by door-to-door intercity trucking for perishables and the growing dominance of supermarket chains which operated their own distribution centres obviating the need for grocery wholesalers. In 1978, for example, 68 per cent of Canada Packers' deliveries in Nova Scotia bypassed the Halifax branch house and were shipped directly to supermarkets from factories as far away as Toronto or Winnipeg (*Canadian Grocer* 1978c: 36).

Until the 1950s retailers still purchased beef direct and in person. Buyers visited sales coolers in branch houses and packing plants that functioned as the meat-packers' showrooms. The buyers would examine each beef carcass, stamping those which they wished to purchase. All of the stamped sides would then be weighed and delivered to individual stores.

Yield grades to quantify the proportion of lean meat in a carcass were established when the federal government revised the beef-grading system in 1972. This eliminated much of the fine judgment required for selecting carcass-beef. With the transition to boxed beef, most meat is now purchased according to precise yield and carcass-grade specifications and buyers no longer visit coolers to select meat in person (Leckie and Morris 1980: 13).

Overcoming Perishability during Shipment: Reefer Cars

Any vessel or vehicle for the chilled shipment of perishable foodstuff is known as a 'reefer' (shortened and adapted from 'refrigerator'). George Hammond was the first to demonstrate the feasibility of shipping chilled beef by rail from the Midwest to the seaboard in 1869, and by the late 1870s Gustavus Swift made the reefer a commercial success. Blocks of river ice cut the previous winter were loaded into bunkers separated from the fresh meat to prevent it from freezing.

The first railway reefer cars appeared in Canada in the 1880s as private cars, bearing brand names such as Armour and Swift. They travelled from Chicago to Boston and New York via Sarnia and the Grand Trunk Railway through southern Ontario to avoid the discriminatory rates being charged by the New York Central Railroad (Skaggs 1986: 93; Stevens 1960: 363). Canadian reefers appeared about the same time (Rennie 1969: 5) to move chilled beef from Toronto to seaports with tidewater access to British markets. However, the export of fresh beef was never terribly large or successful, especially in comparison with live cattle.

In 1936, the railway reefer was redesigned with overhead bunkers to permit icing through hatches in the roof, without entering the food storage area of the car. Ice and salt had to be placed in the bunkers several days prior to shipment to chill the cars before they were spotted in front of the packing plant's loading dock. The ice-cooled cars were used mainly to position bacon for export overseas, but when the bacon trade came to an end, they were also used for shipping beef. Only quarter carcasses could be carried, as full sides of beef were too long to fit in the car without touching the floor and blocking the flow of cool air among the carcasses (*Canadian Food Packer* 1943). Iron rails ran along the ceiling to accept quarters of hanging beef. The cars were loaded by 'beef luggers' who transferred the heavy carcass quarters on their shoulders from the rail in the slaughter plant's holding cooler across the railway platform and hung it on the rail in each car. Considering that each quarter carcass of beef could weigh 100 kilograms or more, the necessity of track-side locations for packing plants is clear.

In the 1920s, Wilson and Company was the first meat packer to experiment with mechanical refrigeration to cool railroad reefer cars (Clemen 1923: 395) but it did not come into general use on railway cars in the United States until the 1950s. In 1966, Canadian Pacific introduced the first railway cars designed and built specifically for mechanical refrigeration. They were built higher than ordinary boxcars, providing eight-foot clearance from the floor to the bottom of the meat hook which permitted the shipment of whole sides of beef instead of quarters. Equipped with a special overhead meat rail, they were also the first reefers in North America designed so that the beef could slide from the plant cooler into the railway car, doing away with many of the luggers who had formerly manhandled carcass quarters. Aluminum was used to reduce the tare and raise the capacity of the new railway reefers to 90 to 100 full beef carcass equivalents (*Canadian Food Industries* 1966). At full capacity, the new rolling stock permitted a saving of 47 cents per hundredweight between Calgary and Montreal, a significant reduction as the shipment of western beef carcasses to Quebec was increasing rapidly (Case 1966: 30). Using their market power,

Quebec beef retailers were able to capture about 75 per cent of the savings in transportation costs from this innovation (Canada 1982: 23). Nevertheless, improved rail transportation of whole sides of beef was an incentive to produce and process more cattle in Alberta for the eastern market.

Truck transportation of fresh meats began in the early 1920s. Vans were backed up to loading docks and the fresh meat was simply piled on the straw-covered floor of insulated vans. In this way fresh meat could be delivered in prime condition as far as thirty miles away (Clemen 1923: 403–4). In 1947, the first ever use of a semitrailer to carry hanging beef on overhead rails was reported by Essex Packers to make the run from Hamilton to Windsor (Bowman 1947). By the 1950s, mechanically refrigerated trucks were coming into use for local deliveries, and by 1962 reefer semitrailers specially equipped for hanging sides of beef had appeared. They were equipped with overhead rails at a height to match the rails at the packing plant's loading dock, tie downs to prevent the sides from swaying, and the flow of cool air was specially designed to reduce dehydration and shrinkage in transit (*Canadian Food Industries* 1959; *Food in Canada* 1963).

Development of Beef Retailing

William Davies and Canada's First Food Store Chains

While William Davies was best known as a pork packer, the firm originated as a retail butcher stall in Toronto's St Lawrence market and later developed Canada's first chain of food stores. Through the late 1880s and 1890s its chief source of revenue gradually shifted from the local market for pork products to exporting bacon to the British market. However, the firm maintained and expanded its locally oriented retail operations in Toronto, in part to provide a local market for the less desirable snouts, feet, heads, lard, and offal trimmed from its high quality export cuts. Under the leadership of Joseph Flavelle, the firm added to its chain of retail stores in the 1890s. By 1900, the company had fifteen retail stores in Toronto which jumped to twenty-four outlets by 1903. Just as late twentieth-century shopping malls followed the map of divided arterials and freeway interchanges, Canada's first grocery store 'chain' located its new stores along the fast-growing streetcar lines in Toronto's turn-of-the-century streetcar suburbs. Flavelle wrote: 'Where the trolley goes it is fair to assume we shall shortly follow' (Bliss 1978: 112). In the absence of serious competition, the main locational strategy was to cover the market area uniformly and to be within walking distance of as many pedestrian clients as possible. The only competitors for Davies stores were other Davies stores.

Beginning in 1902, the firm began to expand its retail chain into the smaller cities and towns in southern Ontario from Windsor in the west, to Brockville in the east, and to Collingwood in the north in an attempt to interdict and pre-empt rival chain stores from becoming established (Child 1960: 62–4; Bliss 1978: 112). With forty stores in Ontario by 1904, Davies began to expand its retail operations to the Montreal market in 1905. The firm also diversified into many products such as cooked meats and sausage, pickles, pies, and even tea, thus William Davies became Canada's first true grocery store chain. Most of the goods sold in Davies stores bore the Davies brand name (Bliss 1978: 116), pioneering the house brand that has become a distinctive feature of Canadian food retailing.

By 1919, the William Davies chain of food stores had peaked with eighty outlets: forty-nine in Toronto, eighteen in Montreal, and thirteen in smaller centres throughout southern Ontario (Child 1960: Appendix B). But the bacon scandal of 1917 destroyed the reputation for quality and honesty that had given William Davies its edge in retailing. Davies's premium quality image gave way in the public mind to an association with profiteering and adulteration that no amount of exoneration could erase. The remaining stores were spun-off to a new company in a vain attempt to disassociate them from the Davies name, but to little effect. The chain of meat and food stores was finally sold in 1927 and after contraction and several changes in ownership it became part of another Toronto-based chain: Dominion Stores (Bliss 1978: 437; Child 1960: 80, 90).

William Davies was not alone in operating retail stores to provide a captive market for its meat products. P. Burns and Company owned a chain of ninety-five retail meat stores in Alberta, British Columbia, and the Yukon until they, too, were sold in 1928 (MacEwan 1979: 161). One motivation for the near simultaneous decisions by the Canadian packers to exit retailing was the packer consent decree in the United States which introduced regulations to limit vertical integration and required the big five meat packers to divest their retail stores (Skaggs 1986: 106–7). In Canada, it appears the meat packers exited the retail sector voluntarily, before it might have been mandatory.

But another motive for the divestment was the growing competition from a new generation of Canadian supermarket chains. Sobeys began as a Stellarton, Nova Scotia, butcher shop in 1907; Overwaitea acquired its first store in New Westminster in 1915, providing an extra measure of tea to its customers; Dominion Stores got its start in Toronto in 1919; Loblaws Groceterias expanded from one store in 1920 to eighty Ontario stores by 1927; and U.S.-based Safeway invaded the western Canadian market in 1929 by acquiring an existing western Canadian chain. The chain stores had the sales volume and market clout to negotiate directly with the growing food-processing industry and by internalizing central distribution operations, displaced third-party jobbers and wholesalers.

Until 1925, both chain stores and independents were relatively specialized. Grocers such as Dominion Stores did not carry meat, produce, or baked goods; butchers such as Sobeys did not carry tinned or bulk goods such as flour and sugar. Customers waited patiently to be served by counter clerks who tendered every item by hand and routinely sold goods on credit. The 'groceterias' of the 1920s were responsible for a number of retail innovations. Credit and delivery were superseded by the 'cash and carry' principle and counter service gave way to self-service for all but produce and meats (Huston 1929). Preweighed name-brand packages of commodities such as flour, sugar, coffee, and spices were introduced, and the sale of generic 'bulk foods' went into decline for the next fifty years. Finally, stores began to diversify their inventory and carry a wider range of food products. Dominion Stores added meats to its grocery product line when it acquired the surviving William Davies stores in 1927.

As they diversified, grocery stores grew in size. They edged up from 2,000 square feet in the 1920s to 6,000 square feet by 1940, 15,000 square feet by 1945 to the 30,000 square feet that became common in the 1960s. True supermarkets had emerged by the 1930s, carrying a full range of food products with wicker baskets and later shiny chrome-plated grocery carts for customers to serve themselves in ever larger quantities (*Canadian Grocer* 1979). The chains also grew in number of stores: Dominion Stores, for example, jumped from twenty stores in 1919 to a peak of 572 by 1931, before contracting as the Depression took hold (*Canadian Grocer* 1979: 19–20).

By the 1930s, full-line supermarkets had begun to appropriate a growing share of the retail market for meats from the traditional specialized craft butcher. As they did so, the self-service concept grew in popularity, while custom cutting each piece of meat to order became anachronistic. In 1956, Canada Packers reported that since the war there had been a very rapid development in the display and sale of meat items in consumer-size packages, and meats were being prepared in self-serve branded packages right in the packinghouse (Canada Packers 1956, *Annual Report*: 9). Self-service meat departments in the United States jumped from about 300 in 1948 to 7,000 in 1953, when about 20 per cent of meat sales was from open counters (Brody 1964: 242). Meat cutting moved to the back of the store and a tripartite in-store division of labour emerged. Retail clerks stocked the meat case in the main part of the store. Craft butchers cut the meat in the back using mechanized equipment such as electric band saws. Wrapping and weighing became the province of unskilled female operatives.

One of the important measures of success in food retailing has always been the 'number of turns' or 'annual product turnover,' the number of times in a year that the entire store's inventory of a particular product is sold. Unlike many other grocery store products, beef is primarily sold fresh and is very perishable. 'You either sell it or smell it' (Canada 1960: 191). Thus, the average turnover of fresh meat was, and is, very high and for that reason alone, it is an important contributor to grocery store sales volume. In 1958, the average annual turnover of meat in supermarkets was 175 times compared with 225 for vegetables, 45 for frozen foods, 30 for groceries, and 13 for non-food items (Canada 1960: 191).

Differentiating Beef

Food commodities are graded to differentiate a product with inherent natural variation that originates with its organic character. Grading regulations include a protocol to classify different qualities and to justify premium prices for the highest quality foods. Most commodities are graded according to objective standards of size (e.g., eggs), and by more subjective qualitative impressions of appearance. For example, most fruits and vegetables are classified under federal grading regulations as Canada Fancy, Canada Choice, Canada Standard, or Canada Substandard. But no matter how they may be graded for quality, all food products must be sound, wholesome, and fit for human consumption. Most beef is still sold fresh as a commodity. Other than price, the beef-grading system provides the main basis for differentiation available to consumers. However, some Canadian producers and processors are succeeding in their campaigns to sell fresh beef as a national name-brand product, attracting consumer loyalty to a specific label and product image.

Canada's Beef-Grading System

Government standards for grading beef have been in existence in Canada since 1929, only three years after grading was inaugurated in the United States. Canada's two highest carcass grades were choice ('red brand') and good ('blue brand'). As more cattle came to be grain-finished on commercial feedlots, a growing proportion of carcasses qualified as red brand (Leckie and Morris 1980: 105). Canada's system of beef grading has changed several times to reflect consumer tastes and cattle-feeding practices. The system was revamped in 1992, with marbling standards comparable to those used by the U.S. Department of Agriculture. Beginning in 1997, the responsibility for grading beef was transferred from Agriculture Canada to the Canadian Beef Grading Agency (CBGA). The CBGA is a non-profit corporation that is accredited by the Canadian Food Inspection Agency to deliver grading services for bison, beef, and veal in Canada. Grading may only be performed by a beef grader trained, tested, and certified in accordance with the Canada Agricultural Products Act. The graders are no longer public service employees; they are all self-employed, working under contract for the CBGA.

Grading must be done on a hanging chilled side of beef, typically in the cooler, the day after slaughter. The carcass must be intact from shank to butt, and fat may not be trimmed off prior to grading, except to remove contamination. The beef must be presented as two sides of a split, but otherwise intact carcass. Prior to grading, the left side of the carcass is 'ribbed,' that is, sliced open between the twelfth and thirteenth ribs at the longissimus dorsi muscle, conventionally known as the 'rib-eye.' The rib-eye must be exposed to air for a full fifteen minutes and illuminated by an incandescent light source (CBGA 1997).

Canada's beef-grading system is based on gender, maturity, yield, marbling, and colour. All masculine-looking carcasses (having features such as a large erector muscle, pronounced pizzle eye, or massive neck crest) are graded E, irrespective of age. Mature carcasses that do not appear masculine receive a D grade. These are invariably cows. The main criterion for judging physiological maturity is the level of ossification of the cartilage in the thoracic and lumbar vertebrae. Chronological age is not assessed, and date of birth is not recorded, but the D grades are generally assigned to animals over two-and-a-half years of age. These 'cow grades' range from D1 to D4. D1 cows, known in the trade as 'white fat cows,' sell at a premium relative to the other D grades, as they have good muscling and less than 1.5 centimetres of fat covering; they have become quite popular with the discount steak house chains. D2 cows are slightly thinner or have yellow fat (indicating a diet of grass or hay), while D3s tend towards emaciation (typically an older cow that has just weaned her last calf). D4 cows are known as 'overfats' because they have more than 1.5 centimetres of fat covering. They are heavily discounted because of the extensive trimming required.

Youthful cattle are identified primarily by a lack of ossification in the vertebrae; they are typically under two-and-a-half years of age. Youthful high quality carcasses receive an A grade, while those with deficiencies are downgraded to one of the B grades. B1 carcasses are devoid of marbling or have less than four millimetres of back fat at the point of minimum fat thickness, B2s have yellow fat indicating that they were finished on grass or hay. Yellow fat is associated with cow meat and the trade discriminates against it. B3s have deficient muscling in the round and loin or the meat is lacking in firmness. B4s are dark cutters, instantly identifiable by the colour of the muscle which ranges from port wine to almost black. Producers suffer a substantial discount of 20 to 35 cents per pound on the rail price of B grade carcasses.

To grade in the A category, a carcass must be youthful and there must be at least trace marbling on the rib-eye, the beef must be bright red in colour, the fat covering must be white or only slightly tinged and not less than four millimetres in thickness, the texture must be firm, and the carcass must be well muscled. The A grades are further broken down based on marbling. At minimum, A has 'trace marbling'; AA has 'slight marbling'; AAA has 'small marbling' while Canada Prime has 'slightly abundant marbling.' A carcass devoid of marbling or has less than four millimetres of back fat would be down-graded to B1, even though all other features would qualify it as an A. Each of the marbling classes is defined according to the abundance or scarcity of white flecks of fat in the rib-eye muscle as portrayed on specimen photographs officially sanctioned by the National Cattlemen's Beef Association in the United States. The assessment of the degree of marbling is ultimately subjective; no rib-eye in the cooler looks exactly like the official photographs of the marbling standards, and graders can only use their best judgment to categorize an infinite variety of lean and fat mixtures into four categories. The marbling classes were clearly designed with exports in mind: Canada Prime is equivalent to U.S. Prime; AAA is the equivalent of U.S. Choice, while AA is equivalent to U.S. Select (Morgan-Jones 1991).

The four marbling categories also assist in meeting consumer preferences which vary by region (Jeremiah 1981). In the eastern markets, especially in Quebec, consumers prefer lean beef, thus eastern Canada is the primary destination for carcasses grading single A. In western Canada, a more highly finished carcass with a higher intramuscular fat content is preferred. Thus, AA beef tends to be more popular from Manitoba to British Columbia. Beef graded AAA and Canada Prime have the highest amount of marbling and are targeted towards export markets in the United States and the Pacific Rim (Scheideman 1991: 42).

It is clear that a high-energy grain ration produces white fat between the muscle fibres (intramuscular fat or marbling) once cattle have reached physiological maturity. By encouraging rapid growth, grain feeding allows the production of a carcass which is both large and youthful. For youthful carcasses, the grade depends largely on the diet used to finish cattle for slaughter. The link between marbling and consumer preferences is more controversial. Studies in the 1970s indicated that marbling had no influence on palatability (eating satisfaction), in general, or on shear force values (objective measures of tenderness). Consequently, Canada's grading system was revamped in 1988 to eliminate marbling as a requirement for the highest quality grades. Another series of studies suggested just the opposite, that marbling was indeed positively associated with favourable palatability characteristics, prompting the return of marbling criteria to grading standards in 1992 (Jeremiah 1996).

The grade is marked on both sides of the carcass using a 'ribbon roll' stamping device which runs a continuous stripe down the loins and ribs. The letter grades are emphasized by the use of colour in the edible stamp ink: red for A grades, blue for B, and brown for D and E grades. The term 'no-roll' has become colloquial for ungraded beef as the carcass has no ribbon roll markings.

In 1999, over 90 per cent of all the beef carcasses graded in federally and provincially inspected plants in Canada received one of the A grades (Table 9.1). This is not to say that 90 per cent of all cattle killed were in the A grade category as only about 90 per cent of the total provincial and federal cattle kill is graded. Plants that kill only cows, for example, often do not bother with the expense of grading, as everything they produce is destined for further processing, largely for grinding into hamburger. All ungraded beef that is imported or shipped across provincial borders must be clearly marked as ungraded.

Cattle killed in Alberta and Ontario stand out as having the greatest

Table 9.1 Beef carcass grades by region, 1999

	British Columbia	Alberta	Saskatchewan and Manitoba	Ontario	Quebec	Atlantic Provinces	Total
			Total gradings (%)[a]				
Prime	0.6	0.4	0.2	0.9	0.4	0.9	0.5
AAA	34.0	40.2	12.6	37.3	14.3	24.0	37.4
AA	49.6	50.2	25.8	49.6	61.4	43.9	48.6
A	7.0	4.1	7.3	8.1	21.0	17.8	5.7
B	3.9	1.0	2.3	2.5	1.9	6.0	1.5
D	3.8	3.9	51.1	1.2	0.5	5.8	6.2
E	1.1	0.2	0.8	0.2	0.5	1.6	0.2
Total graded	22,012	2,181,789	179,729	556,684	46,027	34,100	3,020,341

[a]Percentages do not total 100 because of rounding.

Source: Agriculture and Agri-Food Canada, *Livestock Market Review 2000.* Table, 24.

percentage of cattle grading AAA, while Quebec carcasses grade the lowest, reflecting the relative scarcity of feed grain in that province and consumer preferences for less marbling. The percentage receiving the Canada Prime marbling grade is low across the board. Canada Prime was inaugurated midway through 1997, and producers have not yet had time to raise cattle that reach this standard. The large percentage of D grades (cow grades) in Saskatchewan and Manitoba reflects the presence of one large federally inspected plant in Moose Jaw, which kills both choice grain-fed cattle and spent dairy cows.

Brand-Name Beef

Processed pork products have long been branded and sold at a substantial premium. Nationally advertised labels such as 'Lazy Maple,' Swift's 'Premium,' 'Brown 'n Serve Sausages,' or Hormel's famous 'Spam' luncheon meat are well-known examples. More recently, poultry producers such as Tyson in the United States and Lilydale and Maple Leaf in Canada have begun to introduce brand-name chicken. Unlike processed pork or poultry, beef, especially fresh beef, has been difficult to differentiate either for the retailer or for the packer. Like fresh produce, most beef sells as a commodity, differentiated only by grade and price. Until recently, attempts to differentiate beef have not been very successful. Loblaws test marketed its 'Natural Choice' brand beef as free of growth hormones, antibiotics or preservatives, and fed on natural sources of forage, silage, and grain (*Canadian Grocer* 1987; 1988). The experiment was later abandoned.

Branded beef products have been more successful in the United States. Cargill uses the 'Excel' brand, IBP supplies its case-ready beef under the 'Supreme Tender' label, while ConAgra sells its beef under no fewer than five brand names, each targeted to a different sociodemographic market. Clearly, brand-name beef can only succeed if it can achieve a quality reputation and become so attractive to consumers that it will justify a premium price. In Canada, branded beef products are differentiated mainly by the region of production or the breed of cattle. For example, XL Foods differentiates its AA or AAA grade beef as 'the Original Alberta Beef' and ages it for at least fourteen days prior to shipping and portioning. 'Canadian Angus Beef' comes only from Canadian-processed cattle with a red or black Angus influence and it must be aged twenty-eight days, while 'Certified Angus Beef' is a U.S. brand.

Some brand-name programs have also been retail initiatives. In 1989,

Quebec's Provigo chain established a '*Le Connaisseur*' brand for certified Grade A beef that was shipped in special high quality boxes (*Canadian Grocer* 1989a: 184). Steinberg's Ontario stores introduced a 'Slice 'n Save' program in which sub-primal cuts of beef were specially labelled with instructions for the consumer to cut and cook to taste (*Canadian Grocer* 1985: 16). This downloads the butcher's job to the consumer, justifying a caveat: 'some disassembly required.'

Retailing Beef

Boxed Beef

The advent of beef fabrication and boxed beef was described from the meat packer's point of view in Chapter 8. From the retailer's perspective, fabricated beef comes in three formats, each with progressively more value added before it reaches the store. 'Block-ready' beef is fabricated into sub-primal cuts which are fully trimmed and yield 100 per cent saleable beef. The retailer can delay opening a sub-primal package until the day it is required in the meat case, avoiding waste, reworking, and repackaging. With further central fabrication sub-primals may be presliced, reassembled, and then vacuum packed 'tray-ready.' All the wrapper needs to do is open the package, place an individual cut on a foam tray, weigh it (deducting the tare weight of the tray itself), wrap it, label it, and place it in the case. No skilled meat cutting of any sort is required; thus, the whole job can be done by a lower paid wrapper.

The ultimate in centralized meat fabricating is 'case-ready' beef. Individual portions may be shipped to the store already weighed, wrapped, and priced on a Styrofoam tray. The only task left to the retailer is to open the carton and stock the refrigerated meat showcase. In Canada, only the most popular cuts such as the rib-eye or strip loin, are currently being shipped in case-ready format. Case-ready beef eventually turns brown, limiting its shelf-life. The distribution of centrally over-wrapped, case-ready beef has been limited by the distance between the fabricating plant and the retail store.

When it is first cut, and for as long as it is vacuum packed, beef has a purplish cast. Some thirty minutes after coming in contact with air, an oxidation reaction converts the myoglobin in the muscle to oxymyoglobin, and the beef 'blooms' a bright red. Because consumers prefer this bright red colour, vacuum-packed beef is opened and exposed to the air, placed on a Styrofoam tray, and wrapped in an oxygen permeable polyvinyl chloride film for display in the meat case. However, if beef remains on a wrapped tray for too long, it turns brown, as the myoglobin is converted to metmyoglobin. The colour change does not affect flavour, but it does indicate that the meat is not freshly packaged and is rejected by consumers. The challenge for meat department managers is to balance consumer preferences for bright red beef with the limited shelf-life of beef once it has been cut and exposed to air. Retailers are experimenting with special 'Promolux' light bulbs, which are reputed to increase the shelf-life of meat and, more importantly, show meat to its best advantage with more natural colour distinctions (Pocock 1993: 104).

The most recent development in central processing is modified atmosphere packaging (MAP) which allows beef to maintain its colour and increases shelf-life, further reducing the need for in-store packaging and reworking. MAP replaces natural atmospheric air with a mixture of oxygen and carbon dioxide which increases shelf-life and gives the meat a more natural red bloom, unlike the purplish cast of meat in conventional vacuum packaging. Using the regular film overwrap, ground beef has a shelf-life of two days, but with MAP technology this increases to six to ten days (Lazar 1997; Smith 1997).

Case-ready branded beef is beginning to make real in-roads in the U.S. market, not only for steaks but for whole muscle cuts such as roasts. The new generation of vacuum packaged case-ready beef will have a shelf-life as long as forty-five days, allowing the meat to age in the package. Vacuum packed case-ready meats will appeal because they are less prone to leakage: 'The package is so clean you can put it in a bag with a sweater and not worry about leaks' (quoted in Bjerklie 1999b: 60). Ingeniously, the industry could turn the purplish colour of vacuum-packed meat, formerly the greatest source of consumer resistance, into a colour-coded meat freshness indicator. When the vacuum film is broken, the cut will 'bloom' a bright beef red within twenty to thirty minutes, reassuring the consumer that it is fresh and wholesome. And if a package in the store or domestic refrigerator is blooming bright red, it will be clear that the vacuum seal has been accidentally broken and the beef should be eaten right away (Bjerklie 1999b).

The transition to boxed beef has offered many advantages for the retailer. There are economies of scale in the large-scale disassembly of sides and quarters of beef with material handling equipment dedicated to swinging beef, specialized meat, and bone-cutting machinery, and conveyors for large-scale breaking operations that are not feasible at the smaller scale of operations typical of a meat department or butcher shop. Boxed beef is far easier to unload and store than swinging beef. Capital costs for in-store rails, saws, and coolers are reduced, and the store needs only a band saw to complete the cutting process. The retailer is relieved of the need to store large quantities of perishable waste (chiefly fat and bone) until it can be picked up by a rendering company. There is always some potential for contamination of hanging sides of beef should they fall off the overhead rail onto an unsanitary floor. Sides of beef were sometimes shipped in a heap on the floor of trucks, and luggers had to walk on the beef itself in order to unload it (Huff and Mehr 1976: 10–11). Case-ready meat appeals to grocers, as it permits them to download liability for contamination and sanitation to the packinghouse, a growing concern as food safety becomes a consumer issue. Shrinkage of vacuum-packed beef is reduced to 1 per cent from the usual 3 per cent for hanging carcasses, and it has a much longer shelf-life.

The store can target a merchandising strategy for a specific cut to a particular sociodemographic market profile without having to dispose of all the other cuts from the carcass which are not popular with the market segment it is trying to serve. The retailer can pinpoint the precise mix of cuts required for its market, avoiding those which are difficult to move. Other advantages include economies in transportation, simplified retail inventories, improved in-store product handling, and reduced in-store processing. Block-ready beef costs the retailer about 33 per cent more per pound than conventional sides of beef, but the freight cost saving is in the order of 20 per cent. In-store meat-cutting labour costs are reduced so much that the net margin for fabricated beef is higher than for carcass beef (*Canadian Grocer* 1976b: 34; *Canadian Grocer* 1978b: 20).

By 1975, block-ready beef accounted for 17 to 18 per cent of all the beef moved through Canadian food stores (*Canadian Grocer* 1976a: 26). This had jumped to 42 per cent by 1979, 55 per cent in 1981, 60 per cent in 1982, and roughly 65 per cent by 1993 (Canada Packers 1982, *Annual Report*; Canada Packers 1983, *Annual Report*; Canadian International Trade Tribunal 1993: 80–1). There are substantial regional variations, however. In western Canada and in Newfoundland boxed beef is more extensively used than in Quebec and the Maritimes, where carcass beef is still common.

One reason for resistance to boxed beef was that retailers felt that whole carcasses of beef gave them more room to manoeuvre in pricing individual cuts to obtain a competitive advantage. A chain might feature prime rib at a loss-leader price and attempt to recover at least some of that loss with higher prices on other parts of the carcass (*Canadian Grocer* 1976a: 26). If boxed beef took away some of the scope for creative pricing by meat retailers that would see some margins reduced and others padded, consumers benefited from a more uniform retail sales margin.

The slowest retailers to adopt boxed beef have been the small-scale independent grocers and specialized butcher shops. One reason for this is that such stores use the crudest of all measures of retail performance – gross margin – as the guide for making their procurement decisions. Gross margins for fresh meats average 17 per cent compared with 25 per cent on poultry and 30 per cent on packaged meats such as bacon, sausage, and frozen boxed meats (Stonehouse 1996: 14). The net margins on fresh meats are even lower because fresh meat sales must also support the labour costs of meat-cutters, capital costs of meat cutting equipment, spoilage, and shrinkage, and expensive refrigerated display space (Lesser 1993: 412). 'Bacon is put on the counter by a stock clerk making seven dollars an hour. A T-bone steak is cut by a meat cutter making $22 an hour and wrapped by a wrapper making $17 an hour ... The saw to cut it cost $10,000 and the scale to weigh it cost another $30,000. There's no equipment for bacon. The cost of the T-bone to the retailer is enormous compared to the cost of the bacon. And bacon has a 25 per cent gross margin and the T-Bone has a seven per cent margin' (Jeff McMullen, quoted in Stonehouse 1996: 16). For these reasons case-ready beef is an attractive option. The gross margin may appear to be lower, but the net margin is considerably higher. If small retailers were able to measure net product profit, carcass beef would appear to be much less cost efficient than boxed beef.

'Attention Shoppers': The Modern Meat Counter

In the average Canadian supermarket, beef contributes 10 to 12 per cent of total store sales and nearly one-half of meat department sales (Lesser 1993: 409; Leckie and Morris 1980: 14). The meat department's 20 per cent of store sales is accomplished in only 10 per cent of total store space, including back-room cutting and wrapping areas. Yet these percentages belie the actual importance of meat in general and beef in particular. Meat has always been a critical component in supermarket competition. Dominion Stores launched a new jingle in 1963: 'It's Mainly Because of the Meat!' Meat departments in general and beef in particular are heavily featured in food store advertisements, and consumer surveys show that meat departments and meat quality are vital criteria in store selection (Canada 1982: 25; Lesser 1993: 412). Fresh meat is critical to supermarket profitability for another reason: it has the greatest potential of all retail departments to lose money when products do not sell as quickly as planned.

Poultry products have become the largest single retail meat category, with about 30 per cent of meat sales, while packaged meat products (fresh and frozen) account for about 25 per cent. The remaining 45 per cent is divided among fresh beef, pork, lamb, and fish. Poultry is increasingly shipped in tray-ready form reducing in-store labour and the opportunity for cross-contamination, especially important because of the presence of salmonella on poultry. Fresh poultry has a shelf-life of four to five days but once fresh beef is taken out of the box and the Cryovac seal is broken, its shelf-life is forty-eight hours. Even then, it must be 'reworked.' If fresh beef does not sell the day it is wrapped, it has to be retrieved from the meat case, unwrapped, retrimmed, rewrapped, and replaced in the case (Macrae 1991: 22). While beef has higher gross margins than most other food products, the net margins are lower, not only because of the labour required but also because of its short shelf-life.

Demand for beef is price inelastic, according to one recent measurement, its own-price elasticity was –0.69. For every 1 per cent increase in price, consumers will decrease their consumption by only 0.69 per cent. The implication is that discount pricing will not cause a commensurate increase in consumption; a price reduction causes a decrease in the total amount spent on beef. Put another way, beef consumption in Canada is not very sensitive to changes in its price (Eales 1993). Yet consumers remain very price sensitive in their meat purchases, and most meat is purchased on special. Consumers are more influenced by the price of the package than the selling price per kilogram. Thus, one of the secrets of meat merchandising is to select the portion size that will maximize convenience at an attractive price (Macrae 1991: 19).

Another challenge for meat retailers is the need for consistency and standardization in fresh meat products. Labour-displacing technologies in meat packing have always been stymied by the organic variability in live cattle. One might think that the fresh meat consumer wants the natural variety of an organic product not too far removed from its animal origins. But it has been argued that consumers have become so accustomed to standardized, mass-produced food products that they are coming to expect greater consistency in palatability, size, price, and availability in fresh meats: 'A consumer cannot count on the size of roasts or steaks from one shopping day to the next. Contrast this to a McDonald's Restaurant or to a package of Lean Cuisine or to a can of Coke. They are all the same no matter where you go' (Kliner 1990: 5). Taken to its extreme, this observation suggests that standardization from seedstock to the meat counter may pose one of the next challenges to meat marketing, as meat cutters attempt to provide as much consistency in a New York strip sirloin as found in a fast food hamburger patty.

Beef Consumption and Beef Preferences

The role of meat in the diet was once extolled as essential to a balanced diet. Indeed, it was 'proven' that 'normal men' in a temperate climate could live for a whole year with no other food but meat (Hinman and Harris 1939: 238). The eating of meat was portrayed as the hallmark of human progress through the ages and the root of civilization itself: 'We all know the place occupied by meat in human civilization today. We know it is the largest single item in the food budget of the average American family. We know that it is an excellent body-building and energy-making food. We know it is easily digestible. We know it is appetizing. We know it appeals to young and old. We know meat-eating races have been and are leaders in the progress made by mankind in its upward struggle through the ages' (Hinman and Harris 1939: 1). From 1960 to 1976, per capita consumption of beef in Canada increased from just under 32 kilograms per year to peak at 50 kilograms per year (equivalent to 4.9 ounces – a generously sized beef patty – per person per day). Consumption increased particularly quickly just as it peaked, gaining 8 kilograms per capita between 1974 and 1976 (Figure 9.1).

Unlike staple agricultural products such as potatoes, beef has a positive income elasticity of demand. Higher incomes lead to higher per capita consumption. This makes beef unlike many farm staples that are classed as 'inferior goods,' for which consumption *decreases* as income *increases*. The income elasticity of demand for beef was determined to be 0.64 based on measurements of family food expenditure spanning 1982 to 1990 (Eales 1993). This means that a 1 per cent increase in income will cause consumers to increase their consumption of beef by 0.64 per cent. The booming 1960s and early 1970s were years of rapid growth in real income, a significant factor driving rising beef consumption.

It is no surprise that the growth phase in red meat consumption

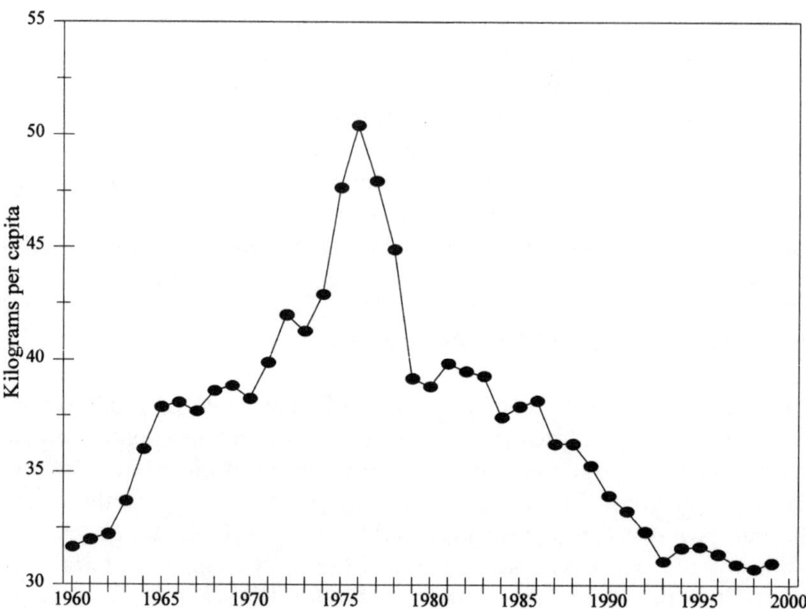

Figure 9.1. Per capita beef consumption in Canada, 1960–1999. Note: Consumption is calculated on a carcass weight basis. Source: Statistics Canada, Cansim Time Series D263633.

coincided with a period of economic growth and rising standards of living. The barbecued steak in the suburban backyard, and the standing rib roast on the dining-room table for Sunday dinner, were part of the good life and rising expectations after the hardship and abstinence of the Depression and war years. In addition, the palatability of beef improved steadily through the 1950s and 1960s as twelve- to sixteen-month-old grain-fattened cattle took the place of three- and four-year-olds fed on grass and hay.

From an all-time high in 1976, beef consumption per capita dropped very rapidly from 1976 to 1979, before entering a more gradual fourteen-year decline. By the mid-1990s, per capita beef consumption had stabilized back where it had been in the early 1960s (Figure 9.1). The major meat packers were apparently unaware of the potential for beef consumption to slide so profoundly. The first reduction in consumption in 1977 was dismissed as merely a 'cyclical effect'; the long-term trend of increasing beef consumption per capita was expected to resume. Future prospects for beef producers were considered to be even brighter as producers were actually reducing their herds, raising prices for those who remained in the industry (Canada Packers 1978, *Annual Report*: 4).

The twenty-year slide in beef consumption had a number of causes. One factor is clearly the health and nutritional concerns created by the widely publicized cholesterol content in the Canadian diet. Influenced by tracts such as Jeremy Rifkin's book *Beyond Beef* (1992), consumers cut back on meat consumption to improve their diet and reduce their weight. High levels of saturated fats in the diet were linked to increased heart disease, stroke, and even colon cancer. Rightly or wrongly, reducing beef consumption was perceived to reduce dietary fat intake. The effect of these dietary concerns about beef was exacerbated by an aging population that is less active, eats less protein, and is more conscious of its vulnerability to cardiovascular disease. Older consumers purchase less beef, regardless of price or income (Canadian International Trade Tribunal 1993: 79). Metropolitan Canada's growing ethnic population may be another source of the sliding preference for beef. Roasting and grilling large cuts of beef in ovens and barbecues is an unfamiliar practice to many recent immigrants.

The decline in beef consumption is also closely related to growth in poultry consumption. Until the Second World War, poultry was considered a luxury. Chicken was reserved for Sunday dinner, while turkey was confined to Christmas and Thanksgiving. When beef and pork were rationed during the Second World War, poultry consumption began to increase and large-scale broiler operations in the 1950s made poultry more price competitive with beef and pork. Thus, chicken made the transition from luxury to food staple (Willis [1964]: 67) and per capita consumption of poultry has grown steadily, while beef has declined ever since 1976.

As the long-term nature of the decline in beef consumption became clear, industry interests such as the Canadian Cattlemen's Association launched public relations and marketing programs to encourage beef consumption. No matter how much the industry attempted to present the facts in objective fashion, the various public relations programs tended to be reactive, vainly attempting to reverse a slide in consumers' red meat preferences that were rooted in the very notions of consumer sovereignty and free markets that they themselves advocated. According to a former plant manager at Canada Packers' Red Deer beef plant: 'Another important factor impacting beef consumption has been the negative publicity our product received from the health nuts of the world. It has been proven that beef is just as healthy to eat as other meats, however, we've been very slow as an industry to combat this negative publicity, and equally slow to promote the attributes of beef in our diets. These issues aside, we must face the reality that others competing for that almighty consumer's food dollar have seemingly better addressed the consumer's changing needs for more appropriate products' (Kliner 1990: 2). This view demonstrates three important features of contemporary meat marketing. First, there is an attitude of scorn towards the motives and preferences of consumers as 'health nuts.' Second, it is reactive; it is concerned with counteracting, combatting, and competing. Third, it seems fixated on the consumer's needs, however irrational they may be.

The notion of consumer sovereignty has been a fundamental concept in food marketing for many years. The marketer surveys and measures what the consumer wants and then makes sure that she gets it. But some of the most brilliant product and market innovations defy this logic. The postmodern approach to marketing observes the great success of products and services that create a hyperreality; something so imaginative, novel, and attractive that the consumer will buy it even though it was not needed: 'Apple's Macintosh computer was not a consumer-driven innovation but a compellingly seductive vision of a computer that could be a *friend* ... The computer – the product – was then developed to fill this vision' (Firat et al. 1995: 46).

The hyperreality imagineered in the promotion of mass-produced agroindustrial commodity foods is often portrayed as a vision of simplicity and wholesomeness. Eating Quaker Oats is 'the right thing to do,' Canadian dairy products are 'Nourishing, naturally,' and the Canadian Egg Marketing Agency exhorts us to 'Get cracking!' The National Cattlemen's Beef Association uses a similar postmodern vision: 'Beef: It's what's for dinner,' while Canada's Beef Information Centre enjoins consumers to 'Savour the sizzle.' No assurances are offered about its sanitary preparation, nutritional value, or low fat content – which are unlikely to change many attitudes. Instead, the consumer is offered simple declarative visions: dinner and the sizzle.

Beef consumption trends have stabilized since 1993, suggesting that the most recent health-related concerns have not had much impact on consumer preferences. Bovine spongiform encephalopathy (BSE) was first identified in England in 1986. Known colloquially as mad cow disease, it began to spread quite rapidly, peaking in 1993, with 1,000 new cases each week. Canada banned imports of British cattle in 1990, but Britain took little concrete action until 1996 when the European Union voted en bloc to impose a worldwide ban on all British beef and cattle exports, which was not lifted until 1999 (*Guardian Weekly* 1996; Barnett and Wintour 1999; Fearne 1998). While BSE began as a threat to beef producers, there is now considerable evidence to link the cattle malady to Creutzfeldt-Jakob disease (CJD), a rare and fatal disease that destroys the brain in humans. Like BSE, the cause of CJD and the agent of its transmission is not known and the full impact of the BSE epidemic on the human population may not be known for many years (Radford 1996).

The incidence of BSE in Britain declined steadily after 1993, but the number of occurrences grew quite rapidly in France and elsewhere in Europe in 1998 and 1999. Amid some gruesome accounts of the wasting effects of CJD on human victims, charges that British authorities had failed to reveal the human health risks created by the spread of BSE among the cattle of the United Kingdom, a growing number of countries have banned the import of beef from individual countries in Europe. In early January 2001, Australia and New Zealand banned the import of beef or processed beef products from anywhere in the European Union (*Economist* 2000; *Guardian* 2001). Thus, the world trade in beef seems to be polarizing into great trading blocs based on the presence or absence of BSE, just as the global cattle trade has long been shaped by the presence or absence of hoof-and-mouth disease.

Canada's single case of BSE appeared on a ranch in central Alberta in 1993. The cow had been imported from Britain in 1987, and she was euthanized before the disease was identified. Once BSE was confirmed, the remainder of the 270-head herd and sixty-seven other cattle that had been imported from Britain were destroyed or returned to the United Kingdom (Carter 1993b).

'Hamburger disease' has become another source of consumer concern about beef. While they are an infrequent event, the grave and occasionally fatal epidemics of enteritis have received much attention in the popular press in recent years. In 1993, four children died and hundreds more were hospitalized as a result of contaminated hamburger which was insufficiently cooked and served by a Jack-in-the-Box fast food restaurant in California. The cause was traced to contamination from a bacterium first recognized in 1982 as *Escherichia coli* O157:H7.

Millions of the *E. coli* species of symbiotic bacteria live harmlessly in the intestine of every mammal. However, the O157:H7 strain of *E. coli* is unique to the alimentary tract of cattle and causes severe bleeding in the lining of the human intestine. The main symptom of *E. coli* O157:H7 infection is a bout of bloody diarrhea which seldom lasts more than a few days. But in about 10 per cent of cases, especially in young children and in elderly or frail adults, the infection leads to hemolytic-uremic syndrome which may damage or destroy kidney function, requiring dialysis. In some cases, it has led to death.

In terms of mortality, one of the most severe institutional outbreaks ever attributed to *E. coli* O157:H7 occurred in a nursing home in London, Ontario, in 1985. Of 169 residents, fifty-five became ill and nineteen died. While the source of the pathogen was never determined with certainty, it appears that the culprit was unrefrigerated ham, turkey, and cheese sandwiches which were prepared on a marred wooden surface several hours prior to consumption by a food handler who had recently recovered from a bout of diarrhea (Carter et al. 1987; *Canadian Nurse* 1986: 14). There is no evidence that beef was involved in this outbreak, nevertheless *E. coli* has become the 'hamburger disease.' Ever since the Jack-in-the-Box episode in the United States, the potential for food poisoning by contaminated meat has been a grave concern for both consumers and the meat-packing industry.

The main source of *E. coli* O157 is fecal waste from cattle. While eating beef contaminated with fecal material without proper cooking is commonly held to be the most likely cause of infection in humans, epidemics such as the London outbreak suggest that other avenues of infection may also be responsible. The potential for fecal contamination of carcasses in the United States is commonly linked to inadequate food inspection resulting from budgetary cutbacks by the USDA's Food Safety and Inspection Service and the increasing chain speed in large-scale kill plants. While the final barrier against *E. coli* O157 infection should be in the kitchen (it is easily killed by cooking for two minutes at 70ºC), unsanitary practices in the slaughterhouse have been held responsible for the spread of the bacterium from the bovine intestine to the surface of meat (Eisnitz 1997; Featherstone 1997).

This has been a powerful motive for the inauguration of steam pasteurization of carcasses in large-scale packing plants and more rigorous meat-inspection procedures (Langman and Bacon 1999). As testing for the presence of *E. coli* O157 in fresh meats and especially in hamburger is becoming more widespread, product recalls are growing more frequent. In June 2000, Lakeside Packers recalled 77,000 kilograms of ground beef scant weeks after an outbreak of *E. coli* contamination in the municipal water supply of Walkerton, Ontario, was responsible for at least seven deaths and was implicated in eighteen more (Foss 2000). The risk of *E. coli* contamination may be sufficient to overcome consumer resistance to the irradiation of fresh meats to kill bacteria in the packinghouse. But, in any case, consumer health concerns about the safety of beef products promise to be a continuing public policy issue.

Beef Consumers: Where Stated Preferences and Behaviour Diverge

The entire commodity chain from calf producers to cattle feeders to meat packers has become more conscious of changing consumer preferences than ever before. Consumer studies have shown that large exposures of fat are perceived as undesirable, and consumers prefer to purchase beef that is closely trimmed. A clear signal has been sent down the commodity chain: 'Fat is out, lean is in.' In other words, the production of excess subcutaneous fat on beef is undesirable, and the industry must strive to remove fat either by trimming or with genetics. Therefore, the future of the beef industry will depend on the ability to develop a more efficient production system through a new and improved technology' (Pelton 1990: 1).

Until 1986, the typical external fat trim standard in the United States for retail beef cuts was in excess of one-half inch. By 1989, the maximum fat thickness was one-eighth of an inch, and 42 per cent of retail cuts had no external fat. In just three years, U.S. meat retailers were putting 27 per cent less fat in the display case. For this and other reasons, the U.S. beef industry is shifting from a commodity orientation to a consumer orientation (Cross 1989: 1). Consumer preferences are transmitted to the retailer to trim more fat, then to the meat packer, then to the cattle-feeding and -finishing operation, and finally, to the seed-stock producer.

But it is wrong to conceive of food preferences as an unambiguous and monolithic message, for two important reasons. First, like any social attitude, consumer preferences have enormous variance and span a broad range. While consumer preferences may have changed on average, the distribution has very long tails. Second, there is a significant amount of hypocrisy in 'stated preferences.' There is a contradiction between what consumers say about their diets and the foods they actually purchase in the supermarket. Survey evidence shows that the preferences of Canadian and U.S. shoppers are decidedly contradictory when it comes to dietary fat. In the display case, consumers invariably choose the leanest cuts. Yet in blind taste tests they tend to prefer the juiciest and tenderest cuts which are typically those with the highest level of intramuscular fat or marbling.

Survey results on display case preferences are legion. According to the January 1956 edition of the *Farm Journal*, visual preferences of consumers favoured a lack of visible fat:

> The little woman just isn't picking out what we've long thought of as premium beef cuts.
>
> In Denver, 500 homemakers expressed a decided preference for Good grade cuts over any other. Second pick was Commercial, with Choice running third, and Prime last. Again in this survey, price was not a factor in their decision.
>
> Housewives in the Pacific Northwest feel the same way. Given a choice of Choice, Good and Commercial T-bone steaks, only 23 per cent of the women in Spokane, Portland, and Seattle surveys chose a Choice-graded cut, 30 per cent selected Good and 41 per cent Commercial. In other words, 71 per cent chose the two leaner grades even though the price was the same. (Bay 1956: 41)

Consumer preferences in regard to dietary fat remain as contradictory today as they were in the 1950s: 'The split personality of the Canadian carnivore is what makes beef such a tricky meat to sell' (Allemang 1995: A1). In a Beef Information Centre survey, consumers complained that the quality of beef had declined from 1977 to 1987, a period in which the leanest grades gained ground over fattier grades of beef. Leanness is the most important and sought-after trait when consumers select steaks from the meat case, although one in five also consider marbling to be a positive selection criterion. Trace marbling is clearly preferred, while modest marbling is rejected at the display case. But these visual preferences are reversed in blind taste tests of cooked samples: samples from steaks with traces of marbling were least preferred, followed by slight, small, and modest marbling. Among the steaks with only trace marbling that were rejected, the most common complaints were toughness, blandness, excessive connective tissue, and lack of juiciness (Jeremiah et al. 1992). Consumers say they want lean meat, and they pick out the leanest cuts in the meat case, but in taste tests they prefer higher levels of intramuscular fat: 'This disparity between consumer acceptance based upon visual assessment at the point of purchase and upon palatability during consumption constitutes a major concern to the Canadian beef industry. Leanness (lack of marbling) is necessary for consumers to purchase the product initially. However, it appears at least a small degree of marbling is required for most consumers to continue to purchase the product' (Jeremiah et al. 1992: 384–5). Canada's new grading system comes closer to judging beef on the basis of the intramuscular fat that consumers prefer in taste tests. But beef consumers are notoriously contradictory in what they say they would like to eat and what they say after they have eaten it.

Meat in general and beef in particular is viewed by a growing number of consumers as an ingredient or even a garnish rather than the main dish and substance of a meal. Portion sizes have become smaller. In 1970, consumers in both restaurants and retail stores wanted ten- to twelve-ounce boneless steaks and sixteen- to twenty-ounce bone-in steaks. By 1990, six- to eight-ounce boneless and twelve-ounce bone-in portions had become the norm. To achieve this and still have a steak that is at least three-quarters of an inch thick, smaller carcasses and smaller cattle are in demand (Carruthers 1990: 1): 'Whatever the market is, heavy weight cattle are quickly becoming less desirable. If anyone still has difficulty with this idea just think of yourself as the consumer that ends up purchasing a T-bone steak off a heavy animal that is a quarter of an inch thick and covers a full size plate when cooked. What are the chances you'll be satisfied? What are the chances you'll buy another?' (Kliner 1990: 3).

Consumer preferences have not only influenced the quantity of beef produced for domestic markets, they have also prompted a reduction in the size of finished cattle. Heavy cattle, one of the most notable characteristics of the exotics and exotic cross-breeds, are becoming less desirable. Despite the economies of scale offered by carcasses in the 800- to 900-pound range (it costs little more to slaughter, break, chill, and grade a large carcass relative to a small one), heavy cattle are discounted in price. Restaurants and steakhouses proclaim that they serve only prime steer beef, and many older consumers believe they are purchasing steer beef in the grocery store (Jeremiah 1981). In fact, the smaller heifer comes closer to providing the portion size that the food service industry is looking for and that people are coming to prefer. Experimental evidence shows that sex has no influence on cooking or palatability attributes (Jeremiah et al. 1997b).

Postmodern Beef Retailing

While postmodernism is normally considered a literary paradigm, it is also being felt in a host of prosaic economic activities including retail sales. In retailing, postmodernism is expressed in an enormous variety of ethnic and culinary styles and in a rejection of apparently mass-produced and standardized goods. Food shopping reverts to a form of entertainment in its own right, rather than a chore to be endured before going back to the standardized suburban home or anonymous high-rise apartment.

The traditional 'modern' supermarket had ten or more identical aisles with a meat counter at the back, produce to one side, and dairy on the other. Each aisle was filled with symmetrical, flush-stacked displays of identical packages of a particular class of foodstuff. Prevailing merchandising orthodoxy holds that the more label faces consumers see, the more they will buy. The postmodern supermarket avoids symmetry and standardization in favour of variety. Supermarkets are introducing an exciting if sometimes bewildering array of 'value added departments,' each creating a unique image of fresh quality and variety. Wonder Bread gives way to the in-store bakery. Identical heads of size-graded iceberg lettuce are replaced by in-store salad bars. The peg-board for sliced and packaged meats is contracting, while the perceived freshness of the in-store deli is growing in popularity, especially among younger consumers. Pyramid displays of homogenized meat blends such as Hormel's Spam, Maple Leaf Kam, or Swift's Prem are boring and *passé* compared with Save-On-Foods' 'Chef's Cut' department which makes a show of seasoning and marinating steaks for the grill before our eyes. The drudgery of 'doing the marketing' has become a spectacle.

The whole layout of the store is designed to increase revenues. And for good reason: 80 per cent of all retail food buying decisions are made at the point of sale, while only 30 per cent of food store customers use any sort of shopping list (Knell 1992: 117). The layout of Ontario's Loblaws stores, for instance, is planned to place impulse items near the entrance, to make sure that 'Ziggy's' delicatessen is always the first display that customers encounter. 'Power aisles' are lined with high margin items and fresh foods. Only later does the shopper encounter the milk and dairy items with low margins which are competitively priced with other stores (Knell 1992: 118). This attractive and varied design invites the customer to stay in the store, to walk the entire track, seeing as much different merchandise as possible, increasing the probability that she or he will purchase more. Coloured floor tiles may be arranged to create a path drawing consumers to departments they might otherwise skip. Cool wall colours such as blue, green, and grey create a more relaxed atmosphere, helping to slow the pace of shoppers, keeping them in the store longer and increasing their purchases (Pocock 1993: 108–10).

The modern meat case was all about sanitary uniformity with red meat on identical white trays and a consistent pricing display. Meat managers would try to position one 'stopper' in each six-foot length of meat display space. Techniques to create a stopper included using double the quantity of every other item in the case, a raised tray of a different shape or a larger than normal price tag. Postmodern supermarket marketing tools include novel packaging, foam trays in a variety of colours, point-of-sale displays, seasoning sachets, and innovative fonts to display pricing information, all in an effort to indulge a consumer image. Refrigerated display cases in sinuous curves have replaced the rectilinear logic of the modern food store, while bunker islands exposed on all sides provide more linear feet of display space to expose more meat to shoppers (Vidoczy 1993: 10).

Traditional retail meat marketing was influenced by its roots as a commodity. Retailers segmented meat according to a rational classification system: first by species (beef, pork, and chicken), and then by anatomical class: brisket, rib, sirloin, and rump. Red meat cuts in a display case are all roughly the same size and colour, and they tend to blend together as a pile of undistinguishable red meat. Particular cuts cannot be identified as something good to eat and are not very appetizing: 'Women never buy just "meat" – they buy particular items like pork chops, liver, steaks, roasts, bacon, ham, etc., and therefore, the job is to arrange the case so they will see items quickly, easily, and from the greatest possible distance away from the case' (Hinman and Harris 1939: 189). Postmodern meat retailing recognizes that consumers are not at the meat case to buy meat, but they are not there to buy a New York sirloin, or butterflied pork chop, either.

According to Margaret Thibault of the Beef Information Centre, 'You're not selling pieces of anatomy on a diaper, you're selling a meal' (Macrae 1991: 19). The motives and images brought by consumers to the meat counter are as varied as consumer behaviour itself: to present oneself as a gourmet, to win prestige, to experience novelty and offset boredom, to save money, to save time for other pursuits, or to enhance health and nutrition. The postmodern approach to merchandising attempts to create variety and interest geared to the meal as a special event or even extravaganza. The prescriptive strategy for the retailer is to reconstruct the meat case to indulge the food image of the consumer.

Merchandisers construct sales categories such as 'heat 'n eat,' 'slim 'n trim,' or a 'sauté centre' that have nothing to do with a meat's anatomical origins and everything to do with the consumer's image of the meal (Vidoczy 1995: 11). Retailers 'cross-merchandise' grocery items such as sauces, spices, marinades, or specialty seasonings at the meat counter, coaxing the consumer into buying a full suite of ingredients to prepare the meal and realize the vision. More or less elaborate value added items such as crown rack of lamb, teriyaki stir fry, or oven-ready meat loaf offer the consumer a gastronomic fantasy in response to the simple motive to buy something to cook. Even small additions to packaged cuts such as a parsley sprig garnish or a recipe card on a meat tray make it appear more fresh and appealing to consumers. Sirloin tip trimmings were once merchandised as just that. Now those very same leftovers are 'fajita strips,' 'fondue cubes,' or 'kabobs.' In some cases these specialty items are prepared in-house from trimmings. But many stores do not have the staff or machinery to make the cuts that generate these trimmings. So, for example, specialty items such as 'oriental stir-fry' are increasingly sliced from outside round and vacuum packed in bulk in centralized beef-processing plants. The retailer merely repackages, weighs, and labels the beef in consumer-sized tray packs before it goes in the display case (*Canadian Grocer* 1989b: 7).

To encourage the consumer to translate a vague meal concept into the purchase of a specific beef product, a new system for retail beef marketing was introduced in 1998. A committee composed of Agri-Food Canada, the Canadian Food Inspection Agency, the Beef Information Centre, the Canadian Meat Council, the Canadian Council of Grocery Distributors, and the Consumers' Association of Canada was struck to examine the existing nomenclature for different cuts of beef and to propose an alternative. Most consumers do not understand the anatomical name of the cut when purchasing beef. They are thinking of dinner on a plate, not a schematic of a bovine carcass. Many consumers do not know how to cook more than a very limited repertoire of all the muscle cuts available. People generally know how to cook cuts from the rib and loin, but they are less familiar with cuts from the hip and chuck.

The committee developed a new classification system for selling beef based on how the meat should be cooked, as well as from where on the carcass it was obtained. For example, rump roast is now labelled as a 'rump oven roast,' blade roast becomes 'blade pot roast,' a rib-eye steak is now known as 'rib-eye grilling steak,' while the tougher inside round steak is more succulently described as an 'inside round marinating steak.' In addition to the official new names for the various cuts, the label includes simplified cooking instructions appropriate to the cut. The layout of the meat case in many of the larger chain stores is being reorganized according to the type of cooking required. By incorporating cooking method into the official names and including detailed instructions, consumers are more likely to cook beef properly, enjoy it more, and increase their consumption. Cooking instructions are becoming especially important as consumers have less personal contact with the in-store butcher in the modern meat department, and many younger and ethnic shoppers are confused and even intimidated by the many cuts of beef that are available (Brand 1998).

Another feature of the postmodern approach to retailing is the 'eclecticism of referents.' Consumers change the groups with which they identify, dropping one self-image in favour of another. Brand loyalty, especially to mass-marketed standard brands, may be a thing of the past. Market surveys are done to measure how consumers feel about products and to determine what they would like to buy, under the assumption that the consumer is rational, predictable, and consistent. Not only do consumers change their views and preferences very rapidly (fads are nothing new), but the image of self and consumption preferences may appear to be highly inconsistent, contradictory, and most of all, unpredictable. Food consumers have a greater variety of distinct preferences for organic foods, meat-free diets, genetically unmodified grains, or low fat cuts. Staples such as meatloaf or mulligan which were once unfashionable are back in vogue.

Marketing has always been concerned with selling a material product with the right sort of image. Meat loaf was once frumpy, middle-class fare. Until the neo-traditional became retro-chic, it was the last thing that any meat manager would suggest to inspire a bored consumer. Now the value added frozen meat purveyors are doing just that: 'We sell a pre-cooked pot roast at Jeffries. No one has time to cook a pot roast anymore. It's in a plastic bag and you boil it in water to heat it up. People buy it like crazy. It's a huge hit' (Jeff McMullen, quoted in Stonehouse 1996: 16). Nevertheless, could a consumer derive much satisfaction from a piece of brisket that had to be steamed in a pressure cooker for half an hour to make it even chewable?

But that was what modern marketing tried to do. It sold a product to satisfy perceived needs and then grafted a complementary image on top of it. 'Sell the sizzle, not the steak!' has been a marketing adage for many years and long predates postmodern thinking (Kenney 1944: 39). Nevertheless, selling the sizzle has become the quintessence of the post-modern approach. Instead of selling a product that has an image, post-modern marketing is projecting and selling an image, an image as reassuring as pot roast, and the marketer shapes a product – any product – to represent or complement that image: 'Successful marketing organizations, such as Nike, realize that they are not in the business of selling shoes but of crafting images. Such organizations communicate the image, not the product in their promotional campaigns. In fact, Nike advertisements are often a form of video poetry – high art that elevates human physical achievement to the level of the sublime. The product – the sneaker – is a mere representation of this image. In the post-modern marketplace, products do not *project* images; they *fill* images' (Firat et al. 1995: 45–6). Consumers pay hundreds of dollars to appropriate the image of a famous athlete. And they buy pot roast, like crazy.

The mass production of a standardized seasonal cutting list (one-inch T-bones for the barbecue in summer and rib roasts for the oven in winter) has given way to a new ethos of flexibility, as meat departments attempt to respond to regional idiosyncrasies of market areas. Average family size continues to shrink, rate of female participation in the labour force continues to rise, and single-person households are growing more quickly than any other size group. There is less time for home cooking than ever before, as the evening meal must be assembled by someone who has already put in an eight-hour day. Thus, lean boneless cuts in small portions are becoming more popular as the traditional eight-pound roast declines in favour. Beef sales were increased in Quebec by developing new, mainly boneless, prime cuts from traditional bone-in roasts (*Canadian Grocer* 1985: 16).

If meat retailers are doing more, not just to meet changing consumer preferences, but to create and shape those preferences, they are also doing less of the repetitive carcass breaking than was the case when sides of beef came straight into the grocery store. Tasks formerly performed in the back room, out of sight, are either done in the packing-house, or they have been brought out into the open – creating an image of animation and activity. Produce trimming and washing, in-store baking, fish preparation, and meat cutting and wrapping are all coming out of the closet. Indeed, the closet walls are coming down, giving food stores a more spacious feel. With the exposure of retail food preparation, stores have a more animated ambience. This also requires that food preparation areas be kept cleaner than may formerly have been the case, and it displays the labour-intensive value added services that postmodern food retailing requires. The supermarket meat department has become less of a back-room value added manufacturing operation and more of a meat merchandiser to satisfy the consumer's image of what is good to eat.

TEN

Conclusion

It is a long way from the Calderwood Ranch to the postmodern supermarket. But that is the nature of the commodity chain. It links diverse industries and distant regions creating production systems on a variegated economic landscape beginning with Prairie grass and ending with a consumer's purchase decision at the supermarket meat counter. Beef consumption by the urban consumer is ultimately articulated with the environmental constraints of finite range land and biological imperatives of animal reproduction. And when consumers vote at the cash register, their preferences, no matter how contradictory, irrational, or inconsistent they may seem, are transmitted up the chain to the producer.

It is impossible to examine the cattle–beef commodity chain over time and space without reference to events and conditions south of the longest undefended border. With few exceptions, innovations in Canada followed events in the United States. The nineteenth-century Canadian cattle boom in the east and after a short lag, in the west, followed the pattern set first in the United States. Much of the nineteenth-century mixed farming in the east was influenced by the United Empire Loyalists from the Middle Atlantic states, while the earliest ranching in the west was a northern variant of the land-intensive methods first developed along the Gulf coast of Louisiana and Texas (Jordan 1993). Large-scale capital intensive cattle feedlots were developed first in California and later transplanted to the high plains of the Ogallala aquifer before they were replicated on the irrigated lands of the Alberta Plain. The cross-breeding revolution occurred first in the United States and then in Canada, although Canada led the way in the invasion of the European exotics.

Toronto's Union Stock Yards was established in 1903 as Canada's first large-scale full-service stockyard, thirty-six years after the creation of Chicago's Union Stock Yards. The first stockyards became the nucleus for the first industrial complex of fully integrated meat packers in the United States. Thirty years later the Chicago experience was repeated at Toronto Junction. The earliest industrial-scale meat packers in Canada gained significant cost advantages over less progressive firms and they parlayed this advantage into an apparently hegemonic oligopoly only decades after the U.S. meat-packing firms had demonstrated the possibilities. The Canadian industry was organized by the United Packinghouse Workers of America, scant years after the CIO affiliate had organized the U.S. industry. Once all the big three plants were organized, the UPWA's Canadian district resolved to copy the accomplishments of its American brothers and sisters in their every detail. And eventually it did. But almost as soon as national negotiations, pattern bargaining, and the master agreement seemed to be enshrined as articles of faith, the big three demonstrated the fragility of that faith and the thirty-eight-year-old collective bargaining structure came crashing down in the mid-1980s, in the same way that it had been destroyed in the United States only a few years previously.

Most regulatory initiatives in Canada were a direct response to U.S. developments. Some western Canadians are concerned that their government plays too active a role in agriculture and economic activity – especially in relation to the United States. But consider federal meat inspection, public stockyards, humane slaughter, combines investigation, and beef grading. Every one of these developments was based on Parliamentary legislation that followed very closely upon acts of the U.S. Congress. Many other trends mirror those in the United States. The cyclical behaviour of cattle supplies and cattle prices follows that in the United States, the temporal pattern of beef consumption in Canada is almost identical to that in the United States. Opposed by Canada's retailers, the boxed beef revolution only came to Canada after IBP had proven its cost effectiveness on a large scale in the United States.

Yet control of Canada's meat-packing industry remained largely in Canadian hands until the 1990s. In 1967 a meat-packing executive proclaimed its Canadian character: 'The Canadian meat packing industry today is very largely the product of native Canadian enterprise and capital. Most companies are owned and managed by Canadians' (Lasby 1967: 17). Swift Canadian, the first foreign-owned subsidiary of Swift and Company of Chicago, was the first meat packer in Canada to operate on a truly national scale with plants and branch houses from Moncton, New Brunswick, to Victoria, British Columbia. But with that notable exception, the Canadian packing firms guarded their little market so fiercely that once Armour, Morris, and Wilson withdrew from the Canadian market in the 1920s, they never re-entered. Pat Burns rescued Gunns in 1921 to prevent it from falling into the hands of Armour and Company. The complex merger that created Canada Packers was largely motivated to keep the eastern Canadian packers out of the hands of the U.S. giants who would have used them as a springboard into Canadian domestic markets and to exploit the British bacon preference as well.

Addressing the commodity chain over time, structural changes of various sorts characterize virtually every link. The cattle look different as a handful of straight-bred British breeds of cattle were joined and crossed with the big European exotics. The emergence of the specialized 25,000-head feedlots in southern Alberta based on barley grain and barley silage is the most dramatic development in the livestock sector. Cattle feeding is no longer a seasonal activity for underemployed grain and dairy farmers. It is a full-time, full-year activity that fairly straddles the divide between farm and factory. Rail transportation of livestock, the public stockyards, and the private treaty transaction between buyers and 'commission men' have completely disappeared. New institutions (the rural auction marts), new modes of transportation (cattle liners), and new transactions (direct to packer sales) have replaced them. But the eighty-year transition from one cattle-marketing structure to a new one was almost imperceptibly slow. By contrast, the transformation in meat packing was completed within ten years.

The No-Name Kill and Chill Plants and the Beef Bonanza

It is always fascinating to learn how simple yet fundamental geographic ideas which are discovered and learned in one era end up being rediscovered and relearned decades later when the principles are finally applied. For many decades the west-to-east shipment of crude resource materials permitted central Canada to specialize in manufacturing – high technology capital-intensive processes creating large amounts of skilled employment directly in the factory and indirectly through the multiplier effect. Western Canada specialized in crude resource extraction, losing the opportunity to add much value to its natural resource wealth. This has been one of the important causes of western alienation and the driving ideology behind many populist reform movements. Cattle are a crude product of the grassland resource. The increasing perishability of the product as value is added to beef was for many years the binding constraint, inhibiting the packing industry from becoming localized where most cattle are raised and finished for slaughter. Incremental improvements to refrigeration, freight transportation, and meat-packaging technology eventually made the benefits of a raw material orientation so large that the inertia of the massive investment in existing meat-packing plant could be overcome. But it took a long time. As early as 1914, J.S. McLean, then secretary-treasurer of the Harris Abattoir, observed: 'Now it is more economical to ship dressed beef than live cattle from Winnipeg to Toronto and Montreal. This statement is self-evident. It will be more than ever true when, instead of one line of track from Winnipeg to Toronto, there will be four, with three companies competing by means of service, for the transcontinental trade' (quoted in Child 1960: 145).

The big three first began to act on this self-evident geographic fact when they built no fewer than three new meat-packing plants in St-Boniface (Harris Abattoir in 1925, Swift Canadian in 1936, and Burns in 1964) directly adjacent to the stockyards. The multistory St-Boniface plants were horizontally integrated and killed all species. Each one produced a full line of both fresh and processed red meat products. They sold and distributed fresh swinging sides of beef, canned, smoked, and cured pork products, and whatever was left went into sausages, the lard refinery or the rendering tank.

In the 1960s and 1970s there was a flurry of new construction as the big three built, bought, and expanded their western beef plants (Canada Packers in Lethbridge, Red Deer, and Moose Jaw; Swift Canadian in Lethbridge; Burns in Lethbridge and Medicine Hat), reciting in deed the lesson that McLean had taught so well in 1914.

The market structure of meat packing has remained heavily concentrated for the past ninety years. But in a span of only ten years, replacements emerged for all of the main players as the multilocational and horizontally integrated big three meat packers gave way to two new U.S.-based concerns (IBP and Cargill Foods) each operating a single continental-scale beef plant in the heart of Alberta's feedlot country. With the boxed beef revolution, the kill and chill plants became packers once again, but they were packing boxes, not barrels, with hermetically sealed beef, not salt cured pork.

While the new generation of packing plants are not horizontally integrated, they have become more vertically integrated than ever before. They have integrated forwards and appropriated the value added activities that were once performed by the in-store butcher and later were transferred to the central meat processing plants of the big supermarket chains. IBP in Brooks, Alberta, was the first in Canada to own, operate, and integrate the feed mill, feedlot, processing plant, and fabricating plant. A significant proportion of its slaughter cattle needs are met by weaned calves which take six to nine months to become transformed into block-ready boxed beef. Once performed by discrete firms at arm's length, the feeding of the raw material and fabrication of the finished product are internalized on one property in one establishment and firm. Parts of separate industries operate as an old-fashioned chain of separate yet articulated links while vertically integrated firms forge the links into one seamless operation following the vision of Henry Ford's great River Rouge assembly plant. This is the essence of Fordist restructuring in the cattle–beef commodity chain.

References

Abattoir Question. n.d. 'The Abattoir Question: How It Interests the Farmers of Quebec.' Ottawa: Canadian Institute for Microreproductions Catalogue 93907.

Acton, B.K., and E.D. Woodward. 1961. *Cattle Ranching in the Interior of British Columbia 1958–59*. Ottawa: Economics Division, Canada Department of Agriculture.

Agriculture Canada. 1983. *Beef Production in the Atlantic Provinces*. Publication 1494/E. Ottawa: Minister of Supply and Services.

– 1989. *National Tripartite Stabilization Committee for Beef: Report for the Year Ended December 31, 1988*. Ottawa: Agriculture Canada.

– 1991. *Recommended Code of Practice for the Care and Handling of Farm Animals: Beef Cattle*. Publication 1870/E. Ottawa: Minister of Supply and Services.

– 2000. *Livestock Market Review*. Table 23. Retrieved 13 June 2000 from the world wide web http: //www.agr.ca/misb/aisd/redmeat/99toce.html.

Akyeampong, Ernest B. 1999. 'Unionization – an Update' *Perspectives on Labour and Income*. Statistics Canada Catalogue 75-001-XPE 11(3): 45–65.

Alberta. 1908. 'Report of the Beef Commission.' *Annual Report of the Department of Agriculture of the Province of Alberta 1907*. Edmonton: Government Printer, 31–46.

Alberta Agriculture. 1986. 'Winter Feeding Programs for Beef Cattle and Calves.' Agdex 420/50-1. Edmonton: Alberta Agriculture.

– 1991. 'National Tripartite Stabilization Program Red Meat Programs Sales and Inventory Report.' 1(1) Statistics Branch.

– Food and Rural Development. 1995. *Code of Practice for the Safe and Economic Handling of Animal Manures*. Edmonton: Alberta Agriculture, Food and Rural Development.

– 1999a. *Addendum to the 1995 Code of Practice for the Safe and Economic Handling of Animal Manures*. 3 May Edmonton: Alberta Agriculture, Food and Rural Development .

– 1999b. *Alberta Irrigation Districts: Crop and Water Information*. Lethbridge: Alberta Agriculture, Food and Rural Development.

Alberta Environmental Protection. 1998. 'Cattle Feedlot Sentenced for Polluting Stream.' 28 Oct. press release 98–074. Edmonton.

Alberta History. 1990. 'The Beef Ring.' 38(4): 29–30.

Alberta, Human Resources and Employment (AHRE). 1999. *Occupational Injury and Disease in Alberta: 1998 Summary*. Edmonton: AHRE.

Allemang, John. 1995. 'Canada's Beef Industry on Horns of a Dilemma.' *Globe and Mail*, 21 Oct., A1.

Allen, Del. 1999. 'Dumping Pathogens Down the Drain.' *Meat Processing* (May): 36–42.

Archives of Ontario. 1944. Correspondence of the Deputy Minister of Agriculture. Record Group 16-9, vol. A-120.

Arkell, H.S. 1914. 'The Cattle Industry,' in Henry J. Boom, ed., *Twentieth Century Impressions of Canada*, 247–54. London: Sells.

Arthur, Eric R. 1937. 'Canada Packers Plant at Edmonton.' *Journal, Royal Architectural Institute of Canada* 14(2): 20, 158–60.

Ayling, R. Stephen. 1908. *Public Abattoirs: Their Planning, Design and Equipment*. London: E. and F.N. Spon.

Aylward, Larry, and Dan Murphy. 1991. 'Robo Shop.' *Meat Processing* (July): 22–32.

Azzam, Azzeddine M. 1998. 'Competition in the U.S. Meatpacking Industry: Is It History?' *Agricultural Economics* 18: 107–26.

Bain, George Sayers. 1964. 'The United Packinghouse, Food and Allied Workers: Its Development, Structure, Collective Bargaining and Future with Particular Reference to Canada.' Master's thesis, University of Manitoba.

Barnett, Antony, and Patrick Wintour. 1999. 'Experiment Gone Wrong Led to Mad-Cow Epidemic: Experts.' *Globe and Mail*. 9 Aug., A9.

Barratt, Ron. 1958. 'New Humane Slaughtering Method Now in Use at Canada Packers Limited.' *Canadian Food Industries* (Sept.): 36–7.

Basarab, John. 1994. 'Crossbreeding in Alberta: It's Come a Long Way.' *Ruminations* 3(1): 3–4.

Bay, Ovid. 1956. 'Now ... the Little Woman Is Changing the Beef Market.' *Farm Journal* 80: 40–1.

Beatty, Carol A. 1994. 'Wanted: The Tiny Perfect Acquisition.' *Business Quarterly* 59(Summer): 51–9.

Bennett, D.R., and E.L. McCarley. 1995. 'Land Availability for Manure Disposal in the LNID Portion of the County of Lethbridge.' Lethbridge: Resource Conservation Section, Irrigation Branch, Alberta Agriculture, Food and Rural Development.

Bentham, Stanley G. 1941. 'Saskatoon "Pork Factory."' *Canadian Food Packer* (April): 13.

Berry, Brian J.L., Edward C. Conkling, and D. Michael Ray. 1997. *The Global Economy in Transition*, 2nd ed. Englewood Cliffs, NJ: Prentice-Hall.

Best, Dunnery. 1984. 'Big Changes in the Meat Industry Bargaining Style.' *Financial Post*, 23 June, 3.

Bjerklie, Steve. 1990. 'Canada's Biggest: A Look Inside Cargill's Big Alberta Kill Plant.' *Meat Industry* (May): 28–32.

– 1997. 'Improving Hide-Pulling Procedures.' *Meat Processing* (May): 40–1.

– 1999a. 'This Year in Meat and Poultry.' *Meat Processing* (June): 24–58.

– 1999b. 'IBP Leaps into Case-Ready Beef.' *Meat Processing* (June): 60–6.

Bliss, Michael. 1978. *A Canadian Millionaire: The Life and Business Times of Sir Joseph Flavelle Bart. 1858–1939*. 1st paperback ed. Toronto: University of Toronto Press.

– 1987. *Northern Enterprise: Five Centuries of Canadian Business*. Toronto: McClelland and Stewart.

Booth, J.F. 1936. 'Ranching in the Prairie Provinces,' in *Agricultural Progress on the Prairie Frontier*, ed. by R.W. Murchie, vol. 5 of Canadian Frontiers of Settlement. Toronto: Macmillan

Bowman, M.W. 1947. 'Trailer Transports Solve Beef Shipping Problem.' *Canadian Food Industries* (Oct.): 20–1.

Brand, Glenn. 1998. 'Meat Counter Makeover.' *Canadian Grocer* (April): 34–5.

Braverman, H. 1974. *Labor and Monopoly Capital: The Degradation of Work in the Twentieth Century.* New York: Monthly Review Press.

Breen, David H. 1983. *The Canadian Prairie West and the Ranching Frontier, 1874–1924*. Toronto: University of Toronto Press.

Brethour, John R. 1994. 'Estimating Marbling Score in Live Cattle from Ultrasound Images Using Pattern Recognition and Neural Network Procedures.' *Journal of Animal Science* 72: 1425–32.

Broadway, Michael J. 1998. 'Where's the Beef: The Integration of the Canadian and American Beefpacking Industries.' *Prairie Forum* 23: 19–30.

Brody, David. 1964. *The Butcher Workmen: A Study of Unionization*. Cambridge, MA: Harvard University Press.

Broehl, Wayne G., Jr. 1998. *Cargill: Going Global*. Hanover, NH: University Press of New England.

Bronson, H.E. 1973. 'The Saskatchewan Meat Packing Industry: Some Historical Highlights.' *Saskatchewan History* 26: 24–38.

Burn, Doug. 1999. 'Rib Removal Robot a Canadian First.' *Food in Canada* (Mar.): 18.
Burns, John. 1942. Correspondence from John Burns, Burns and Company to A. MacNamara, Associate Deputy Minister of Labour, 4 December, 1942. National Archives of Canada, RG 36, vol. 27, National War Labour Board 1942 Correspondence, File 907-2-2.
Business Week. 1979. 'A Meat Packer Discovers Consumer Marketing.' 28 May, 164–70.
– 1980. 'Iowa Beef: Moving in for a Kill by Automating Pork Processing.' 14 July, 100–1.
Byfield, Mike, and Terry Johnson. 1987. 'Cargill's New Plant Creates a Furore.' *Western Report* 19 Oct., 29.
Canada-Alberta Environmentally Sustainable Agriculture Committee. 1998. *Agricultural Impacts on Water Quality in Alberta*. Edmonton: Alberta Agriculture Food and Rural Development.
Canada. 1895. 'Report of the Minister of Agriculture for Canada, 1894.' *Sessional Papers* (no. 8).
– 1934. *Special Committee on Price Spreads and Mass Buying*. Minutes of Proceedings and Evidence. Ottawa: King's Printer.
– 1935. *Report of the Royal Commission on Price Spreads*. Ottawa: King's Printer.
– 1944. *Labour Gazette*. Terms of Settlement of Dispute between United Packinghouse Workers of America and Packinghouse Managements. Commissioner, Justice S.E. Richards, 1486–7.
– Privy Council. 1945. 'Orders-in-Council PC 6481, PC 6557, and PC 6558.' Oct. 11, 1945.
– 1960. *Report of the Royal Commission on Price Spreads of Food Products*. Volume 3. Ottawa: Queen's Printer.
– 1961. *Report of the Restrictive Trade Practices Commission Concerning the Meat Packing Industry and the Acquisition of Wilsil Limited and Calgary Packers Limited by Canada Packers Limited*. Ottawa: Queen's Printer.
– 1969. *Canadian Agriculture in the Seventies*. Report of the Federal Task Force on Agriculture. Ottawa: Queen's Printer.
– 1976. *Report of Commission of Inquiry into the Marketing of Beef and Veal*. Ottawa: Minister of Supply and Services.
– 1982. *Industry in Turmoil: Report on the Long Term Stabilization of the Beef Industry in Canada*. Standing Senate Committee on Agriculture. Ottawa: Minister of Supply and Services.
– Department of Agriculture (DOA). 1950. *Livestock Market Review*. Ottawa: DOA. Markets Information Section, Production and Marketing Branch.
– 1957 *Livestock Market Review*. Ottawa: DOA. Markets Information Section, Production and Marketing Branch.

– Minister of Agriculture. 1925. *The Safe Handling of Commercial Livestock: A Producer to Consumer Campaign*. Leaflet published by authority of the Hon. W.R. Motherwell.

Canada Packers Limited. 1943. *The Story of Our Products*. Kingston: Jackson Press.

Canadian Beef Grading Agency. 1997. *Beef Carcass Grading Reference*. Calgary: Canadian Beef Grading Agency.

Canadian Cattlemen. 1938. 'Public Markets and Direct Shipments.' 1(3): 115.

Canadian Food Industries. 1959. 'Some New Food Transportation Trends.' (Feb.): 26.

– 1960. 'Develop New Humane Slaughter Device.' (Oct.): 36.

– 1961. 'Ontario Pork Packers Bid by Wire.' (June): 34–5.

– 1962. 'Kill-Dress Plant Specialty.' (Dec.): 58–60.

– 1966. 'New Reefers Can Load Beef or Frozen Food.' (July): 22–4.

Canadian Food Packer. 1942. 'Conveyors in Meat Packing.' (Feb.): 18–19.

– 1943. 'Overhead Refrigerator Cars for Bacon Shipments.' (Aug.): 11–12.

Canadian Grocer. 1902. 'Embalmed Beef "Scandal."' 16 (31 Jan.): 40.

– 1976a. 'Sees Steady Growth for Block-Ready Beef Systems.' 40 (May): 26.

– 1976b 'Western Trade Moves Strongly to Block-Ready; Burns Responds.' 40 (Sept.): 34.

– 1978a. 'Cryovac Surveys Boxed Beef Progress.' 42 (Feb.): 5–6.

– 1978b. 'Boxed Beef Said to Have Numerous Advantages.' 42 (March): 20.

– 1978c. 'Canada Packers to Close Halifax Warehouse.' 42 (May): 36.

– 1979. 'Dominion Stores 60th Anniversary October 1919–1979.' 43. (Oct.): 19–32.

– 1985. 'Awareness Ups Beef Sales.' 49 (Dec.): 16.

– 1987. 'Loblaw Tests "Natural" Beef.' 51 (July): 10.

– 1988. 'Loblaws' Natural Beef Wins at SIAL.' 52 (Dec.): 45.

– 1989a. 'No-Roll has Role for Some.' 53 (Feb.): 181.

– 1989b. 'Meat Strips for the 90's.' 53 (Dec.): 7.

Canadian Illustrated News. 1877. 'Fattening Cattle for Shipment.' 15(7): 99.

Canadian International Trade Tribunal (CITT). 1993. *An Inquiry into the Competitiveness of the Canadian Cattle and Beef Industries*. Ref. no. GC-92-001. Ottawa: Minister of Supply and Services.

Canadian Labour. 1962. 'Health Board, BCFL Ask Meat Inspection.' 7(6): 31.

Canadian Labour Relations Board Reports. 1985. 'Burns Meats Ltd. and United Food and Commercial Workers International Union and United Food and Commercial Workers International Union, Local 139.' New series, 7: 355–70 Scarborough: Butterworth.

Canadian Nurse. 1986. 'Foodborne Illness: The Problem That Just Won't Go Away.' (Feb.): 14–15.

Canadian Transportation Commission (CTC). 1975. *Transportation Factors and the Canadian Livestock and Meat Industries*. Research Branch ESAB 75-19, Nov. Ottawa: CTC.

CanFax 2000. 'Cattle on Feed – Feedlot Capacity by Region.' Retrieved 8 May 2000 from the World Wide Web: http://www.cattle.ca/canfax/cof_region_capacity.htm

Cargill Foods. n.d. 'Career Opportunities in the Beef Processing Industry.' High River: Cargill Foods.

Carruthers, R. Don. 1990. 'Beef Carcass Requirements to Meet the Needs of the Food Service Industry.' *Proceedings of the Ultrasound Beef Production Strategy Conference March 12–13*. Saskatoon: Agriculture Canada and Saskatchewan Agriculture and Food.

Carter, Anne O., Alexander A. Borczyk, Jacqueline A.K. Carlson, Bart Harvey, James C. Hockin, M.A. Karmali, Chandrasekar Krishnan, David A. Korn, and Hermy Lior. 1987. 'A Severe Outbreak of *Escherichia coli* O157:H7-Associated Hemorrhagic Colitis in a Nursing Home.' *New England Journal of Medicine* 317(24): 1496–1500.

Carter, Toni Owen. 1993a. 'From "Bad" Subsidies to "Good" Ones.' *Alberta Report* 5 April, 22–3.

– 1993b. 'Ag-Can's Mad Cow Crackdown.' *Alberta Report* 21(2): 16.

Case, Peter A. 1966. 'Mechanical Reefers: Ship More and Pay Less.' *Food in Canada* (March): 29–31.

Cash, C. 1907. *Our Slaughter-House System: A Plea for Reform*. London: George Bell.

Chandler, Alfred D. 1977. *The Visible Hand: The Managerial Revolution in American Business*. Cambridge: Belknap Press of Harvard University Press.

Cheeke, Peter. 1993. *Impacts of Livestock Production*. Danville, Ill.: Interstate Publishers.

Child, A.J.E. 1960. 'The Predecessor Companies of Canada Packers Limited: A Study of Entrepreneurial Achievement and Entrepreneurial Failure.' Master's thesis, University of Toronto.

Chilled Meat Committee. 1909. 'Report on the Desirability of Establishing throughout the Dominion a Complete System of Meat Chilling, Packing and Exporting.' Report to Sydney Fisher, Minister of Agriculture, Ottawa. Canadian Institute for Historical Microreproductions microfiche no. 76654.

Clemen, Rudolph Alexander. 1923. *The American Livestock and Meat Industry*. New York: Ronald Press.

– 1927. *By-Products in the Packing Industry*. Chicago: University of Chicago Press.

Commons, John R. 1904. 'Labor Conditions in Meat Packing and the Recent Strike.' *Quarterly Journal of Economics* 19 (Nov.): 1–32.

Cosh, Len. 1967. 'Quebec Meat Industry sees Advancement.' *Canadian Food Industries* (May): 47–8.

Craig, Alton Westwood. 1964. 'The Consequences of Provincial Jurisdiction for the Process of Company-Wide Collective Bargaining in Canada: A Study of the Packinghouse Industry.' Doctoral thesis, Cornell University.

Craypo, Charles. 1993. 'Strike and Relocation in Meatpacking,' in Charles Craypo and Bruce Nissen, eds., *Grand Designs: The Impact of Corporate Strategies on Workers Unions, and Communities*, 185–208. Ithaca, NY: ILR Press.

– 1994. 'Meatpacking: Industry Restructuring and Union Decline,' in Paula B. Voos, ed., *Contemporary Collective Bargaining in the Private Sector*, 63–96. Madison: Industrial Relations Research Association.

Creative Research Group. 1983. *A Survey of Attitudes among Ontario Beef Producers*. Toronto: Ontario Ministry of Agriculture and Food.

Cronon, William. 1991. *Nature's Metropolis: Chicago and the Great West*. New York: W.W. Norton.

Cross, H. Russell. 1989. 'Advances in Ultrasound Procedures for Determining Carcass Merit in Cattle.' *Proceedings of Beef Improvement Federation*. Annual Convention, 11–13 May, 1–6, Nashville, TN.

Daly, Clyde C. 1988. 'Welfare of Cattle During Slaughter: Comparison of Conventional and Religious Methods.' *Journal of the Science of Food and Agriculture* 42: 87–8.

Dawes, Colin Jonathan. 1987. *The Relative Decline of International Unionism in Canada Since 1970*. School of Industrial Relations Essay Series No. 19. Kingston: Industrial Relations Centre, Queen's University.

Dawson, C.A. 1936. *Group Settlement: Ethnic communities in Western Canada*, vol. 7, *Canadian Frontiers of Settlement*, ed. W.A. Mackintosh and W.L.G. Joerg. Toronto: MacMillan.

Dickstein, Morris. 1981. 'Introduction,' in *The Jungle*, by Upton Sinclair, 1906. Bantam Classics Edition. New York: Bantam Books.

Douglas Lake Ranch. 2000. 'Land' and 'Cattle.' Retrieved 30 April 2000 from the world wide web: http://www.douglaslake.com/home.htm

Downie, Bryan M. 1972. *Centralized Collective Bargaining: U.S.–Canada Experience*. Kingston: Industrial Relations Centre, Queen's University.

Drummond W.M. n.d. 'Wartime Controls in the Meat Packing Industry.' Committee on Reconstruction. Ottawa: National Library of Canada.

Dun's Review. 1967. 'Hog Butcher for the World.' (Feb.): 36–7.

Eales, James. 1993. *North American Meat Demand*. Report no. 8. Winnipeg: Manitoba Red Meat Forum.

Economist. 2000. 'France's Mad Cows Go Political.' 11 Nov., 67.

Ehrensaft, P. 1987. *Structure and Performance in the Canadian Beef Sector*. Production Analysis Division, Policy Branch. Ottawa: Agriculture Canada.

Eisnitz, Gail A. 1997. *Slaughterhouse: The Shocking Story of Greed, Neglect, and Inhumane Treatment Inside the U.S. Meat Industry*. Amherst, NY: Prometheus Books.

Enchin, Harvey. 1989. 'Canada Packers Patriarch Prefers to Avoid Limelight.' *Globe and Mail*. 21 Oct., B1.

Evans, Mark. 1991. 'Maple Leaf's Newton a Turnaround Master.' *Financial Post*. 16 Dec., 8.

Evans, Simon M. 1979. 'Canadian Beef for Victorian Britain.' *Agricultural History* 53: 748–62.

– 1983. 'The Origins of Ranching in Western Canada: American Diffusion or Victorian Transplant?' *Great Plains Quarterly* 3: 79–91.

Excel Meats. 2000 'Excel Locations.' Retrieved 30 June, 2000 from the world wide web: http://www.excelmeats.com/about/locations.htm

Fairbairn, Garry. 1989. *Canada Choice: Economic, Health and Moral Issues in Food from Animals*. Ottawa: Agricultural Institute of Canada.

Fairbank, W.C. 1983. 'Manure Management.' In G.B. Thompson and Clayton C. O'Mary, eds., *The Feedlot*, 3rd ed. 197–212. Philadelphia: Lea and Febiger.

Fancher, Diana. 1999. 'Stock Photography: A Pictorial History of Canada's Greatest Livestock Market.' *The Leader and Recorder*. Toronto: West Toronto Junction Historical Society.

Fearne, Andrew. 1998. 'The Evolution of Partnerships in the Meat Supply Chain: Insights from the British Beef Industry.' *Supply Chain Management* 3: 214–31.

Featherstone, Carol. 1997. '*Escherichia coli* O157: Superbug or Mere Sensation?' *Lancet* 349(9056): 930.

Fink, Deborah. 1995. 'What Kind of Woman Would Work in Meatpacking, Anyway? World War II and the Road to Fair Employment.' *Great Plains Research* 5: 241–62.

Firat, A Fuat, Nikhilesh Dholkia, and Alladi Venkatesh. 1995. 'Marketing in a Postmodern World.' *European Journal of Marketing* 29(1): 40–56.

Flavelle, Joseph. 1907. Correspondence from Joseph Flavelle, General Manager, William Davies, Company to the Hon. Sydney Fisher, Minister of Agriculture, 15 Jan. 1907. National Archives of Canada, RG 17 I-1, Vol 988, Agricultural Department Correspondence, File 159525.

– 1911. 'Mr Flavelle States Case' Letter to the editor, *Toronto Daily Star*. 7 Sept., 2.

Food in Canada. 1957. 'Slaughter Methods-Progress Report' (Dec.): 27.

– 1958. 'Swift 50th Jubilee at Edmonton.' (Dec.): 27.

– 1960a. 'December 1st Deadline for Real.' (March): 33.

– 1960b. 'Free Plan for Humane Schechitah.' (Sept.): 32–3.
– 1962a. 'Meat Inspection Crash Program.' (April): 28.
– 1962b. 'The Meat-Scare Cost.' (Aug.): 20.
– 1963. 'New Reefer Reduces Dehydration.' (Jan.): 33.
– 1964. 'How an Ontario Plant Halved Labor with a Hog-Beef Floor.' (July): 30–1.

Foran, Max. 1998. 'Mixed Blessings: The Second "Golden Age" of the Alberta Cattle Industry, 1914–1920.' *Alberta History* 46(3): 10–19.

Force, L.T. 1951. 'Beef Dressing on the Rail.' *Canadian Food Industries* (April): 20–5.

Forrest, Anne. 1989. 'The Rise and Fall of National Bargaining in the Canadian Meat-Packing Industry.' *Relations Industrielles* 44: 393–406.

Foss, Krista. 2000. 'Alberta Meat Packer Issues Massive Recall.' *Globe and Mail.* 24 June, A3.

Freeze, Brian. 1993. *Impact of Irrigation on the Competitive Advantage of the Southern Alberta Cattle Feeding Industry.* Lethbridge: Alberta Irrigation Projects Association.

– and T.G. Sommerfeldt. 1985. 'Break-Even Hauling Distances for Beef Feedlot Manure in Southern Alberta.' *Canadian Journal of Soil Science* 65: 687–93.

Freeze, Brian S., A. Gene Nelson, Wesley N. Musser, and R. Hironaka. 1990. 'Feeding and Marketing Portfolio Effects of Cattle Feeding in Alberta.' *Canadian Journal of Agricultural Economics* 38: 233–52.

Friend, H.M. 1957. 'Let's Take a Look at Sharp-Frozen Red Meats.' *Canadian Food Industries* (July): 14–15.

Friesen, Leonard. 1995. *Cows, Cowboys, Cattlemen, and Characters: A History of the Calgary Stockyards, 1903–89.* Airdrie: Friesen Cattle Company.

Gardner, Robert L. 1983. *Industrial Development in Metropolitan Toronto: Issues, Prospects and Strategy.* Toronto: Economic Development Office of the Chairman, Municipality of Metropolitan Toronto.

Gibbons, N.E. 1951. 'Should We Treat Pigs with More Consideration?' *Canadian Food Industries* (Dec.): 19–23.

Giedion, Siegfried. 1948. *Mechanization Takes Command: A Contribution to Anonymous History.* New York: Oxford University Press.

Gill, C.O. 1998. *Apparatus for Pasteurizing Red Meat Carcasses.* Technical Bulletin 1998-5E, Research Branch, Agriculture and Agri-Food Canada.

Gilson, J.G., and A.G. Wilson. 1993. *Commercial Aspects of National Agricultural and Trade Policies for the Red Meat Industry in Western Canada.* Winnipeg, Man.: Red Meat Forum.

Globe. 1934a. 'Evasion of Laws is Charged Freely in House Speeches.' 23 Feb., A1.

Globe. 1934b. 'Ottawa Committee Shocked by Disclosures, Official Cites Low Wages of Toronto Firms.' 28 Feb., A1–A2.

Globe and Mail. 1962a. 'Commit Man to Trial on Meat Sale Count.' 3 Feb., 9.

– 1962b. 'Youth Jailed in Sale of Dead Animal Meat.' 9 Feb., 8.

– 1983. '4 Meat Firms Settle Conspiracy Suit.' 21 Nov., 10.

– 1992. 'Trillium Meats Plants Cargill Firmly in Ontario.' 22 Sept., B14.

– 1998a. 'Feedlot Charged in River Pollution.' 7 May, A3.

– 1998b. 'Animals Butchered Alive, Former USDA Inspectors Say.' 4 April, A16.

Goldberg, Patricia A.M. 1989. 'Canada Approved – The Meat and Canned Foods Act of 1907: Federal Veterinary Inspection for the Export Trade.' Master's thesis, University of Guelph.

Grandin, Temple. 1991. 'Double Rail Restrainer for Handling Beef Cattle.' Paper no. 915004 for presentation at the 1991 International Summer Meeting, American Society of Agricultural Engineers, Albuquerque.

– 1993a 'Introduction: Management and Economic Factors of Handling and Transport.' In Temple Grandin, ed., *Livestock Handling and Transport*, 1–9. Wallingford, Oxon: CAB International.

– 1993b. 'Handling and Welfare of Livestock in Slaughter Plants.' In Temple Grandin, ed., *Livestock Handling and Transport*, 289–311. Wallingford, Oxon: CAB International.

– 1994a. 'Farm Animal Welfare During Handling, Transport, and Slaughter.' *Journal of the American Veterinary Medical Association* 204(3): 372–77.

– 1994b. 'Euthanasia and Slaughter of Livestock.' *Journal of the American Veterinary Medical Association* 204(9): 1354–60.

– 1995. 'Report on Handling and Stunning Practices in Canadian Meat Packing Plants.' Prepared for Agriculture Canada, Canadian Federation of Humane Societies, Canadian Meat Council and Canadian Poultry and Egg Processor's Council. Fort Collins, CO: Grandin Livestock Handling Systems.

– 1999. 'Canadian Animal Welfare Audit of Stunning and Handling in Federal and Provincial Inspected Slaughter Plants.' Unpublished report sponsored by Federal Food of Animal Origin Division, Agriculture Canada, Canadian Meat Council, and Canadian Federation of Humane Societies.

– and Joe M. Regenstein. 1994. 'Religious Slaughter and Animal Welfare: A Discussion for Meat Scientists.' *Meat Focus International* (March): 115–23.

Green, Evelyn. 1997. 'Islamic Foods Move Slowly into Marketplace.' *Meat Processing* (Feb.): 34–6.

Grey, Mark A. 1999. 'Immigrants, Migration and Worker Turnover at the Hog Pride Pork Packing Plant.' *Human Organization* 58: 16–27.

Grier, Kevin. 1988. *Ontario Beef Packer Situation Outlook*. Toronto: Ontario Ministry of Agriculture and Food.

– 1999. 'Out with the old ... Will Meat Packers Pay a High Price for Confrontational Style Labour Negotiations?' *Food in Canada* (March): 23.

Grover, John Hanley. 1996. 'Winnipeg Meat Packing Workers' Path to Union Recognition and Collective Bargaining.' Masters thesis, University of Manitoba.

Guardian. 1996. 'EU Backs Beef Ban.' 23 March, 1.

– 2001. 'Special Report: The BSE Crisis.' Retrieved 5 January, 2001 from the world wide web, http://www.guardianunlimited.co.uk/bse/

Hammons, Donald R. 1961. *Improving Methods and Facilities for Cattle Slaughtering Plants in the Southwest*. Washington, DC: U.S. Department of Agriculture, Agricultural Marketing Service, Marketing Research report no. 436.

Haney, Ted. 1997. Canada Beef Export Federation 'Industry Background, Production.' Calgary. Retrieved 15 July, 1999 from the world wide web: http://www.cbef.com/ind_prod.htm

Harding, Myrick D. 1937. 'Mechanical Progress in the Meat Packing Industry.' *Journal of the Western Society of Engineers* 42(1): 16–30.

Harrap, G.T., and Loudan M. Douglas. 1901. *Public Abattoirs and Cattle Markets*. London: Ice and Cold Storage Publishing Company.

Hart, John Fraser, and Chris Mayda. 1998. 'The Industrialization of Livestock Production in the United States.' *Southeastern Geographer* 38: 58–78.

Heiss, Hugo. 1907. *The German Abattoir*. In *Our Slaughter-House System: A Plea for Reform*. Translated by C. Cash. London: George Bell.

Helmer, Joanne. 1998a. 'County Won't Block Feedlot Expansions.' *Lethbridge Herald*. 27 May, A1.

Henderson Commission. 1918. 'Report of the Henderson Commission on Canadian Packers' Profits.' Reprinted in Saskatchewan, 1918, *Final Report of the Live Stock Commission of the Province of Saskatchewan 1918*. Printed by order of the Legislative Assembly, 47–52. Regina: King's Printer.

Hill, William. 1907. Correspondence from William Hill, Clerk of Hamilton Market to The Hon. Sydney Fisher, Minister of Agriculture, 8 Jan., 1907. National Archives of Canada, RG 17 I-1, vol. 988, Agricultural Department Correspondence, File 159525.

Hinman, Robert B., and Robert B. Harris. 1939. *The Story of Meat*. Chicago: Swift and Company.

Hironaka, R., and B. Freeze. 1992. *Feedlot Finishing Cattle*. Revised Agriculture Canada Publication 1591/E. Ottawa: Minister of Supply and Services.

Hobbs, E.H. 1970. *The Agricultural Climate of the Lethbridge Area, 1902–1969*. Agrometeorology Publication 1. Lethbridge Research Station: Canada Department of Agriculture.

Horner, Hugh M. 1981. *A Review of the Meat Industry in Alberta*. Consultant report for Alberta Economic Development. Barrhead, AB: Author.

Horner, W.H. 1980. *Western Canadian Agriculture to 1990*. A Canada West Foundation Special Task Force Report. Calgary: Canada West Foundation.

Hossie, Linda. 1984. 'Jobless by Design? Slaughterhouse Shutdown Put 600 on Street.' *Globe and Mail*. 27 Oct., 1.

Houston, Mary. 1985. *White River – 100 Years*. White River: Author.

Huff, H. Bruce, and Barry D. Mehr. 1976. *Developments in Central Processing of Beef in Canada*. Commission of Inquiry into the Marketing of Beef and Veal, Research Report no. 6. Ottawa: Minister of Supply and Services.

Huston, Bertram T. 1929. 'The Chain Store.' *Queen's Quarterly* 27 (Spring): 313–25.

IBP. 2000. 'The IBP Story.' Retrieved 30 June 2000 from the World Wide Web: http://www.ibpinc.com/about/IBPNewHistory.stm

Institute of American Meat Packers. 1925. *Readings in Packing House Practice: Part II – Beef, Mutton and Veal Operations*. Institute of Meat Packing, School of Commerce and Administration. Chicago: University of Chicago Press.

Irvine, Michael J. 1978. *The Guelph Abattoir Programme: An Innovative Approach to Correctional Facilities*. Toronto: Ontario Ministry of Correctional Services.

Ives, J. Russel. 1966. *The Livestock and Meat Economy of the United States*. Washington, DC: American Meat Institute.

Jacobs, Frank. 1993. *Cattle and Us*. Calgary: Detselig.

Jeremiah, L.E. 1981. 'Factors Affecting Consumer Selection and Acceptability of Beef in Central Alberta.' *Journal of Consumer Studies and Home Economics* 5: 257–68.

– 1996. 'The Influence of Subcutaneous Fat Thickness and Marbling on Beef.' *Food Research International* 29: 513–20.

– J.L. Aalhus, W.M. Robertson, and L.L. Gibson. 1997a. 'The Effects of Grade, Gender, and Postmortem Treatment on Beef. I. Composition, Cutablity, and Meat Quality.' *Canadian Journal of Animal Science* 77: 33–40.

– 1997b. 'The Effects of Grade, Gender, and Postmortem Treatment on Beef. II. Cooking Properties and Palatability Attributes.' *Canadian Journal of Animal Science* 77: 41–54.

– G.C. Smith and J.K. Hillers. 1970. 'Utilization of Breed and Traits Determined from the Live Beef Steer for Prediction of Marbling Score.' *Journal of Animal Science* 31: 1089–95.

– A.K.W. Tong, S.D.M. Jones, and C. McDonnell. 1992. 'Consumer acceptance of Beef with Different Levels of Marbling.' *Journal of Consumer Studies and Home Economics* 16: 375–87.

J.M. Schneider. 1989. *A Legacy of Quality: J.M. Schneider Inc. A Centennial Celebration*. J.M. Schneider Inc.

Johnson, Terry. 1993. 'Send Us Your Calves and Yearlings: Alberta Has Quietly Become a Leading North American Feeding Centre.' *Alberta Report* 20(46): 20–1.

Johnston, Alex, and Andy den Otter. 1991. *Lethbridge: A Centennial History*. Lethbridge: Lethbridge Historical Society.

Johnston, Tom R., and Marvin Sundstrom. 1995. 'Irrigation Agriculture and Local Economic Development: The Case of Lethbridge, Alberta.' In Christopher Bryant and Claude Marois, eds., *The Sustainability of Rural Systems*, 290–303. Montreal: University of Montreal.

Jones, Robert Leslie. 1946. *History of Agriculture in Ontario, 1613–1880*. Toronto: University of Toronto Press.

Jordan, Terry G. 1993. *North American Cattle-Ranching Frontiers: Origins, Diffusion, and Differentiation*. Albuquerque: University of New Mexico Press.

Josling, J.T., and G.I. Trant. 1966. *An Empirical Study of Interdependence among Agricultural and Other Sectors: An Input-Output Model*. Ottawa: Agricultural Economics Research Council of Canada.

Kenney, C. Hamilton. 1944. 'The U.K. Bacon Market – Will Canada Hold It?' *Canadian Food Industries* (Dec.): 40–1.

– 1945. 'Hog Singeing – Vital Wiltshire Operation.' *Canadian Food Industries* (March): 21–3.

– 1949. 'Chuting the Bull.' *Canadian Food Industries* (Sept.): 22–5.

Kerr, William A., and S. Monica Ulmer. 1984. *The Importance of the Livestock and Meat Processing Industries to Western Growth*. Discussion Paper 255. Ottawa: Economic Council of Canada.

Klassen, Henry C. 1999. *A Business History of Alberta*. Calgary: University of Calgary Press.

Kliner, Miles. 1990. 'Ultrasound beef production.' *Proceedings of the Ultrasound Beef Production Strategy Conference*, 12–13 March. Saskatoon: Agriculture Canada and Saskatchewan Agriculture and Food.

Kneen, Brewster. 1994. *Trading Up: How Cargill, the World's Largest Grain Trading Company Is Changing Canadian Agriculture*. Toronto: Ram's Horn.

Knell, Michael J. 1992. 'Profits by Design.' *Canadian Grocer* (Feb.): 116–19.

Kolko, Gabriel. 1963. *The Triumph of Conservatism, A Reinterpretation of American History, 1900–1916*. London: Collier-Macmillan.

Krause, Kenneth R. 1991. *Location and Feedlot Size*. Commodity and Economics Division, Economic Research Service, U.S. Department of Agriculture. Agricultural Economic Report no. 642.

Langman, Brent. 2000a. 'Keep sharp! Look sharp!' *Meat Processing* (March): 52–7.
– 2000b. 'ConAgra Strives to Become America's Premier Beef Company.' *Meat Processing* (May): 20–31.
– Todd Bacon. 1999. 'Monfort Aims New Weapons at Contamination.' *Meat Processing* (May): 44–51.
Lasby, W.W. 1967. 'A Century of Progress in the Canadian Meat Industry.' 47th Annual Meeting, Meat Packers Council of Canada, 13 February. Toronto. Archives of Ontario, C262-7-6, CPFZ.
Lazar, Virginia. 1997. 'MAP innovations.' *Meat Processing* (Oct.): 28–30.
Leckie, Keith, and John Morris. 1980. *Study on Government Regulation in the Red Meat Industry.* Working Paper Number 8. Ottawa: Economic Council of Canada.
Lemon, James. 1985. *Toronto: Since 1918*. Toronto: Lorimer.
Lesser, William H. 1993. *Marketing Livestock and Meat*. New York: Food Products Press.
Lethbridge Herald. 2000a. '*E. coli* Prompts Packer to Try Irradiating Beef.' 27 June, A4.
– 2000b. 'Three More Deaths Linked to Walkerton.' 27 June, A4.
– 1999. 'Province Cracking Down on Cattle Rustlers.' 9 Aug., A4.
– 1950. 'Public Livestock Market Opening Here Next Monday.' 4 Feb., 11–13.
Leung C.Y., S.N. Kulshreshtha, and W.J. Brown. 1991. 'Economies of Size in Beef Cattle Production in Saskatchewan.' Saskatchewan Beef and Hog Sector Study, Report 6. Saskatoon: Department of Agricultural Economics, University of Saskatchewan.
Logan, Samuel H., and Gordon A. King. 1962. *Economies of Scale in Beef Slaughter Plants*. California Agricultural Experiment Station, Giannini Foundation of Agricultural Economics, Giannini Foundation Research Report 260.
Logan V.S., and P.E. Sylvestre. 1950. *Hybridization of Domestic Beef Cattle and Buffalo*. Ottawa: Central Experimental Farm, Department of Agriculture.
Lutz, John S. 1980. 'Interlude or Industry? Ranching in British Columbia, 1859–1885.' *British Columbia Historical News* 13(4): 2–11.
MacAlpine, N.D., D.F. Engstrom, John Kirtz, and Sandra Cooke. 1997. *Resources for Beef Industry Expansion in Alberta*. Edmonton: Alberta Agriculture Food and Rural Development.
MacDonald, Jac. 1993. 'Plant Still a Bad Buy – Burns.' *Edmonton Journal*. 11 Sept., C3.
MacDougall, Heather A. 1982. 'The Genesis of Public Health Reform in Toronto, 1869–1890.' *Urban History Review* 10(3): 1–10.
MacDowell, G.F. 1971. *The Brandon Packers Strike*. Toronto: McClelland and Stewart.

MacEachern, G.A. 1978. *Retention of the Crow Rate and the Alberta Livestock Economy.* Prepared for the Alberta Cattle Commission. Ottawa: Agricultural Economics Research Council of Canada.

MacEwan, Grant. 1979. *Pat Burns: Cattle King*. Saskatoon: Western Producer Prairie Books.

– 1980. *Illustrated History of Western Canadian Agriculture*. Saskatoon: Western Producer Prairie Books.

– 1982. *Highlights of Shorthorn History.* Calgary: Comprint Publishing.

Mackintosh, W.A. 1934. *Prairie Settlement: The Geographical Setting*. Toronto: Macmillan.

MacLachlan, Ian. 1998a. 'Hammond, George Henry,' in Neil L. Shumsky, ed., *Encyclopedia of American Cities and Suburbs*. New York: ABC-Clio Publishing, 335–6.

– 1998b. 'Stockyards.' In Neil L. Shumsky, ed., *Encyclopedia of American Cities and Suburbs*. New York: ABC-Clio Publishing, 744–5.

– 1998c 'Swift, Gustavus Franklin.' In Neil L. Shumsky, ed., *Encyclopedia of American Cities and Suburbs*. New York: ABC-Clio Publishing, 769.

Macrae, Barbara. 1991. 'Sales on a Skewer.' *Canadian Grocer* (Oct.): 19–28.

Manitoba Labour Relations Board Decisions. 1984. 'Burns Meats and United Food & Commercial Workers International Union, Local 111.' Case No. 521/84/ LRA Quicklaw: QL Systems.

Manitoba Red Meat Forum. 1993. 'Initial Submission to Canadian International Trade Tribunal Inquiry into the Competitiveness of the Canadian Cattle and Beef Industries.' Reference No. GC-92-001. Winnipeg: Manitoba Red Meat Forum.

Manning, E.S. 1956. 'The Right Type of Slaughter is Good Business.' *Canadian Food Industries* (Dec.): 14–15.

Manning, Richard. 1995. *Grassland: The History, Biology, Politics and Promise of the American Prairie*. Harmondsworth: Penguin Books.

Marlowe, Thomas J. 1983. 'Preweaning, Conditioning and Stocker Management.' In G.B. Thompson and Clayton C. O'Mary, eds., *The Feedlot*, 3rd ed. 73–97. Philadelphia: Lea and Febiger.

Marsh, E.L. 1931. *A History of the County of Grey.* Owen Sound: Fleming Publishing.

Matthews, Garth R. 1955. 'Intercontinental Packers Limited.' *Canadian Food Industries* (Aug.): 14.

McAuley, Julie. 1995. 'The Canadian Cattle Industry: A Complete Industry Profile.' Livestock and Animal Products Section, Agriculture Division. Ottawa: Statistics Canada.

McDonald, D.R. 1985. *The Stockyard Story.* Toronto: NC Press Limited.

McFall, Robert James. 1927. *The World's Meat*. New York: Appleton.

McIntyre, A.W. 1941. 'Golden Jubilee of Gainers Limited.' *Canadian Food Packer* (Sept.): 11–16.

McKnight, Tom L. 1979. 'Centre Pivot Irrigation: The Canadian Experience.' *Canadian Geographer* 23: 360–7.

McLean, W.F. 1964. 'Address to the Toronto Society of Financial Analysts.' 9 Dec. Archives of Ontario, C263-7-3, CPC3.

McTague C.P. 1947. 'Settlement in Meat Packing Dispute: Arbitration Award of Hon. Mr. Justice C.P. McTague in dispute between Canada Packers Limited and Burns and Company Limited and the United Packinghouse Workers of America (CIO-CCL).' *Labour Gazette* 47: 1791–6.

Meat Processing. 1990. 'The Top 200.' (June): 21–32.

– 1993. 'The Top 200.' (June): 18–20.

Mendel, Frederick S. 1972. *The Book and Life of a Little Man*. Toronto: Macmillan.

Metcalfe, William H. 1939. 'Swift's New Plant in St. Boniface.' *Canadian Food Packer* (July): 9–25.

Mitchell, Alanna. 1996. 'White-Collar Rustlers Going After Beef.' *Globe and Mail*, 12 August, 11.

Montague, John Tait. 1950. 'Trade Unionism in the Canadian Meat Packing Industry.' Doctoral thesis, University of Toronto.

Moore, W.W. 1904. *The Food Products of Canada*. Commissioner of Agriculture and Dairying. Ottawa: Department of Agriculture.

– 1906. 'Report on the Conditions in Canadian Meat Packing Houses.' National Archives of Canada, RG 17 I-1, vol. 988, Agricultural Department Correspondence, File 159525.

Moore, William. 1820. *Remarks on the Subject of Packing and Re-Packing Beef and Pork*. Montreal: Canadian Institute for Historical Microreproductions, microfiche no. 57435.

– 1838. *Remarks on the Subject of Curing and Packing Beef and Pork in Conformity with the System of Inspection of Lower Canada*. Montreal: Canadian Institute for Historical Microreproductions, microfiche no. 52898.

Morgan-Jones, S.D. 1991. 'The New Canadian Beef Grading System.' *Lacombe Research News* 3(6). Lacombe, AB: Lacombe Research Station, Agriculture Canada.

Morris, J.L., and D.C. Iler. 1975. *Meat Processing Capacity: Processing Capacity in Canadian Meat Packing Plants*. Ottawa: Food Prices Review Board.

Morton, Arthur S. 1938. *History of Prairie settlement*, vol. 2 of *Canadian Frontiers of Settlement*, ed. by William A. Mackintosh and W.L.G. Joerg. Toronto: Macmillan.

Mulvany, C. Pelham. 1884. *Toronto: Past and Present until 1882*. Toronto: W.E. Caiger.

Murphy, L.W. 1952. 'Mercy killings hogs – for profits.' *Canadian Food Industries* (Dec.): 26–7.

Nation's Business. 1976 'Restructuring a Company for Greater Earnings.' 64 (Feb.): 39–48.

Noël, Alain, and Keith Gardner. 1990. 'The Gainers Strike: Capitalist Offensive, Militancy and the Politics of Industrial Relations in Canada.' *Studies in Political Economy* 31(Spring): 31–72.

Novek, Joel. 1992. 'The Labour Process and Workplace Injuries in the Canadian Meat Packing Industry.' *Canadian Review of Sociology and Anthropology* 29(1): 17–37.

– Annalee Yassi, and Jerry Spiegel. 1990. 'Mechanization, the Labour Process and Injury Risks in the Canadian Meat Packing Industry.' *International Journal of Health Services* 20(2): 281–96.

O'Mary, Clayton C. 1983. 'Types of Cattle to Feed.' In G.B. Thompson and Clayton C. O'Mary, eds., *The Feedlot*, 3rd ed., 37–46. Philadelphia: Lea and Febiger.

Ontario, Ministry of Agriculture and Food (MAF). 1987. *Processing, Distribution and Retailing Newsletter*, no. 29 (4 May). Toronto: MAF.

– 1988. 'Beef Marketing Task Force Report.' Submitted to Ontario Minister of Agriculture and Food. 29 Sept. Toronto: MAF.

Ontario, Provincial Board of Health (PBH). 1896. *Pamphlet No. 1: Meat and Milk Inspection*. Toronto: PBH.

Ontario, Sessional Papers. 1886. *Fourth Annual Report of the Provincial Board of Health of Ontario Being for the Year 1885*. No. 74: 62. Toronto: Legislative Assembly.

– 1887. 'Report *RE* Abattoirs and Slaughter-Houses.' *Fifth Annual Report of the Provincial Board of Health of Ontario Being for the Year 1886*, 82–8. Toronto: Legislative Assembly.

Oppenheimer, Harold L. 1971. *Cowboy Arithmetic: Cattle as an Investment*. 3rd ed. Danville, Ill.: Interstate Printers and Publishers.

Page, Brian. 1998. 'Rival Unionism and the Geography of the Meatpacking Industry.' In Andrew Herod, ed., *Organizing the Landscape*, 263–96. Minneapolis: University of Minnesota Press.

Parliament, Ralph. 1974. 'Winnipeg Livestock and Meat Processing Industry: a Century of Development.' In Tony J. Kuz, ed., *Winnipeg 1874–1974: Progress and Prospects*, 75–82. Winnipeg: Manitoba Department of Industry and Commerce.

Pawson, H. Cecil. 1957. *Robert Bakewell: Pioneer Livestock Breeder*. London: Crosby Lockwood.

Pelton, Lorna. 1990. 'Using Ultrasound as a Selection Tool in Future Beef Production.' *Proceedings of the Ultrasound Beef Production Strategy Conference*,

12–13 March. Saskatoon: Agriculture Canada and Saskatchewan Agriculture and Food.
Perren, Richard. 1978. *The Meat Trade in Britain 1840–1914*. London: Routledge and Kegan Paul.
Perry, Charles R., and Delwyn H. Kegley. 1989. *Disintegration and Change: Labor Relations in the Meat Packing Industry*. Philadelphia: Wharton School, University of Pennsylvania.
Peters, H.F. 1957. 'A Feedlot Study of Bison, Cattalo and Hereford Calves.' *Canadian Journal of Animal Science* 38: 87–90.
- S.B. Slen. 1966. 'Range Calf Production of Cattle × Bison, Cattalo, and Hereford Cows.' *Canadian Journal of Animal Science* 46: 157–64.
- 1967. 'Brahman-British Beef Cattle Crosses in Canada.' *Canadian Journal of Animal Science* 47: 145–51.
Philo, Chris. 1995. 'Animals, Geography, and the City: Notes on Inclusions and Exclusions.' *Environment and Planning D: Society and Space* 13: 655–81.
Pocock, Kate. 1993. 'Design Therapy.' *Canadian Grocer* (Feb.): 102–32.
Prairie Farm Rehabilitation Administration. 1987. *Prairie Soil Prairie Water: The PFRA Story.* Regina: Agriculture Canada.
Preston, T.K., and M.B. Willis. 1970. *Intensive Beef Production*. Oxford: Pergamon Press.
Purcell, Theodore Vincent. 1953. *The Worker Speaks his Mind on Company and Union*. Cambridge, MA: Harvard University Press.
Putnam, Donald F., and Robert G. Putnam. 1970. *Canada: A Regional Analysis*. Toronto: Dent and Sons.
Raby, Stewart. 1965. 'Irrigation Development in Alberta.' *Canadian Geographer* 9: 31–40.
Radford, Tim 1996. 'Poor Cow.' *London Review of Books* (Sept. 5): 17–19.
Ralph, Julian. 1892. 'Killing Cattle for Two Continents.' *Harper's Weekly* 36 (9 July).
Rasmussen, K. 1995. *Trail Blazers of Canadian Agriculture*. Ottawa: Agricultural Institute of Canada.
Reaman, G. Elmore. 1970. *A History of Agriculture in Ontario*. Toronto: Saunders.
Reed, W.G. 1942. 'Safety in Meat Packing Plants.' *Canadian Food Packer* (Jan.): 19.
Regina v *Canada Packers Inc. et al*. 1988. *Canadian Patent Reporter* (3d) 19: 133–88. Alberta: Court of Queen's Bench.
Regina Public Stockyards. 1977. 'Annual Report of Livestock Marketing at the Regina Public Stockyards.' Ottawa, National Library of Canada.
Rennie, James ed. 1969. *The Growth and Development of Canada's Meat Packing Industry*. A Documentary Commemorating the 50th Anniversary of the Meat Packers Council of Canada. Prepared by *Food in Canada*.

Reshef, Yonatan. 1989. 'Negotiating Wage Settlements: A Structural Approach.' *Relations Industrielles* 44(3): 532–50.

– 1990. 'Union Decline: A View from Canada.' *Journal of Labour Research* 11(1): 25–39.

– Alan I Murray. 1991. 'Union Decline: Lessons from Alberta.' *Relations Industrielles* 46(1): 185–201.

Rifkin, Jeremy. 1992. *Beyond Beef: The Rise and Fall of the Cattle Culture*. New York: Dutton.

Rode, L.M., R. Hironaka, and D.M. Bowden. 1992. *Feeding Beef Cows and Heifers*. Agriculture Canada Publication 1670/E. Ottawa: Minister of Supply and Services.

Rosaasen, K.A., and J.S. Lokken. 1986. 'Economic, Marketing and Policy Constraints affecting Animal Production in Canada.' *Canadian Journal of Animal Science* 66: 845–57.

– and Andrew Schmitz. 1984. *The Saskatchewan Beef Industry: Constraints and Opportunities for Growth*. Technical Bulletin BL 84-02. Saskatoon: University of Saskatchewan.

Rose, Alison. 1997. 'A Cut Above.' *Report on Business Magazine* (May): 78–81.

Ross, Carlyle, Rudy Susko, Dale Kaliel, Kathleen MacDonald-Date, and Elwyn Smith. 1990. *The Location of Cattle Production in Alberta*. Edmonton: Alberta Agriculture.

– Dale Kaliel and Darren Chase. 1988. *Economics of Cow-Calf Production in Alberta*. Edmonton: Alberta Agriculture.

Rowe, P.A. 1952. 'Canada Packers' New Conveyor System for Beef Dressing.' *Food in Canada* (March): 15–18.

Ruston, Derek. 1983. *The Red Meat Packing and Processing Industry in Ontario*. A Background Study for the Red Meats Studies. Toronto: Ontario Ministry of Agriculture and Food.

Rutherford, J.G. 1909. *The Cattle Trade of Western Canada*. Special Report. Ottawa: Department of Agriculture.

Ruttan, Vernon W. 1954. *Technological Progress in the Meatpacking Industry, 1919–47*. Marketing Research Report No. 59. Washington: United States Department of Agriculture.

Saskatchewan. 1917. *Interim Report of the Live Stock Commission of the Province of Saskatchewan 1917*. Printed by order of the Legislative Assembly. Regina: King's Printer.

– 1918. *Final Report of the Live Stock Commission of the Province of Saskatchewan 1918*. Printed by order of the Legislative Assembly. Regina: King's Printer.

Saturday Night. 1917. 'Ins and Outs of the Bacon Business.' 20 Oct., 23.

– 1926. 'Swift Canadian Company Extends.' 6 Feb., 13.

Scheideman, Brenda. 1991. 'Marbling and Lean Meat Yield Factor into New Grading System.' *Grainews* (Dec.): 42.

Schissel, Bill, Ken Matthews, and Ken Nelson. 1995. 'The Cow-Calf Industry in Canada and the United States: A Comparison.' *Canadian Journal of Agricultural Economics*, special issue: 177–94.

Schmidt, Glenn. 1998. 'How to Keep the Hot Box Clean.' *Meat Processing*, (Feb.): 34–8.

Schmidt, Ken. 1995. 'Dark, Firm, Dry (DFD) Beef.' *Beef Carcass Grading Training Manual*. Ottawa: Canadian Beef Grading Agency, 20–3.

Schoenberger, E. 1988. 'From Fordism to Flexible Accumulation: Technology, Competitive Strategies, and International Location.' *Environment and Planning D: Society and Space* 6: 245–62.

Schwarz, Oskar. 1901. *Public Abattoirs and Cattle Markets*. G.T. Harrap and Loudon M. Douglas, eds., London: Ice and Cold Storage Publishing Company.

Schweisheimer, W. 1957. 'Why must Beef Hang to become Tender?' *Food in Canada* (Jan.): 16–36.

Scott, A.J. 1988. 'Flexible Production Systems and Regional Development: the Rise of New Industrial Spaces.' *International Journal of Urban and Regional Research* 12: 171–85.

Shaw, A.M., and J.W.G. MacEwan. 1938. 'An Experiment in Beef Production in Western Canada.' *Scientific Agriculture* 19(4): 177–98.

Shilliday, Greg. 1991. 'Killing Floor Horror.' *Alberta Report* 18(6) 21: 34.

Silver, Jim. 1994. 'The Origins of Winnipeg's Packinghouse Industry: Transitions from Trade to Manufacture.' *Prairie Forum* 19: 15–30.

Sinclair, R.D. 1931. 'Report of the Beef Cattle Committee.' *Scientific Agriculture* 11(7): 433–5.

Sinclair, Upton. 1981 [1906]. *The Jungle*. New York: Bantam Books.

– 1962. *The Autobiography of Upton Sinclair*. New York: Barcourt Brace and World.

Skaggs, Jimmy M. 1986. *Prime Cut: Livestock Raising and Meatpacking in the United States, 1607–1983*. College Station: Texas A&M University Press.

Smith, Greg. 1996. 'Steam is the Theme on the War on Pathogens.' *Meat Processing* (Feb.): 32–4.

– 1997. 'Case-Ready Ground Beef Finding a Niche at Retail.' *Meat Processing* (Jan.): 34–5.

Smith, Lyle. 1980. *Economics of Feeding Cattle in South Central and Southern Alberta*. Production Economics Branch, Economics Services Division. Edmonton: Alberta Agriculture.

Smoliak, S., and H.F. Peters. 1955. 'Climatic Effects on Foraging Performance of

Beef Cows on Winter Range.' *Canadian Journal of Agricultural Science* 35: 213–16.

Snavely, King and Associates. 1982. *1980 Costs and Revenues Incurred by the Railways in the Transportation of Grain under the Statutory Rates*. Prepared for the Grain Transportation Directorate, Transport Canada. Washington, DC: Snavely, King and Associates.

Spencer, J.B. 1913. *Beef Raising in Canada*. Bulletin no. 13, rev. ed. Ottawa: Minister of Agriculture.

Spry, Irene M., ed. 1968. *The Papers of the Palliser Expedition 1857–1860*. Toronto: Champlain Society.

Statistics Canada. 1997. *Profile of Farm Operators*. Catalogue 93–359–XPB. Ottawa: Minister of Supply and Services.

Stevens, O.B.E. 1960. *Canadian National Railways*, vol. 1. Toronto: Clarke, Irwin.

Stonehouse, Darrell. 1996. 'The Secret World of Supermarket Meat Sales.' *Alberta Beef* (Aug.): 14–17.

Suzuki, David, and Keibo Oiwa. 1996. *The Japan We Never Knew*. Toronto: Stoddart.

Swanson, Wayne, and George Schultz. 1982. *Prime Rip*. Englewood Cliffs, NJ: Prentice-Hall.

Swift, Louis F., and Arthur Van Vlissengen Jr. 1927. *The Yankee of the Yards: The Biography of Gustavus Franklin Swift*. Chicago: A.W. Shaw.

Tamarkin, Jerry. 1980. 'Growing by Shrinking.' *Forbes* 126 (21 July): 33–4.

Tarrant, Vivion, and Temple Grandin. 1993. 'Cattle Transport.' In *Livestock Handling and Transport*, ed. Temple Grandin, 109–26. Wallingford, Oxon: CAB International.

Taylor, Don, and Bradley Dow. 1988. *The Rise of Industrial Unionism in Canada – A History of the CIO*. Research and Current Issues Series No. 56. Kingston: Industrial Relations Centre, Queen's University.

Thomas, Larry. 1989. 'Cargill Plant on Schedule.' *Canadian Cattlemen* (Jan.): 10–11.

– 1991. 'It's a Tough Road for the Lowly Magpie.' *Cattlemen: The Beef Magazine* 54(10): 11–12.

Tinstman, Dale C., and Robert L. Peterson. 1981. *Iowa Beef Processors Inc: An Entire Industry Revolutionized!* Newcomen Publication Number 1137. New York: Newcomen Society in North America.

Toronto. 1919. Abattoir Committee Records. City of Toronto Archives, RG 244.

– 1958. 'Municipal Abattoir Inquiry' Evidence presented before his Worship the Mayor and the Board of Control in the Council Chamber, City Hall, Toronto, on Thursday 16 January, 1958. City of Toronto Archives RG2 Series D, vol. 1.

– 1983. *Report on the Stockyards, Meat Packing and Related Industries in the Stockyards Industrial District*. Toronto: Stockyards Task Force, Planning and Development Department, City of Toronto.

– n.d. 'Abattoir Department, Administrative History.' City of Toronto Archives, RG 3.

– 1911. 'Invoices Show the Stores and Prices at which Articles in Star's Exhibit were Purchased; Comparisons Fair' *Toronto Daily Star*. 15 Sept. (Last ed.): 1.

Toronto Star. 2001. 'The Walkerton Story: Bad policies Bad decisions Bad water.' Retrieved 6 January, 2001 from the world wide web: http://king.thestar.com/editorial/walkerton/

Trepp, Leo. 1980. *The Complete Book of Jewish Observance*. New York: Behrman House.

Trow-Smith, Robert. 1959. *A History of British Livestock Husbandry 1700–1900*. London: Routledge and Kegan Paul.

United Packinghouse Workers of America. 1942 (UPWA). 'Agreement between Toronto Employees Plant Council and Canada Packers,' 3 March 1942. Typewritten Manuscript, Collective Agreements File, United Food and Commercial Workers, Canadian District Office, Rexdale, ON.

– 1945. Correspondence UPWA – Regional Labour Board for Manitoba, 6 June. National Archives of Canada, MG28 I 186, vol. 7.

– 1947. 'Reasons Why Geographical Wage Rate Differentials should be Eliminated.' Union submission to the McTague Arbitration of 1947. National Archives of Canada, MG28 I 186, vol. 9.

– 1956. Correspondence Sam Hughes to J. McKnight, President Local 180, New Westminster dated 4 September. National Archives of Canada, MG28 I 186, vol. 14.

– 1958 Press Release, 14 Aug. National Archives of Canada, MG28 I 186, vol. 8.

– 1964. Report by Peter Uganecz dated 22 December 1964. National Archives of Canada, MG28 I 186, vol. 24.

– 1965. Correspondence Sam Hughes to Swift locals dated 26 May. National Archives of Canada, MG28 I 186, vol. 12.

U.S. Department of Agriculture. 2000a. *Cattle on Feed*. National Agricultural Statistics Service. Retrieved 12 June 2000 from the world wide web: http://NASS/USDA.gov.

– 2000b. *Livestock Slaughter 1999 Summary*. National Agricultural Statistics Service. Retrieved 12 June 2000 from the world wide web: http://NASS/USDA.gov.

U.S. International Trade Commission (U.S. ITC). 1987. *The Competitive Position of Canadian Live Cattle and Beef in U.S. Markets*. Washington, DC: USITC Publication 1996.

– 1993. *Live Cattle and Beef: U.S. and Canadian Industry Profiles, Trade and Factors of Competition*. Washington, DC: USITC Publication 2591.

U.S. Congress, House of Representatives. 1906. *Conditions in the Chicago Stock Yards*. 59th Congress, 1st Session Document no. 873. Reprinted in A.R. Miller, 1958, *Meat Hygiene* 2nd ed., 15–23. Philadelphia: Lee and Febiger.

Uvacek Jr., Edward. 1983. 'Economics of feedlots and financing.' In *The Feedlot*, 3rd ed., G.B. Thompson and Clayton C. O'Mary, eds., 11–29. Philadelphia: Lea and Febiger.

Vidoczy, Jim. 1995. 'Meat Merchandising: Making the Grade.' *Canadian Grocer* (Oct.): 10–14.

Vrooman, C.W. 1941. 'A History of Ranching in British Columbia.' *Economic Annalist* 11(2): 20–3.

Wade, Louise Carroll. 1987. *Chicago's Pride: The Stockyards, Packingtown, and Environs in the Nineteenth Century.* Urbana: University of Illinois Press.

Ward, Clement E. 1988. *Meatpacking Competition and Pricing*. Blacksburg: Research Institute on Livestock Pricing, Virginia Tech.

Watkins, M.H. 1963. 'A Staple Theory of Economic Growth.' *Canadian Journal of Economics and Political Science* 29: 141–58.

Watson, Harrison. 1906. Correspondence from Harrison Watson, City [of London] Trade Branch to J.A. Ruddick, Dairy Commissioner, Department of Agriculture, 20 Nov. 1906. National Archives of Canada, RG 17 I-1, vol. 988, Agricultural Department Correspondence, File 159525.

Weijs, J.H., and A. Contini. 1963. 'Marketing Practices and Opinions of Ontario Beef Producers, 1960.' Toronto: Ontario Department of Agriculture, Farm Economics and Statistics Branch.

Weir, Thomas R. 1964. *Ranching in the Southern Interior Plateau of British Columbia*, rev. ed. Memoir no. 4, Geographical Branch, Mines and Technical Surveys. Ottawa: Queen's Printer.

Western Report. 1993. 'Dumping the Latest of Getty's Disasters: Dinning Unloads Gainers to a hesitant Burns, while an Ontario Subsidiary Collapses.' 8(44): 11–12.

Williams, Willard F., and Thomas T. Stout. 1964. *Economics of the Livestock Industry.* New York: Macmillan.

Willis, J.S. [1964]. *This Packing Business.* Toronto: Canada Packers Limited.

Wilson, Barry. 1981. *Beyond the Harvest*. Saskatoon: Western Producer.

Winnipeg Free Press. 1962. 'Consumers Worried about Tainted Meat.' 7 Feb., 11.

Winsberg, Morton D. 1996. 'Geographical Changes in the Distribution of the Nation's Agricultural Production between 1929 and 1992.' *Agricultural History* 70: 525–36.

Winters, Laurence M. 1948. *Animal Breeding*, 4th ed. New York: Wiley.

Wooliams, Nina G. 1979. *Cattle Ranch: The History of the Douglas Lake Cattle Company.* Vancouver: Douglas and McIntyre.
Yeager, Mary. 1981. *Competition and Regulation: The Development of Oligopoly in the Meat Packing Industry.* Greenwich, Conn.: JAI Press.

Index

abattoir 123; in contrast to slaughterhouse 132–3. *See also* public abattoir
Abattoir Colbex 287
Abattoir La Villette 132, 136
Abattoir Les Cèdres 279, 287
Aberdeen Angus 40, 41, 44, 45
accidents: hazards in packing plants 220; rates 220–1
acid wash 256
adulteration 153; and William Davies 157. *See also* scandal
aftosa: and imported exotic cattle 47; in Saskatchewan 187
African Americans: in packing plants 221
aging: of beef carcass 259–60
Agricultural Products Act (Canada) 301
air knife 162, 164
aitch bone 173
Alberta: beef cattle in 21; effect of boxed beef on economy 260; cattle feeding 55–6, 59; cattle flows 120; cattle slaughter 262; climatic disadvantage relative to the U.S. 72; Code of Practice and minimum distance separation 84; Code of Practice for spreading manure 82–3; effect of Crow rate in 76; Feed Grain Market Adjustment Program 77–8; government seizes Gainers 197; growth in cattle on feed 74–5, 115; labour climate 246, 279; meat-packing wages 278; northern compared with southern for cattle feeding 59–60; origins of cattle feeding in 70–2; provincial meat inspection 182; rationalization and packing-plant closures 285, 287; spatial distribution of beef cows 24
Alberta Cattle Commission 78
Alberta Labour Relations Board 246
Alberta Meat Company 195
Alberta Meat Inspection Act 182
Alberta Processing and Marketing Agreement 262
Alberta Railway and Irrigation Company 58

Alberta Stock Yards Company 115
Alberta Western Packers: and Burns Foods 200
Allied Packers 152
Amalgamated Meat Cutters and Butcher Workmen of North America 223, 224
Amarillo, Texas: and IBP 264
American Federation of Labour 223
animal welfare 250. *See also* downers; humane handling
Armour and Company: and by-products 142; Chicago packing plant 137; Hamilton plant 151; Regina plant 149
Armour, Philip 212, 292
artificial insemination. *See* cattle breeding
Atlantic Canada 55
auctions: Dutch 91; electronic 93–4; satellite 94; stockyards 105. *See also* cattle marketing; community auction

backer 140
backgrounding 38, 64–6; recreational 61–2, 65
bacon: and Burns and Company 149; exports 130, 144–5; during Second World War 187; and Swift Canadian 153, 195; and William Davies 133
Bakewell, Robert 40
bargaining 234, 270. *See also* pattern bargaining
barley 66, 72
barrels: beef packing 124; regulating 125–6
beef bulls 30–1; herds on community pastures 37; grades for marketing 105. *See also* cattle breeding
beef commission 158–9
beef consumption: health and diet 311–13; per capita trends 186, 187, 284, 311–12. *See also* consumer preferences
beef cows: breeding 29–33; grades for marketing 105; regional structure 19; management 28–9; size distribution of herds 26; spatial distribution of 21–4
beef demand, elasticity of 310–11
beef differentiation: beef as commodity 300, 321; branded beef 300; kill and chill plants 328
beef dressing. *See* dressing beef
beef exports: of chilled meat 123, 146, 159; and meat inspection 130, 131; and public abattoirs 133–4; wartime embargo of U.S. 187, 204. *See also* carcass beef; reefers
beef grading: Canadian system 301; dark cutter 248, 302; differentiation of food commodities 300; first system of grades 72; marbling 302; regional differences 303; white fat cows 301–2; yellow fat cows 53, 302
beef luggers 233, 245, 296, 308
beef marketing: and beef consumption 313; branch house system 293–5; image of a meal 321–2; nomenclature for cuts and cooking methods 322; and reefer cars 292; slogans 314, 324
Beefmaster 44
beef packaging 306–7; shelf-life and repackaging 310; vacuum

packing 306–7. *See also* boxed beef
beef packing: pre-industrial for export 124–6. *See also* cattle slaughter; meat packing
beef ring 124
Beef Terminal 112
beef trade. *See* beef exports; beef packing; meat inspection
beef transportation 97; boxed beef 259; west-east shipments of beef 98, 284, 296, 329
beef trust: and new generation of meat packers 261; and Upton Sinclair 129, 131, 185; and Toronto Municipal Abattoir 135. *See also* big three
Benson, Bruce 210
Better Beef 287; and boxed beef 259; origins 265; and Temple Grandin 248
big three 185, 187; decline 186–7; lead in kill and chill plants 283; motives for diversification 200; spatial distribution 281. *See also* Burns and Company; Canada Packers; Swift Canadian
bison 44
black eyes: on beef carcasses 164, 217
bloat 68
block-ready beef 306, 308
blood 143, 222. *See also* exsanguination
blue brand beef 72, 301. *See also* beef grading
Boer War: and adulteration of tinned beef 154
boning 246
bovine spongiform encephalopathy (BSE) 314–15
boxed beef: aging 260; block-ready 306; Cryovac 257, 258, 260; and Burns Foods 202; and Cargill Foods 262; as commodity 277; growth in use 258; handling in packing plant 257; IBP 263; origins 258; and railway transportation 97; and retail 306, 307, 308; tray-ready 306; vacuum packaging 246, 306. *See also* fabrication
brackets. *See* labour grade system
Brahman 44, 45
branch houses 293–5; Canada Packers 188, 235
branded beef 307
branding 13–14; preconditioning 32–4
Brandon: and Pool Packers 200
Brangus 44
British breeds 44, 65
British Columbia: cattle in 21; cattle flows 120
British War Office 157
Brooks, Alberta 56. *See also* Lakeside Packers
Brown Swiss 44
Bruce County, Ontario 56
brucellosis 183
buffalo 44
bulls. *See* beef bulls
Burakumin 221
Burlington, Ontario: and Tender-Lean Beef 192, 193
Burns and Company 197; branch houses 294; principle of regional wage equality 225; renamed 150, 198; Royal Commission on Price Spreads 207. *See also* P. Burns and Company
Burns Foods 197, 269; accounting

system 199; A.J. Child as President 198, 203; and Canada Packers 198; and Canadian Dressed Meats 112; Conspiracy to Reduce Competition 210; exit from fresh beef and divestment of assets 186, 201, 203; expansion and diversification 198, 200; and Gainers 197, 202; ownership change 198; pattern bargaining 270; processed meat brands 202; renamed 198; turnaround, expansion, and reinvestment 200; wages taken out of competition 226. *See also under city locations of plants*
Burns Meats: acquired by Maple Leaf Foods 203; Conspiracy to Reduce Competition 210
Burns, Senator Patrick 144; cattle king 148–50; divests meat-packing interests 150, 198; and Harris Abattoir 152; and Regina plant 201
bung 173
butcher aristocracy 217
butchers: and beef commission in Alberta 158; of Hamilton 130–1; in supermarkets 291; of Toronto 133
butcher shop: nuisance created in urban areas 127, 132; public abattoir supporters 133
by-products: and boxed beef 259; as cattle feed 66, 69–70; markets for 147; and profitability of Harris Abattoir 142; enhanced by-product harvesting in large-scale packing plants 141–2; importance of cattle hide 141; in small plants 164; transportation of 170
Cadet Roussel (Charolais bull) 47
calf production 17–19; calving season 32–3; economies of scale 27–8; regional structure 19–21; scale of production 25–6; spatial distribution 21–4. *See also* cattle breeding; cow-calf producers
Calgary 149; and Burns Foods 202, 270; and Canada Packers plant 190, 259; and P. Burns and Company 159; and Swift Canadian plant 173, 195, 196; and Union Packers 195; and XL Foods 193
Calgary Packers 169; and Canada Packers 190; Restrictive Trade Practices Commission 208, 209
Calgary Stock Yards 103, 108; and Burns plant 149; and Calgary Packers 169; and Lethbridge Stockyard 115
calves: backgrounding 64; preconditioning 32–3, 53; weaning 28, 34–5; heifer vs steer calves 39
Canada Agricultural Products Act 301
Canada Packers: 188; accounting methods 191; and A.J. Child 198; boxed beef system 259; branch houses 294–5; Can-Pak on-the-rail dressing (*see under* kill floor); as combine 209; competition with Burns 198; Conspiracy to Reduce Competition 210; creation by merger 152, 188, 208; gradual exit from fresh beef 192; growth and diversification 189, 273; and Hoffman Meats 182, 192; and Hunnisett 189; and humane slaughter 179; mechanized hide removal

137; and Ontario Stock Yards 112; and pattern bargaining 273; post-merger rationalization 188–9; and reverse takeover by Maple Leaf 193; Restrictive Trade Practices Commission 208; and Royal Commission on Price Spreads 206; 1966 strike 235, 274; strike avoidance 275; and Tender-Lean Beef 192, 193; UFCW 268–9; UPWA 224, 225; wages 234, 235, 273; wage convergence 243; western beef plants 192, 193. *See also* Maple Leaf Foods *and under city locations of plants*
Canada Safeway 264, 299
Canadian Beef Grading Agency 301
Canadian Cattlemen's Association 78–9, 94
Canadian Dressed Meats: and Burns Foods 200, 202; and Maple Leaf Foods 203; and Ontario Stock Yards 112
Canadian Food Inspection Agency 301
Canadian Meat Council 249. *See also* Meat Packers Council
Canadian Pacific Railway 58, 96; and beef commission 158; Lethbridge Stockyard 114–15; Union Stock Yards of Toronto 111; reefer cars 296
Canadian Packing Company 152; and Canada Packers 188
Canadian shield 55, 97, 147, 150
Canbra Foods 200
CanFax 94
canola 200
Can-Pak on-the-rail dressing. *See under* kill floor
carcass beef 308; aging 259–60; and railway transportation 97; cost of bruising 100
carcass breaking. *See* fabrication
carcass contamination: acid wash 256; kill floor procedures 253; pasteurization 255–6
carcass tracking 255
carcass weight. *See* rail grade
Cargill Foods 261; and Excel 261; and Trillium Meats 262–3. *See also under city locations of plants*
case-ready beef 306
cash and carry 299
catch basins: to contain feedlot runoff 85
Cattalo 44–5
cattle: age at slaughter 38, 70, 74; and beef grades 301; as commodity 17; population growth 17–18, 74; regional structure of 19–21. *See also* beef cows; beef bulls; calves; heifers; oxen; steers; stocker cattle
cattle breeding: artificial insemination 30, 49–50; Canadian cross-breeding experiments 43–4; Cattalo experiments 44–5; exotic cross-breeds 46–7; Manyberries breeding experiments and hardiness 45; Robert Bakewell 40; selection criteria in breeding beef cattle 41–2, 47–8; and ultrasound 48
cattle breeds 29; exotics 46–7, 65; origins 39–40; pure breed associations 45; pure breeds 40–2. *See also under breed names*
cattle brokers. *See* commission firms
cattle buyers 89–90

cattle exports 70, 71, 72; from Alberta 262; disease and embargo 123, 126, 146; exports and live cattle inspection 130
cattle feed 54; by-products 66, 69–70; effect of Crow rate 76; feedlot rations 66–8; grain prices 74; subsidies 78. *See also* barley; corn; grazing; sorghum; wheat
cattle feeding: and beef grades 74; conversion efficiency 67; digestion difficulties 67–8; on grass 53, 74; growth of in Alberta 70–2, 74–5, 115; integration with calf producers and packing plants 68–9; and marketing options 38–9; early methods 71; minimum cost size 63; number of cattle on feed 74; origins 69–70; part-time and small scale 61–2; and packing plants 246; winter feeding, 29, 35, 43, 70. *See also* backgrounding; cattle feed; feedlots; irrigation
cattle feet. *See* by-products
cattle grades 105
cattle grazing. *See* grazing
cattle hide. *See* hide
cattle liners 28, 53, 88; origins of 98; preferred to rail 97
cattle marketing: and feeding options 38–9; livestock exchange 103; overview 89–91; price discovery process 91; in stockyards 105, 106; unfair practices in stockyards 106–7
cattle markets: eighteenth- and nineteenth-century markets and fairs 100–1; municipal 101–2. *See also* Smithfield; St Lawrence Market; Western Cattle Market
cattle prices: hedging 70, 79; direct-to-packer pricing systems 95–6
cattle prod 93
cattle slaughter: in Alberta 285; ante mortem health of cattle 164, 182–3; contraction 285; dark cutters 248; flexibility of small-scale packers 167; large-scale and urban 146, 163, 281; pre-industrial 124–6; raw material oriented 117, 120, 202; by region 284; rural and small-scale 124, 163. *See also* farm slaughter; kill floor; meat inspection; packing plants; humane slaughter of cattle; stunning
cattle trade: interprovincial flows of cattle 116–20; shipments from stockyards 108–9; west–east cattle shipments 76, 88, 89, 329; west-east cattle shipments by railway and highway 97–8. *See also* cattle exports; cattle markets
cattle transportation 21, 28; cattle liners 98–9, 108; driving on the hoof 69, 89, 124; freight rates 96, 97; railway shipment 96, 170; regulations for feed and water stops 100; stockyards 96–7, 106; streets of Toronto 110; trailed into Calgary 108. *See also* cattle liners; cattle trade; humane handling of cattle
Celtic cattle breeding 69
centralized processing facilities 257; shift to packing plant in 1960s 258
Charlottetown: and Canada Packers plant 190, 192, 238
Charolais 47, 65
Chatham: meat-packing strike 223;

and Wilson and Company plant 150–1
Chicago: closure of Cudahy plants 266; industrialization of meat-packing 136, 145, 159; labour conditions 215; packing plants 69, 107; setting for *The Jungle* 128
Chicago Union Stock Yards: establishment 102; closure 107; model for Toronto 110
Child, Arthur J. 197, 203; and Intercontinental Packers 204; and J.S. McLean 198, 211; profits in meat-packing industry 211; turn-around of Burns Foods 199
Chilled Meat Committee 143
Chinook belt 25
Cincinnati, Ohio 125, 136
Civil War (American): and Canadian cattle markets 101, 144
cold storage. *See* coolers
collective bargaining 226
Combines Investigation Act: Restrictive Trade Practices Commission 209; Conspiracy to Reduce Competition 210
commission firms 90; and Ontario Stock Yards Board 111
Commission of Inquiry into the Marketing of Beef and Veal 107
commodity chain 4; articulation of places 6; concentration 89; comparison with U.S. 326; disappearance of stockyards 107; structural change 328
commodity cycle: of cattle 17–18, 186; cattle slaughter 284; meat-packing firms 200
Commons, John 215, 241, 244, 276
community auctions 91–3; agricultural service centres 110; compared with public stockyards 105; growth in numbers 107
community pastures 36–8, 43
computer-assisted manufacturing 254–5, 288; carcass tracking 255
ConAgra Beef 264
concentration. *See under* commodity chain
Congress of Industrial Organizations (CIO) 224, 266
conservatism of cattle producers 15, 47, 72, 75
consumer preferences: and behaviour 317; identity and food as image 323; marbling 318–19; portion sizes 319; regional variation 303, 324
Consumers' Association of Canada 181
contamination 253–4
Cookstown, Ontario: auction market 39, 109
coolers: aging 260; branch houses 293; carcass weight 96, 142; beef dressing process 172, 175; grading in 48, 246; limitation on packing-plant output 283; small-scale meat packers 166, 167; shipping 170, 233, 245; and William Davies 157; working conditions 222, 237
corn: as cattle feed 66, 72, 76
corn belt 55, 69
counter service 291, 299
countervailing duties (U.S.) 78, 79
cow-calf producers: feeding and marketing options 38–9, 53; gender division of labour 15–16, 27; integration with backgrounding and feeding 39, 65, 68; full-time/

part-time operation 15, 26–7, 61–2; strategy 15; tradition-bound 15, 17, 50–1. *See also* calf production
cows: white fat cows 301. *See also* beef cows; dairy cattle
credits: value of by-products 142
Creutsfeldt-Jakob disease 314
Crow Benefit Offset 77–8
Crow rate 75; disincentive for raising livestock 76
Crowsnest Pass 97, 148, 150
Cryovac 257–8. *See also under* boxed beef
cube square law 60–1
custom feeding 68
custom slaughter: The Beef Terminal 112; hide and by-products as payment 143; small-scale meat packers 166

dairy cattle: artificial insemination 49; culling 19, 29; regional distribution 19–21
Dakota City, Nebraska: and IBP 266
dark cutters 248–9, 302
dark, firm, and dry (DFD) beef. *See* dark cutters
Davies, William. *See* William Davies (meat-packing firm)
Davis and Fraser 190
D.B. Martin and Company 153
dehorning 14, 34, 37; to avoid bruising 100; in feedlots 53; methods 32–3
Denmark 144
Dennison, Iowa: and IBP 263
Department of Regional Industrial Expansion 195
Depression. *See* Great Depression
deskilling 215, 234, 244; on-the-rail dressing 276–7
direct-to-packer sales 94–5; decline of stockyards 106, 107; pricing systems 95–6
disassembly line 125, 137, 142, 145, 288; by-products 142; inspiration for Henry Ford 137; machine-driven chains 137, 141; manual labour process 247. *See also* kill floor; fabrication
division of labour: community branding 13; on kill floor 215, 218, 244, 247, 288; in meat retailing 300
Dodge City, Kansas: and Cargill 261
Dominion Packers 198
Dominion Securities 150
Dominion Stores 73, 291, 298, 299, 309
double-rail restrainer system 250
Douglas Lake Ranch, British Columbia 25
downers 183, 249
dressing beef: appearance of beef carcass 175, 259; bed dressing procedure 140–1, 175; Can-Pak on-the-rail 173–5; compared with hogs 217; machine-paced 247. *See also* carcass contamination; disassembly line; speed-up
dryland: and grazing 24; feedlots 59
Duchess of Geneva, Eighth (Shorthorn bull) 42
dugouts 36, 58, 59
Dumart's Limited 198
Durham Cattle Fair 101
Durhams. *See* Shorthorns
Dutch auction. *See under* auctions

E. coli 85–6, 315–17. *See also* carcass contamination
economies of scale 288; in cow-calf operations 27–8; in feedlots 60–3; in packing plants 213, 246, 283, 285
economies of scope 288
Edmonton: and Burns Foods 202; and Canada Packers plant 171, 189, 190, 192; and Gainers 196, 197; and Maple Leaf Foods plant 203, 278; and Swift Canadian plant 153, 173; early union organizing 225; wages 226
Edmonton Stock Yards 103, 197
Eighth Duchess of Geneva (Shorthorn bull) 42
electrical carcass stimulation 255
electric prod 93
electrification of packing plants 138
electronic auction. *See under* auctions
embalmed beef scandal 154
Eschem Canada: Conspiracy to Reduce Competition 210
Escherichia coli. See *E. coli*
Esmark 195
Essex Packers 297
estrus: in cows 54
ethnicity of meat-packing labour force 221–2
evisceration 140, 145, 174
Excel. *See* Cargill Foods
exotic cross-breeds. *See* cattle breeds
exports. *See* beef exports; cattle exports; Wiltshire sides
exsanguination 138; bleeding rail 140, 173; collection of blood as by-product 143; kosher procedure 138, 180
fabrication 256–7. *See also* boxed beef; central processing facilities
Faminow, Merle 210
fancy meats 218. *See also* offal
farm slaughter 163, 165–6
Fearman's Meats 144; and Maple Leaf Foods 203
Fedération des Producteurs de Bovins du Québec 93
feed. *See* cattle feed
Feed Grain Adjustment Program, Saskatchewan 77
Feed Grain Market Adjustment Program, Alberta 77–8
Feedlot Alley 79, 86. *See also* Lethbridge Northern Irrigation District
feedlots: Alberta's first 149; ambience 87; custom 68; diseconomies of scale 63; facilities layout 52–3, 54; packing plants 262; IBP 264; preference for backgrounded cattle 65; processing of new cattle 53–4; runoff and manure contamination 85; scale 53, 55, 87; scale economies 60–3; supply and demand as cause of growth 73. *See also* cattle feed; cattle feeding; heifers; Holsteins; manure; steers
feed mill 52, 54
federal inspection 247: and Temple Grandin 249; meat exports 187; large horizontally integrated plants 169; meat produced 181; procedures 182–4; supermarkets 171, 181
fell 174, 217, 218
finishing. *See* cattle feeding
First World War 145; African Americans 221; meat-packing strike 223; postwar recession in

meat packing 151; profiteering scandal 154, 157
Flavelle, Sir Joseph: and Canada Packers 199; and Harris Abattoir 146; and J.S. McLean 188, 191; profits 155, 212; profiteering during First World War 157–8; regulation of large and small meat packers 130, 131; retailing 297; and Swift Canadian 153
Fletcher's Fine Foods 278
flexible specialization 287–8
floorsmen 140, 217
Ford, Henry 137, 330. *See also* disassembly line
Fordism 288, 289
Fordney-McCumber Tariff 150
foreign ownership 150, 327; new generation of meat packers 261, 287; used to enter British market 153, 195. *See also under* meat-packing industry
formaldehyde 154
forward contract 69
Fowler's Canadian: sanitary conditions in packing plants 129–30; and Swift Canadian 152

Gainers 194; acquires Swift Canadian 196; acquisition by Burns Foods 197, 202, 203; acquisition by Peter Pocklington 197; and Alberta government 197; boycott and strike 267; Conspiracy to Reduce Competition 210; establishment 196; and Hoffman Meats 192
Gallagher, Holman and Company 149; early cattle slaughter plant 159
gambrel 140
gendered work 218, 219
geographic wage differentials 227, 232, 244; interregional standardization 239; intraregional standardization 238; why elimination of differentials was important 239–44
George Matthews 144
Gordon, Ironside and Fares 144, 148, 153, 158; branch houses 294; early cattle slaughter plant 159
government policy: programs to encourage cattle production 75. *See also* Alberta Processing and Marketing Agreement; Crow rate; Feed Grain Market Adjustment Program; National Policy; National Tripartite Stabilization; Prairie Farm Rehabilitation Administration; subsidy; Western Grain Transportation Act
Grace Meat Packers: and Ontario Stock Yards 112
grading. *See* beef grading; cattle grades
grain finishing. *See* cattle feeding
Grand Trunk Railway 101; reefers 295; and Union Stock Yards of Toronto 111
Grandin, Temple 247; design of cattle-handling equipment 248; humane slaughter practices 250; survey of packing plants 249, 250, 252
grazing: community pastures 36–8, 43; grazing leases 36; pasture management 28; pasture rental 35–6; in prairies 24–5, 72. *See* cattle feed

Great Depression; and Dominion Stores 299; Ottawa Agreements 187; Prairie Farm Rehabilitation Administration 36; Royal Commission on Price Spreads 205, 207
Great Western Railway 101
groceterias 299. *See also* supermarkets
Grosse Isle 47
Gunns Limited: and Canada Packers 152, 171, 188; and Morris and Company 150; and Ontario Stock Yards 112; and P. Burns and Company 151; and Union Stock Yards of Toronto 111, 135, 147
gutter 140

halal slaughter 252–3
Halifax, Nova Scotia: cattle market 102
hamburger disease 315–17. *See E. coli*
Hamilton: market 131; and Armour and Company plant 151; and Fearman's Meats 144, 203
Hammond, George 136, 295
Harris Abattoir: 145; beef specialist 145; blocked entry by U.S. packers 152; branch houses 294; by-products and profitability 142; and Canada Packers 152, 188; early cattle slaughter plant 159; establishment and growth of 145, 147; and Gunns 151–2, 171; sanitary conditions in packing plants 129; and Union Stock Yards of Toronto 111, 135; and Western Cattle Market 111; and Ontario Stock Yards 112
Harris, William 145, 146, 149; as butcher 150
Haussman, George Eugène 132
Hays Converter 44
Health of Animals Act 100
heifers 28; development centres 30; in feedlots 54, 64; grades for marketing 105
herd books 40
Herefords 40, 41, 44, 45, 52, 149
heterosis 46
hide: dropper 140; mechanical hide puller 174, 218, 233; removal and carcass contamination 253; removal as labour-intensive process 137, 217; value 33, 164
High River, Alberta: and Cargill Foods 248, 259, 262–3, 285; and Cargill's workforce 281
Hillsdown Holdings PLC 193, 194
hobby farms 27, 65
Hoffman Meats 182; acquisition by Canada Packers 192; and Maple Leaf Foods 203
hogs: carcass dressing 217; commodity cycle 17; countervailing duties 78; industrialization of pork packing 125; manure 84; pre-industrial slaughter and packing 125; price in national market 210; processed pork products 169, 203–4; PSE pork 248
Holsteins 44, 64
hoof-and-mouth disease 47. *See also* aftosa
Hornepayne, Ontario 97
house brand 298
hot box. *See* coolers
hotel, restaurant, institutional markets 168

Hub Meat Packers 287
Hull, Quebec: and Canada Packers plant 190, 192
Hull, William Roper 149
humane handling of cattle: meat quality 248; shrinkage and bruising in transport 99–100, 177; and Temple Grandin 247
Humane Slaughter of Food Animals Act 178, 180
humane slaughter of cattle: beef commission 176; principle of 171, 176, 178; public abattoir movement 132–3; survey of plants in Canada 250–1. *See also* stunning
Hunnisett Limited: and Canada Packers 189; and Ontario Stock Yards 112
Huron County, Ontario 56
hybrid vigour 45–6
hyperreality 314

IBP 263–4; integrated feedlot 265, 330; name change 263, union avoidance strategy 266–7, 276. *See also* Lakeside Packers *and under city locations of plants*
immigrants: in meat-packing labour force 221
inbreeding of cattle 40
Indian Reserves 144, 148
industrialization of meat-packing 123, 136, 288; by-products utilization 141–2; of hog and cattle processing 125; lags behind developments in U.S. 159–60; postdates meat inspection 137; public abattoir movement 137. *See also* disassembly line; hide
inedibles. *See* by-products
Innis, Harold Adams 19
Institute of American Meat Packers 217
intensive livestock operations (ILOs) 80
intensification of labour process. *See* speed-up
Intercontinental Packers 203; and A.J. Child 198; Conspiracy to Reduce Competition 210; and Frederick Mendel 203; growth and acquisition 204; and Mitchell's Gourmet Foods 205
intervening opportunity 55
inventory control 255
Iowa cattle feeding 55; and IBP 264
Iowa Beef Processors: name change 263. *See* IBP
irrigation: cattle feeding 59, 85; origins of in Alberta 58; land under irrigation 58; and Lethbridge Stock Yards 115; manure spreading 84; pollution of canals with manure 85; technology 58; water sources in Alberta 56. *See also* dryland; dugouts
Islamic countries 252

Jewish dietary laws 178
J.M. Schneider: cattle slaughter 170, 171; federally inspected 187
Jungle, The 128, 130
just-in-time: boxed beef 259; delivery of cattle to packing plants 90
J.Y. Griffin 152

Kamloops, British Columbia 97
Kansas: cattle feeding 55, 69; cattle slaughter 246, 264
key bargain 227; goal of pattern

bargaining 238; and Swift Canadian in 1947 232
kill and chill plants 281, 328; Burns Foods 202; locations 283
kill floor: bed dressing of beef carcass 140–1; Can-Pak on-the-rail dressing of beef 171–5, 218, 233; Can-Pak kosher slaughter 180; carcass contamination 253; contemporary developments 247; double-rail restrainer system 250; electrical tools 137–8; hazards (*see* accidents); and Intercontinental Packers 204; procedures in a small plant 161–3, 164; robots 255; sources of power 137, 170; technological change 137, 171–3, 233; workers 222 (*see also* labour); women 219. *See also* division of labour; stunning; exsanguination
Kitchener: and Burns plant 198, 202, 270–1; and Hoffman Meats plant 182, 192; and J.M. Schneider plant 171
Kitchener Packers 200
Kitchener-Waterloo, Ontario 56
Klondike 148
knife work 218–19, 257
Kootenay 150
kosher kill 178; cattle reaction 180–1; compared with halal 252; procedures 179–81; origins of exsanguination 138
knocking. *See* stunning
knocking box: in Can-Pak system 173; Can-Pak kosher slaughter 180; development 138; large-scale slaughter 250; in small plant 164

labour: age of workforce 280; in Alberta 279; alienation 216; dangerous work 219–20; dehumanizing 222; ethnicity of workforce 221, 280; gendered work 218, 219; new packinghouse workers 280; stigmatized 219, 222. *See also* accidents; working conditions
labour costs in meat packing 215
labour grade system 227–8; technological change 233; standardization of 238; value of brackets 236–7
Labour Relations Code (Alberta) 279
labour relations in meat packing: collective bargaining 226; fear of plant closures 214; 1944 negotiations 228; 1945–6 negotiations 229; 1947 negotiations 231. *See also* geographic wage differentials; labour grade system; pattern bargaining
Laing Packing and Provision Company 144
Lakeside Farm Industries 264
Lakeside Packers 214; acquired by IBP 264; boxed beef 259, 265; integrated feedlot 264; labour force 281; strike 245, 268; and Temple Grandin 248; UFCW defeated 268, 281; wages 278–9, 281
Laver, A.W. 206
legger 162, 173
Lethbridge, City of: and Burns Foods 202, 258; and Canada Packers plant 192, 193, 235, 258; and Canadian Dressed Meats 200; cattle shipments 97; and Gainers plant 197; irrigation 58, 79; kill and chill plants 283; and Maple

Leaf plant 203; and Swift Canadian 195
Lethbridge County, Alberta 56, 59, 79, 115; bunk capacity of feedlots 80; debates on intensive livestock operations 84
Lethbridge Northern Irrigation District (LNID) 79, 83
Lethbridge Stock Yards 103, 114; facilities for cattle 116; origins and growth 114–15; location at railway junction 115; packing plants 116
Limousin 47, 65
live weight: basis for pricing cattle 96; carcass bruising in transport 100
Liverpool: destination for chilled meat exports 133
Livestock and Livestock Products Act: stockyards 102, 103
livestock dealers 90
Livestock Development Program, Manitoba 77
Loblaws: groceterias 299; natural beef 305; Ziggy's 320
longissimus dorsi 48, 301
Lucerne Foods 265

Macdonald, Sir John A. 75
MacEwan, Grant 43
mad cow disease 314
Manitoba: cattle flows 117, 120; Livestock Development Program 77
manure 53, 60, 63, 87; Alberta Code of Practice 82–3, 84; composition 80; cost of transportation 81; management 82; odour 84–5; pollution from Western Cattle Market 110; spreading 81–4; as tag on hide 174, 222, 253; water pollution 85, 86
Manyberries Range Research Station 45
Maple Leaf Foods: acquisition of Burns Meats 203; acquisition of Unox and Fearman's Meats 194; branded processed meats 194; creation by merger 186, 193–4; Hillsdown Holdings 194; and Wallace McCain 194
Maple Leaf Mills 193
marbling: categories 303; feeding 53; grading 302; palatability 303; ultrasound 48
margin: on meat sales 5, 212, 309
Martin, Larry 210
master agreement 227, 228; bargaining units covered 236
Matthews-Blackwell Packers 171
MBPXL Corporation 261
McCain, Wallace 194
McDonald's Restaurants 311; animal welfare 252; halal 252
McLean, James S. 152; accounting methods 191, 199; architect of Canada Packers merger 188; death of 190; and A.J. Child 198; evidence before Royal Commission on Price Spreads 206; profits in meat-packing industry 212; and Sir William Flavelle 211
McLean, William F. 190, 193
McTague, C.P. 232; case for wage standardization 240–4
meat: as intimate commodity 154; processed brands 194, 202
Meat and Canned Foods Act 131
Meat Board 230

meat counter 73; beef sales 309; counter service 291, 300; postmodern 321; reorganized by type of cooking 323; packaged meats and self-service 300; shelf-life and repackaging 310
meat cutting 257
meat inspection (Canada): ante mortem 127, 182–3; early Ontario legislation 127; large and small packers 130, 131; Meat and Canned Foods Act 131; Meat Inspection Service 130; in municipalities 127–8; post mortem 127, 174, 183–4; provincial 163, 166, 182, 187, 249; to safeguard export markets 130; supermarkets 168, 169, 171; in U.S. 128–9, 130, 160. *See also* federal inspection
meat inspectors 161
Meat Packers Council (Canada): and Ontario Society for the Prevention of Cruelty to Animals 178, 179; and Ontario Stock Yards Board 111; tainted meat 181. *See also* Canadian Meat Council
meat packing. *See* beef packing; industrialization of meat packing; packing plants
meat-packing firms: diversification and price fluctuations 200; economies of scale 213, 246, 283, 285; fresh vs processed 273–4; high turnover 155, 211; importance of marketing 292; low margin and profitability 155, 211–12; new generation of meat packers 260–261; strikes debilitating 274; as victims in spite of market power 186
meat-packing industry: continental scale 227; depression years 207; economies of multiple plant operation 208–9; foreign ownership of 150–2, 186, 194, 261, 327; growth in wartime 144; heterogeneous 166; market concentration 207; new competitive conditions 285, 287; oligopoly 9, 123, 135, 184, 185; oligopsony 5, 184; postwar recession 151, 187; rationalization and plant closure 285. *See also* big three; industrialization of meat packing; labour relations in meat packing
Medicine Hat: and Alberta Western Packers 200; and Burns plant 200, 201, 283; and Lakeside Packers workforce 281
Melengestrol acetate 54
Mendel, Frederick 203–4
mesentery 174
metmyoglobin 307
Mexico 55
MGI Packers 287: halal 252
milk 19
Missouri Beef Processors 261
Model Abattoir Society 132
Modern Packers 198, 202
Moncton: and Swift-Canadian plants 153, 196
monopoly: humane slaughter 249; new generation of meat packers 261; market power of meat packers 155, 184, 185, 205; and Pat Burns 158; Royal Commission on Price Spreads 205; and William Davies 154–5. *See also under* price fixing inquiries; scandal
Montreal: and Burns plants 198, 202;

and Canada Packers plants 173, 188, 190; meat-packing strike 223; and Wilsil plant 190, 192
Montreal Abattoir 190
Montreal Stockyard 103
Moore, W.W.: report on conditions in packing plants 130, 154
Moose Jaw 97, 153; and Canada Packers plants 192, 193, 283; and Intercontinental Packers 193; stockyards 103; and XL Foods 193
Mormons: irrigation in Alberta 58
Morris and Company: and Gunns 151
multiplier: agricultural commodities 76
multispecies: public abattoirs 134; give way to single species 192, 246, 276
municipal abattoirs. *See* public abattoir; Toronto Municipal Abattoir
Muslim community 252
myoglobin 306

National Cattlemen's Beef Association (U.S.): slogan 314; specimen photographs 302
National Labour Relations Act (U.S.) 223
National Policy 75
National Tripartite Stabilization Program 60, 78–9
National War Labour Board (Canada) 224, 225
National War Labor Board (U.S.) 227
Nebraska cattle feeding 55, 69; cattle slaughter 246, 261, 264
Neill-Reynolds Report (U.S.) 129
Nelson, British Columbia 97
New Deal 223
Newell County, Alberta 56
Newfoundland: dairy cattle in 21; labour force recruiting for Lakeside Packers 281
New Westminster: and Swift-Canadian plants 196
New York Central Railroad 296

Occidental Petroleum 263
occupational safety. *See* accidents
offal 142, 164; consumption by working class 222. *See also* by-products
Ohio River 125
Oldman River 79, 86; dam 58
Ontario: cattle feeding 55, 70, 76; cattle flows 117, 120; cattle production 20–1; provincial meat inspection legislation 127, 182; spatial distribution of beef cows in 24
Ontario Livestock Exchange (OLEX) 93
Ontario, Provincial Board of Health 110
Ontario Society for the Prevention of Cruelty to Animals 178, 179
Ontario Stock Yards 103, 110; creation by government 111; closure 109, 114; employment in stockyards industrial complex 112–14; inaugurates auction selling 105; nucleus of Toronto manufacturing 114; size and sales volume 111–12; wages in meat-packing plants 278. *See also under* Toronto, Union Stock Yards of
Ontario Stock Yards Board 111
Ontario Teachers' Pension Plan 194
Ontario Securities Commission 232

on-the-rail dressing. *See under* kill floor
order buyers *See* cattle buyers
Order in Council P.C. 1003 224, 244
organizing packing plants 215, 245
Ottawa Agreements 187, 189, 195
Overwaitea 299
oxen 40, 41, 101
oxymyoglobin 306

packaged meats 309
packer direct sales. *See* direct-to-packer sales
packer consent decree (U.S.): stockyards ownership 111; retail sales 298
packinghouse, 170; separate from slaughterhouse 125
Packinghouse Workers Organizing Committee (PWOC) 224
packing industry. *See* meat-packing industry
packing plants: beef specialists 169, 192, 246, 276; boxed beef 258; decline of metropolitan plants and stockyard decline 107; hazards (*see* accidents); instability of prices and costs 199, 200; integration with feedlots 68–9; large horizontally integrated 169–71; livestock supply and raw material orientation 117, 120, 202, 283; location of in nineteenth-century Toronto 111; minimum efficient scale 246, 283; multistorey design 170–1, 246; real estate value of inner city locations 193, 197; rationalization and closure 285; sanitary conditions 129, 254; segregated to reduce cross-contamination 253–4; small and medium scale 163, 166–9; spatial distribution 227, 281; very large-scale beef specialists 246, 285, 329. *See also* fabrication; kill floor
pack-off 254, 257
pale, soft, exudative (PSE) pork 248
Palliser, John 25, 56
Palliser's Triangle 24, 56
Palm Dairies 150
Paris 132
Park belt 24, 60
Park-Blackwell 111
Pasco, Washington: and IBP 264
pasteurization: of beef carcass 255–6
pasture. *See* grazing
Patrician Land Corporation 197
pattern bargaining 227: advantages 230, 272; bargaining units included 235; Burns Foods determination to break system 202, 270; Canada Packers leads 232, 272; Canada Packers follows 269; goal of 238; labour relations board decisions 271; modelled on system in U.S. 225, 227, 244; national bargaining 227, 228, 230, 232; reversion to plant-level bargaining 269; process 234; technology change 233; unravels 266–7, 271–2. *See also* key bargain; master agreement
paunch manure 141, 170
paunch truck 140
P. Burns and Company 148; beef shipments to Indian reserves and Klondike 148; early cattle slaughter plant 159; growth by acquisi-

tion 149; and Gunns 151; and Harris Abattoir 151–2; monopoly power and meat prices 158; name change 150; origins 148; retail store chain 298. *See also* Burns and Company
Peat, Marwick Mitchell 199
pedigreed cattle. *See* cattle breeds
Peterborough: and Canada Packers plant 171, 192; and George Matthews 144; and Matthews-Blackwell 171
Philip Armour and Company 142
pigs. *See* hogs
Playtex 196
pleuropneumonia 126
pluck 162, 174
Pocklington, Peter 197
policy. *See* government policy
polyvinyl chloride film 306
Pool Packers 200
possum belly. *See* cattle liner
pot roast 323–4
poultry 310; and beef consumption 313
Prairie Farm Rehabilitation Administration 36. *See also* community pastures
Prairie Provinces: cattle production 20–1; cattle grazing 24–5, 72; effect of Crow rate 77; spatial distribution of beef cows in 24
Presswood Brothers 195; and Maple Leaf Foods 203
price discovery 89, 91, 107
price discrimination 207–8
price-fixing inquiries 205; beef commission of 1908 and P. Burns and Company 158; Royal Commission on Price Spreads 205; Restrictive Trade Practices Commission 208; Conspiracy to Reduce Competition 210
Pride of Canada 150
primal cuts 246; fabrication 257
prime grade 302
Prince Albert, Saskatchewan 97, acquisition of Russel Baker Packing Company 149; and Burns plant 230, 269
Prince Albert Stock Yards 103
Prince Rupert Meat Company 153
principle of bulk transactions 61
principle of multiples 61
pritch plate 140
private treaty: selling process 91
profiteering. *See under* scandal
progeny testing 40
progesterone 54
Promolux 307
provisions 144, 169
public abattoir: in Britain and Europe 132, 159; in Canada 132, 159; construction standards in Ontario 127; favoured by farmers 133–4; and Harris Abattoir 146; movement to promote 131; multi-species handling 134; small-scale butchers 133; system of feeder abattoirs and depots 134. *See also* Toronto Municipal Abattoir
public stockyards. *See* stockyards

Quality Packers 135, 278
Quebec: cattle feeding 55; cattle flows 117; cattle production 20; farmers 133; provincial meat inspection 182; spatial distribution of beef cows in 24
Quebec City: all-season port 133

railway transportation. *See under* cattle transportation; reefers
rail grade 47, 96; carcass bruising in transport 100
receiving yards 96, 103; in Lethbridge, Alberta 114
red-brand beef 73–4, 301. *See also* beef grading
Red Deer: and Canada Packers plant 192, 193, 259, 283, 313; and Intercontinental Packers plant 204
Red Deer Packers: Conspiracy to Reduce Competition 210
Red Deer River 150
reefers 123; branch houses 293; compared with cattle shipments by rail 96; icing 296; industrialization of meat packing 136; loading rails 233–4; mechanical refrigeration 296; railway cars 295; trucks 297
refrigerated railway cars. *See* reefers
refrigeration: beginning of mechanical 140; of ships for beef exports 146. *See also* coolers; reefers
Regina 149; and Burns plant 201; and Intercontinental Packers plant 204
Regina Stock Yards 103
Regional Development Incentives Act 195
regulatory paradox 130, 131, 249
rendering: condemned beef carcasses 183, 184; odour 222; waste 308
Restrictive Trade Practices Commission 208
retail 168; boxed beef 307–8; discount pricing 310; diversification of food stores 299; grocery store chains 297; postmodern store design 320; sales margin 309; sales from packing plants 182, 295; visibility of in-store value added 324–5. *See also* supermarkets
rib eye 48, 301
Richards, Justice S.E. 229
right-to-work states 246, 279
risk reduction. *See under* cattle prices
ritual slaughter 252. *See also* halal; kosher
robots 255
Rockefeller, John D. 185
Roosevelt, President Franklin D. 223
Roosevelt, President Theodore 128
Royal Commission on Price Spreads 205
rumper 140
Russel Baker Packing Company 149
Rutherford, J.G.: cattle feeding methods 70, 71; meat inspection 127, 130

Saint Helen's Meat Packers 287
Saint John, New Brunswick: and Canada Packers plant 190, 192
St-Boniface, Manitoba 88; and Burns Foods 198, 202; and Canada Packers plant 190, 193; technology change on kill floor 137, 172–3; and Swift Canadian plant 170, 173, 195, 196; and UPWA organizing 224–5
St-Boniface, Union Stock Yards of 103, 117
St-Hyacinthe auction market 109
St Lawrence Market 102, 110
St Mary River Dam 58, 115
Safeway 264, 299

San Antonio, Union Stock Yards 103
sanitation 254
Saskatchewan: aftosa 187; beef cattle in 21; cattle flows 117; Feed Grain Adjustment Program 77
Saskatchewan Hog Marketing Commission 201
Saskatchewan Livestock Commission 131
Saskatoon: and Intercontinental Packers plant 203, 204; and Mitchell's Gourmet Foods 205; and P. Burns and Company 148
Saskatoon Stock Yards 103
satellite auction. *See under* auctions
Saxon cattle feeding 69
scales. *See* weigh scales
scandal 153–4, 160; adulteration and price fixing 153–4; and *The Jungle* 128; meat inspection 129–30, 181; profiteering during First World War 157, 298; tainted beef 171, 181; Toronto Union Stock Yards land subsidy 135; and William Davies 154–5, 186. *See also under* monopoly; price-fixing inquiries
Scott National 150
Second World War 169; African Americans in packing plants, 221; bacon exports 187, 204; growth of meat packing in postwar era 187, 190, 216; union organizing 215, 224
self-service: in retail 299. *See also* supermarkets
shambles. *See* slaughterhouse
Shamrock 150
shechitah 179
shelf-life: of beef 306
shift work 247, 281, 283
shipping fever 126
shochet 179, 252
Shorthorns 40, 41, 44, 45
shrink 89; driving cattle 124; in transportation 99 (*see also* humane handling of cattle); vacuum-packaged beef 308
shrouding of beef carcass 174, 259
shut-in grain 77
siders 140
silage 54, 66, 67
Simmenthal 47
Sinclair, Upton: *The Jungle* 128, 129, 131, 185
skill: cattle butchers 217; skilled labour 216, 218; specialized skills and division of labour 216; unskilled labour 217. *See also* butcher aristocracy
slaughterhouse: nuisance created by 127, 134; reform 126, 176; separate from packinghouse 125
Smithfield: cattle market 101–2, 108
Smoot-Hawley Tariff 150
Sobeys 298–9
sorghum 66
Spanish-American War 154
spatial division of labour: boxed beef 259; cattle breeding and feeding 69; global scale 288; slaughter and packing 125
species wage differentials 217, 226, 276–7
speed-up 218, 257, 283
splitter 140
staples theory 19
steam pasteurization. *See* pasteurization
steers: in feedlots 63; in Lethbridge County 59; life-span 38; regional

distribution of 20; size distribution of herd 26, 61–3; grades for marketing 105
sticking. *See* exsanguination
stocker cattle 64, 72, 94, 109
stockman's cane 93, 101
stockyards 102; auction selling 105; cattle shipment trends 109; decline of 106, 107–8; direct-to-packer sales 106; federal regulation protects farmers 106; location in metropolitan regions 108; of northern Ontario 97; as nucleus of agroindustrial complex in Canadian cities 5, 105; origins 102–3; packing plants 108, 170; redevelopment of land in cities 109; seasonal peaks and troughs 105. *See also* cattle marketing *and under city names*
Stockyards Act (Ontario) 111
strike: UPWA strategy 228, 230, 232; of 1947, 231; IBP 263, 266; McTague arbitration 232; votes 228
stunning: Alberta regulations 164; with a captive bolt stunner 173, 178, 217, 250; with carbon dioxide 178; double-rail restrainer system 250; exsanguination 178; with a knocking hammer 173, 176, 179, 217; with a pole-axe 138; by shooting 138, 161, 164
stunning pen. *See* knocking box
subsidy: inducements to build packing plant in High River 262; – at Union Stock Yards of Toronto 111, 147; – in Vancouver 149. *See also* government policy
Sudbury 147
supermarkets 299; beef sales contribution to revenues 309; centralized processing facilities 257, 258; demand for grain-finished beef 73–4; federally inspected meat 168, 169, 171; importance of meat counter 309; meat retailing techniques 321–2; visibility of in-store value added 324–5
Swift and Company (U.S.) 146; branch houses 293; Canadian operations 160; corporate restructuring 195–6; and D.B. Martin and Company 153; working conditions 237. *See also* Swift Canadian
Swift, Gustavus 136, 212, 292, 295
Swift Canadian: 152, 194; acquisition by Gainers 197; lack of autonomy 194; Conspiracy to Reduce Competition 210; divestment and closure of packing plants 186, 196, 203; and Fowler Canadian 152; and Intercontinental Packers 204; and J.Y. Griffin 152; large horizontally integrated packing plant 170; and Ontario Stock Yards 112, 196; and PWOC 224; and Royal Commission on Price Spreads 207; sanitary conditions in packing plants 129; and Union Stock Yards of Toronto 111, 135, 147; and UPWA 194–5, 231–2; working conditions 237. *See also under specific locations of plants*
Swift-Eastern 112. *See also* Swift-Canadian
Swift Independent Packing Company 196
swinging beef 308. *See also* carcass beef

tag. *See under* manure
Taggert, James G. 230
Teamsters 223; and IBP 263
technological change. *See under* meat-packing industry
Tender-Lean Beef 192, 193
terminal yards 103; in Toronto 110
Texas: cattle feeding 55, 69; cattle slaughter 246, 261
Toronto: and Canada Packers plant 171, 173, 188, 193; and Canadian Dressed Meats 200, 202; and Harris Abattoir 147; location at railway junction 110–11; meat-packing strike 223; nuisance posed by slaughterhouses 134; origins of 110; and PWOC charters 224; scandal over free land provision 135; and Swift-Canadian plants 196, 197; Union Stock Yards of 103; and UPWA organizing 224–5. *See also* Ontario Stock Yards
Toronto Junction 110, 147, 149
Toronto Municipal Abattoir 278; cruelty to animals 178; motives for establishment 135
Trades and Labour Congress of Canada (TLC) 224
transit-pneumonia 126
transportation. *See* beef transportation; cattle transportation
tray-ready beef 306
Trillium Meats 262–3
Tripartite Stabilization Program. *See* National Tripartite Stabilization Program
Truman, President Harry S. 229
tuberculosis 130, 183
turnover 5; of feeder cattle 53, 70; of meat packing 155, 211; of labour in meat packing 245, 280, 281; in food retailing 300
Tyson Foods: merger with IBP 263

ultrasound 48
Underwood Tariff (U.S.) 71
unfair labour practices 270
union density: Alberta 246, 280; in meat packing 215
Union Packers 195
union stockyards 103. *See also under city names*
United Auto Workers 224
United Food and Commercial Workers (UFCW): Lakeside Packers strike 268; failure to impose same terms on all firms 275–6; failure to reorganize Lakeside Packers 245, 276; and IBP 263; pattern bargaining collapse 266. *See also* United Packinghouse Workers of America
United Nations Relief and Rehabilitation Agency 187
United Packinghouse Workers of America (UPWA) 223, 224; big three plants organized 228, 272; chain committees 234; committed to industry-wide bargaining process 228, 230, 244; early agreements 225; merges to create United Food and Commercial Workers 266; organizing failures 275; organizing tactics in St-Boniface and Winnipeg 224–5
United States International Trade Commission 78

United Steel Workers 224
United Stockyards Corporation 111
Upper Canada: cattle markets 101

vacuum packing. *See under* boxed beef; beef packaging
Valley Meats (pseudonym) 161–3, 164, 288
Vancouver: Alberta Meat Company 195; and Burns plant 149; and Canada Packers plant 189, 190, 192; and Gainers plant 196, 197
Vancouver Stock Yards 103
viscera 174
Vulcan County, Alberta 59

wages: at Canada Packers 234; at Lakeside Packers 281; compared with manufacturing industries 263; under master agreement 235–6; pattern in 1999 278; principle of regional wage equality 225; taking wages out of competition 226, 228, 238; two-tier wage system 278. *See also* geographic wage differentials; species wage differentials
Wagner Act (U.S.) 223, 244
Walkerton, Ontario 86, 317
War Labor Disputes Act (U.S.) 229
War Measures Act 229–30
Washington Cattlemen's Association 79
water: pollution (*see* manure). *See also* irrigation
Webster, Howard 198
weasand 173
weigh scales: at stockyards 106; truck scales at feedlots 96
Western Canadian Seed Processors 200
Western Cattle Market (Toronto) 102; cattle driven through city 110; and Harris Abattoir 145; packing plants 111; pollution from 110; and Toronto Municipal Abattoir 135; and Union Stock Yards of Toronto 110
Western Feeders 82
Western Grain Transportation Act (WGTA) 77, 78
Western Stock Yards 103
wheat 21, 24; as cattle feed 67, 73; exports and Crow rate 76
white fat cows 301
White River, Ontario 88, 97
Wholesome Meat Act (U.S.) 129
William Davies: bacon exports 144, 203; bacon processing 133; branch houses 294; and Canada Packers 152, 188; divests retail stores 299; and Harris Abattoir 145, 146, 147–8; monopoly position 156; profit record and scandal 154–5, 186; retail stores 297–8; sanitary conditions 129, 154; and Union Stock Yards of Toronto 111
Williamson Brothers 149
Wilsil 190, 192; Restrictive Trade Practices Commission 208, 209
Wilson and Company 150, 296
Wiltshire side 145, 156, 203, 204
Windsor-Quebec Axis 55
Winnipeg: cattle transportation 97, 111; and Gordon Ironside and Fares 159; meat packing 144, 149; and Swift Canadian 152. *See also* St-Boniface

winter feed. *See under* cattle feeding
women: in meat-packing occupations 219, 280
working conditions: fabrication 256; hours worked 230, 235–6; Royal Commission on Price Spreads 206; packinghouse odour 222; U.S. influence 237
XL Foods 193, 259, 262, 287

yield grades 295